Theater as Metaphor

Theater as Metaphor

Edited by
Elena Penskaya and Joachim Küpper

DE GRUYTER

This book is published in cooperation with the project DramaNet, funded by the European Research Council

ISBN 978-3-11-073653-3
e-ISBN (PDF) 978-3-11-062203-4
e-ISBN (EPUB) 978-3-11-062210-2

This work is licensed under a Creative Commons Attribution-NonCommercial-NoDerivatives 4.0 License. For details go to https://creativecommons.org/licenses/by-nc-nd/4.0/.

Library of Congress Control Number: 2019936229

Bibliographic information published by the Deutsche Nationalbibliothek
The Deutsche Nationalbibliothek lists this publication in the Deutsche Nationalbibliografie; detailed bibliographic data are available from the Internet at http://dnb.dnb.de.

© 2020 Elena Penskaya and Joachim Küpper, published by Walter de Gruyter GmbH, Berlin/Boston
This volume is text- and page-identical with the hardback published in 2019.
Cover image: photodeedooo/iStock/Thinkstock
Typesetting: Integra Software Services Pvt. Ltd.
Printing and binding: CPI books GmbH, Leck

www.degruyter.com

Acknowledgments

The present volume contains the revised versions of papers read at the conference "Theater as Metaphor", which took place on June 1 and 2, 2018 on the premises of the Fritz Thyssen Foundation in Cologne, Germany. The editors as well as the contributors wish to express their gratitude towards the Fritz Thyssen Foundation for funding and hosting the event. Our discussions benefitted enormously from the atmosphere of the location (a high modernist building right in the historic center of Cologne, vis-à-vis one of the city's famous medieval monuments, the Church of the Apostles), the friendliness of the staff, and the Foundation's generous hospitality.

The publication of this volume was facilitated by a grant from Freie Universität Berlin. De Gruyter Publishing was ready to print the book and make it available in a hardcover and an open-access electronic version.

Samuel B. Walker took up the task of bringing the linguistic quality of the papers to a level suitable for their publication in the language that has become the lingua franca of our age.

The obvious fact that the participants came either from Russian or from German academic institutions is not meant in the sense that the conference's topic is genuinely Russian or German—as is evidenced alone by the papers dedicated to texts from England, France, Italy, Spain, and Brazil. Neither is it to claim that scholars teaching in the two countries have a specific competency when it comes to discussing this particular topic. Cooperation between scholars teaching in Russia who are not Germanists in the strict sense and scholars teaching in Germany who have not been trained as Slavicists continues to be rare—an astonishing circumstance given the undeniable fact that cultural exchange between the two countries has been formative for both over several centuries. The reasons behind this present state of affairs are, evidently, political. The devastations caused by Nazi Germany in Eastern Europe and the reciprocal fear of invasion during the period of the Cold War belong to the past, but to a past that is still alive mentally. Current politics have extreme difficulties dealing with this twofold burden in a way that would benefit both countries. Scholars are certainly not politicians; but they are citizens of their respective countries. Especially in times of strained political relations they may have the task, if not the obligation, to demonstrate, *ad oculos* of the Republic of Letters, that a mutual exchange of ideas is meaningful and may enrich both countries' academic culture. In that sense, this volume is meant to be a first step towards a more sustainable cooperation, which will be open, in the future, to colleagues from other countries as well.

Moscow/Berlin, December 2018
Elena Penskaya, Joachim Küpper

Open Access. © 2019 Elena Penskaya and Joachim Küpper, published by De Gruyter. This work is licensed under the Creative Commons Attribution-NonCommercial-NoDerivatives 4.0 License.
https://doi.org/10.1515/9783110622034-201

Contents

Acknowledgments —— V

Elena Penskaya/Joachim Küpper
Introduction —— 1

I: Early Modern Variations

Peter W. Marx
Between Metaphor and Cultural Practices: *Theatrum* and *scena* in the German-Speaking Sphere before 1648 —— 11

Julia V. Ivanova
Spectacularity before the "Renaissance" of Theater: Visuality and Self-Image of the *Quattrocento* papacy —— 30

Sandra Richter
Literal and Figurative Uses of the *Pícaro*: Graded Salience in Seventeenth-Century Picaresque Narrations —— 45

Andrey Golubkov
Theater as Metaphor and Guiding Principle: The French Anecdote Tradition from the Seventeenth to the Nineteenth Century —— 65

Jan Mosch
"Dressed for life's short comedy": *Desengaño* and *connivere libenter* as Ethical Paradigms in William Shakespeare's Plays —— 77

Joachim Küpper
The Conceptualization of the World as Stage in Calderón and Cervantes – Christian Didacticism and its Ironic Rebuttal —— 101

Kirsten Dickhaut
The King as a "Maker" of Theater: *Le ballet de la nuit* and Louis XIV —— 116

Ekaterina Boltunova
War, Peace, and Territory in Late Eighteenth-Century Russian Outdoor Performances —— 133

Pavel V. Sokolov
Lucis an caliginis theatrum: Theatrical Metaphors in the Early Modern *historia literaria* —— 143

II: The Romantic Turn

Petr Rezvykh
Theater, World History, and Mythology: Theatrical Metaphors in Schelling's Philosophy —— 159

Elena Penskaya
The Philosophical Narrative as a Semiotic Laboratory of Theatrical Language: The Case of Jean Paul in the Context of the Russian Reception —— 168

Tatiana Smoliarova
Theatrical Metaphor and the Discourse of History: Nikolai Karamzin —— 191

Olga Kuptsova
Theater as Metaphor in the Drama of Alexander Ostrovsky —— 207

III: Twentieth-Century Experimentations and Theoretical Explorations

Juana Christina von Stein
The Theater of the Absurd and the Absurdity of Theater: The Early Plays of Beckett and Ionesco —— 217

Susanne Zepp
Chico Buarque's *Gota d'água, uma tragédia carioca*: Theater as Metaphor in Brazil during the Military Dictatorship, 1964–1985 —— 238

Erika Fischer-Lichte
From *theatrum mundi* to Theatricality —— 253

Notes on Contributors —— 264

Elena Penskaya/Joachim Küpper
Introduction

The papers of the present volume investigate the potential of the metaphor of life as theater for literary, philosophical, juridical, and epistemological discourses from the Middle Ages through modernity proper, with a focus on traditions as manifold as those of France, England, Spain, Italy, Russia, Germany, and Latin America.

The history of the metaphorical usage of the concept of theater is a very venerable one; the idea as such seems to emerge not much later than the establishment of drama-writing and theatrical performances in classical Greek antiquity. This early presence of a metaphorical understanding of the concept may be linked to the fact that, according to Aristotle, (good) drama and theater is *mimesis*, that is, the truthful imitation of "pragmatic" human interaction on a *lieu autre* (M. Foucault) called the stage. Such a conceptualization leads almost automatically to configurations in which pragmatic human interaction on the one hand and stage performances on the other tend to become difficult to distinguish. It is not astonishing that a corresponding reverse conclusion—prohibited by the basic laws of logic, but productive in the realm of rhetoric—emerged: namely, that pragmatic ("real") life is, in the final analysis, similar or even identical to a theatrical performance. The utilization of the metaphor was favored since antiquity by the prominent role attained by two schools of thought that are both—albeit for different reasons—committed to assessing the physical world and its enjoyments as "vain" and transitory: Stoicism and Christianity.

Given this background, it is not surprising that the tradition of this metaphor was "reborn" in an age of European intellectual and literary history that chose exactly this name with a view to fashioning itself. What is striking, however, is the high frequency the usage of the metaphor attained particularly in that period that we tend nowadays to call, with a more neutral term, early modern. Most of the essays contained in this volume are dedicated to texts from that age. One of the chief aims of the discussions at the conference from which this volume emerged was to produce convincing hypotheses concerning the reasons for this remarkable and, in comparison, outstanding presence of the metaphor.

Provisionally, we would like to suggest two different tendencies, both characteristic of the early modern age, as being at the origin of this massive presence. On the one hand, there is the importance of the religiously inflected meaning of the metaphor in an age characterized by the Reformation, the Counterreformation, and the Thirty Years' War. In a period steeped in religious controversies whose intensity might be hardly imaginable from a present-day perspective, the denunciation of the material world as vain—or, from a Protestant viewpoint, as radically vain—may have provoked a resurgence of the metaphor from ancient times that is far more extensive than what one might expect before having studied the relevant text corpora.

In that same age, there is a massive instrumentalization of the metaphor for aims and purposes one might consider to stand in diametrical opposition to a religiously informed conceptualization of the physical world. Starting at the latest with the tracts of Machiavelli and Castiglione, real-world life, especially life in the public sphere, becomes more and more equated with the concept of role play. In the treatises by these two theoreticians, "performing as if being on a stage" is the most important way to gain worldly success. This strand is continued, particularly in the age of absolutism, by theatrical devices and techniques whose primary function is to overwhelm the "audience" of the "play", that is, court society, by means only available in fictional worlds, for example apotheosis understood literally or metaphorically, and to thus make its members ready to unconditionally surrender to the absolute monarch in the real world.

It is fascinating to observe that the self-same conceptualization is used in that age to denounce worldly success as futile, though, in contrast to the religiously inflected interpretation, without reference to any sort of metaphysical horizon. The lasting success of the pieces of the only dramatist of that period whose works remain at the center of the canon into the twenty-first century, Shakespeare, may not least be due to the fact that his casting of the world as a stage, but without spectators and, most prominently, without a "real", more substantial reality surrounding this stage, is compatible with sociological theses that became highly influential in twentieth-century intellectual discussions, e.g. Erving Goffman's theorization of social interaction as being based on permanent role play. In a certain way, this evolution might be regarded as a re-emergence of the at first sight striking classical Greek concept of *prosopon*, of the mask worn by actors that is at the same time the "real" face—there is no "real" reality beyond the confines of the play.

The huge task that the age of Romanticism set for itself, philosophically, literarily, and, partly, theologically, was to find a way to deal with the destabilization of religion and tradition in more general terms that started in the Age of Discovery and reached its apogee during the Enlightenment. How to preserve a link between the present and the past?—this was the central question which emerged as a consequence of the insight that a radical "cut" in the historical continuum, a revolution, finally leads by necessity to civil war and unheard-of bloodshed. The "solution" devised by philosophy was, more a less, the historicization of the concept of revelation. If History, from the beginning to the end, is the "book" in which the Godhead reveals itself, it becomes conceivable to assume that there is, beyond the constant alterations of the physical world, a transcendent agency whose identity may be arcane but whose interaction with the human world is observable.

Such a re-conceptualization provokes a fundamental shift as to the usage of theater as metaphor. Since the philosophy of (German) idealism contests the strict opposition between the physical world and the beyond, the concept of theater as metaphor becomes flexibilized in a way one might consider an anticipation of tendencies observable in theater proper only in the twentieth century, in the work of authors like Pirandello or stage-directors like Mnouchkine. If there is no longer a strict separation between role play and action in the proper sense, between a (metaphorical) stage and a "real" world surrounding it, the metaphor comes to be transformed into one of the many devices applied in literary texts of Romanticism in order to illustrate the never-ending undecidability of what is "real" and what is "phantasy", what is "original" and what is a "copy", what is the "object" and what is its "mirror"-image, what is the "genuine" thing and what is its "simulacrum". The controversy regarding the question of whether it is literature or philosophy that "came first" in this move towards a destabilization of the dichotomies implied in the original usage of the concept of theater as metaphor might be much less important than the fact itself. Considered from the interpretative perspective briefly outlined, it is not even particularly striking that the frequency of the metaphor decreases in Romantic times when compared with its astonishing presence in the early modern age.

Is the metaphor's usage in twentieth-century literary texts nothing more than the aftermath of a long history that reached its peak in the early modern age and began to wane in the age of Romanticism? As is demonstrated in essays contained in the present volume that deal with outstanding twentieth-century literary texts from quite different ideological horizons, the metaphor seems to remain active in our age. Compared to the period of Romanticism, where its presence was already a reduced one, the frequency of the metaphor's usage in modernity proper seems to recede even more. This might be due to the undeniable fact that one of the two terms of the dichotomy on which the traditional meaning of the metaphor relied was not only flexibilized in the twentieth century, but became blurred to such an extent that one might hold that it vanished almost completely. The conviction that there is a "real" world beyond the physical one whose existence alone suggests conceiving of all action in the physical world as a sort of theatrical play has evaporated more and more, for various reasons, in Western thinking of the last 100 years. At the same time, the massive problematization of the dichotomy of "sincerity" and "simulation", initiated, with different implications, by both

Nietzsche and Freud, might have led to the insight, ratified in the works of twentieth-century sociological theory, that there is nothing but constant role playing—the distance separating the proper and the oblique, that is, the metaphorical dimension of the concept may have collapsed.

The volume starts with an essay by Peter W. Marx ("Between Metaphor and Cultural Practices: *Theatrum* and *scena* in the German-Speaking Sphere before 1648"). The argument draws attention to the fact that the metaphor existed in early modern Germany even before theater proper in the modern sense emerged there. The expression used for conveying the meaning and the message familiar from posterior times was *scena mundi*. Marx's article proposes to investigate in more detail a terrain yet unexplored in the research dedicated to the metaphor of theater, namely the Middle Ages, which had a rich tradition of performances, mostly religious, without the strict separation of stage and audience, of performers and viewers, as it became current from the sixteenth century onward.

Julia V. Ivanova ("Spectacularity before the "Renaissance" of Theater: Visuality and Self-Image of the *Quattrocento* Papacy") deals with an important chapter in the instrumentalization of "spectacularity" that is situated several decades before the humanist "Renaissance" of theater. Focusing on Enea Silvio Bartolomeo Piccolomini, who acceded to the papacy under the name of Pius II (1458–1464), the essay examines the "theatrical" restructuring of Piccolomini's place of birth, Corsignano, renamed Pienza by the Pope himself. The numerous buildings (churches, palaces, public places) that the Pope had erected in his hometown are, according to Ivanova, meant to metaphorically represent his self-image as a human being elected by God with a view to leading profane and sacred history to an apogee never seen before. This self-stylization via the "stage" of the town of Pienza is corroborated, as Ivanova shows, by Pius's textual self-interpretation in his *Commentarii rerum memorabilium quae temporibus suis contingerunt* (1463).

Sandra Richter ("Literal and Figurative Uses of the *Pícaro*: Graded Salience in Seventeenth-Century Picaresque Narrations") makes a point that is crucial for the investigation of the metaphor of life as theater in general: It is not only in plays or on stages (in the proper or in the figurative sense) that the image is exploited. Narrative texts—and as may be said in anticipation, theoretical texts—also make use of the metaphor. Its frequency seems to be particularly high in the "new" genre of the picaresque novel which emerged in Spain and exercised considerable influence on French, German, and English early modern literature. The *pícaros* may be the first to have emancipated the concept of life as simulation and dissimulation from the courtly background from which it indubitably stems and thus may have been an important inspiration for the generalization of the metaphor observable in twentieth-century sociological theory.

Andrey Golubkov ("Theater as Metaphor and Guiding Principle: The French Anecdote Tradition from the Seventeenth to the Nineteenth Century") deals with the genre of anecdote, first documented in Late Antiquity and "resurrected" in the Renaissance. The article focuses on the observation that there is, in addition to the religiously inflected and the courtly interpretations of the metaphor of life as theater, a significant presence in the comic genres. The denunciation of personages' actions as mere play or simulation, which frequently appears in the genre of the Renaissance anecdote, becomes a device that is formative for the seventeenth-century "canonical" comedy (Shakespeare, Molière).

Jan Mosch ("'Dressed for life's short comedy': *Desengaño* and *connivere libenter* as Ethical Paradigms in William Shakespeare's Plays") highlights the omnipresence of the metaphor in Shakespeare's plays. By drawing on medieval texts (John of Salisbury, twelfth century CE) and on texts immediately preceding Shakespeare's own period (Erasmus of Rotterdam), the essay documents the fact that Shakespeare's interpretation of the topos was not original at all, but rather belonged to the patrimony of a discourse that was particularly linked to milieus one might anachronistically call "intellectual".

Joachim Küpper ("The Conceptualization of the World as Stage in Calderón and Cervantes: Christian Didacticism and its Ironic Rebuttal") deals with the play in the Western tradition that exploits the metaphor at issue in the most detailed and systematic manner, i.e. Calderón's *The Great Theater of the World*. It then proceeds to discuss the striking fact—one that is nonetheless characteristic of the versatile usage of the metaphor of theater in that age—that there are, even in Counterreformation Spain, additional variations of the metaphor apart from the standard religious one, namely ironic functionalizations that target in particular those dogmatic and moral-theological positions to whose divulgation the Calderonian play is committed.

Kirsten Dickhaut ("The King as a 'Maker' of Theater: *Le ballet de la nuit* and Louis XIV") discusses a usage of the metaphor which aims to stabilize the system of political absolutism. By performing on stage as the sun, the (young) French king Louis XIV tried to convey that his rule over France, reasserted by the defeat of the *fronde*, was as "natural" as the predominance of the sun is in the cosmos. The entire world of Versailles may thus be assessed as a grand stage upon which the play of power is performed on a daily basis. The concept's (political) effectuality, however, is based on the fact that there is a "real" reality beyond this stage. As soon as the king divests himself of his role within the performance, he is able—in contrast to an actor in the proper sense—to punish those who are reluctant to react appropriately to the message contained in the play.

Ekaterina Boltunova ("War, Peace, and Territory in Late Eighteenth-Century Russian Outdoor Performances") demonstrates that "theatrical" techniques of staging power in eighteenth-century Russia, in particular under the Tsarina Catherine the Great, constituted a continuation yet at the same time a most impressive elaboration of devices invented in Italy and France one century before. The victory over the Ottoman Empire and the subsequent annexation of Crimea, which opened the way to ice-free ports for Russia, were celebrated by a grand open-air performance festival in Moscow in 1775 whose intention was to demonstrate not only the monarch's power over her enemies, external as well as internal, but also the claim that the Tsarina is able to transform nature as if it were nothing but a theater coulisse.

Pavel V. Sokolov's "*Lucis an caliginis theatrum*: Theatrical Metaphors in the Early Modern *historia literaria*" is another one of those essays in this volume which remind readers of the frequently forgotten fact that the metaphor at issue here is present in non-theatrical texts also. Sokolov makes the striking observation that there is an intense discussion of the problem of plagiarism in an age without copyright regulations. The intricacies involved in the question of what is an "original" and what is a (perhaps plagiarized) "copy" were highlighted in contemporary treatises by drawing on the resources offered by theatrical metaphors, especially on one specific semantic strand inherent to this metaphorical complex, namely, the difficulty to decide between what is "real" action and what is (only) an imitation of real action.

Petr Rezvykh's essay ("Theater, World History, and Mythology: Theatrical Metaphors in Schelling's Philosophy") opens the second section of this volume, which is dedicated to the transformation of the metaphor in literary and philosophical texts commonly referred to as "Romantic". Rezvykh argues that the metaphor of theater holds a central role in Schelling's philosophy. Humans in their real lives continue to be conceived as actors. But, according to the transformation of the highest being from transcendent to transcendent and at the same time immanent, the dichotomy between actors and author is destabilized: the actors take part in designing their roles. It is interesting to observe that drama proper did not make use of this re-conceptualization before the first half of the twentieth century (Pirandello).

Elena Penskaya ("The Philosophical Narrative as a Semiotic Laboratory of Theatrical Language: The Case of Jean Paul in the Context of the Russian Reception") discusses a Germanophone Romantic author whose works were particularly well received in Russia, where they continued to exert influence up to the era of the avant-garde of the first two decades of the twentieth century. Especially in the *Flegeljahre*, but also in his *Ästhetik*, Jean Paul makes conspicuous use of the metaphor of life as theater. There is no longer any religious dimension linked to it, nor is there the courtly inspired concept of the necessity of simulation and dissimulation. In anticipation of phenomena observable in particular in twentieth-century high modernist texts, the metaphor assumes in Jean Paul the function of a focal point in the problematization of the concept of reality as opposed to imagination.

Taking as a starting point the works of Karamzin, Tatiana Smoliarova ("Theatrical Metaphor and the Discourse of History: Nikolai Karamzin") demonstrates the presence of pan-European Romantic concepts in nineteenth-century Russian literature. In Karamzin, whose texts are paradigmatic of Romanticism, the metaphor of life as theater is functionalized with a view to questioning the dichotomies of sensory perception and phantasy, of representation and (mere) imagination, of—as may be said in anticipation of Freud's theorizing—the conscious and the unconscious, the real and the unreal which is, however, real at the same time.

Olga Kuptsova ("Theater and Metaphor in the Drama of Alexander Ostrovsky") presents the meta-theatrical dramas of Ostrovsky as an intermediate stage between the functionalization of "theater as metaphor" to be found in plays by Lermontov on the one hand and that to be found in the plays of Chekhov on the other. Focusing in particular on *The Forest*, Kuptsova shows that the extent of its meta-theatricality is astounding, even if measured by the standards of Romanticism: the play references at the same time *Hamlet*, *The Robbers* (by Schiller), and archetypes drawn from Molière's comedies, Sganarelle in particular. The surprising result of this—at first sight—erratic mix of meta-theatrical structures is, as Kuptsova argues, not only a "hymn to Romanticism", but at the same time "a sober recognition of its problematic effects".

There are three articles dealing with twentieth-century texts in the present volume. They demonstrate the extremely high versatility of the metaphor in modernity proper, a phenomenon that is accompanied by the fact of its receding overall frequency.

Putting Ionesco's pieces at the center of her essay, Juana Christina v. Stein ("The Theater of the Absurd and the Absurdity of Theater: The Early Plays of Beckett and Ionesco") introduces the thesis that in many avant-garde pieces, the metaphor no longer serves as a means of illustrating what ("real") life is, but rather as a device for the self-reflection of theater. Briefly put: in contrast to the assumptions dominant in current research, v. Stein argues that Ionesco's and also Beckett's early theater is meant to demonstrate not the absurdity of life, in the sense of the human condition, but rather the absurdity of traditional theater. The metaphor is utilized with a view to providing a meta-theatrical comment on what (traditional) theater is.

Susanne Zepp ("Chico Buarque's *Gota d'água, uma tragédia carioca*: Theater as Metaphor in Brazil during the Military Dictatorship, 1964–1985") demonstrates, however, that twentieth-century literature also exhibits a sort of continuation of the early modern usage of the metaphor. By recourse to the famous play *Gota d'água* (1975) by Chico Buarque, Zepp shows that much of twentieth-century Latin American literature (or, as may be said, literary texts produced under authoritarian regimes in general) makes use of famous dramas, in this case, dramatizations of the story of Medea, in order to comment on political and societal problems pertaining to the present. The intention is, however, not Nietzschean; it is not about conveying that reality consists of nothing but the "eternal recurrence". The play, including the metaphor implied by its dramatic plot, is meant to problematize the productive role of theater, and of art in general, within political processes.

The last article of the present volume is linked to theoretical explorations and their relation to the metaphor of life as theater. Erika Fischer-Lichte's essay ("From *theatrum mundi* to Theatricality") pays homage to the (frequently "forgotten") theoretician who first created a term that is linked to the traditional usage of the metaphor but at the same time transcends its limits: "theatricality" or, in the original wording: *teatraln'ost'*. The expression coined by Nicolaj Evreinov is contextualized in Fischer-Lichte's essay by reference to the Foucauldian concept of a "crisis of representation" that emerged at the end of the nineteenth and the beginning of the twentieth century. While the episteme of analogism, dominant in medieval times and partly in early modern times also, provides a quasi-ideal terrain for a strictly allegorical interpretation of the metaphor of *theatrum mundi*, the episteme of representation—substituting the concept of (arbitrary) sign for the concept of (God-given) "signatures"—leads to a new and highly multi-faceted functionalization of the metaphor. As is evidenced by texts such as Hofmannsthal's *Lord Chandos Letter* and Nietzsche's *Fourth Untimely Meditation*, the conviction that there is a tenable differentiation to be made between sign and signified becomes, however, unstable at the beginning of the twentieth century. A blurring of the distinction between life and stage, as is implied in the concept of theatricality, thus seems to suggest itself. Evreinov's concept may also owe its conspicuous popularity in present-day intellectual discourses to the fact that an essentialistic theorization of "selfhood" has become more and more obsolete.

I: **Early Modern Variations**

Peter W. Marx
Between Metaphor and Cultural Practices: *Theatrum* and *scena* in the German-Speaking Sphere before 1648

Introduction

Whereas the early modern period is celebrated as the hour of birth for many European theatrical traditions, the German-speaking sphere seems to come late to the table; some older works of literary history even speak about a theater-less period. As such a leap seems to be implausible—*cultura non facit saltus*—I would like to take a closer look at the period between the spread of the printing press (after 1460) and the end of the Thirty Year's War, a period often lamented as lacking a genuine "German" (whatever that might be) theatrical culture. With the juxtaposition of theater as a metaphor and as a cultural practice, I try to unfold a panorama that allows for a different and more nuanced assessment of this period of theater history. As framing assumptions, I would like to state:

- Theater and drama describe more or less autonomous forms of theatrical phenomena—the concept of the "theater of drama",[1] based on the temporal and hierarchical succession of drama being first and theater second, does not fully apply to the period I am talking about.
- The practices of "performing theater" and "printing play" constitute two poles of a complex configuration that comprises not only semiotic models of production and reception (including a special temporal and spatial order) but also different materialities and economic modes.

Following these two assumptions, I will first discuss a metaphorical concept of theater in this period and will then contrast it with some observations on scenic practice.

---

[1] H.-Th. Lehmann's influential *Postdramatisches Theater* (Frankfurt/Main 1999) popularized a historical periodization centered on the concept of the "theater of drama", which the author identifies with the bourgeois theater emerging in the eighteenth century. Accordingly, the classical drama of Greek antiquity is classified as pre-dramatic theater, whereas twentieth-century theater is called post-dramatic theater. This periodization has been criticized for its inherent evolutionary logic as well as for its focus on drama.

∂ Open Access. © 2019 Peter W. Marx, published by De Gruyter. [CC BY-NC-ND] This work is licensed under the Creative Commons Attribution-NonCommercial-NoDerivatives 4.0 License.
https://doi.org/10.1515/9783110622034-002

Theater as a metaphor and the absence of theater

Among the first books printed (as early as in the 1490s) are various editions of Terence's comedies, which were obviously widely read by students of Latin. The frontispieces are symptomatic in their claim to present "theater": The 1493 edition presents a two-storied building; on the ground floor we see a *fornices* (Lat.: brothel) forming the foundation for a somewhat distorted auditorium—apparently the social prejudice about theaters and actors had been more successfully transmitted through the ages than the actual practice.

The 1496 edition presents a picture that makes it rather obvious that the engraver probably had no idea of what a *theatrum* actually was: it shows a tower from which the spectators look at the world—not a place to look at itself. It is evident that the engraver had no real point of reference, but literally illustrated an abstract concept. J. Stone Peters, in her seminal study *Theatre of the Book* (2003), acknowledges the importance of these editions—together with the "re-discovery" of Vitruvius' *De architectura*—even claiming that the printing created a boost in the rise of theater:

> Print, then, was central to the late fifteenth- and sixteenth-century theatrical revival, and it continued to shape its unfolding history. As the press began to circulate dramatic texts and images of the ancient theatre, as the multiple late-medieval entertainment genres were interwoven with the classical genres in the new plays being circulated by the press, an institution (or, more accurately, a set of institutions) was created. Theatres used exclusively for the production of plays sprang up.[2]

While this assumption is true for the Italian Renaissance and the influence of the Italian humanists, the German-speaking sphere again seems to have failed to keep up with its neighbors: As O. Brockett and F. Hildy show in a diagram about purpose-built playhouses in Europe,[3] the German-speaking sphere is significantly absent. Whereas France (1548: Hôtel de Bourgogne), England (1567: The Red Lion), Spain (1579: Corral de la Cruz), and Italy (1584: Teatro Olimpico) can proudly point to this tradition of theater architecture, the German-speaking sphere could only refer to the *Ottoneum* in Kassel, a theater of which we do not

---

[2] J. Stone Peters, *Theatre of the Book 1480–1880: Print, Text, and Performance in Europe*, Oxford 2003, p. 7.
[3] Cf. O. G. Brockett and F. J. Hildy, *History of the World Theatre*, 9th ed., Boston, MA 2003, p. 138.

Fig. 1: Frontispiece of Terence edition 1493.

Fig. 2: Frontispiece of Terence edition 1496.

really know whether it was ever used as a playhouse,⁴ and to a theater built in Ulm in 1640/41 by the legendary Joseph Furttenbach (1591–1667). Stone Peters follows the tempting equation of printed texts and purpose-built playhouses to argue for the constitutive impact of printed play texts:

> In disseminating ancient drama, in producing texts about the Greek and Roman theatre, in identifying comedy and tragedy with gesturing actors, in publicizing the classical rubrics around which theatrical institutions formed themselves, in circulating images of buildings called "theatres," in printing and circulating vernacular playtexts that could be performed in them, in identifying the textual drama as the paradigmatic performance art, print gave the theatre an image of itself.⁵

While this assumption is consistent with the *grand récit* of the "re-discovery" of antiquity at the end of the Middle Ages, a glance at the usage of the term *theatrum* in German-speaking publications from that period gives us a different impression: As N. Roßbach⁶ has shown in an extensive survey of printed books of the seventeenth and eighteenth centuries, the term *theatrum* did not refer to theater in our sense of the word but rather to a heightened point of observation—as we might see it in the 1496 edition of Terence—from which to look at the world. Stone Peter's argument applies to Italy, France, and partly to England, but the development in the German-speaking sphere was symptomatically different.

While some research does exist about the discourse of theater in England in the sixteenth century—for example on stage directions⁷—comparable studies for the German-speaking sphere are still a desideratum. Apart from some older studies,⁸ there is no systematic exploration of the semantic field (and scenic practices) of theater in this period. If one examines these older studies, they soon reveal the terminological confusion noted above: R. Stumpfl, for example,

---

4 For further details, cf. H. Hartleb, *Deutschlands erster Theaterbau: Eine Geschichte des Theaterlebens und der englischen Komödianten unter Landgraf Moritz dem Gelehrten von Hessen-Kassel*, Berlin and Leipzig 1936.
5 Stone Peters, *Theatre of the Book*, p. 98.
6 Cf. http://www.theatra.de, accessed 13 January 2019, for a complete list of the titles included in the project.
7 Cf. A. C. Dessen and L. Thomson, *A Dictionary of Stage Directions in English Drama: 1580–1642*, Cambridge 1999; A. C. Dessen, "Stage Directions and the Theater Historian", in: *The Oxford Handbook of Early Modern Theatre*, ed. R. Dutton, Oxford 2009, pp. 513–527.
8 Cf. R. Stumpfl, "Die Bühnenmöglichkeiten im XVI. Jahrhundert: Bausteine zur deutschen Theatergeschichte (I)", in: *Zeitschrift für deutsche Philologie*, vol. 54, 1929, pp. 42–80; R. Stumpfl, "Die Bühnenmöglichkeiten im XVI. Jahrhundert: Bausteine zur deutschen Theatergeschichte (II)", in: *Zeitschrift für deutsche Philologie*, vol. 55, 1930, pp. 49–78; S. Mauermann, *Die Bühnenanweisung im deutschen Drama bis 1700*, Berlin 1911; P. E. Schmidt, *Die*

notes that the term *theatrum* covers a very broad and almost undistinguishable semantic horizon; the term is even applied to town halls. For more specific elements of the theatrical art, the historical discourse uses terms that today no longer refer to theater: for example, the stage (i.e. the scaffold on which the performance took place) is often described as *Brücke [brüge]* (bridge).[9] The terminological conflation is an index of theatrical activities that just might have been captured by different expressions. W. N. West—departing from a different angle—comes to a comparable conclusion:

> Before theatre was a real space in which to enact plays, the theatre was an idea built around a word that referred to an object that no longer existed except in texts, in which its attributes, functions, and powers changed.[10]

Conversely, in the following we will look at the real spaces in which theater was performed and how its *Sitz im Leben* was defined.

Interjection: *scena* as a concept

A terminological alternative to *theatrum*—that is already present in the early modern period—is the concept of *scena* and its various vernacular variations. The OED lists various meanings of *scene*, ranging from a subdivision of a dramatic text to the "material apparatus" or "the place where an action is carried out". These two latter meanings can already be found in the sixteenth century—i.e. in the period when the modern notion of theater is formed. In contrast to the rather broad and vague term *theatrum*, *scena* has a very practical, material reference to the place and apparatus and to the action taking place. A later semantic twist includes "a view or picture presented to the eye". The comparison with further historical dictionaries reveals a comparable semantic profile: In his Latin-German dictionary of 1536, Petrus Dasypodius defines *scena* as "hütte od. gemach/in welchen sich die Comedispyler uebeten"[11]—further German dictionaries follow suit, providing translations that usually refer to *Schau-Platz*, often implying a scaffold and some kind of temporary construction designed for better viewing.

Bühnenverhältnisse des deutschen Schuldramas und seiner volkstümlichen Ableger im sechzehnten Jahrhundert, Berlin 1903.
9 Cf. Stumpfl, "Bühnenmöglichkeiten (II)", pp. 67–71, and also C. H. Kaulfuß-Diesch, *Die Inszenierung des deutschen Dramas an der Wende des sechzehnten und siebzehnten Jahrhunderts: Ein Beitrag zur älteren deutschen Bühnengeschichte*, Leipzig 1905, pp. 3 and 8.
10 W. N. West, *Theatres and Encyclopedias in Early Modern Europe*, Cambridge 2002.
11 Petrus Dasypodius, *Dictionarium latinogermanicum*, intr. G. de Smet, Hildesheim 1995.

The term has also gained some scholarly interest recently. In his essay on the concept of *scene*, B. R. Smith has discussed the term with its specific dimension in the early modern discourse; he concludes:

> And what does "scene" mean in these cases? It certainly includes the act of acting and the physical structure of the playing place as well as the fictional location. What is remarkable about all the remarks upon "scene" that I have assembled here is their solid grounding in scene as stage structure. This firm connection between physical means and theatrical ends in early modern usage constitutes the most significant difference from our own understanding of scene.[12]

I would like to highlight the three key components in Smith's reading of *scena* that make the term so attractive for further discussion:
- act of acting
- physical space of acting
- fictional locale (created through the acting).

Smith's emphasis of the physical space as the center of the various semantic dimensions is helpful in understanding *scena* not only as a synonym of theater but rather as a narrower, more specific term that emphasizes the material conditions of theatrical practices. In contrast to the general term theater (*theatrum*), which lends itself in the early modern period rather to a metaphorical usage, the term *scena* focuses on historically (and culturally) specific conditions—highlighting the amalgamation of material conditions, conceptual framings, and techniques and practices.

Taking its point of departure in a spatial order, *scena* is also parallel to anthropological considerations. In his *Homo Ludens* (1944), J. Huizinga has provided a definition of play that is based on temporal limits as well as spatial seclusion:

> More striking even than the limitation as to time is the limitation as to space. All play moves and has its being within a playground marked off beforehand either materially or ideally, deliberately or as a matter of course. Just as there is no formal difference between play and ritual, so the "consecrated spot" cannot be formally distinguished from the play-ground. The arena, the card-table, the magic circle, the temple, the stage, the screen, the tennis court, the court of justice, etc., are all in form and function play-grounds, i.e. forbidden spots, isolated, hedged round, hallowed, within which special rules obtain. All are temporary worlds within the ordinary world, dedicated to the performance of an act apart.[13]

---

[12] B. R. Smith, "Chapter 5: Scene", in: *Early Modern Theatricality*, ed. H. S. Turner, Oxford 2013, pp. 93–112.
[13] J. Huizinga, *Homo ludens: A Study of the Play-Element in Culture*, London and Boston, MA 1980, p. 10.

The play-ground is a sphere in its own right: "Inside the play-ground an absolute and peculiar order reigns."[14] Reading *scena* as a play-ground in Huizinga's sense allows not only for the identification of theatrical spaces but also for a discussion of the framing conditions and the specific "jurisdiction" that enabled the space and its practices.

Practice (1): *Scenae* without theater

To get a better sense of the specificities of the theatrical landscape in the German-speaking sphere of the sixteenth and seventeenth centuries, I will pick two exemplary locales: Nuremberg and Cologne. The two cities display symptomatic similarities, as both were important centers of trade and commerce, and both were Free Imperial Cities with a strong magistrate; both cities had been important urban centers already in the Middle Ages. Yet, they also differ significantly: While Nuremberg declared itself a Protestant city in 1525, Cologne remained Catholic. Thus, a comparison between the two cities might also provide a glimpse of the different paths of transformation along the denominational divide in early modern Europe.

Nuremberg

At the beginning of the twentieth century, Nuremberg became a central point of reference for cultural politics as well as for the emerging discourse of cultural history: Epitomizing the German Renaissance as the hometown of artists such as Hans Sachs (1494–1576) and Albrecht Dürer (1471–1528), the town also represented the high art of German Protestantism. Turning to Protestantism in 1525, Nuremberg became a symbol of the German Reformation—also by bridging the gap between the "new" doctrine and the tradition of the medieval concept of the *Kaiser*. These references were in particular fashionable in late nineteenth-century Germany and its attempt to define itself through a great tradition.

At the same time, the focus on the Reformation offered a hidden dramaturgy for the history of Nuremberg's theater that fit the general *grand récit* remarkably well. Nuremberg was known for its *Fastnachtsspiel* (Shrovetide play) and its masked pageants, documented in the illuminated *Schembart* manuscripts.

---

14 Ibid.

Accordingly, the emergence of theater in the sixteenth century was often read as part of the process of overcoming rites and customs of the "Old Faith" and preparing for the secularization and rationalization of the Enlightenment. Hans Sachs became the most prominent representative of this early form of German drama.

Yet, if we take a closer look, the relation between these carnivalesque traditions and the emergence of theater appears more problematic: Whereas the first *Schembart* pageants are documented starting in 1449, and the first performances of plays in 1517, the documents that give proof to this tradition are the product of a legislative campaign to tame the wild activities of Nuremberg's citizens during carnival.[15] "Purging" itself from the stains of irrational (i.e. Catholic) rites and costumes, the *Fastnachtsspiel* appears as a first mode of literary drama: still imperfect, but certainly a medium of enlightenment and national/bourgeois formation.

At the end of the sixteenth century (since 1593), English comedians visited Nuremberg regularly. Their lasting impact can be seen in the works of Jacob Ayrer (1544–ca. 1605). His *Opus Theatricum*, published as an extensive Folio in 1618, contains 69 of his alleged 109 plays. Thus, Nuremberg figures as an example for the process of "literarizing" theater and performance in the sixteenth century.

If we take a closer look at the specific locales in which these performances took place, it becomes evident to what extent theatrical activities in these periods used existing spaces: while the carnival performances usually did not require any specific place—the *scena* was strictly performative in the sense that it was created through the action itself[16]—later performances of the *Meistersinger* (Hans Sachs was part of this social institution) also used the church St. Martha—a usage that obviously was enabled through the impact of the Reformation.[17] While this repurposing of ecclesiastical spaces was rather common in the sixteenth century,[18] the English comedians used the yard of the *Heilbronner Hof*—a space surrounded by buildings with open galleries. Eventually, in 1628, the magistrate of Nuremberg decided to build a *Fechtschule* (fencing school) which

---

15 Cf. Th. Hampe, *Die Entwicklung des Theaterwesens in Nürnberg von der zweiten Hälfte des 15. Jahrhunderts bis 1806*, Nuremberg 1900; H.-U. Roller, *Der Nürnberger Schembartlauf: Studien zum Fest- und Maskenwesen des späten Mittelalters*, Tübingen 1965.
16 Cf. Hampe, *Entwicklung*, pp. 24f. and 61.
17 Cf. M. Herrmann, *Forschungen zur deutschen Theatergeschichte des Mittelalters und der Renaissance*, Berlin 1914.
18 The rise of the private playhouses in London is a comparable phenomenon.

was equally usable for public fencing exercises and for performances.[19] The architectural similitude to the public playhouses of Elizabethan England is striking and probably not accidental. According to Th. Hampe, the space allowed for up to 3,000 spectators. It is symptomatic that this space was open for multiple usages such as public fencing exercises, bear- and ox-baiting—and theatrical performances. Aesthetically, it is clear that the performances could not rely on any form of scenery or stage machinery. Visual illusion obviously was no part of this theatrical tradition. The *scenae* of Nuremberg were defined by performance and scenic narratives—the locales might not have been purpose-built but they provided an "interface" in the sense of "a means or place of interaction between two systems or organizations" (OED).

Cologne

The situation in Cologne is strikingly similar, but the historical account differs: Whereas Nuremberg serves as a prime example of a linear, evolutionary development, Cologne, in contrast, has been widely perceived as symptomatic of a medieval community and its failing struggles to adjust to the new era. Whereas Nuremberg opted for the Reformation in 1525, Cologne—quite the opposite—firmly rejected the new doctrine. Being one of the key sites for European pilgrimages—with its cathedral and the relics of the Magi—it was also one of the major centers of European trade. Since Cologne was a member of the Hanseatic League, it was connected to cities in Norway and Scotland in the North, Sicily, Spain, and the Canary Islands in the South, Lisbon in the West, and Novgorod in the East. Despite its firm stand with the Roman church, Cologne also became the safe haven for Protestant refugees from the Netherlands (the *Geuzen*) in the sixteenth century. Artists such as Peter Paul Rubens or the dramatist Joost van den Vondel partly lived in Cologne and held close ties to the city.

Cultural and theatrical life in Cologne was correspondingly multifaceted: The commonwealth is determined politically by its status as a Free City (with the archbishop officially not residing in Cologne), but its social and cultural status is determined by the presence of various monasteries and religious orders—some of them heavily involved in the system of education, such as the Jesuits or the Franciscans—, by being one of Europe's main centers of trade, by its

---

19 Cf. Hampe, *Entwicklung*, pp. 111–116.

university, and by a community of urban dwellers who developed a strong sense of local identity and independence early on.

Cologne was also an important location for the rising print and book market: As early as 1464, Ulrich Zell opened the first book printing shop in Cologne.[20] Very soon, Cologne became one of the most productive printing locations in Europe. Its central position in Western Europe also made Cologne one of the most influential printing places for the Flemish-speaking regions.

The theatrical landscape of Cologne mirrored this vibrant and multi-faceted profile:

- As early as 1526, school performances are documented; with three different *Gymnasia* (grammar schools) in town—two of these being municipal institutions, the third taken over by Jesuits in 1556—there was a fierce competition for students but also for public recognition and performances as an additional source of income for the principal and the school.
- Due to its lively scene of book printers, the practice of printing plays was established early on. An interesting case in point is the printer Jaspar van Gennep (ca. 1500–1564). Gennep published various plays, but his biggest success was *Homulus: Der sünden loin ist d. Toid* (staged 1539; published 1540). The play—an adaptation of *Everyman*—was widely circulated, translated, and performed.[21]
- The files of the city council also provide proof of the fact that there were many local performance initiatives: in 1576–78, Adam von Trier received permission to perform comedy three times; the printer Conrad Lewen staged three productions in 1591 and continued to receive permission for various performances until 1602, so we might consider the existence of a local tradition of setting up shows.
- In 1592 we have the first proof of an appearance of an English troupe in Cologne. The English troupes kept appearing until 1670—when they disappear altogether. According to older statistics, Cologne was the second most visited city: 34 performances in comparison to 53 in Frankfurt and 28 in Nuremberg.

---

20 For the history of printing in Cologne, see P. Norrenberg, *Kölnisches Literaturleben im ersten Viertel des sechszehnten Jahrhunderts*, Viersen 1873; E. Voulliéme, *Der Buchdruck Kölns bis zum Ende des fünfzehnten Jahrhunderts: Ein Beitrag zur Inkunabelbibliographie*, Bonn 1903; W. Schmitz, *Die Überlieferung deutscher Texte im Kölner Buchdruck des 15. und 16. Jahrhunderts*, Cologne 1990; W. Schmitz, *500 Jahre Buchtradition in Köln*, Cologne 1999.

21 J. Bolte, *Unbekannte Schauspiele des 16. und 17. Jahrhunderts*, Berlin 1933, p. 4. The play was performed in Vienna in 1553; see C. Niessen, "Nachträge zur alten Kölner Theatergeschichte (2)", in: *Jahrbuch des Kölnischen Geschichtsvereins*, vol. 42, 1968, pp. 199–260, p. 208.

But what is probably even more significant is that Cologne was also a widely sought-after destination for troupes of various other countries/traditions, such as France, Italy, the Netherlands, Poland (probably English actors), and the German-speaking lands. Thus, Cologne's theater audience must have been treated to a rather broad variety of theatrical styles and traditions—much more diverse than the city itself would have been able to entertain permanently.

But why is this variety registered so minimally in most historical accounts? The reason is twofold: On the one hand, most of these theatrical enterprises were rather short-lived—their existence was based on the often opaque system of seeking permission for performances from the magistrate. Secondly, the linguistic variety lacks the homogeneity which is conventionally associated with literary theater.

But this is a nineteenth century perspective which takes especially the *Comédie Française* as its ideal model. In the process of nation-building in the nineteenth century,[22] theater was conceived as one of the formative elements—and so was theater history: The longing for the nation as an essence included the concept of a shared language and a shared cultural identity. The Cologne model seems to have followed an (at least partly) different pattern: Linguistically situated not only in the German-speaking but, through the Ripuarian dialect, also closely connected to the Flemish-speaking sphere, the city entertained a certain polyglot atmosphere. Theater and theatrical activities were not understood as creating a national identity, but were part of an urban life that was fueled by trade and exchange.

It is in line with this practice that, as early as 1441–47, the magistrate of Cologne decided to build a municipal warehouse and banquet hall, called the *Gürzenich*, for public events of all sorts. Since the demand soon exceeded the capacities of the building, the magistrate acquired a nearby building in 1561, called *Quattermart*, which was then refurbished as a public space for banquets, festivities, and also for theater performances.[23] As in Nuremberg, Cologne institutionalized the option to provide a *scena*, but it was politically conceived of as a temporal, ephemeral space.

---

[22] Cf. B. Anderson, *Imagined Communities: Reflections on the Origin and Spread of Nationalism*, London and New York, NY 1983, as well as *The Invention of Tradition*, ed. E. Hobsbawm and T. Ranger, Cambridge 1983—these studies have drawn attention to the nineteenth-century demand for historical narratives to foster the idea of the nation state.

[23] Cf. J. J. Merlo, "Haus Quattermart zu Köln", in: *Annalen des Historischen Vereins für den Niederrhein*, vol. 20, 1869, pp. 218–247.

Practice (2): Theater made out of other performances

In 1581, the Laurentius Gymnasium (one of the grammar schools of Cologne) produced a St. Lawrence play, a common and rather conventional subject for a Catholic school. What was so remarkable about this production was the organization of set and scene: Built on a provisional stage—mounted on barrels—the scene depicted ancient Rome. All loci of the play are marked by the painted backdrop that depicts the places in which the plot is situated. Thus, the scenery marks a transformation from the medieval practice of the *stage of simultaneity*, where every location of the plot has its own physical space, towards the *stage of succession*. C. Niessen, who first discussed the visual material of this production in his dissertation in 1913 (published in 1917), understood this material as one of the rare visual documents of a major shift in the practice of creating performance spaces (*scenae* in our terminology).[24] What might look like a rather minor change is actually a radical step that called for a very different form of *spectating*, a literacy that required the audience to conceive of the scenic space as an integral space in time, to perceive the painted backdrops as constitutive parts of the performance. Whereas earlier performances used textile backdrops either as mere confinements of the scenic space or as tools to veil parts of the space, here the paintings were a direct index of the locale of the scenic plot. The audience had to learn how to "read" this new decoration and this new scenic space as it also required a different understanding of time and space: The previous model presented all locales at once—hence the term *stage of simultaneity*—while the new model presented only one locale through which time runs (hence *stage of succession*).

These scenic changes were clearly not fueled by a new dramaturgical model—the text was rather conventional in its form. It was the spatial structure that fostered innovation and change. In order to understand the cultural constellation that allows for this new form, we need to broaden our scope and to look at related phenomena. West has offered such an approach by adapting J. Bratton's concept of *intertheatricality*[25] to the early modern drama:

---

[24] Cf. C. Niessen, *Dramatische Darstellungen in Köln von 1526–1700*, Cologne 1917; C. Niessen, "La scène du 'Laurentius' à Cologne et le noveau document sur le Heilsbrunner Hof à Nuremberg", in: *Le lieu théâtral à la Renaissance*, ed. J. Jacquot, Paris 1964, pp. 191–214.

[25] Cf. J. Bratton, *New Readings in Theatre History*, Cambridge and New York, NY 2003; J. Bratton, *The Making of the West End Stage: Marriage, Management and the Mapping of Gender in London, 1830–1870*, Cambridge 2011.

> Instead of reading the historical record of early modern theatricality as a collection of allusions and references, it opens the possibility of understanding theatre as made out of other performances.²⁶

"Theatre made out of other performances"—this is a precise description of a *scena* that is not confined to a fixed framework but is determined as a space that is permeable to different forms of performances. The use of painted, textile backdrops is known in this context, for example tapestries that were also used in churches or in aristocratic abodes. The empty spaces of the *Gürzenich* and the *Quattermart* as well as their bare walls required furnishing with movable textiles and decoration to fashion them for the respective occasions. Aristocratic courts also used tapestries to add an additional symbolic layer to various festivities. In this sense, the emptiness of public spaces such as the *Gürzenich* or *Quattermart* (or the *Fechtschule* in Nürnberg) clearly was functional and effective in the sense of being open to multiple occasions and meanings.

But the transfer of these meaningful backdrops to the *scena* of the St. Lawrence play of 1581 adds a new quality: the backdrop becomes an integral part of the narrative of the play, conveying important information to the audience. This information was not—as in the case of tapestries at court—located on a commenting meta-level, but was essential information in the sense of providing spatial orientation. Thus, the transfer of a performative technique to the realm of theater fostered the emergence of a new literacy in spectating theater.

The extent to which this *circulation* of techniques, narratives, forms of spectating, and economies was a hallmark of pre-Thirty Year's War theater in the German-speaking sphere can be determined with the help of another performance in the year 1627, when the Jesuits of Cologne celebrated the dedication of their new church *Mariae Himmelfahrt* with a theatrical production of the story of St. Stephen.²⁷ The opening took place on November 16 and 17, 1627. In the main nave of the church, a massive stage was erected, divided into three parts: there was an exterior stage for the people, an interior for the regal and aristocratic scenes, and an upper stage for the scene situated in heaven.

---

26 W. N. West, "Intertheatricality", in: Turner (ed.), *Early Modern Theatricality*, pp. 151–172, p. 154.
27 Cf. C. Niessen's unpublished second dissertation (Habilitation): *Studien zur Geschichte des Jesuiten-Dramas in Köln*, Universität zu Köln, Cologne 1919.

Fig. 3: Sketch of the Lawrence play by Broelman, Cologne 1581 (Stadtmuseum Köln).

As Niessen has stated, the Jesuits had taken this form of stage design from the English comedians, who worked with a similar scenic structure.[28] The similitude of descriptions is actually striking—and astonishing at the same time as the English comedians were not only mostly Protestants, but also came from very different social strata. The structure of intertheatricality—"theatre made out of other performances"—allows us to understand that the circulation of narratives, techniques, and devices was not restricted to a homogenous field in terms of religious denomination.

In light of this fact, it is even more astonishing that Niessen assumes—without any form of evidence—that the artistic consultant for the construction of the stage was probably Valentin Boltz, a Cologne Jesuit who is known for having designed and built the main altars of the church. The altar in the northern nave shows a similar tripartite structure—the two lower parts present paintings, while the third one is decorated with small figures and represents the Resurrection.[29] This upper section contains two interesting references. In depicting the Resurrection it builds an intertheatrical relationship to the emblematic scene of Christian theatricality: the Easter plays. The presentation of

---

28 Cf. ibid., p. 41.
29 *Die Kunstdenkmäler der Stadt Köln*, ed. P. Clemen, Düsseldorf 1911, p. 143.

Fig. 4: Model of the St. Stephanus stage, Cologne 1627.

small figures, indicating through their distinctive proportions a spatial distance, also reminds us of T. Stern's much-discussed hypothesis of an early modern practice of presenting plays with human actors and puppets at the same time.[30] This altar might give us an idea of how these mixed performances

---

[30] Cf. T. Stern, "'If I could see the Puppets Dallying': Der Bestrafte Brudermord and Hamlet's Encounter with the Puppets", in: *Shakespeare Bulletin*, vol. 31, 2013, pp. 337–352, pp. 343–345.

might have looked: using the puppets in structures like the *discovery space*[31] not as a breach of aesthetic devices, but rather to signal and demonstrate spatial and temporal dimensions.

What is remarkable here is that the circulation obviously was not restricted to homogenous groups or strata (sacred vs. profane), but ran across all these categories. Even further, I would argue that the *scenae* of the pre-1648 theater world in the German-speaking sphere were of high importance as they allowed for cultural, social, and intellectual mobility in a period that otherwise was determined by an aggressive policy of distinction and the creation of differences.

Epilogue

The above arguments can hardly do more than scratch the surface of a complex, polyphone, and sometimes contradictory theatrical landscape. It should have become obvious by now that concepts well established in literary or art history can be misleading when it comes to describing and analyzing the early modern theater of the German-speaking sphere. Even the notion of such a sphere might be misleading as it suggests reading the various developments in light of the later nation-building process. Instead, micro-histories of specific cities or regions seem to be a genuine desideratum when it comes to getting a better picture.

In order to revise earlier positions, we might need to reconsider our own historiographic toolbox and catalogue of concepts. As D. Niefanger has pointed out, the lament about the lack of a national theater (like the *Comédie Française*) neglects that the German countries had one of the most diverse theaterscapes in Europe.[32] The reason for this distorted retrospective view is—of course—that the nationalist paradigm that fueled the emergence of historiography in the nineteenth century favored homogeneity and autochthony over diversity and transcultural exchange. In light of this, Nuremberg becomes the textbook example for an autochthonous culture transformed from a performative and oral tradition into a "proper" literary culture. Professionalization and

---

31 As to this technique in the English theater see R. Leacroft, *The Develoment of the English Playhouse: An Illustrated Survey of Theatre Building in England from Medieval to Modern Times*, London 1988, pp. 40–42.
32 "Die ältere Kulturgeschichte hat es als Manko angesehen, dass im 17. Jahrhundert ein deutsches Nationaltheater nicht existierte [...]. Eine solche Kritik an den spezifischen deutschen Zuständen im 17. Jahrhundert übersieht aber, dass gerade im Austausch der Kulturen auf deutschem Boden ein Vorteil bestand. In keiner anderen Region gab es ein so vielfältiges Theater" (D. Niefanger, *Barock: Lehrbuch Germanistik*, 2nd ed., Stuttgart and Weimar 2006, pp. 144f.)

"literarization" appear as the governing forces behind the emergence of German theater. When one looks at the actual cultural practices, it becomes evident that this functions as a "principle of limitation"[33]: The publication of prestigious Folio editions of the works of Hans Sachs and Jacob Ayrer should be regarded as intertwined with the larger discourse about taming the time-bound, spontaneous, ephemeral practices that grow out of carnival traditions. *Sola scriptura*—Luther's famous dictum—gains here a rather different resonance.

The concept of *scena*—as suggested here—is at the same time a point of intersection and a prism to get the different fields and institutions at play into view. The usage of theater as a metaphor, or as an abstract cipher for a relation of observation and overview, as we have encountered it in the frontispieces of the Terence editions, relates to the discourse of epistemology as it meanders from medieval axioms to early modern attempts to define humans' attitude vis-à-vis the world anew.[34]

Related to this discursive thread is the rise of poetic discourses about genres and the formation of drama. Throughout Europe, the seventeenth century is filled with normative attempts to define drama "proper"—most clearly by the French in the *doctrine classique*. But again, the German-speaking discourse displays a symptomatic discrepancy: While the plays of the English comedians were printed in at least three editions between 1620 and 1630, Martin Opitz does not even mention them (or any other itinerant troupes) in his *Buch von der deutschen Poeterey* (1624). To acknowledge this bias against theatrical practices is the first step to understanding the contradictory development of theater in the German-speaking sphere.

The rise of the genre and of the poetological discourse related to it is rooted in the emergence of book printing as a praxis of circulating knowledge and formal patterns. While centralist states such as France, with its epicenter of Paris, i. e. the Royal Court, created institutions to secure cultural homogeneity and specific formal standards giving expression to it already in the early seventeenth

---

33 M. Foucault, "The Order of Discourse", in: *Untying the Text: A Post-Structuralist Reader*, ed. R. Young, Boston, MA 1981, pp. 51–78, p. 59.

34 The prototypical—but by far not the only—example for this is certainly Michel de Montaigne (1533–1592), whose essays can be understood as impressive documents of the development of a sense of individual subjectivity through self-observation. While Shakespeare's interest in Montaigne has been widely discussed, the question of the extent to which the essays can be read as contributing to the metaphorical discourse about theater is still to be investigated more broadly.

century,[35] the situation in Germany was categorically different. The rising tensions and conflicts between Protestants and Catholics were catalyzed by the political system of numerous small principalities with secular and clerical princes. In this sense it is also important to note that neither the territories nor the linguistic borders were clear-cut. As pointed out in the case of Cologne, the Ripuarian dialect most likely was easily understood by most speakers of Flemish. Again, the clear conjunction of territory and a homogenous language is a nineteenth-century fiction created with a view to nation-building. The book market had a homogenizing effect with regard to these pre-modern structures—but economically speaking it was less profitable than theater. In this sense, the title pages of Quarto editions of Elizabethan play texts are indicative as they often do not mention the author but announce past performances as decisive selling points. The printed scripts of the English comedians make a similar claim to a theatrical practice.

The various theatrical practices form a broad horizon that mirrors the manifold tensions constituting the profile of this historical period: from liturgical and para-liturgical practices, through carnival rites, to school performances and the emergence of professional troupes—all these forms are fueled and enabled by the social, political, intellectual, and economic developments of this period before the beginning of the Thirty Year's War, which marks an interruption of all cultural development in central and northwestern Europe.

To acquire a view of these processes of cultural formation, it is necessary to develop a refined understanding of the cultural mechanisms of transformation and transmission of ideas, techniques, narratives, ideas, and economic models; to acknowledge that innovation is but one aspect of these developments, often accompanied, thwarted, or even promoted by phenomena of anachronism, residues, and simultaneities of contradicting developments.

---

35 The French model clearly becomes the ideal for all European states in the process of nation building. It is remarkable how the close connection between the foundation of the *Académie Française* (1635) and the *Comédie Française* (1680) is indicative of the concept of theater as a secular institution and art form designed to grant expression to the idea of national identity.

Julia V. Ivanova
Spectacularity before the "Renaissance" of Theater: Visuality and Self-Image of the *Quattrocento* Papacy

The humanist culture of the *Quattrocento* has left no visible traces in dramatic genres. Humanists paid a most respectful attention to the legacy of ancient theater, but their attention was scholarly in nature, manifesting itself in commentaries on plays by Plautus and Terence and citations of the playwrights' words in research papers—but rarely, with very few exceptions, in imitations. The whole *Quattrocento* era produced about fifty comedies, but only two plays, *Polyxena*, attributed to Leonardo Bruni (Aretino), and *Chrysis*, by Enea Silvio Bartolomeo Piccolomini (Pope Pius II), can be considered as outstanding products of the humanist culture.[1] It seems that tragedies were even more rare; their study seems to be a matter for the future. It could be assumed that, given the weakness of theater as a social institution, humanists invested all of their potential as playwrights into the dialogue, the genre that prevails in humanist literature.[2] Dialogue was particularly in demand as it not only served the purpose of "art for art's sake" successfully, but, being close to Menippean satire, it also allowed the author to probe the limits of any accepted truth freely, testing its resistance to various kinds of critique, putting it into serious and funny contexts alternatively, and listening to how it sounded in a polyphony of voices, stated by different characters. In that period, searching for solutions to scholarly or ethical problems was considered to be more important than aesthetic objectivizations of possible solutions through individual characters, and the logic of scholarly inquiry was more attractive to intellectuals than the attempt at building a well-wrought dramatic plot. It was not until the late fifteenth

---
1 On the latter play see E. O'Brien, "Aeneas Silvius Piccolomini's *Chrysis*: Prurient Pastime—or Something More?", in: *MLN*, vol. 124, 2009, pp. 111–136.
2 On the genre of the humanist dialogue, see D. Marsh, *The Quattrocento Dialogue: Classical Tradition and Humanist Innovation*, Cambridge, MA 1980.

Note: The research that is at the basis of this paper was conducted within the framework of the Basic Research Program at the National Research University Higher School of Economics (HSE) and supported within the framework of a subsidy granted to the HSE by the Government of the Russian Federation for the implementation of the Global Competitiveness Program.

Open Access. © 2019 Julia V. Ivanova, published by De Gruyter. This work is licensed under the Creative Commons Attribution-NonCommercial-NoDerivatives 4.0 License.
https://doi.org/10.1515/9783110622034-003

century that Giovanni Pontano's dialogues began to present scenes the very emergence of which announced the (re-)birth of comedy.

The dramatization of ideological positions developed in the genre of the dialogue is one of the processes leading to the renaissance of theater. However, this study will focus on another aspect—namely on the spectacularity of political life in *Quattrocento* Europe, i.e. spectacularity as a means of self-presentation for authorities during that era.

The transformation of the sociocultural construct of power that Italy witnessed throughout the fifteenth century has been a frequent object of historical and sociological research. R. Fubini sees one of the origins of humanism in Italy of the late *Trecento* in the mutation of the self-image of papal authority,[3] which had been transformed from the force embodying and implementing the Law, uniform and unalterable for every member of society, into nothing more than a representation of the personal will of an individual (or a group of individuals) within the power echelon. Having lost its legal justification and broken the link with the social context of traditions (whether feudal/patriarchal or municipal/republican) that had endowed it with power, this new guise of papal authority needed to identify and legitimize itself. This was the situation in which heroism of the ancient type, with its strong mythological element and blatant unconventionality manifested in the motif of resisting fate, ever-present in the hero's journeys, became the center of rhetorical deliberations among the advocates of the new order representing the rising humanist movement. These were able, relying on their historical erudition and oratorical endowment, to dignify the crude materiality of the tyranny of power as a truly heroic conduct, which transcended the boredom of everyday traditions with an imperious gesture to create a "brave new world".

The strategy of "classicizing" becomes one of the pivotal aspects of internal and external policies pursued by the numerous Italian city-states of differing sizes in the fifteenth century. During that period, the Holy See's economic and political weakness was balanced by the stability and conservatism of the symbolic institution of the papacy. The means of representing the power of St. Peter's successors were produced at a rapid-fire pace and in huge volumes: the concept of strong individual rule in Rome was far ahead of the full-fledged actual consolidation of this type of power throughout the fifteenth and even in the early sixteenth century. The strategy of materializing the symbolic capital adopted by the See of Rome was as ambitious as it is hard for us to understand, being an attempt to *directly produce* real out of symbolic power. At the basis of this strategy was

---

[3] R. Fubini, *L'umanesimo italiano e i suoi storici: Origini rinascimentali, critica moderna*, Milan 2001, pp. 30ff.

the attempt—after having created an all-embracing, integral, and impeccably shaped *image of authority* in the verbal and figurative arts, first of all in architectural forms—to translate that image into real life, as if it were possible to make historical reality a function of such a fabricated image by exerting purely *aesthetic* influence on the public and producing a performance with real-world authorities occupying the lead role.

This paper focuses on the strategies (mainly aesthetic and gravitating toward visuality) that the Holy See, represented by Pope Pius II as one of its most prominent agents,[4] used during that period to construct its self-image and proclaim its mission and intentions.[5] This new type of power largely drew on the means of self-representation, enabling the subject of power to mark his position as exclusively significant—both in space and in historical time. But in fact, the Pope remains in the same space as his subjects (among whom are many of his relatives, friends, opponents, and rivals—i.e. those who know him closely and have no reasons to acknowledge his superiority over them) and lives the same historical moment with them. Therefore, the Pope was looking for spatial-visual means that would create a radical contrast between him and his audience. In addition, he needed a narrative and self-image that would confirm his supremacy as uncontested. He finally came to the solution to use the perspectival organization of space and self-staging, the positioning of himself at the point of intersection of the convergence of visual rays and sightlines of the spectators, as a visual means of portraying the exclusiveness of his position. Elaborating, in addition, narrative means of self-presentation, the Pope drew on the methods of typological exegesis—a specifically Christian way of interpreting texts as containing a "veiled" prophetic dimension. Typology presupposes that the events depicted in the Old Testament are not ontologically complete in themselves, because their authentic sense is revealed only in analogous events narrated in the New Testament: the "true" meaning of Abraham's (finally not performed)

---

4 On Piccolomini's "Renaissance world", see A. White, *Plague and Pleasure: The Renaissance World of Pius II*, Washington, D.C. 2014.
5 On Piccolomini's visual and performative strategies of self-representation, see M. Maskarinec, "Mobilizing Sanctity: Pius II and the Head of Andrew in Rome", in: *Authority and Spectacle in Medieval and Early Modern Europe: Essays in Honor of Teofilo F. Ruiz*, ed. Y.-G. Liang and J. Rodriguez, New York, NY 2017, pp. 186–215; F. Nevola, "'La più gloriosa solemnità che a di de padri nostri giammai fusse veduta': Feste ed apparati urbani durante il pontificato di Pio II Piccolomini", in: *I luoghi del sacro: Il sacro e le città fra medioevo ed età moderna*, ed. F. Ricciardelli, Florence 2008, pp. 173–188; F. Nevola, "Metaurbanistica e ceremoniale: Pio II e la corte papale in Siena", in: *Enea Silvio Piccolomini: Arte, storia e cultura nell'Europa di Pio II*, ed. R. Di Paola, A. Antoniutti, and M. Gallo, Rome 2006, pp. 357–369; F. Nevola, "Le patronage architectural du Pape Pie II Piccolomini à Sienne", in: *Médiévales*, vol. 47, 2004, pp. 139–152.

sacrifice of his son, for instance, becomes manifest in the Crucifixion. The implication of typological exegesis consists in the claim that the *raison d'être* of the events portrayed in the Old Testament is to indicate those of the New, to be the "typoi"— the "prefiguration" of these latter events, with a view to pedagogically preparing the Israelites and the pagans of the ancient world so that they will be able to perceive the "true truth" of Christian dogma. Pius II uses the resources offered by this approach, traditionally confined to biblical exegesis, in two ways: at times, he constructs prophecies concerning himself; the *typoi* he makes use of for that purpose are not only the characters of Christian salvation history (first of all, Jesus himself), but also the heroes of the pagan world, above all Aeneas and Cesar.

I shall now consider the visual means of self-representation that Piccolomini applied in his two most ambitious cultural-political projects: the architectural ensemble of Pienza, conceived by Bernardo Rosselino with the active participation of the Pontiff, and the narratives created by Piccolomini to be staged on the occasion of mass festivities in different regions of Italy, directed by the Pope himself.

The few literary works of the second third of the *Quattrocento* that could be labelled as relating to the theory of art present the principles of perspectivism and architecture as a rather abstract, rigidly regulated model of "proper" artistic and architectural creation. E. Panofsky was the first to emphasize the entirely abstract nature of the early works of perspectivism, their deliberate, often excessive resistance to the conventional (medieval) logic of the viewer's gaze.[6] The simple mimetic reproduction of a spatial body evolves into rational harmonization and structural decomposition of the space perceived, elevating the deliberation concerning the organization of space to a reflection on the very conditions and patterns of visual perception. For instance, Alberti's books on artistic and architectural works contain spatial metaphors that serve to overcome the limitations and habits of trivial visual experiences.[7] Alberti suggests devising a wall as a row of pillars punctuated by the spaces between them, a house as a series of openings connecting it to other spatial zones in the city, a town district as a frame of outdoor open spaces, and a network of streets as a frame of an urban open space. He also recommends representing a town as a house in which all the rooms must be interconnected; all of his architectural plans of houses and villas include an "antique" patio that interconnects all the

---

[6] E. Panofsky, *Perspective as Symbolic Form*, New York, NY 1991, pp. 47–66.

[7] On Alberti's notion of space and the social-political significance of architecture and city-planning, see B. Mitrović, "Leon Battista Alberti and the Homogeneity of Space", in: *Journal of the Society of Architectural Historians*, vol. 63, 2004, pp. 424–439; C. W. Westfall, "Society, Beauty, and the Humanist Architect in Alberti's *De re aedificatoria*", in: *Studies in the Renaissance*, vol. 16, 1969, pp. 61–69, p. 66.

residential premises and is used for relaxation and communication, similar to an urban open space. Meanwhile, the vertical structure of the town is levelled and smoothed so that the horizontal space has a uniform size and represents an ideal model of a linear geometrical perspective.[8] Such ascetic discipline designed to "geometrize" the viewer's gaze is supposed to eventually result in the pure perception of the inner space of a picture or architectural landscape as an ideal system of coordinates in which a visual narrative evolves, whether it is a fictional plot or real events in the town's political life.

Being guided by the seemingly "natural" laws of visuality, the early art of perspectivism in fact creates a space that is not inherently consistent with any real perception. Rather than imitating real-life spatial forms, artistic and architectural perspectivists uncover the principles of their construction. They expose visual *patterns* of reality—and only when such patterns have been calculated and measured do they translate them into an image, allowing the abstract geometric principle to become an ideal platform for images and events. They thus create a *new*, totally fictional reality relying on the laws and rules that are subject to calculation, articulation, and replication. The field of visual perception becomes dominated by the logic of structuring rational space. The urban planners who created the architectural utopias of *Quattrocento* perspectivism would first draw perfect geometric shapes and perfectly straight lines and only then try plotting structures and, rarely, human figures on city maps. As for urban landscapes, it was obviously extremely rare that the architectural ideas of perspectivism, perceived in the context of consolidating the power of some prominent political figure, were brought to life in full, probably with the only exception of the small town of Pienza with its unique central square ensemble.

Piccolomini, who called himself Pius II at the beginning of his pontificate, attached enormous importance to perspective: he perfectly realized its semantic potential and used it skillfully to represent his own personality. This is manifest, apart from the architectural plan of Pienza that he designed in cooperation with Rossellino,[9] in his autobiographical *Commentarii rerum memorabilium quae temporibus suis contingerunt* (1463), in which he describes every part of his architectural concept and explicates to his readers and to visitors of the town the meaning that should be recognized in the plan of the *borgo* and its structures. If

---

[8] See I. Danilova, "Gorod v italyanskikh arkhitekturnykh traktatakh Kvatrochento" [The Town in Italian Architectural Tractates of the Quatrocento], in: I. Danilova, *Italyanskiy gorod XV veka: real'nost', mif, obraz* [Italian City-States of the 15th Century: Reality, Myth, and Image], Moscow 2000, pp. 29–84.

[9] On Pienza as a *Quattrocento* city, see *Pienza: The Creation of a Renaissance City*, ed. Ch. R. Mack, Ithaca, NY 1987.

the *Commentarii* contain Pope Pius's verbalized self-image, Pienza is his self-image carved in stone. In order to convey this dimension, the Pope had renamed his small native *borgo* Corsignano this way. The verbal image of the Pope's personality and biography is illustrated by the Pienza ensemble, while the details of the latter find their explication as well as interpretation in the *Commentarii*.[10]

The lack of space into which the newly designed central square ensemble—the cathedral as well as the Pope's, the Bishop's, and the Municipal Palaces—had to be squeezed encouraged Rossellino to invent new methods of creating an illusion of perspective centered around the cathedral façade, despite all the disadvantages as to landscape and topography that marked Corsignano. The small town of a few streets sits on a cliff overlooking the Val d'Orcia. Its central avenue (now named after Rossellino), as conceived by the architect, separates the square with the cathedral at its back from the Municipal Palace, the square being only slightly wider than the avenue. The lanes running perpendicular to Corso Rossellino and leading away from the cathedral are aligned so that the sight of the cathedral is lost as soon as one dives into any of them. For this reason, it is virtually impossible to observe the cathedral and the Pope's Palace from a remote perspective; meanwhile, a perspective was indispensable to grasp the meanings intended by the contractor and the architect. The square paved with dark stone was divided into nine rectangles by straight lines of pale tufa and flanked by four more trapezoids (two on either side), quadrilaterals truncated by the buildings of the Pope's and the Bishop's Palaces that frame the square in front of the cathedral on both sides. A passer-by would think that the palace façades are perpendicular to the façade of the cathedral, but a bird's-eye viewer will see that they actually form a trapezoid with the line of the cathedral's façade as its shorter base; in fact, the outer corners of the palaces facing the Corso Rossellino diverge from each other while the inner ones converge and almost reach the cathedral.[11]

D. del Grande called the Pienza ensemble a collage of Piccolomini's personal impressions and memories, comparing Pienza to Hadrian's Villa, which was also designed in the so-called genre of "architecture of a philosopher king's memories". Piccolomini commissioned the Cathedral of Assumption of the Virgin Mary; the

---

[10] On the ensemble of Pienza as Piccolomini's "project" and as a manifestation of the "humanist worldview", see J. Pieper, *Der Entwurf einer humanistischen Weltsicht*, Stuttgart and London 1997; S. J. May, "Pienza: Relics, Ritual and Architecture in the City of a Renaissance Pope", in: *Foundation, Dedication and Consecration in Early Modern Europe*, ed. M. Delbeke and M. Schraven, Leiden 2012, pp. 99–128.

[11] See D. del Grande's article "Pienza: La città di Pio" in a digest of studies and materials on the issues of the history of Pienza's architecture and its restoration: *Pio II, la città, le arti: La rifondazione umanistica dell'architettura e del paesaggio*, ed. G. Giorgianni, Siena 2006, pp. 17–34.

Pope, consistently referring to himself in the third person, says: "Pius wished the cathedral to be built by the example of churches that he had admired in Austria, the land of German peoples."[12] At the same time, the massive pilasters and large vault arches give the visitor an impression of being inside a Romanesque structure rather than a Gothic one. The low, regular-shaped triangular roof and the pillars splitting the façade into three parts and making the cathedral resemble an ancient triumphal arch are to bring, in addition, an image of a classical pagan temple to the viewer's mind: "The seventy-two-feet-high cathedral façade made of travertine-like stone as glittering as marble has a form similar to that of ancient temples; it is magnificently adorned with pillars, vaults, and semicircular niches that could hold statues."[13] The complexity and polysynthetism of Rossellino's architectural plan can partly be explained by the landscape: the cathedral erected on a cliff seems to be hanging over the valley, so those who conceptualized the building sought to take as much advantage of the location as possible, trying to transform the topographical challenges into unique strengths of the structure.[14] By no means did Piccolomini intend to reproduce fragments of familiar examples of Gothic or ancient architecture. His project is an ambitious (if not unprecedented) combination of features of all the styles known at his time, subordinated to the single idea of representing the builder's self-image. On the one hand, the cathedral is meant to become a sort of microcosm embodying the whole history of Western European architecture; on the other hand, both the cathedral and the palace are involved in a special type of elaborated relationship with the space they belong to.

The Palazzo Piccolomini and the Cathedral of the Assumption of the Virgin Mary, representing secular and religious power, capture precisely the semantics of supremacy in their respective domains not only by their appearance but also by the way they are organized spatially. The palace, which looks strikingly similar to Florentine palaces of those times to a viewer in the street (its façade resembling the Palazzo Rucellai most of all), is bordered by hanging gardens on the side of the valley. While the façade represents ancient times and the windows are a tribute to Gothic architecture, the gardens evoke the distant age of Queen Semiramis, to whom the construction of the Hanging Gardens of Babylon is attributed. The Pope could enjoy the view of the gardens from the palace loggia, which also provided a magnificent view of the whole Val d'Orcia. The

---

[12] The text of Piccolomini's "Commentaries" is quoted after the Italian edition: Enea Silvio Piccolomini, *I commentari*, ed. G. Bernetti, vol. 2, Milan 1981, pp. 840–841, IX, 24.

[13] Ibid.

[14] For example, the choir adjacent to the hall area and bordering the base of the cliff on the outside required devising an intricate form of a rectangular with a trapezoid based on one of its sides (a hexagon obtained by truncating a regular octagon).

valley is dominated by the dark silhouette of Mount Amiata, the "sacred mountain", as Enea Silvio himself called it.[15] The symbolic meaning of the three planes of landscapes that one was able to observe form the loggia is obvious: the hanging gardens supported by pillars represent nature that has been refined and transformed into a work of art by man; the Val d'Orcia is nature cultivated by man and serving the needs of humans; Mount Amiata is nature untamed, unbowed by human dominion. Piccolomini's gardens, built around a four-sector regular quadrilateral with a bowl in the middle, enclosed by a high wall and raised above the ground, recall the image of Eden, where man used to live when he had absolute power over nature.

The cathedral was constructed so that the noon shadow cast by its façade on an equinox day is exactly aligned with the travertine-lined boundaries of the square; the church thus assumes the role of a giant sundial. "The façade has three finely refined doors of appropriate size; the middle one is wider than the other two and has an open eye above it, similar to that of a cyclops; above the eye looms the Piccolomini family's coat of arms with the Keys of Heaven, and above it all there are the Pope's mitre and the papal triple tiara."[16] The circle—a round window in the upper part of the façade referred to as the "eye"[17]—is echoed by a white tufa circle in the middle of the central regular quadrilateral (which is one of the nine into which Pienza's square is divided). The two circles of the same size are located at the same distance from the façade-square plane intersection line. The "living" eye of the church is symmetrical to the dead, blind one on the ground. Opposing Christianity, associated with life and vision, to all other religions and philosophies as dead and blind has always been an extremely popular motif in Christian iconography, and the shadow of the cathedral crawling over the square and covering it completely from time to time is another symbol of false knowledge and death—the architect and his contractor bear in mind the antithesis of light and shadow, pagan (subterranean heathen sanctuary) and Christian (cathedral, erected by the Pope). Del Grande points out that the figure '9', which is at the basis of the square's spatial organization, has been associated with death in both pagan and Christian contexts.[18] The travertine-covered cathedral, the source and home of light and truth, is opposed to the ground from which it rises, the square, which is on behalf of its geometry a symbol of everything that is opposed to light and truth. Within the urban context,

---

15 The mountain is situated 47 km from Pienza and is more than 1,500 m high.
16 Piccolomini, *Comm.*, IX, 24.
17 Piccolomini uses the term *occhio*, which was regularly used at his time to denote a small round window in the upper part of a façade.
18 Del Grande, "Pienza", pp. 24–25.

the cathedral and the square thus realize the same idea of contrast that determines the relationship between the palace with its hanging gardens and Mount Amiata outside the town[19]: the gardens are anthropogenic images of spiritual power and beauty dominating the chthonic ones of earth and death. However, the latter are not allowed to reign supreme even underground, as the crypt—the lower part of the cathedral—occupies the area that had allegedly been home to an Etruscan sanctuary in most ancient times.

An orientation of pure space that does not inhibit the viewer's gaze toward a distant visual object does not only organize the optics of inanimate objects. The Pope's throne inside the cathedral is situated opposite the central choir chapel so that on a sunny day the pontiff is shaded by the silhouette of Mount Amiata, which is well discernible through the chapel window. It cannot go unnoticed by the reader of the *Commentarii* that the author attaches an extremely high importance to the visual effects that accentuate the central, dominant, and exclusive status of the protagonist. Piccolomini creates a literary correlate to composition in perspectivist art by elaborating his fabulous ekphrases of the buildings to be constructed in Pienza, which must have saved trouble for Pinturicchio, who was commissioned to paint frescoes based on plots from Pope Pius's life for the so-called Piccolomini Library in the cathedral of Siena almost half a century after the Pope died. If in the ekphrases of the popular feasts the figure of the Pope becomes the point of convergence of the geometrical lines, structuring the perspectivist image, in the episodes of the *Commentarii*, dealing with miracles centering around the figure of Pius, the epiphany of the Pontiff becomes the culmination of history; time becomes a manifestation of Providence—it provides a transcendent justification of Piccolomini's exclusive position.

Piccolomini was not the first to utilize this strategy of self-positioning, which was based on methods of Christian typological exegesis.[20] It existed prior to as well as during the Pope's lifetime, but nobody had ever reached such a virtuosity and versatility in dealing with it. The strategy as such can be traced back to the tendency of the fourteenth and fifteenth-century authors to comment on and evaluate their own achievements against the background of the literary tradition they belonged to. Dante, for instance, presents his appearance on the literary stage as the coming of the "fullness of time", prefigured by earlier poets. He

---

19 On the Pope's hydraulic utopias concerning the Val d'Orcia and the Monte Amiata, see F. Pellegrini, *L'utopia idraulica di Pio II nell'immaginario antico e moderno della Val d'Orcia*, San Quirico d'Orcia 2006.

20 Cf. the classical work on typology as an exegetical method, including its differences from allegory: H. de Lubac, "Typologie et Allégorisme", in: *Recherches des sciences religieuses*, vol. 34, 1947, pp. 180–226.

thematizes this self-conceptualization in the *Vita Nova*, in the *Convivio*, and in the *Divine Comedy*.[21] Petrarch stylizes himself in a similar way: in his *Africa*, he has Scipio and Ennius prophesy a "son of the Etruscan land", named Franciscus, who will become the glorious restorer of Latin poetry after centuries of decline.[22] When Lorenzo Medici, Pius II's junior contemporary, writes "A Commentary on my Sonnets" ("Comento de' miei sonetti"), he obviously suggests that he should be perceived as a new Dante: the plot, shaped by the sequence of poems and interpolated fragments of comments, is very similar to that of the *Vita Nova*.[23] In a letter to Lorenzo, Giovanni Pico della Mirandola traces the prehistory of the Magnifico's poetic genius: his arrival in the world of poetry is considered as a culmination of the whole history of literary production in *volgare*.[24] The head of the first Neapolitan Academy, Gioviano Pontano (1429–1503), exposes in the final part of his eclogue "Lepidina"[25] a version of the history of literature culminating in his own literary activity. This lengthy—more than 800 lines long—eclogue deals with the festivities on the occasion of the (mythical) wedding of the nymph Parthenope and the river god Sebes. A huge number of deities—protectors of a variety of Neapolitan villages, forests, fields, and rivers—take part in the procession. The eclogue ends, rather than with a praise of Parthenope and Sebes, with the apotheosis of Pontano himself. The nymph Antiniana, the patroness of a *villa urbana* in Antignano which belonged to the poet, predicts in her song the coming of Virgil and of Pontano—the latter appearing on Neapolitan soil some centuries later than the descendants of Parthenope and Sebes. In the song, both poets are said to have supernatural creative abilities; and the nymph even predicts the rituals of the Academia Pontaniana established by the author. Another of Picolomini's junior contemporaries, Marsilio Ficino (1433–1499), stated that Cosimo de' Medici the Elder decided, when Ficino was only six years old, to make of him a son of the Medici family and

---

21 O. Holmes, *Assembling the Lyric Self: Authorship from Troubadour Song to Italian Poetry Book*, London and Minneapolis, MN 1999, p. 123.
22 Petrarch, *Africa*, I, vv. 237–245. On the typological way of thinking of Petrarch in its relation to Virgil and Dante, see G. Regn and B. Huss, "Petrarch's Rome: The History of the *Africa* and the Renaissance Project", in: *MLN*, vol. 124, 2009, pp. 86–102.
23 On Lorenzo's commentary, see M. Shapiro, "Poetry and Politics in the *Comento* of Lorenzo de' Medici", in: *Renaissance Quarterly*, vol. 26, 1973, pp. 444–453; on the chronological inversion of the biographic events, effectuated by Lorenzo in order to reach a closer similarity to the plot of the *Vita Nova*, see Ch. Poncet, "The Judgment of Lorenzo", in: *Bruniana & Campanelliana*, vol. 14, 2008, pp. 541–561; esp. on Simonetta Cattaneo and Lucretia Donati, see pp. 545–547.
24 The date of Pico's letter is 15 July 1484; see Lorenzo de' Medici, *Selected Writings*, ed. C. Salvadori, intr. L. Bartoli, Dublin 1992, p. 192.
25 *Poeti latini del Quattrocento*, ed. F. Arnaldi, L. Gualdo Rosa, and L. Monti Saba, Milan and Naples 1964, pp. 316ff.

predicted that one day he would be a physician and a Platonic philosopher.[26] Ficino, indeed, conceived a full-fledged historiosophic design according to which he, together with the Florentine rulers from the Medici family, was the one in whom the history of the pagan world and Christianity found its completion.

In his *De christiana religione* (Ital. 1474, Lat. 1476), Ficino divides the history of mankind into the periods of inspiration (*inspiratio*) and interpretation (*interpretatio*). In the periods of inspiration, the Creator granted knowledge of the divine law and mysteries only to the chosen, to whom Moses and other Hebrew prophets as well as Plato and further pagan theologians belonged. Christ's incarnation marks the beginning of the era of interpretation: the disciples and, subsequently, all Christian believers obtain the key to the full truth of divine Revelation, hidden in the law and the prophecies. The era of interpretation reaches its peak in the figure of Dionysius the Areopagite (Ficino identifies the author of the *Corpus Areopagiticum* with Paul's disciple from Athens). After Dionysius, religious wisdom suffers a new decline, but is restored by the *platonici*, who have read the writings of St. Paul, St. John, Hierotheos, and Dionysius, and reaches perfection once again in the works of Origen and St. Augustine. After that, there were again "Dark Ages" that lasted until the times of Ficino, who, backed by Cosimo and Piero Medici, dedicated himself to Platonic philosophy and was ordained a priest not least thanks to the support of Lorenzo de' Medici. The coming of Ficino, who combined in his person a priest and a philosopher, brings to an end the thousand-year (!) silence of God.

Dante, Petrarch, Boccaccio, Ficino—all of them exploit the same myth in order to mark the position they lay claim to in the pantheon of culture: they present their arrival as an epiphany that is predicted in a number of prophecies and prefigured in a variety of prototypes, which would never have obtained the plenitude of the meaning implied in them had the latter men not been born. Typology allows for the endowment of each particular period with the attribute of the "plenitude of time", of being more perfect in comparison to the epoch of the founding of the tradition; the "plenitude of time" comes only in the present and involves all who are fortunate enough to witness the coming of the messianic hero. The series of events which come to pass between the founding of the tradition and the epiphany of the hero are provided with a vector. And the significance of the personality of the hero grows to such an extent that this personality becomes commensurable with all that took place during the lifetime of this tradition. Thus the author's

---

[26] On Ficino's biography and legacy, see R. Marcel, *Marsile Ficin (1443–1499)*, Paris 1958; *Marsilio Ficino e il ritorno di Platone: Studi e documenti*, ed. G. C. Garfagnini, 2 vols., Florence 1986; on Ficino's Platonism in its connection with his historiosophy, cf. J. Hankins, *Plato in the Italian Renaissance*, Leiden, Cologne, and New York, NY 1990.

narration about himself finds a resource of auto-justification in the exploitation of the entire tradition including its inherent antinomies.

In order to illustrate this rhetorical strategy with respect to Piccolomini, I will present two examples from the *Commentarii* dealing with the taming of the elements—majestic deeds comparable not merely to those of the Christian saints, but rather to those of the Old Testament prophets: As the Pope was on a visit to Perugia, a severe storm churned up the waters of Lake Trasimeno for many days—sailing was unthinkable.[27] However, as soon as the pontiff finally decides to approach the lake, the gale suddenly drops to a calm, "as if obeying a divine sign", and by the moment the Pope reaches one of the islands located in the lake, the elements "resemble a tamed beast". Crossing the still waters, the protagonist enjoys the wonderful sounds of flutes greeting him from the island. The fishermen he passes by will have an almost miraculously abundant catch of fish later that day. The Pope spends a night and the following morning on the island, the lake remaining still all the time; but as soon as his boat touches mainland, the storm rages again. Those who observed the Pope sailing and landing are left bewildered—everyone knows that navigation on Trasimeno Lake is impossible in winter.

The cycle of scenes describing the events related to the translation of Andrew the Apostle's relics to Rome is probably one of the most spectacular examples of self-representation created by Piccolomini, not least due to its aesthetic coherence.[28] It seems that the author was eager to perform in every genre he was skilled in: refined descriptions of preparation for the event flow smoothly into an elaborate epideictic speech pronounced by the Pope in front of vast crowds of people of all ranks and classes; this is followed by Sapphic stanzas from a hymn composed by Agapito Rustici-Cenci, Archbishop of Ancona, and an elegant impromptu Latin poem created by the Pope himself, while the description of the clergy's procession is reminiscent of Homer's Catalogue of Ships. Piccolomini describes the blooming meadows that line the road from Ostia to the Gates of Rome; subsequently, there is the description of the procession carrying the Honorable Head of Apostle Andrew from the harbor to the city. Amidst a vast field of flowers, the pontiff orders the erection of a wooden tribune with an altar in the middle. This had to be spacious and durable enough to hold all the clergy present, and high enough to allow anyone in the meadows to view every detail of the ceremony. Accompanied by nearly all the members of the senate, by numerous clerics, legates, princes, and other grand

---

27 Piccolomini, *Comm.*, pp. 162–164, II, 19.
28 Ibid., pp. 708–731, VIII, 2; the following quotes are from the same section. See also the above-mentioned article by Maskarinec, "Mobilizing Sanctity".

people of Rome, and followed by an endless crowd, the Pope exits the Porta Flaminia holding a palm branch—the day before was, indeed, the *Domenica delle Palme*. Palm branches are also held by all the clerics. The crowds cover the whole area as far as the eye can see, leaving no single section of meadow or vineyard visible. Having reached the field with the wooden tribune, the Pope orders the prelates to dismount their horses and walk the distance of a bowshot by foot before mounting the tribune together with him. Pius admires the majestic scene greeting him: the white brightness of luxurious clerical robes looks even more splendid against the background of lush greenery. "As if spellbound, the gazes were anchored on the miraculous order, the dignified and glorious procession of many priests divided in pairs, with palm branches in their hands, walking slowly beside the pontiff and praying together with him, surrounded by a massive crowd resembling a halo."

The tribune can be mounted by two sets of steps, one on the side of the city and the other on the side of the harbor. According to the ceremonial procedure, the Pope and his retinue ascend the former, while the latter one is reserved for Basilios Bessarion carrying the sacred head. After the keys and seals have been presented to the public, the urn containing the relics is opened in complete silence. Bessarion "passes the head to the Pontiff, crying with excitement". Before accepting the relics, the Pope kneels before the altar "and then speaks, his pale face down, his eyes filled with tears, his voice trembling"—next comes a two-page speech, which makes everyone weep. According to Piccolomini, there was no one left on the tribune, whether layman or cleric, who did not cry or pray for the Apostle's protection and pound his or her chest. Some even recorded the Pope's speech verbatim immediately after returning home and then showed the manuscript to the Pope. The ceremony ends with a Sapphic hymn, and the whole giant procession sets off to Rome. The sacred head is left overnight in a suburban church. The next day, according to Pius's plan, it should cross the City and arrive at St. Peter's Basilica. Suddenly, the weather changes, and the bright sun that lit the festive event the day before gives way to a heavy rain. Crowds of pilgrims, countless ambassadors, the clergy and folks of Rome are all in dismay and sorrow, for the procession which began so solemnly, as it seems, cannot be completed appropriately on account of the elements. The Pope is likewise aggrieved. He begins to pray, and a miracle happens: shortly after dawn, the clouds are blown away by the wind and the sun shines brighter than ever.

The list of miracles performed by the Pope is nearly endless: supernatural phenomena occur in the protagonist's life every now and then. Most often, they are witnessed by the public. As they are mainly described from the viewer's perspective, they do not appear as something actually *performed* by the main actor of the scenario. Presented as eyewitness testimony, a description of a miracle looks more credible. However, feigned humility, which is in fact an ill-disguised craving for public recognition, is not the only reason to recount one's own deeds in the third person. As a writer, Piccolomini needs a spectator whose admiring or jealous gaze would follow Pius, the protagonist of his narration. This is one of the constants in his writing style: third-party observers shape the Pope's image, making it integral. It does not even matter who the observer is—a peasant watching the papal retinue pass by, an unknown cleric attending a papal mass, or a noble seignior obliged to carry the gestatorial chair. Piccolomini's audience is indiscriminate with regard to social rank, the spectator only being required to have feelings strong enough to match the protagonist's grandeur and perfection. It could be jubilance at seeing the Pope, anger, envy, etc. Yet, admiration is what the overwhelming majority of spectators feel. The reactions of people as background actors, be it to the Pope's arrival, his departure, the festivities organized by Pius himself or in his honor, never remain unaddressed by the author. They vary from ordinary expressions of joy and awe worthy of the occasion to emotional extremes such as tears, crying, and pounding one's chest. Justifying the strong reactions of people observing the self-presentation of Pope Pius, the pontiff—whose self-description in the third person may be inspired by Julius Caesar—indulges in self-laudations that are far from being moderate.

It should be noted that Piccolomini uses this method of self-positioning not only in his literary works, but in his political activity as well. After his election to the papacy, he "confirmed" his first name—Aeneas—with the epithet of "Pius", which had been that of the legendary ancestor of the founders of Rome and of the whole *orbis romanus*.[29] The scale of Piccolomini's ambitions becomes clear when he—at first sight—modestly summons his flock "to reject Aeneas and to accept Pius". The pattern of third-person autobiography and the very title of *Commentarii* refer to Caesar, the founder of imperial Rome.[30] In this way, the Pope explicitly indicates his predecessors on the Roman throne, mythical as well as authentic ones. In the *Commentarii*, he does not refrain from praising his own integrity (*integritas*), strength of mind (*vis animi*), perseverance (*animus invictus*), large-heartedness (*magnanimitas*), piety (*pietas*), prudence (*prudentia*), invincible constancy (*invicta constantia*), unlimited benevolence (*imminuta benignitas*), justice (*iustitia*), humility (*clementia*), and determination (*firma deliberatio*). Ekphrasis, which has its origin in classical antiquity, together with medieval Christian hagiography, are the templates

---

29 Virgil apostrophized the protagonist of his epic as *pius Aeneas*.
30 The authentic title of the text known as *De bello Gallico* is, indeed, *Commentarii de bello Gallico*.

Piccolomini draws upon alternatively to create his own image. Enea Silvio's intentions as a writer bring these two genres into a complementary relationship: ekphrasis is used to demonstrate the "exterior" perfection of the protagonist, while hagiographic techniques with a generous touch of ancient moralist literature (for the most part classical historical writings) expose his perfect inner qualities. In other words, the exemplary form is filled with equally exemplary content, either pious or heroic.

In order to present the protagonist, i.e. himself, as an agent of Providence, the papal autobiographer has to isolate him aesthetically as much as possible by placing every single event in his life in a transcendental context, raising his image far above ordinary human existence and attributing extremely high spiritual and moral qualities to his character. The pious effort of an exegete trying to understand the design of Providence for his own life is thus merged with a narcissistic desire for self-completion and the sheer obsession with others' opinions. Pius's self-reflective I is only able to perceive himself in forms dependent on others. This dependence on the viewer is embodied spatially in the protagonist's position in the point of convergence of perspectives and verbally in the concentration of epithets indicating superiority and excellence around his own figure, in ekphrastic self-admiration from a third-person perspective, and in the assertion of his life as unique by means of a self-exegesis based on the concept of divine mission.

In the scenes depicting the Pope's triumph, which constitute the semantic axis of imagery in the *Commentarii*, the appearances of the protagonist and the way they are perceived by admiring audiences seem to be perfectly in unison; they are organized according to a phenomenon that could be described as a *predetermined harmony of contemplation*. The other's position turns out to have been utterly and completely predetermined in a unified panoptical perspective: taking no active part in self-affirmation on the outside, the protagonist has already made use of the author's absolute power over the audience and taken possession of their will in advance. Piccolomini transforms the entirely predetermined opinions of others into moments of his own aesthetic self-assertion, thus avoiding any personal responsibility for his self-image: individual others conceal the figure of the Absolute Other, the author of the *Commentarii*, who has become the source of divine will and justification of himself. Transcendental intuition of an unseen deity is thus translated into aesthetic language, providing ultimate descriptive visualization—that is how the aesthetic microcosm of the *Commentarii* (and Piccolomini's life as such) reaches the ontological extremes of faith and reason, leaving nothing but itself on or above the earth.

Sandra Richter
Literal and Figurative Uses of the *Pícaro*: Graded Salience in Seventeenth-Century Picaresque Narrations

Hans Jakob Christoffel von Grimmelshausen's *Abentheuerlicher Simplicissimus Teutsch / The Adventurous Simplicissimus Teutsch* (1668/1669) opens with an impressive frontispiece, structured in the form of an emblem. A multiform creature presents a book containing icons and stands on a sort of stage, with masks scattered around and beneath its feet. The title of this picture gives insights into what to expect: "Der Abentheuerliche Simplicissimus Teutsch" / "The Adventurous Simplicissimus Teutsch". Perhaps this creature is Simplicius: a fish tail, a duck's webbed foot, a goat's cloven hoof (thereby citing the devil), wings, an epee, a human torso, fingers making the sign of the devil, a Pan-head with horns and large ears as though it were a mask. In the book presented by this creature, a crown suggests the sovereign, a cannon indicates war, a fool's head the picaro, a wine glass and a cooked fowl food and the culture of the still life, evoking *vanitas*. This frontispiece seems to be conveying the meaning of the novel—but in what way? Is the fool real and the *theatrum mundi* our stage? Or is being a fool a transitory state of every human until he or she embraces Christian belief?

Research on picaresque narratives has focused on the one hand on what this way of writing, still new in the seventeenth century, takes over from the chivalric novel of the medieval past, and on the other hand it has explored the varieties within what had previously been viewed as a more-or-less homogeneous European genre, the "picaresque novel".[1] In the form of a pseudo-autobiography, the picaro, often a young man, belongs to the lower ranks, but moves quickly between them, changing his roles. He explores the world and experiences contingency and unreliability. From 1618 onwards, depictions of the Thirty Year's War feature prominently in picaresque narratives. As a result of war, the picaro gains

---

[1] U. Wicks, "The Nature of Picaresque Narrative: A Modal Approach", in: *PMLA: Publications of the Modern Language Association of America*, vol. 89, 1974, pp. 240–249; G. van Gemert, "Gibt es einen deutschen Picaro-Roman im siebzehnten Jahrhundert? Überlegungen zu einer kontroversiellen Gattungsbezeichnung", in: *Kontroversen, alte und neue: Akten des VII. Internationalen Germanisten-Kongresses Göttingen 1985*, ed. A. Schöne, Tübingen 1986, pp. 103–109; J. Mohr, C. Struwe, and M. Waltenberger, "Pikarische Erzählverfahren", in: *Pikarische Erzählverfahren*, ed. J. Mohr, C. Struwe, and M. Waltenberger, Berlin and Boston, MA 2016, pp. 3–34.

Open Access. © 2019 Sandra Richter, published by De Gruyter. This work is licensed under the Creative Commons Attribution-NonCommercial-NoDerivatives 4.0 License.
https://doi.org/10.1515/9783110622034-004

Fig. 1: Frontispiece of Hans Jakob Christoffel von Grimmelshausen's "Adventurous Simplicissimus Teutsch", 1668/69 (German Schleifheim von Sulsfort [i.e. Hans Jakob Christoffel von Grimmelshausen], *Der Abentheurliche Simplicissimus Teutsch*, Monpelgart [i.e. Nuremberg] 1669, s.p., p. [1]. http://www.deutschestextarchiv.de/book/view/grimmelshausen_simplicissimus_1669?p=7, accessed 17 December 2018).

insight into the corrupted nature of man. He observes the very nature of men: affects and emotions, virtue and vice. He himself tries to find his way past obstacles. These episodes make for an entertaining read, give detailed accounts even of erotic issues, and develop their own recognizable topography and plot. Disillusioned in his old age the picaro often turns to the life of a hermit, emigrates to foreign islands,[2] and, in turn, his narration could be viewed either as utopian, alluding to unknown paradises,[3] or as a penitential parable or sermon (consisting of three parts: *contritio, confessio, satisfactio*), an allegorical pilgrimage (in the form of the *navigatio hominis*) in which the ageing former picaro condemns his previous behavior,[4] sometimes taking in exempla literature. Some of the picaresque narratives are dominated by moral or religious teaching.[5] Francisco Gómez de Quevedo's *Historia de la vida del Buscón / History of the Life of Buscón* (1626), one of the few picaresque narratives to deny the moral effect of this type of writing, may serve to confirm this rule thanks to its harsh opposition to moralistic doctrines. The moral teaching of most picaresque narratives represents a mixture of ascetic Christianity and neostoicism.[6] Picaresque narratives can, to some extent, be interpreted as an escape from an overly rigid neostoic mentality. This literary flight allows for narrative and rhetorical experiments within the neostoic and Christian mental framework.[7]

Over the course of the eighteenth century the picaro was transformed, excluded from some parts of literature while being inserted into the other ever-changing literary and mental frameworks of the time. One reason for the

---

[2] J. Mohr, "Inseln und Inselräume: Kontingenz in Grimmelshausens und Dürers Schelmenromanen", in: *Inseln und Archipele: Kulturelle Figuren des Insularen zwischen Isolation und Entgrenzung*, ed. A. E. Wilkens, P. Ramponi, and H. Wendt, Bielefeld 2011, pp. 225–243.

[3] N. Kaminski, "Narrator absconditus oder Der Ich-Erzähler als 'verschwundener Kerl': Von der erzählten Utopie zu utopischer Autorschaft in Grimmelshausens 'Simplicianischen Schriften'", in: *Deutsche Vierteljahrsschrift für Literaturwissenschaft und Geistesgeschichte*, vol. 74, 2000, pp. 367–394; W. Voßkamp, "Figuren produktiver Negation: Interferenzen zwischen pikareskem und utopischem Erzählen bei Grimmelshausen", in: *Spielräume: Ein Buch für Jürgen Fohrmann*, ed. J. Brokoff, E. Dubbels, and A. Schütte, Bielefeld 2013, pp. 13–25.

[4] G. van Gemert, "Vom Pícaro zur Leitfigur interkonfessioneller Konfrontationen: Kompilatorisches Verfahren und neuer Sinngehalt im deutschen 'Gusman' von 1615–1626", in: *Morgen-Glantz: Zeitschrift der Christian Knorr von Rosenroth-Gesellschaft*, vol. 6, 1996, pp. 265–290; J.-M. Valentin, "Die Indienstnahme der Pikareske durch die Gegenreformation: Aegidius Albertinus' Adaptation (1615) des Alemanschen *Guzman de Alfarache*. Narratio und catechisatio", in: *Die Bedeutung der Rezeptionsliteratur für Bildung und Kultur der Frühen Neuzeit (1400–1750): Beiträge zur ersten Arbeitstagung in Eisenstadt (März 2011)*, ed. A. Noe and G.-G. Roloff, Bern 2012, pp. 325–341.

[5] U. Knapp, *Der Roman der fünfziger Jahre: Zur Entwicklung der Romanästhetik in Westdeutschland*, Würzburg 2002, pp. 9f.

[6] M. Watson, "The Stoicism of the Picaro in the Picaresque Novel of Sixteenth- and Seventeenth-Century Spain", in: *Furman Studies*, vol. 21, 1974, pp. 37–40.

[7] Th. Althaus, "Topische Radikalisierung und allegorische Kontrolle des Pikaresken in den frühen deutschsprachigen Adaptionen", in: *Pikarische Erzählverfahren*, pp. 67–94.

exclusion of the picaro is the changing anthropology of the eighteenth century, an anthropology that proclaims the constructive function of reason. Classical ideas of literature also play a role: although some characters in eighteenth-century drama acted as though they were fools, the fool and his representatives were not among the favorite figures either of French classicism or of Johann Christoph Gottsched's adaptations of Pierre Corneille and others. In contrast to French and German literature in the "classical" tradition, English literature (long after Thomas Nashe's early *Unfortunate Traveller: or, the Life of Jack Wilton*, 1594) invented ever new picaros. For instance, Henry Fielding was fascinated with Cervantes and in his *History of Tom Jones, a Foundling* (1749) he imitated *Don Quixote*. Only ten years later, Voltaire published his *Candide* (1759), which portrays the picaro as a sceptic; Laurence Sterne with *The Life and Opinions of Tristram Shandy, Gentleman* (1761–1767) followed suit. The two latter novels in particular served as role models for contemporary German literature, for instance for Christoph Martin Wieland. However, they were dedicated to a specific question: to what extent can reason serve as a means to understand and plan life? The idea of the picaro has been taken further: he has been regarded as a character with parallels to the court jester through to present-day Nigerian drama,[8] as a companion to the American trickster as well as his counterpart,[9] as a forerunner of Joseph von Eichendorff's "Taugenichts" (good-for-nothing),[10] of the figure of the clown in its various guises,[11] of the Mexican Chicano,[12] of the pirate in colonial contexts,[13] of the main characters in Günter

---

[8] H.-J. Mahl, "Narr und Picaro: Zum Wandel der Narrenmotivik im Roman des 17. Jahrhunderts", in: *Studien zur deutschen Literatur: Festschrift für Adolf Beck zum siebzigsten Geburtstag*, ed. U. Fulleborn and J. Krogoll, Heidelberg 1979, pp. 18–40; K. G. Kofoworola, "The Court Jester in Nigerian Drama", in: *Clowns, Fools and Picaros: Popular Forms in Theatre, Fiction and Film*, ed. D. Robb, Amsterdam and New York, NY 2007, pp. 101–114.
[9] F. Ballinger, "Ambigere: The Euro-American Picaro and the Native American Trickster", in: *MELUS*, vol. 17, 1991, pp. 21–38; M. Y. Bennett, "Dominance and the Triumph of the White Trickster over the Black Picaro in Amiri Baraka's *Great Goodness of Life*: A Coon Show", in: *Callaloo: A Journal of African Diaspora Arts and Letters*, vol. 36, 2013, pp. 312–321.
[10] A. von Bormann, "Joseph Von Eichendorff: *Aus dem Leben eines Taugenichts* (1826)", in: *Romane und Erzählungen zwischen Romantik und Realismus: Neue Interpretationen*, ed. P. M. Lützeler, Stuttgart 1983, pp. 94–116.
[11] A. Tobias, "The Postmodern Theatre Clown", in: Robb (ed.), *Clowns, Fools and Picaros*, pp. 37–55.
[12] E. R. Lamadrid, "The Rogue's Progress: Journeys of the Picaro from Oral Tradition to Contemporary Chicano Literature of New Mexico", in: *MELUS*, vol. 20, 1995, pp. 15–34.
[13] J. Mander, "Picaros, Pirates, and Colonial History", in: *Philological Quarterly*, vol. 89, 2010, pp. 55–74.

Grass's *Die Blechtrommel* / *The Tin Drum* (1959),[14] Patrick Süskind's *Das Parfum* / *Perfume* (1985),[15] in Edgar Hilsenrath's *Der Nazi und der Friseur* / *The Nazi and the Barber* (1971/77),[16] Wladimir Kaminer's novels,[17] and in postcolonial and postmodern writing.[18]

These concepts of the picaro deviate considerably from the one that was dominant in the early stages of his construction. Therefore, this article will restrict itself to the early development of the role of the picaro and explore its specific theatrical characteristics. What exactly was a picaro and how was his stage conceived? Although research has certainly provided extensive knowledge about the picaresque novel and seventeenth-century anthropology, the ways in which "being a fool" is introduced and described have seldom been analysed. Furthermore, the exact etymology of the term "picaro" has remained unclear.[19] The noun *pícaro* was first used in sixteenth-century Spanish contexts. The term "picaresque novel", of course, was coined only in late nineteenth-century research literature.

My thesis is that picaresque narratives display a wide variety of motifs and roles which require differentiation. Some of these narrative variations do not use the concept of the picaro at all but do contribute to the traditional characteristics of fools and similar figures and, consequently, to the vast field of picaresque writing. Other variations use the notions of the picaro, *Schelm*, rascal, rogue, and the like as though they denote a real being and as though the

---

14 G. R. Dimler, "Simplicius Simplicissimus and Oskar Matzerath as Alienated Heroes: Comparison and Contrast", in: *Amsterdamer Beiträge zur neueren Germanistik*, vol. 4, 1975, pp. 113–134.
15 E. Borchardt, "Caricature, Parody, Satire: Narrative Masks as Subversion of the Picaro in Patrick Süskind's *Perfume*", in: *State of the Fantastic: Studies in the Theory and Practice of Fantastic Literature and Film*, ed. N. Ruddick, Westport, CT 1992, pp. 97–103.
16 B. Malkmus, "Picaresque Narratology: *Lazarillo de Tormes* and Edgar Hilsenrath's *Der Nazi und der Friseur*", in: Robb (ed.), *Clowns, Fools and Picaros*, pp. 211–229.
17 A. Wanner, "Wladimir Kaminer: A Russian Picaro Conquers Germany", in: *Russian Review: An American Quarterly Devoted to Russia Past and Present*, vol. 64, 2005, pp. 590–604.
18 R. Rosenthal, "Gravity's Rainbow and the Postmodern Picaro", in: *Revue française d'études américaines*, vol. 42, 1989, pp. 407–426; H. Williams, "Hatterr and Bazza: Post-Colonial Picaros", in: *Commonwealth Review*, vol. 2, 1990, pp. 204–211; I. Almond, "Rogues of Modernity: Picaresque Variations in the Postcolonial Genre of the Enlightenment Missionary", in: *Orbis Litterarum: International Review of Literary Studies*, vol. 61, pp. 96–113; R. Bartosch, "The Postcolonial Picaro in Indra Sinha's *Animal's People*: Becoming Posthuman through Animal's Eyes", in: *Ecozon@: European Journal of Literature, Culture and Environment*, vol. 3, 2012, pp. 10–19; Robb, *Clowns, Fools and Picaros*.
19 On the unresolved puzzle of the etymology, see J. L. Laurenti, *Catálogo bibliográfico de la literatura picaresca (siglos XVI–XX)*, 2 vols., 2nd ed., Kassel 2000.

concept of the picaro has to be understood literally. Yet others use these notions figuratively, with the help of comparisons ("like a picaro") or as if-clauses. The same applies to the adjective "picaresque" which is also used both literally and figuratively.

Drawing on a large body of rhetorical and linguistic research, it can be assumed that members of the figurative language family such as metaphor, metonymy, and synecdoche express the ordinary in extraordinary or even poetic ways.[20] Interpretation of the relevant texts will show how this is done and allow for speculation about the exact functions that may be relevant for contemporary and later readers. One or more functions may be dominant in a given context but the others are present at the same time. Recent experimental research on a dataset of Italian literary metaphors has shown that, while in non-literary utterances context supports metaphor comprehension, literary metaphors are understood differently: context makes them "only slightly more predictable" and reduces familiarity with them.[21] Accordingly, it may be assumed that literary texts leave metaphors—and possibly all members of the figurative language family—open to various and different interpretations. And, in contrast to ordinary metaphors, literary ones do not seem to lose their power after repeated exposure.[22] It would seem that there are peculiar poetic mechanisms at work that render figurative uses of language even more difficult to understand.

However, this observation may also hold true for the literal use of language, especially as regards a newly created and not yet conventionalized adjectival noun such as "picaro". Also, literary uses of such a word could fulfil emotive, cognitive, possibly also appellative, referential, phatic, and perhaps even metalingual functions. Yet the word seems to have been meaningful and concrete. In addition, in languages other than Spanish, the Spanish word may have raised attention. Following the Graded Salience Hypothesis, all occurrences of the word picaro in the seventeenth-century novel could be accessed directly and regardless of literal and figurative use.[23] At the same time, it would

---

[20] See the standard works by R. Jakobson, "The Metaphoric and Metonymic Poles", in: *Fundamentals of Language*, ed. R. Jakobson and M. Halle, The Hague 1956, pp. 76–82; G. Lakoff and M. Johnson, *Metaphors We Live By*, Chicago, IL and London 1980.
[21] V. Bambini, D. Resta, and M. Grimaldi, "A Dataset of Metaphors from the Italian Literature: Exploring Psycholinguistic Variables and the Role of Context", in: *PLOS ONE*, vol. 9, 2014, p. 10. https://doi.org/10.1371/journal.pone.0105634, accessed 18 December 2018.
[22] Ibid.
[23] Regarding the Graded Salience Hypothesis see R. Giora, *On Our Mind: Salience, Context and Figurative Language*, New York, NY 2003.

be interesting to study whether literal and figurative uses make a difference to the ways in which the word "picaro" is activated in these texts, that is: in which ways does its meaning become salient? I would like to identify the features associated with the picaro and his role, the emotive, cognitive, and other dimensions that the concept conveys, and, consequently, why it had to be made salient in its own narrative. The result will point to contemporary theater and theatrical concepts.

Three texts will serve as examples. They all originated after the publication of initial literary picaresque innovation, the anonymous *Vida de Lazarillo de Tormes y de sus fortunas y adversidades / The Life of Lazarillo de Tormes and of His Fortunes and Adversities* (1554), a work not explicitly called a "picaresque" narrative (nor indeed a "novel"). The first example is Mateo Alemán's *Guzmán*, the second Paul Scarron's *Roman comique*, the third Grimmelshausen's *Simplicissimus Teutsch*, the most famous German picaresque text aside from Johann Beer's works and Christian Reuter's parodistic travel report *Schelmuffskys warhafftige Curiöse und sehr gefährliche Reisebeschreibung zu Wasser und Lande / Schelmuffsky's true, curious, and very dangerous travel description by water and land* (1696).[24]

Spanish picaros and early picaresque writing

Lazarillo seems to have been responsible for a number of literary innovations. The text deals with a marginalized character, a boy of humble (possibly Jewish) origins who has to serve a blind beggar and several other masters while using the narrative technique of the "worm's eye view" and various other rhetorical and narratological techniques of deception (e.g. the unreliable narrator).[25] Lázaro observes the world as though it is unknown to him, uncovering its contingency and injustice. With the help of the "worm's eye view", the text refers to various levels of society, to the working conditions and domestic life of the

---

[24] See inter alia, I. Wirtz, "Mausköpf, Fuchsschwänz und Bärenhäuter: Schimpfreden und Picarofiguren in Johann Beers Romanen", in: *Johann Beer: Schriftsteller, Komponist und Hofbeamter 1655–1700. Beiträge zum Internationalen Beer-Symposium in Weißenfels, Oktober 2000*, ed. F. van Ingen and H.-G. Roloff, Berlin and Bern, 2003, pp. 615–630; M. Bergengruen, "Der große Mogol oder der Vater der Lügen des Schelmuffsky: Zur Parodie des Reiseberichts und zur Poetik des Diabolischen bei Christian Reuter", in: *Zeitschrift für Deutsche Philologie*, vol. 126, 2007, pp. 161–184.
[25] R. Cacho Casal, "Hide-and-Seek: *Lazarillo de Tormes* and the Art of Deception", in: *Forum for Modern Language Studies*, vol. 44, 2008, pp. 322–339, p. 324.

poor, and even to children. The mirror the text holds up to contemporary Spain presents multiracial life, referring to Lazarillo's black stepfather and a *negrito* half-brother. The church and the aristocracy are among the groups and ranks that are attacked extensively, and core beliefs and ceremonies of Christianity such as Holy Communion are parodied.[26] In sum, the novel not only contradicts established literary forms such as the chivalric romance with its superhuman heroes, it also proved to be an anticlerical, ironic, and metafictional document, which was consequently banned by the Spanish crown and included on the *Index Librorum Prohibitorum*, the Index of Forbidden Books.[27]

The character of the anti-hero Lázaro, however, is described as a sinner, not as a picaro.[28] A selective overview of the literary traditions and the character of this pre-picaresque picaro is appropriate at this juncture. Research has identified a few likely forerunners of *Lazarillo* and his adaptations, for instance Apuleius' tale of the Golden Ass (allusions to donkeys figure prominently in picaresque narratives), in which a servant—a man metamorphosed into a donkey—serves many masters. The humanists' letters and, last but not least, interrogation documents of the inquisition (directed against so-called *judaizantes*, converted Jews) have been named as further sources that may have inspired the pseudo-biographical life-writing in *Lazarillo*.[29] The heritage of *Lazarillo* reflects the ways in which this innovative text was appreciated: the anonymous novel (or, more correctly: a censored version of it) was translated into many European languages, among them German, already in the sixteenth and seventeenth centuries. The first German translation of the text appeared in Breslau in 1614. Its translator may have been an erudite Protestant of Silesian origin who was enthusiastic about its criticism of the Catholic clergy.[30] In Spain, however, 45 years passed without any notable publications of picaresque stories. The reason may have been the rigid courtly culture in Spain as well as the strict publication policy that had apparently made it difficult for any picaresque novels to appear.

---

26 S. Zepp, "Ironie, Inquisition und Konversion: Parodien von Inklusionsdispositiven im *Lazarillo de Tormes*", in: *Romanistisches Jahrbuch*, vol. 56, 2006, pp. 368–392, p. 372.
27 E. H. Friedman, "From Inside Out: The Poetics of *Lazarillo de Tormes*", in: *Philological Quarterly*, vol. 89, 2010, pp. 13–30.
28 H. Mancing, "The Mind of a Pícaro: Lázaro de Tormes", in: *Cognition, Literature, and History*, ed. M. J. Bruhn and D. R. Wehrs, New York, NY 2014, pp. 174–189.
29 Zepp, "Ironie, Inquisition und Konversion", pp. 375–388.
30 A. Martino, "Die Rezeption des *Lazarillo de Tormes* im deutschen Sprachraum (1555/62–1750)", in: *Daphnis: Zeitschrift für Mittlere Deutsche Literatur und Kultur der Frühen Neuzeit*, vol. 26, 1997, pp. 301–399, p. 304.

In the next canonical text to be published in the vein of *Lazarillo*, Mateo Alemán's popular Spanish novel *Guzmán de Alfarache* (1599/1604), the main character does not become a picaro either but calls his "office" and life picaresque—a figurative use of the word which denotes his existence, rank, and role in society. There is no comparison of the picaresque existence to theater; Guzmán takes up a social role with which his whole being is, in part, identical. This figurative use of the word "picaro" fits Alemán's way of employing metaphors, such as taste metaphors, to show the extent to which picaresque life enables the protagonist to perceive the world through thought, emotion, and physical sensation.[31]

Need drives Guzmán from his home. Born to a father of Jewish origin who converted to Christianity, a prominent topos of picaresque storytelling,[32] Guzmán takes his mother's maiden name Alfarache and, having lost his servant's job, walks around in torn clothes. "Viéndome perdido, comencé a tratar el oficio de la florida picardía" / "As I found myself lost I began to take up the flourishing office of the picaro", he notes.[33] Feeling ashamed, he joins other beggars and tries to assist them with their work. "Aprendí a ser buen huésped, esperar y no ser esperado" / "I learned to be a good guest, waiting but not awaited."[34] With a Madrilenian host he learns gambling and deceit; Guzmán enjoys the "vida de pícaro" / "life of the picaro".[35] Moreover, he commends his "deseo desta gloriosa libertad" / "desire for this glorious freedom", also defying the authorities.

> I wouldn't trade this rogue life for the best my past has ever had. I took my time at court, I employed my ingenuity for hours, I gave a new edge to my understanding and, seeing that children other than I could do with little wealth, and I could eat without asking or expecting it from someone else's hand—which is bread of pain, bread of blood, even if your father gave it to you—with a desire for this glorious freedom and not to be punished like others for vagrancy, I agreed to bear the burdens that my shoulders could suffer.

---

[31] R. K. Fritz, "Cognition and Redemption in *Guzmán de Alfarache*", in: *Beyond Sight: Engaging the Senses in Iberian Literatures and Cultures, 1200–1750*, ed. R. D. Giles and S. Wagschal, Toronto 2018, pp. 66–93.

[32] R. D. Giles, "Picaresque Fatherhood: Racial and Literary Heritage", in: *Neohelicon*, vol. 40, 2013, pp. 227–244; E. Weissbourd, "Translating Spain: Purity of Blood and Orientalism in Mabbe's *Rogue* and *Guzmán de Alfarache*", in: *Modern Philology: Critical and Historical Studies in Literature, Medieval through Contemporary*, vol. 114, 2017, pp. 552–572.

[33] Mateo Alemán, *Guzmán de Alfarache*, ed. J. M. Micó, vol. I, Madrid 1987, p. 275.

[34] Ibid., p. 276.

[35] Ibid.

> No trocara esta vida de pícaro por la mejor que tuvieron mis pasados. Tomé tiento a la corte, íbaseme sotilizando el ingenio por horas, di nuevos filos al entendimiento y, viendo a otros menores que yo hacer con caudal poco mucha hacienda y comer sin pedir ni esperarlo de mano ajena—que es pan de dolor, pan de sangre, aunque te lo dé tu padre—, con deseo desta gloriosa libertad y no me castigasen como a otros por vagabundo, acomodéme a llevar los cargos que podían sufrir mis hombros.[36]

"¡Ved a lo que se estiende su fuerza!" / "See what constitutes your force!" he cries out proudly.[37] Carrying his belongings on his shoulders the newborn picaro wanders around and reflects upon his previous life as well as the life of his parents, or, more precisely, that of the people he considers to be his parents. Almost everybody, so it seems to him, betrays others and will be betrayed in turn.

Even though Guzmán acquires wealth and falls in love with a woman who seems to love him, this does not last. He loses his wealth, his wife runs away, and he is condemned to serve on the galleys. Having gained insight into this vicious wheel of fortune he pledges to mend his ways. Writing retrospectively, the narrator admits wit only under the veil of morality; he promotes a Christian and moral point of view. The novel sheds a pessimistic light on human life while taking in contemporary developments such as multilingualism and challenging established humanist views.[38] Man cannot escape the state of original sin—which is further expressed and made manifest in the notion of the "life of the picaro". Those protagonists who live the life of the picaro are sinners par excellence. Their only escape, it seems, lies in isolation and, ultimately, in becoming a hermit.

The first description of such a character as a picaro is to be found in the German adaptation of Alemán's text, which was published as *Guzmán: Der Landstörtzer Gusmann von Alfarache oder Picaro genannt* (1615–1626) by the Bavarian Counter-Reformation writer Aegidius Albertinus. He freely adapted the first part of the Spanish original and then omitted some sections of the other parts of the text, while also adding other material—a compilation that has been called the first "picaresque novel" in the German language.[39] Albertinus

---

[36] Ibid., p. 277.
[37] Ibid.
[38] J. C. Parrack, "The Picaresque School of Learning: Modernity and the Critique of Classical Humanism in *Guzmán de Alfarache* and the *Ortografía castellana*", in: *Romance Notes*, vol. 45, 2005, pp. 293–301; J.-L. Brau, "Roman picaresque et prose d'idées: *Guzmán de Alfarache* de Mateo Alemán", in: *Cahiers de Narratologie*, vol. 14, 2008, pp. 1–13.
[39] Van Gemert, "Vom Pícaro zur Leitfigur", pp. 265–290; A. Martino, "Der Erzpicaro in Deutschland: Aegidius Albertinus' Übersetzung des *Guzmán de Alfarache*", in: *Mittlere Deutsche Literatur und Italien: Beiträge zu Ehren von Emilio Bonfatti*, ed. F. Masiero, Bern 2013, pp. 139–203.

identifies the main character as a picaro—a word that was new to the contemporary German language. The German Guzmán literally becomes a picaro, leading a life characterized by idleness, as in the Spanish original. In order to explain what this means and to highlight the importance of the notion, Albertinus adds words in the same semantic field as the picaro or ones that bear an associative relationship with the term, for instance "Schwarack" (a Bavarian expression that could be translated as "buffoon" or "jester") and "Landstörzer" ("vagabond")[40]:

> [...] for they thought I was a Picaro or a Schwarack, who was useless. That caused me to join the laudable picaric company or society, for I had already lost all shame on the way, and, because I had to go on foot, so it [shame] was too heavy for me to carry, therefore I let it go its separate way, and clothed myself in impudence, for it is impossible for hunger and shame to be good friends and be together.
>
> [...] dann man hielt mich für einen Picaro oder Schwaracken, der kein nutz were. Das verursachte mich, daß ich mich in die löbliche Picarische zunfft oder gesellschafft begab, dann die scham hatte ich allbereit auffm weg verlohren, dann weil ich zu Fuß gehen muste, so war sie mir vil zu schwer zu tragen, derwegen ließ ich sie fahren, und bekleidete mich mit der unverschammtheit, dann unmüglich ists, daß der hunger und die scham gute freunde und beysammen sey[41].

Through translations like this, the picaresque being or the picaro becomes one of the literary types of the period. It is interesting that this identification takes place in the German context, whereas the French takes up the pre-picaresque tradition (though not the word) and mingles it with the traditions of theater-writing. In contrast to the direction taken by the French tradition, Albertinus relies much more on penitential literature (especially in the second part of the novel),[42] on character-writing and neostoic morals and, therefore, tends to construct characters not as roles but rather as moral types. In the case of Albertinus these depictions serve a distinct goal: Counter-Reformation moral preaching and Catholic apologetics.

---

40 M. Feltre, "La traduzione del termine Pícaro nel *Gusman* di Aegidius Albertinus", in: *Prospero*, vol. 3, 1996, pp. 117–144.
41 Aegidius Albertinus, *Der Landtstörtzer: Gusman von Alfarache oder Picaro genannt*, vol. I., Munich 1615, p. 54.
42 K. Bremer, "Konversion und Buße: Zur Funktion des Einsiedlers in Aegidius Albertinus' Landstörtzer Gusman", in: *Daphnis: Zeitschrift für Mittlere Deutsche Literatur und Kultur der Frühen Neuzeit (1400–1750)*, vol. 40, 2011, pp. 697–708.

As regards the figurative and literal uses of the word picaro, however, the Guzmán example shows that both uses are salient in literature. The figurative use that is dominant in Alemán's original highlights the numerous changes to Guzmán's biography. Alemán's Guzmán tries to fulfil a role in various lower ranks of society, of which the picaro is just one. Accordingly, Alemán's uses of the picaro highlight the relevance of need: an image of society in which men fight against each other as well as against the contingency of the wheel of fortune. The brief interlude in which Guzmán praises the idea of liberty quickly uncovers the high costs that are the prerequisite of this liberty. In contrast to the original, the literal use of the picaro in Aegidius Albertinus turns Guzmán into an amoral character: a character that could be condemned with the help of moralistic literature—although the translation uncovers some of the wit that is inherent to the story of the "free men".

French "comédiens" and a theater novel

Paul Scarron's *Roman comique* (incomplete, I, 1651; II, 1657) holds a prominent position in picaresque writing. Scarron's cast, however, which consists of wandering actors ("comédiens"), does not have any explicit hero, anti-hero, or picaro. Building on elements of the commedia dell'arte, the farcical and burlesque plays in the novel are reminiscent of the lazzi.[43] Taking up the French tradition of "histoires comiques" as well as of the lower register of the Spanish novel, especially Miguel de Cervantes Saavedra's *Ingenioso hidalgo Don Quixote de la Mancha / The Ingenious Nobleman Sir Quixote of La Mancha* from 1605/1615, (e.g. the character of the wild man, the context of a morally dubious hostel),[44] Scarron's theater troupe enjoys rather flat hierarchies—and may soon even be governed by the servants:

> The comedy troupe was made up of Le Destin, L'Olive, and La Rancune, each of whom had a valet aspiring to one day become chief actor. Some of these valets were already reciting without blushing or stumbling; Le Destin's servant, among others, did quite well, listened enough to what he said, and was witty.

---

[43] J. Vos-Camy, "Theatrical Intersections in the Novel: Scarron's *Roman comique*", in: *Intersections: Actes du 35ᵉ congrès annuel de la North American Society for Seventeenth-Century French Literature, Dartmouth College, 8–10 mai 2003*, ed. F. E. Beardsley and K. Wine, Tübingen 2005, pp. 53–58.

[44] G. Hautcœur, "Scarron et l'héritage quichottesque: une lecture comparatiste du *Roman comique*", in: *Cahiers de l'association internationale des études françaises*, vol. 63, 2011, pp. 215–228.

> La troupe comique était composée de Destin, de L'Olive et de La Rancune, qui avait chacun un valet prétendant à devenir un jour comédien en chef. Parmi ces valets, il y en avait quelques-uns qui récitaient déjà sans rougir et sans défaire; celui de Destin, entre autres, faisait assez bien, entendait assez ce qu'il disait et avait de l'esprit.[45]

They all act within the realm of the artificial environment of theater—representing roles themselves to which their self-explanatory names allude. The *Roman comique* mocks the tradition of courtly writing and acting, especially the doctrine of "bienséance". When Le Destin and his fellow actors discover a version of the *Chanson de geste*, for instance, Le Destin's plan is to create a play according to the rules. Yet he is ridiculed and his creation is turned into a version of the fairy tale *Peau d'âne / The donkey's hide*.[46]

Acting comes as naturally to the troupe as drinking, or, to be more precise: drinking makes them more inclined to play and they will all adopt their roles more easily.[47] Moreover, the personnel imitates numerous roles in quick succession; they play everybody and all kinds of roles. La Rancune, for instance, plays the roles of the nurse, the porter, the confidants, the ambassador, and the bailiff "under the masks".[48] La Caverne represents the queen and the mothers at the same time. Their genres are comedy and farce; the comedians have no aim but to entertain. Though the characters seem to be closely interwoven, or at least acquainted, with their roles, they study, repeat, and practice them regularly or out of habit. Much of their acting appears to be driven by the techniques of the commedia dell'arte or stand-up comedy, but they perform written roles. Yet they do not follow any erudite or noble playwright; on the contrary, Léandre, the servant of Étoile's brother, devises the texts and roles, amusing himself over the comedians and killing them off on stage even when they want to continue. The *Roman comique* presents the world as a never-ending play within a play.

Grimmelshausen's *Adventurous Simplicissimus Teutsch*

Building on various picaresque narratives, and in the context of the Thirty Year's War, Grimmelshausen's *Adventurous Simplicissimus Teutsch* combines

---

45 P. Scarron, *Le Roman comique*, ed. R. Garapon, Paris 1980, p. 62.
46 Ibid., p. 64.
47 Ibid., p. 48.
48 Ibid., p. 53.

both the peculiar state of the picaro, termed "Schelm", and theater.[49] Simplicissimus deals with three roles: the "Bestia" or the state of original sin; the Christian manchild ("Christenkind"); and the picaro.[50] The narrator describes his development from the "Bestia" to the Christian human being—two states of existence which he claims to be in—using literal meaning of the words, a type of meaning that is not applicable in the same way or to the same degree for the notion of the picaro. In the hut of his biological father, the man he calls Einsiedel, he is taught the Law of Moses, the Ten Commandments, and the Bible. Referring to a doctrine of the soul which Simplicius terms Aristotelian (but is, in fact, largely derived from Descartes), he illustrates how his soul had been empty like a blackboard and was then filled with Christian ideas.[51] Apparently Einsiedel taught Simplicius a lot about life and erudition.[52]

Once educated in this way, Simplicius is immune to bad influences. Although he may commit sins, act against the law, and play many controversial roles in the theater of the world, he remains Christian in nature. What is more: he cannot be manipulated by drink, dancing, or sexual seduction. Normal people act out their animal nature on occasions when these things are present, but Simplicius does not.[53] Simplicius, instead, has only been taken for a fool. He plays the fool but neither fully embraces the role nor becomes identical to it. Instead, he reflects upon himself and his environment while acting. In Grimmelshausen's novel, the word picaro is used figuratively, or, at least, the figurative use is markedly dominant.

For instance, Simplicius clearly states that he is no fool but rather that he is being made into one—by fools. His master's riflemen ("Furienschützen") approach him at night, dressed as devils. He notes "that those who would make a

---

[49] H. G. Rötzer, *Picaro—Landstörtzer—Simplicius*, Darmstadt 1972; P. Joseph, "The *Pícaro* at War: Vernacular Language and Violent Conflict in Grimmelshausen and Saro-Wiwa", in: *PMLA: Publications of the Modern Language Association of America*, vol. 131, 2016, pp. 1284–1298.
[50] "[...] ich war nur mit der Gestalt ein Mensch, und mit dem Namen ein Christenkind, im übrigen aber nur eine Bestia!" (Hans Jacob Christoffel von Grimmelshausen, "Der Abentheuerliche Simplicissimus Teutsch", in: Hans Jacob Christoffel von Grimmelshausen, *Werke*, ed. D. Breuer, vol. I.1, Frankfurt/Main 1997, pp. 9–984, p. 27); U. Zeuch,"Wie wird Simplicissimus zum 'schlime[n] Gesell'? Grimmelshausens Antwort auf die zeitgenössische Ethik", in: *IASL: Internationales Archiv für Sozialgeschichte der deutschen Literatur*, vol. 28, 2003, pp. 133–151.
[51] Grimmelshausen, *Simplicissimus*, p. 40.
[52] B. Hinrichs, "Zum 'Simplicissimus Teutsch': Die Fundierung der Lehre im Lernen Simplicii", in: *Simpliciana: Schriften der Grimmelshausen-Gesellschaft*, vols. 6–7, 1985, pp. 47–80, p. 51f.
[53] Grimmelshausen, *Simplicissimus*, p. 114.

fool of me must be my fools" / "daß diese, so mich zum Narren machen sollten, meine Narren sein mußten."⁵⁴ The riflemen keep him imprisoned in a cellar and abuse him badly. Having been regarded as a fool once, he is then retained in this role—and he plays the foolish role of a calf in order to save his life. Again, the word *fool* is being used only figuratively. The pastor to whom Simplicius confesses his sins pretends to console him and praises his prudent behavior. Or, more precisely, he preaches egoistic dissimulation:

> You must not worry about this, the foolish world wants to be deceived, if your wits have been spared, then use them to your advantage, imagine you have been reborn like a phoenix from ignorance to reason through fire and thus to a new human life: But know that you are not yet safely over the trench, but wear this fool's cap at the risk of your reason, these times are so strange that nobody can know whether you will come out again without loss of your life, [...]. Therefore you will need more caution and reason than at the time when you did not yet know what reason and lack of reason were, remain humble and await in patience the coming change.

> Hierum darfst du dich nicht bekümmern, die närrische Welt will betrogen sein, hat man dir deinen Witz noch übrig gelassen, so gebrauche dich desselben zu deinem Vorteil, bilde dir ein, als ob du gleich dem Phönix vom Unverstand zum Verstand durchs Feuer und also zu einem neuen menschlichen Leben neu geboren worden seiest: Doch wisse dabei, daß du noch nicht über den Graben, sondern mit Gefahr deiner Vernunft in diese Narrenkappe geschlossen bist, die Zeiten sind so wunderlich, daß niemand wissen kann, ob du ohne Verlust deines Lebens wieder herauskommest, [...] darum wird dir mehr Vorsichtigkeit und Verstand vonnöten sein, als zu der Zeit, da du noch nicht wußtest, was Verstand und Unverstand war, bleibe demütig und erwarte in Geduld der künftigen Veränderung.⁵⁵

According to the pastor, the world is foolish and Simplicius finds himself among fools. The clergyman uses the image of the phoenix only figuratively: new human life does not exist. There is no escape. Simplicius thinks and acts differently. He fears that the pastor has indeed discovered that he took up the role of the fool on purpose and without complete identification. In order to keep the pastor well-disposed, Simplicius thanks him for his consolation:

> [...] for I imagine he has read in my face that I think I am great because I have carried through such a masterful deceit and fine art, and I, on the other hand, have surmised from his face that he was reluctant and tired of me, for his expressions gave that away, and what had he of me? So I also changed my rhetoric and knew how to thank him for the wonderful means he had given me to keep my mind intact, yes, I made impossible promises to owe gratefully everything as was my obligation.

---

54 Ibid., p. 134.
55 Ibid., pp. 142f.

> [...], denn ich bilde mir ein, er habe mir an der Stirn gelesen, daß ich mich groß zu sein bedünke, weil ich mit so meisterlichem Betrug und feiner Kunst durchgeschloffen, und ich mutmaßete hingegen aus seinem Angesicht, daß er unwillig und meiner überdrüssig worden, denn seine Mienen gabens, und was hatte er von mir? Derowegen veränderte ich auch meine Reden, und wußte ihm großen Dank für die herrlichen Mittel, die er mir zur Erhaltung meines Verstands mitgetheilet hatte, ja, ich tat unmögliche Promessen, alles, wie meine Schuldigkeit erfordere, wieder dankbarlich zu verschulden.[56]

The pastor follows suit and recommends mental medicine: the mnemonic arts of Simonides Melicus (i.e. Simonides of Keos, 557–467 BC) and Metrodorus Scepticus, which were thought to teach imitative and mellifluous speech. This, of course, confirms that the pastor is less interested in Christian morals than in worldly goods and successful self-presentation—an evident criticism of the clergy. Opposing the pastor without contradicting him, Simplicius testifies to his knowledge as well as his prudence:

> "Yes", I thought, "my dear pastor, at Einsiedel's hut I have read very different things in your own books, concerning what comprises Scepticus's natural memory." But I was clever enough not to say anything, for if I must confess the truth, when I had become a fool, then for the first time I had wit and became more cautious in my speech.

> „Ja", gedacht ich, „mein lieber Herr Pfarrer, ich habe in deinen eigenen Büchern beim Einsiedel viel anders gelesen, worinnen Sceptii Gedächtnis-Gunst bestehet." Doch war ich so schlau, daß ich nichts sagte, denn wenn ich die Wahrheit bekennen soll, so bin ich, als ich zum Narren werden sollte, allererst witzig und in meinen Reden behutsamer worden.[57]

This multidimensional quotation proves that Simplicius has learned about ancient rhetoric—and apparently also about literal and figurative uses of words. In Einsiedel's home he had been able to read about Simonides, who was called "honey-tongued" because of his impressive oratorical skills. Simonides is also said to have possessed an astounding capacity for memory: On one occasion, Simonides managed to antagonize his host, Scopas, by talking less about him than about the twins Castor and Pollux. Simonides left the room in order to receive two young men, but while he waited for them, the roof fell on Scopas and the other guests so that they died disfigured—but Simonides could remember where they had all been sitting and led their family members to their bodies so that they could be buried appropriately.

Yet neither erudition nor the church offer any help. Simplicius, who has acquired some knowledge of Latin, understands and memorizes all that is being

---

56 Ibid., p. 143.
57 Ibid.

said about him but cannot fight against his brutal fellow human beings. Again and again he is punished, dressed up in women's clothes, and treated as a calf—a method of humiliating a person that appears almost theatrical and could have its origins in topical elements of peasant plays on the early modern stage.[58]

The extent to which Grimmelshausen was aware of European traditions of theater and performance is shown in the comedy episode, an inter-theatrical element in Grimmelshausen's novel as well as an early proof of *galant* style in early modern Germany[59]: Simplicius travels to France, finds a master named Monsieur Canard (as though he had stepped out of a *comique* play), and becomes an actor. Alluding to the French tradition of drama and "galanterie", Simplicius takes part in a play within a play. Having impressed some noblemen in a private audience with his lute and German song, he is invited to play Orpheus in a rendering of an Orpheus and Euridice opera, a popular topic at court at the time. The young and handsome Simplicius is fascinated with the French stage, learns the melodies and the foreign language as quickly as possible, and shows a remarkable talent for natural and emotional acting. Creating an enormous impact, especially on the female audience members, he is soon adored as "Beau Alman" (who he, apparently, claims really to be) while the evening of theater continues with ballet and short pieces that are also played around carnival.[60] Simplicius, of course, is conscious of his mock-playing and reflects enthusiastically upon the ways in which he has succeeded in convincing his audience.

To sum up, in Grimmelshausen's novel, the picaro or fool is a mere role that Simplicius plays in order to save his life. Just as in Alemán's novel, the notion of the picaro is used figuratively, or at least the figurative use is dominant, pointing to the conviction that a foolish state of life can only be transitory and/or a mere role, as illustrated in Scarron's *Roman comique*. The role of the picaro allows Simplicius to reflect upon himself, others, and life; it is the meta-role of the era —the role in which all other roles are combined. In circumstances in which human beings tend to play mere roles, the role of the picaro points to reflection upon these roles as such: the picaro distances himself from all-too-frequent and supposedly suitable roles that might lead to superficial success or well-being. In

---

58 See the volume *Poetics and Politics: Net Structures and Agencies in Early Modern Drama*, ed. T. Bernhart, J. Drnovšek, S. T. Kilian, J. Küpper, and J. Mosch, Berlin and Boston, MA 2018.
59 Cf. D. Niefanger, "Galanterie: Grundzüge eines ästhetischen Konzepts um 1700", in: *Künste und Natur in Diskursen der Frühen Neuzeit*, ed. H. Laufhütte (in collaboration with B. Becker-Cantarino, M. Bircher, F. van Ingen, S. Solf, and C.-P. Warncke), Wiesbaden 2000, pp. 459–472.
60 Grimmelshausen, *Simplicissimus*, p. 361.

the role of the picaro, however, the main character barely survives. He suffers and becomes a Jesus-like character—a wise man, a neostoic character who is able to act as a scapegoat for all men, the sinners who cross his path. Simplicius ultimately proves to have enjoyed a quick development from the beast he was to the wise man he has become with the help of Einsiedel, himself a wise man. Late in his life Simplicissimus enjoys his solitude on a lonely island, but even this existence does not remain without comment, for the fictitious editor ponders that the position of the hermit is the only morally acceptable one. Ultimately, however, it is the reader who will have to reflect on these stories within stories, on the roles presented, and on the literal and figurative truths present.

Again, the frontispiece offers a valuable clue for the reader. The *subscriptio* alludes to the pastor's quotation in its comparison of the main character with the mythical phoenix. Yet the meaning differs considerably, highlighting the possibility of escaping the existential state of fool or picaro that is otherwise presented as a life-saving role:

> I was born of fire like the phoenix
> I flew through the air, but I was not lost
> I wandered through water, I traveled over land
> in such swarming around I made myself acquainted
> with that which often saddened and rarely delighted me
> what was that? I put it in this book here
> so that the reader, just like I now do,
> may remove himself from folly and live in peace.

> Jch wurde durchs Fewer wie Phoenix geborn.
> Jch flog durch die Lüffte! wurd doch nit verlorn,
> Jch wandert durchs Waſſer, Jch raißt über Landt,
> in ſolchem Umbſchwermen macht ich mir bekandt
> was mich offt betrüebet und ſelten ergetzt
> was war das? Jch habs in diß Buche geſetzt,
> damit ſich der Leſer gleich wie ich itzt thue,
> entferne der Thorheit und lebe in Rhue.[61]

Looking at the texts selected, the literal use of the word picaro seems to be relatively rare and occurs mainly in the context of moral writing. In Aegidius Albertinus' text, the picaro becomes a type: a funny yet amoral character upon whom every good Christian must express clear moral judgement. The two ways of using the word "picaro", the literal and the figurative, highlight different meanings and different degrees of salience: while Albertinus' literal way of using the word points to a high degree of conventionality, familiarity, and

---

[61] Grimmelshausen (Sulsfort), *Der Abentheurliche Simplicissimus Teutsch*, s.p., [p. 2].

prototypicality, the figurative and more poetic use in Alemán's original text and then in Grimmelshausen's novel increases the options for interpretation. The picaro might not be one at all. On the contrary, he might be the true and—especially in Grimmelshausen—the incorruptible Christian. He needs no conversion, since he has an innate belief and will which protect him against the foolish world. However, Christian purposes may also be the ultimate goal of those texts in which the literary use of the notion of the picaro prevails. Man need only convert to the true religion and turn away from a corrupted world.

Interconfessional "medicina mentis"

This insight points both to the mediating function and the integrative character of picaresque storytelling in the seventeenth century. Picaresque narratives like the ones discussed can be regarded as interconfessional expressions that were attractive because they allowed a fully-fledged picture even of the lower ranks[62] and mirrored the hybridity of contemporary life in ironic, funny, and non-committal ways.[63] They allude to a variety of genres and ways of writing: to utopian and exempla literature, allegorical pilgrimages, penitential sermons, parables, and biographies; they also overlap with travel reports and satirical writing, to name just a few. The human being, sinner per se, experiences the torments of life and men until he finally reaches a state of religious and mental distance from his needs and desires. This bitter pilgrimage is accessible to all human beings; it is a mirror of everyman's martyr legend and everyman's window of rhetorical and narrative opportunities to explore the world as well as to reject its seductions, to embrace a heavenly or earthly paradise, that is—utopia. In the French tradition, however, these legends are presented in more *galant* ways: alluding to the theater metaphor of the century, all characters become fools but may also change their roles.

Thus the attempt to look for differentiation in European picaresque narratives gives insights into their variety. This variety could be related to the linguistic and literary features of specific countries as well as to the traditions on which they build. What is true beyond this is that there are some similarities regarding the common European moral and theatrical heritage.

Christianity features in two respects: on the one hand, as the church, attacked by authors like the anonymous Lazarillo-writer and by Grimmelshausen;

---

[62] Van Gemert, "Vom Pícaro zur Leitfigur", pp. 290.
[63] Zepp, "Ironie, Inquisition und Konversion", p. 392.

on the other hand, picaresque narratives establish and confirm what they consider to be true and honest Christian belief "from below". In combining neo-stoic Christian morals with contemporary images of the theater and roles such as the picaro, these narratives present their literary morals. Picaresque novels teach morality with the help of literal and figurative usages, exempla, roles, and types, in the form of pre-sociological observation, funny or exciting descriptions, meta-critical, inter-, and metatheatrical comments in the satirical tradition.[64] This is the *medicina mentis* that Johann Jacob Breitinger, building on Lucretius's image of the doctor who hides bitter medicine in honey, prettily and figuratively dubbed the "sugared pill".

---

[64] J. Azazmah, *Poetologische Reflexionen in satirischen Romanen des 17. Jahrhunderts, 1615–1696/97*, Heidelberg 2018.

Andrey Golubkov
Theater as Metaphor and Guiding Principle: The French Anecdote Tradition from the Seventeenth to the Nineteenth Century

The topic of theater as metaphor implies reflections not on theater as such, but, rather, on theater turning out to be not only *theater*, comprising, in fact, larger discursive practices. Theatrical and dramatic images used as a definition of theater are not an end in themselves, but a means to convey other, more important content of various kinds related to faith and religion, rituals and etiquettes of power, etc. Theatrical imagery reveals itself as a flexible means of presentation, that is, not the final point of the aesthetic process, but one of its means, a language to describe reality, which is more important than the imagery; in that sense, any discursive practice offering elements from the theatrical lexicon or theatrical method becomes productive. Our analysis shall use as its textual material the tradition of French anecdotes from the seventeenth and the eighteenth centuries, a time when the genre of the anecdote actually received this name and when its poetics were conceptualized.

Our point of reference shall be the text of *Comediana, ou Recueil choisi d'anecdotes dramatiques; bons mots des comédiens, et réparties spirituelles; de bonhomie et de naiveté du parterre*, created by a well-known man of letters, Charles-Yves d'Avallon, who signed his works as Cousin d'Avallon. Cousin d'Avallon wrote over two dozen texts with the suffix *ana* in their titles, on writers (including Molière, Voltaire, Rousseau, Diderot, Chateaubriand, Mme de Staël), on general human features (for example, on avariciousness, which became the main subject of his *Harpagoniana*, with a title based on the main character's name from Molière's comedy), as well as on politicians, including Napoleon Bonaparte. Let us note that the "magic formula" *ana ou anecdotes* is used in this collection's title (as well as those of other collections). Let us also recall that this French literary genre dates back to the late Renaissance. The collections that recorded unpublished remarks and comments by great scholars, scientists, or mighty men appear from the end of the seventeenth until the middle of the nineteenth century. Gabriel Peignot, a contemporary of Cousin d'Avallon, as well as a philologist, bibliographer, and member of the Besançon Academy, faced the necessity to construct a false etymology: as suggested by this bibliographer, the compilers of *ana* giving this title to their works had initially meant an anecdote, but did not use this latter word due to its dissonance when combined with the principal character's name. Seen from this perspective, *ana* becomes an abbreviation of anecdote:

> Let us get back to *ana* and talk about the etymology of this word, which remains a mystery [...]. It is known that the Books whose name ends in ANA usually contain reflections and little-known anecdotes about those who are their object. Could the word ANA be considered as a diminutive of ANECDOTA [...]? Because the word *Anecdota*, added to a proper name, made it very unpleasant to the ear (for example, *Menagianecdota*), a part of the added word fell off, and a plural neuter ending was added to the remaining part; thus, *Menagiana* was formed from *Menagianecdota*, or *Verba non edita*.[1]

Actually, Peignot is asserting the priority of the word "anecdote" and presenting *ana* as a derivative; it is not sufficient for him to merely suggest that the two "matrices" are based on the intent to demonstrate the "interior" of the persons concerned.

One of the anecdotes in the *Comediana*, dealing with Mademoiselle de Champmêlé, a French actress of the seventeenth century, is particularly worthy of our attention:

> Mademoiselle Champmêlé, célèbre actrice, sacrifia Racine au comte de Clermont-Tonnerre. On fit le quatrain suivant sur cette aventure, quatrain dont tout le sel et toute la finesse roulent sur un jeu de mots:
> Au tendre amour elle fut destinée,
> Qui prit long-tems Racine dans son cœur;
> Mais par un insigne malheur,
> Le tonnerre est venu qui l'a déracinée.[2]

This anecdote was told 35 years before the publication of the *Comediana* in the *Anecdotes dramatiques*, a three-volume collection by Jean Marie Bernard Clément and Joseph de la Porte, published in Paris in 1775. In addition to the above-mentioned anecdote, we can read another one, also dealing with love affairs:

> Racine aima la Champmêlé, qui lui fut infidèle; et il s'en vengea par un beau-mot, qu'il adressa à son mari, et que Boileau a rimé dans cette épigramme:
> De six amans contens et non jaloux,
> Qui tour-à-tour servaient Madame Claude,
> Le moins volage était Jean son époux:

---

[1] Gabriel Peignot, *Répertoire de Bibliographies spéciales, curieuses et instructives*, Paris 1809, p. 218.
[2] Charles-Yves Cousin d'Avallon, *Comediana, ou Recueil choisi d'anecdotes dramatiques: bons mots des comédiens, et réparties spirituelles; de bonhomie et de naiveté du parterre*, Paris 1801, p. 25.

> Un jour pourtant d'humeur un peu trop chaude,
> Serrait de près sa servante aux yeux doux,
> Lorsqu'un des six lui dit, que faites-vous ?
> Le jeu n'est sûr avec cette Ribaude ;
> Ah ! voulez-vous, Jean, Jean, nous gâter tous ?
> Despréaux ne lisait cette épigramme qu'à ses meilleurs amis.[3]

Our attention is attracted by the unity of tone and the predetermined character of this anecdote's heroine; within this anecdotic discourse, the French actress is interesting in one respect only; all diversity and features not fitting into the specific one which is underlined are cut off and not mentioned.

Our second example will be the *Arliquiniana*, a book published in 1694. It was written by a lawyer, Charles Cotolendi, a Provençal by origin, living in Paris, who was the author of several hagiographies and biographies of famous people, including the Duke of Montmorency and St. Francis of Sales. In the wake of *Arliquiniana*'s success, Cotolendi published a sequel titled *A Book without Name* (1695), and five years later another one titled *Saint-Evremoniana* (1700). *Arliquiniana* is centered on imaginary conversations between Cotolendi and Harlequin—whose legal name was Domenico Biancolelli (1640–1688)—an Italian actor famous in the 1670s, who had been invited to France by Cardinal Mazarin. Domenico was so talented that he was often fully identified with this well-known *commedia dell'arte* character to the extent that even nowadays the personage of Harlequin is sometimes called "Dominique" in French contexts. It was not the first time that an actor had been identified with the type he represented on the stage within seventeenth-century French cultural practices. A well-known memoir writer, Gédéon Tallemant des Réaux, recounts the story in his *Historiettes* collection of another, chronologically earlier Harlequin—Tristano Martinelli, a *zanni* actor who was very much favored by Marie de Médicis, the second wife of King Henry IV of France. He was one of the first to adopt for his role or mask the name of Alichino (Hellequin), one of the demons featuring in Dante's *Divine Comedy*.[4] In his collection of anecdotes about Henry IV, Tallemant des Réaux describes a meeting between the King and Harlequin:

> In these days Harlequin came to Paris with his company and, while greeting the King, he found a suitable moment when His Majesty got up from the throne, and in his sprightliness he took the King's seat all at once, and then said, addressing him as if the King was Harlequin: 'Well, Harlequin, you came here with your company to entertain me. I am

---

[3] Jean Marie Bernard Clément and Joseph de la Porte, *Anecdotes dramatiques*, vol. 3, Paris 1765, p. 161.
[4] Inferno, Canto XXI.

much pleased with it. I promise to protect you and shall give you such and such wages', etc. The King did not dare to contradict him, but said in the end: 'Whoa, hold on! You have played *my part* long enough, now let me *play it myself*'.[5]

The scene of Henry IV's meeting with a theatrical character, who had actually adopted the name of a demon, has several meanings. The first one alluded to is the concept of the relativeness of the "roles" humans play in real life and the types represented on the stage; it is about the world as a theater and about royal power as a configuration of actions that are similar to stage performances. Harlequin emphasizes that the status of Henry IV is nothing but that of a role; he is questioning the king's claim to be an agent of political will; Harlequin is thus cast as a personification of backstage power able to uncover a face behind the mask and to shuffle destiny's cards.

Let us get back to the *Arliquiniana*. In the foreword and in the part titled *The Appearance of Harlequin*, Cotolendi refers to himself as a collector of "real" conversations with Harlequin; in fact, the conversations represent an imaginary dialogue between Cotolendi and Harlequin, who had died in 1688. Harlequin is elevated above mere mortals, standing between the worlds of life and death; we are witnessing the talks with the dead Dominique or with someone so successfully impersonated by him. Harlequin is providing information from the otherworld, telling, often in sarcastic tones, about the lives led by great men, including scientists and writers, in the Elysian Fields:

> Pray, would you please tell me,—I said to him—what is your pastime in the Elysian Fields?—My lot here is a little easier than before, because where I am, everyone appears as he is, having no possibility to hide his true feelings. During my lifetime, I have often turned against those who would only put on the mask of an honest man *(honnête homme)*. Now I witness only unmasked hearts, and a generous man appears to be generous, I need but a sole look to tell a decent woman from a frivolous one, and I am pleased with this sincerity. Having finished his words, he almost wished to go away...—How so! To leave me so quickly! This is unfair... I have always wanted to learn something about some of my acquaintances, and you could help me with it. Please tell me what Molière is doing twenty years after his death.—He answered me—Terence and Plautus are still chasing him, in order to lessen his fame,—What about Corneille?—This one is conversing with the characters from his tragedies, and his companions are praising his wisdom.[6]

---

5 Gédéon Tallemant des Réaux, *Historiettes*, ed. A. Adam, vol. 1., Paris 1960, p. 12.
6 Charles Cotolendi, *Arliquiniana, ou les bons mots, les histoires plaisantes et agréables recueillies des conversations d'Arlequin*, Paris 1694, p. IX.

Cotolendi is asserting that all his dialogues are true, that he has tried to discover the interior of Harlequin's life, hidden from other people's eyes:

> My purpose is to collect not only the wondrous words said by Harlequin in the guise of his character on the Italian stage, but also to present many pleasant stories told by those with whom he was on friendly footing. I will also speak of serious things, and relate moral maxims so often present in his speech.[7]

The character of Harlequin in Cotolendi's text is stable; he figures as a "demon", often ready to make a "saucy joke". Dominique was a highly appreciated theater actor and a well-respected man; he was valued for his exceptional mind and for his aphorisms full of wisdom. Cotolendi is trying to collect the best of Harlequin's jokes; this results in a transformation of the *Arliquiniana* from a coherent discourse with jokes integrated into its "frame" into a collection of short stories and witticisms:

> In another comedy he was playing a sick man, healed by a doctor. The doctor asked a payment from him, but Harlequin was not even thinking of settling accounts. The doctor sued him, and thus Harlequin appears before the judge, insisting that he has never asked the doctor to give him health, and that he is ready to give it back.[8]

In this way, the character of the dead actor Harlequin becomes an incarnation of reason, a transcendent power possessing information and sharing it with an initiate.

Let us note that the events described are not called "anecdote" in the texts, though one could have intuitively used this word to apostrophize the depicted situations. Let us also recall that the term *anecdote* as a name for a specific variant of historical narrative began to establish itself in France in the first half of the seventeenth century, after the discovery of a pamphlet titled *Anekdota*, attributed to Procopius of Caesarea, a Byzantine historian of the sixth century CE. The manuscript was found in the Vatican Library by the scholar Niccolo Alemanni, who translated the text from Greek into Latin and published this version with his own comments under the title *Procopii Caesarensis Anekdota seu Arcana Historia* (1623). Alemanni, when he published this text by Procopius that the author had left without a title, referred to a Greek encyclopedic lexicon from the tenth century whose title spelled *Suda*, in which this literary work had been actually mentioned for the first time as *Anekdota*, that is, literally translated, "unpublished notes". Actually, Alemanni transformed the word *anecdote*,

---

7 Ibid., pp. 1–2.
8 Ibid., p. 4.

which previously had served to specify the status of a literary work as handwritten and not readily available for a broader public, into a name for this text and its genre; he thereby created a type of historical work breaking with the traditions of ceremonial official historiography.

The official works by Procopius, who lived in the sixth century, celebrating the Emperor Justinian were well known. In medieval Christian Europe and in the early modern period, Justinian was considered as one of the most important historical figures. Let me recall that Justinian tried to restore the Roman Empire and also conducted administrative and judicial reforms, thus earning himself posthumous fame and authority in Europe as a lawgiver. The discovery of the secret notes turned upside down all previous visions of him: Procopius, who praised Justinian in his official works as a lawmaker and conqueror of barbarian peoples, is very severe about the Emperor in the text not intended for publication. In the seventeenth century, the most famous episodes were those related to the debauchery and follies of Justinian's spouse, the Empress Theodora (whose portrait with a nimbus we can see even now in the mosaics in Ravenna). Most of the facts, or rumors, about the Basilissa were presented by Procopius in the ninth book. Procopius describes in detail how Theodora, after growing up in depravity, became a comedian famous for the most disgusting vices, ascribed to the actress by the crowd. The text published by Alemanni on the basis of Procopius (which passed over the most obscene anecdotes, but made allusions to them) became one of the most popular books in the seventeenth-century French intellectual sphere. Procopius' naturalism is striking; he does not resort to restrictions and describes the emperor's and the empress's vices in great detail. It seems here that the anecdote is intended to become a rendering of "true" history, but when studying it more closely, one notices that Procopius cannot help but use rhetoric and poetical schemes. The most well-known example in this respect is the following characterization of Theodora by Procopius:

> And though she made use of three orifices, she used to take Nature to task, complaining that it had not pierced her breasts with larger holes so that it might be possible for her to contrive another method of copulation there. And though she was pregnant many times, practically always she was able to contrive to bring about an abortion immediately.[9]

This famous description is modeled on a well-known description of Neera, an Athenian actress and hetaera; it thus turns out that Procopius

---

[9] Procopius, *Secret History*, tr. H. B. Dewing, Cambridge, MA 1935, p. 109.

as well as Alemanni are following the traditional logic of historical discourse by choosing the events that need to be mentioned in accordance with an initially chosen frame. Hermogenes, one of the famous authors of *progymnasmata*, mentions a speech by Demosthenes, who exclaimed that Neera works "with three orifices".[10] Procopius thus displays his ability to exaggerate; his text is not only a fine sophistical game, but may be considered an inverted praise. Procopius borrows rhetorical and poetical patterns and adapts real characters to them; he uses theatrical *topoi* and metaphors to provide matrices serving to create characters such as he wishes to present them.

One excellent example of the strategy of implementing "general" features in a historical narrative is a text by the French historian Antoine de Varillas; its title is *Anecdotes of Florence, or a Secret History of the House of Medici*. The idea of writing a historical work about the Medici was conceived by Colbert, who in 1662 instructed Varillas to begin to collect, for political ends, materials related to the famous Italian family. In 1662–1663, when Varillas began to study in the libraries the documents in connection with the Medici's history, the Royal Printing House had published a two-volume edition of the book by Procopius. Having familiarized himself with it in detail, as well as with its French translation (1669), Varillas decided to realize the work commissioned by Colbert by emulating Procopius' text:

> Si Procope, qui est le seul auteur dont il nous reste des Anecdotes, avait laissé par écrit les règles de ce genre d'écriture, je ne serais pas obligé de faire une préface, parce que l'autorité de cet excellent historien, que l'Imprimerie Royale vient de nous donner si correct, suffirait pour me mettre à couvert de toutes sortes de reproches, supposé que je les eusse observées avec exactitude.[11]

There are several answers to the question of why it is the Florentine story of the fifteenth century that became the focus of Varillas's attention. Ph. Hourcade hypothesizes that the surge of interest was connected to the marriage, celebrated in 1661, of the King's cousin Marguerite Louise d'Orléans, whose chosen one was Cosimo III, future Grand Duke of Tuscany.[12] But it may be that the cause for the interest in the House of Medici is of a quite basic nature. In his

---

10 Hermogène, *L'art rhétorique*, ed. and tr. M. Patillon, Paris 1997, pp. 422–423.
11 Antoine Varillas, *Les anecdotes de Florence ou: L'histoire secrète de la maison de Médicis*, ed. M. Bouvier, Rennes 2004, p. 43.
12 Ph. Hourcade, "Sur les Anecdotes de Florence", in: *L'Histoire en miettes: Anecdotes et témoignages dans l'écriture de l'histoire (XVI–XIX siècles)*, ed. C. Dornier and C. Pouloin, Caen 2004, pp. 141–156, p. 153.

monograph on Lorenzo the Magnificent, I. Cloulas,[13] discussing the interest in the Florentine ruler in the time of Louis XIV, says that Lorenzo was regarded not simply as an ancestor, but also as a kind of spiritual precursor of the French monarch. In this connection, it is interesting to read in Varillas's text the comparison of young Lorenzo the Magnificent, who had just gained power, with the Sun, which in the 1680s was the symbol of the French monarch. This may reveal the intention of the initiator of the project, Colbert. The characterization of Lorenzo by Varillas reads as follows: "Il s'y fit connaître aux amis de son nom pour ce qui'il y devait être. Il y dit son avis avec une maturité d'esprit qui fut admiré, et commença par cette heureuse adresse à se faire regarder comme un soleil levant".[14] The final version of the text was published in 1685–22 years after the first drafts—in The Hague. In this edition, Varillas's book consists of seven volumes of different size. The first volume covers the period of rule of Cosimo the Elder; the second and the third volumes, which are the main and most voluminous parts, deal with Lorenzo the Magnificent; in the said volumes, much attention is given to the story of the Pazzi conspiracy. At the beginning of the fourth volume, Varillas reports Lorenzo's death and, contradicting actual chronology, offers after that a gallery of portraits of the most outstanding figures of the Renaissance, including Leonardo Bruni, Pico della Mirandola, Angelo Poliziano, etc. The fifth and the sixth volumes cover the period of the Medici's return to Florence after Savonarola's execution and Piero Soderini's and Machiavelli's rule: after 1512, Florence found itself under the rule of the Vatican, where the power soon passed to Pope Leo X, whose secular name was Giovanni Medici; he was the second son of Lorenzo the Magnificent. The seventh (last) volume is the smallest (it is one third of the size of the foreword); the most impressive figures from the milieu of Pope Leo X are described in it; in addition, there are portraits of Savonarola and Marsilio Ficino. It seems that Varillas abruptly ceased to work on the text; in the foreword, many more portraits are announced than there are in the actual volumes; the reasons for this configuration are unknown.

Varillas, who is afraid of being attacked by other historians, reasons that Procopius had not left behind any guidelines of how to write anecdotes because he was not able to finish his work or that the description of such guidelines is not available to us due to a partial loss of the text; these lost passages may have been, according to Varillas, exactly the part in which Procopius had outlined what many consider to be missing in his work. The

---

13 I. Cloulas, *Laurent le Magnifique*, Paris 1982, p. 2.
14 Varillas, *Les anecdotes*, p. 100.

reconstruction of these guidelines is necessary for Varillas in order to provide protection from possible critics:

> Je me crois réduit, comme ceux qui s'engagent dans de nouvelles routes, je veux dire, à prendre toutes les précautions nécessaires pour n'être pas condamné dès l'entrée de mon ouvrage, à m'imposer des lois moi-même sur lesquelles je prétends être jugé par un équitable lecteur, à condition que je ne les emprunterais ni de ma raison, ni de mon caprice, mais seulement des exemples du même Procope, que je l'aurais toujours devant mes yeux, puisque je ne saurais trouver d'autre guide.[15]

Although Procopius' anecdotic narrative was at variance with historical models prevalent in antiquity, Varillas associates it, as well as his own work, with the latter ones also, which implies that there is an entire set of rules and a highly developed structural complexity, that is, an "artistic" nature of the genre in which he tries to excel:

> C'est donc avec son approbation, que je suppose pour le fondement de ce discours, qu'il n'est pas si facile d'écrire des anecdotes qu'on le pourrait figurer, parce que d'un côté l'on ne saurait se dispenser d'aucune des règles qu'Aristote, Cicéron, Plutarque et les autres maîtres de l'art ont si judicieusement prescrites pour l'histoire publique; et de l'autre côté il y en a beaucoup d'autres, que je rapporterai dans la suite de cette préface.[16]

The dichotomy of two kinds of rhetoric, one of them historical and the other anecdotic, is illustrated by Varillas by referring to Procopius, who, as a historian on the one hand and as an anecdotist on the other, has chosen different ways to describe the same event—the recall of the victorious Belisarius from Africa by Justinian. In the second book of his *Vandalic War*, Procopius presents as the cause of the event the Emperor's jealousy of the general's fame, as Varillas highlights:

> Il est certain que Procope s'est acquitté du devoir d'un fidèle historien, lorsque recherchant la cause qui avait porté l'empereur Justinien à rappeler Bélisaire de l'Afrique, d'où il avait chassé les Vandales en trois mois, quoique la présence de ce grand capitaine fût absolument nécessaire pour affermir sa nouvelle conquête; il écrit que ce service était de telle considération, que Justinien, ne se sentant pas capable de la récompense, craignit que Bélisaire ayant les armes à la main ne se fît lui-même justice. Procope en demeure là, parce qu'il croit avoir satisfait aux lois de l'histoire; et certainement il y aurait eu de l'injustice à lui demander alors quelque chose de plus.[17]

---

15 Ibid., p. 43.
16 Ibid.
17 Ibid., p. 44.

As an anecdotist, however, Procopius has developed a different interpretation of the same events, because he could tell about something impossible to include in historical works, where the truth has to be hidden when it is not in line with the "general" laws of historical necessity:

> Mais quand il s'avisa longtemps après de travailler à ces Anecdotes, il crut qu'il n'y avait rien à déguiser sur un fait si bizarre, qu'il en fallait expliquer les particularités les plus cachées, et que la curiosité de son lecteur ne serait pas pleinement satisfaite, à moins que de lui révéler ce mystère de cour; que ce qu'il avait fait passer dans le second livre de la guerre des Vandales pour un effet de l'ingratitude et de la jalousie d'un souverain à l'égard d'un de ses sujets que la fortune élevait trop haut, n'était, à proprement parler, qu'une intrigue d'amour d'Antonienne, femme de Bélisaire, qui se hâtait de retourner à Constantinople pour y revoir l'infâme objet de sa passion.[18]

When Procopius creates the official version of history he cannot mention the true cause of the event (Antonina had made Justinian call Belisarius back to Constantinople because she wanted to meet again with her lover). The anecdote becomes an appropriate way to reveal the actual reason behind this recall.

Varillas rejects the hierarchical principle when he is comparing history and anecdote; at the same time, the author of *The Anecdotes of Florence* highlights the central opposition between official history and private anecdote:

> L'historien considère presque toujours les hommes en public; au lieu que l'écrivain d'anecdotes ne les examine qu'en particulier. L'un croit s'acquitter de son devoir, lorsqu'il les dépeint tels qu'ils étaient à l'armée, ou dans le tumulte des villes; et l'autre essaie en toute manière de se faire ouvrir la porte de leur cabinet. L'un les voit en cérémonie, et l'autre en conversation; l'un s'attache principalement à leurs actions, et l'autre veut être témoin de leur vie intérieure, et assister aux plus particulières heures de leur loisir. En un mot, l'un n'a que le commandement et l'autorité pour objet, et l'autre fait son capital de ce qui se passe en secret et dans la solitude.[19]

The obsession with "secrecy" and small details, with the hidden springs of history, though not recorded in its "official" rendering, is extended to the study of the character's behavior, which reflects his temperament. In this respect also, the logic of affect replaces the logic of necessity. If the historian is allowed to distort the truth, the author of an anecdote has to tell the truth in full, in order to reveal the genuine (the "corporeal", not the "public") causes of great events:

> Ce n'est pas que l'écrivain d'anecdotes ne fasse une peinture des personnes aussi exacte et aussi fidèle pour le moins que saurait faire l'historien; mais il la fait à sa mode. Il ne

---

18 Ibid.
19 Ibid., p. 45.

représente le dehors de l'homme, qu'autant qu'il est nécessaire pour en connaître le dedans; et comme les bonnes ou mauvaises dispositions de l'âme ne se découvrent que dans les mœurs, c'est aussi pour les mœurs qu'il réserve les plus vives couleurs et sa plus fine matière.[20]

The anecdote interprets private facts, tailoring them on the basis of similarity to a specific affective model: the anecdote's author may, of his own volition, reduce the variety of historical events to one particular case that is not a generalization of all the others, and not even the brightest among them, but one chosen solely to show the described event as an ordinary one, oft-recurring and, therefore, not exceptional, just an illustration of a predominant vice or virtue, an outward manifestation of internal aspirations. In this way a private episode, without losing its private nature, is perceived as a potential pattern of similar events and a demonstration of the character's habit, allowing the reader to judge the everyday life and character:

> Une réponse imprévue lui sert à pénétrer le fond des intentions. S'il se fut trouvé à Florence avec Alexandre de Médicis [the first Duke of Florence, 1531–1537], une seule parole de ce duc lui aurait suffi pour en faire le portrait. Il eût supposé que l'impénétrabilité du secret était son véritable caractère, aussitôt qu'il aurait ouï dire qu'il était lui-même un concierge de ses desseins, mais un concierge si jaloux, qu'il ne leur permettait jamais de sortir un moment de son cœur pour prendre l'air sur le bord de ses lèvres.[21]

During the age at issue, passion was considered a weakness opposed to reason; passion transforms the human mind into a slave passively enduring the influence of an external force, most often originating from the body. The description of a dominant passion, that is, of a deviation from the human norm, namely an action silenced by the historians, becomes the anecdotist's principle, making him reduce the whole behavior of his character to a small set of obsessive ideas (the "flaws" of mind):

> Je m'engage à faire le portrait du pape Clément VII, et si je veux réussir, il faut que je découvre sa passion dominante, et que j'en examine jusques aux moindres symptômes. Personne, que je sache, n'a encore dit quelle elle était; et je suis le premier à soutenir, qu'elle consistait dans un désir aveugle et bizarre, dont il fut toujours possédé, de ravir la liberté à ses compatriotes, pour élever à la souveraineté de Florence deux bâtards de sa Maison, quoiqu'elle ne manquât pas alors de plusieurs enfants légitimes [...]. Mais que n'ai-je point à craindre, lorsque la nécessité de mon sujet m'obligera de passer outre, et de mettre la vérité dans tout son jour; lorsque le fâcheux destin des anecdotes, qui ne

---

20 Ibid.
21 Ibid., p. 47.

peuvent souffrir qu'on laisse à la postérité rien de mystérieux sans l'expliquer, ni rien de secret sans le révéler, m'engagera à ôter insensiblement le fard que les historiens avaient mis sur la plupart des actions de Clément, pour montrer combien de faiblesse et de fautes contre la bonne politique pullulèrent de cette première irrégularité.[22]

According to Varillas, an anecdotist has to learn the secret of Plutarchian moral philosophy: a human being is the least secretive about that what is going on in the depths of his heart at the moment when a passion dominating him or her reaches its extreme.[23] This mention of Plutarch's method gives Varillas a free hand; after referring to the analysis of psychological motivations, he presents the characters at the moments of external realization of passions at their peak, in fact fully destroying their inner individuality and transforming them into patterns pre-established according to literary concepts. Varillas ties the description of the characters' external behavior to their morals, addressing the issue of history's causality in his own way. Every action of a character is interpreted according to his temper; Varillas considers affect as a source of historical dynamics, subtly asserting that, if people were perfect, there would be no history. In anecdotes, the history of an individual is reduced to a story of passion; thus Varillas is utilizing, consciously or unconsciously, conceptual elements of classicist theater. As soon as the dominating passion has emerged, historical characters begin to act like Molière's Harpagon and Argan, who are reduced to one passion only. It may seem paradoxical to a modern reader that the psychological perspective claimed by the author leads to a reduction of a historical person to just one passion. This feature is highly reminiscent of the logic of creating characters for comedy, and it dates back to the character studies by a disciple of Aristotle, the philosopher Theophrastus, whose work became immensely popular in seventeenth-century France. Let me recall what is commonplace: Theophrastus, a Greek philosopher who lived in the fourth century BC and was the teacher of Menander, identified 30 types (the liar, the slanderer, the grumbler, the arrogant one, etc.); and thus the New (Attic) Comedy became in many aspects a result of the assimilation of peripatetic psychology. The reductionist strategy of the anecdote goes back to the same conceptual and formal methods.

---

22 Ibid., p. 46.
23 "[...] ce beau secret, que Plutarque a le premier decouvert dans sa philosophie morale, savoir, qu'il n'y a point d'état dans la vie où l'on soit plus négligent à cacher ce qui se passe dans le fond du cœur, que quand la passion qui le domine est arrivée jusque dans l'excès" (ibid., p. 45).

Jan Mosch
"Dressed for life's short comedy": *Desengaño* and *connivere libenter* as Ethical Paradigms in William Shakespeare's Plays

In an oft-quoted passage from Shakespeare's pastoral comedy *As You Like It*, the nobleman Jaques, who has joined the banished Duke Senior in his exile in the Forest of Arden, offers a pessimistic account of human life as an inevitable journey from infancy to "second childishness and mere oblivion" (II.7.164).[1] Alluding to roles familiar from the *commedia dell'arte*—the lover, the soldier, the judge, the old man Pantalone—Jaques' speech conflates two influential Renaissance topoi—that of the seven ages of man and that of the world as a theater, *theatrum mundi*—to prove the point that "[a]ll the world's a stage / And all the men and women merely players" (II.7.138–139). The sentiment, which echoes many other instances in which Shakespearean characters describe the world as a theater or pageant and feel that they must respond to external "cues" and "prompts", is occasionally cited as representative of the worldview encoded in Shakespeare's dramatic oeuvre and, in lieu of any autobiographical evidence, even as potentially indicative of the playwright's personal outlook on life. However, the acceptance of Jaques' perspective as the play's dominant ideology—the equation, to use M. Pfister's terms, of a figure-perspective with the reception-perspective[2]—is highly problematic because it neglects Jaques' peculiar mental state. The character's despondent interpretation of the theater of the world, whose moribund actors can never transcend the passive, heteronomous state of *"mere* players" and are destined to perish "sans [i.e. without] everything" (II.7.168), ought not to be decontextualized.

---

1 Quotations of Shakespeare's works follow *The Norton Shakespeare: Based on the Oxford Edition*, ed. S. Greenblatt, W. Cohen, J. E. Howard, and K. Eisaman Maus, 2nd ed., New York, NY 2008. Subsequent references will provide act, scene, and line numbers only.
2 Cf. M. Pfister, *The Theory and Analysis of Drama*, tr. J. Halliday, Cambridge 1991, p. 58.

Note: I wish to thank J. Küpper, G. Gubbini, and G. Chakrabarti for the opportunity to discuss an early version of this paper and for their helpful remarks, not least on the scholastic views on dissimulation.

Open Access. © 2019 Jan Mosch, published by De Gruyter. This work is licensed under the Creative Commons Attribution-NonCommercial-NoDerivatives 4.0 License.
https://doi.org/10.1515/9783110622034-006

Throughout the play it is emphasized that Jaques suffers from melancholy. Other characters use the term almost as an epithet—when he is first mentioned, he is twice referred to as "melancholy Jaques" (II.1.26, 41)—and the aristocrat himself discusses his affliction in a conversation with Rosalind (IV.1). In early modern England, this ailment was considered a grave illness. This is shown, for example, by Robert Burton's *Anatomy of Melancholy* (1621), which characterizes its subject as "a perpetual agony" that leaves the sufferer restless, fearful, and in constant terror of dying, losing loved ones, or being damned by God.[3] As a consequence, Jaques' interpretation of the theater of the world must be seen as slanted. His unreliability is further substantiated by his inability to overcome his malady: at the end of the play, when Duke Senior is restored to power and returns to court, Jaques takes the first opportunity to leave. Upon hearing that Duke Frederick—the man who once ousted Senior and usurped power—has met "with an old religious man" and has been "converted / Both from his enterprise and from the world" (V.4.149–151), Jaques decides to join him in his solitude, arguing that "[o]ut of these convertites, / There is much matter to be heard and learned" (V.4.173–174). This, again, is a problematic position. While a positive interpretation of the general spirit of reform is conceivable,[4] the scene, if read against Burton's *Anatomy*, rather suggests that melancholy, the "plague subverting kingdoms",[5] is catching: according to Burton, the natural love of God, if corrupted by the fallen state of humanity, will turn people into "mad men"[6]

---

[3] Part. 1, Sect. 3, Memb. 1, Subs. 2. The *Anatomy* is quoted in the following edition (in which Burton's "partitions" correspond to the volume numbers): *The Anatomy of Melancholy*, ed. T. C. Faulkner, N. K. Kiessling, and Rh. L. Blair, 3 vols., Oxford 1989–1994.

[4] A. Wolk points out that Jaques, who initially vows to "[c]leanse the foul body of th' infected world" (II.7.60), is like a "hypocritical physician" who finally listens to the proverb "Physician, heal thyself" (Lk 4:23) and "exchanges his ignorance of the world for a desire for self-knowledge" ("The Extra Jaques in *As You Like It*", in: *Shakespeare Quarterly*, vol. 23, 1972, pp. 101–105, p. 104). In a structural perspective, however, characters who shun communal life are never agents of positive change in Shakespeare—one might consider the misanthropes Timon, Hamlet, who is disgusted by the drinking and carousing of the Danish court, or Malvolio, who, in the final scene of *Twelfth Night*, leaves the lovers with the vow to be "revenged on the whole pack of you" (V.1.365). An additional problem is posed by Jaques' choice of an ineffectual cure. Burton, who devotes the second partition of the *Anatomy* to the treatment of melancholy, suggests the company of friends; only if the illness is caused by the intrigues and abuses of court life, it might help to take one's leave (2.1.6.2). This does not apply to Jaques, though, who has been away from court before. During his voyages (which highlight his restiveness), his condition was only exacerbated, and Jaques himself believes that his sadness is "extracted from many objects, and indeed the sundry contemplation of my travels" (IV.1.15–16).

[5] Burton, *Anatomy*, 1.2.3.12.

[6] Ibid., 1.2.3.14.

who adhere to all sorts of superstitious errors. Predictably, the Anglican cleric mentions Catholicism and non-Christian faiths, but he also maintains that "Monkes, Hermites, &c. may be ranged in this extreame, and fight under this superstitious banner, with those rude Idiots, and infinite swarmes of people that are seduced by them."[7]

The assumption that such an assessment applies to Jaques is borne out by the fact that *As You Like It* offers an alternative model of development through the character of Duke Senior. Senior, too, uses the *theatrum mundi* metaphor when he despairs over his banishment: "Thou seest we are not all alone unhappy. / This wide and universal theatre / Presents more woeful pageants than the scene / Wherein we play in" (II.7.135–138). Unlike Jaques, however, he does not cling to that worldview, which supports the hypothesis that the characters represent two different kinds of melancholy. Senior seems to experience what Burton calls melancholy "in disposition", defined as "that transitory Melancholy which goes and comes upon every small occasion of sorrow".[8] According to the scholar, this temporary depressiveness is common to all humans: "from these melancholy dispositions, no man living is free, no stoic, none so wise, none so happy, none so patient, so generous, so godly, so divine, that can vindicate himself."[9] Burton contrasts this largely inconsequential dejection with melancholy as "a habit, *morbus sonticus*, or *chronicus*, a chronic or continuate disease, a settled humour"[10] that requires treatment and therefore defines the purpose of his investigation. Jaques, from this point of view, is seriously ill, even at the end of the play, and this diagnosis calls the viability of his moral stance into doubt. As a result, we can state that *As You Like It* offers two ways to understand the *theatrum mundi* metaphor: as a metaphysical comment on the ephemerality of the world and as a secularized description of the theatricality of social life, not least the intrigues at court. In the same vein, two ethical positions can be derived: on the one hand, the flight from this world, possibly in conjunction with pious preparation for the next one—the loss of illusions aptly captured in the Spanish term *desengaño*; on the other hand, the (re-)engagement in political structures as practiced by Senior.

---

7 Ibid., 3.4.1.1. Burton previously criticizes monks and hermits because they "contemne the world, contemne themselves, contemne all titles, honours, offices" and are thus "more proud then any man living whatsoever" (1.2.3.14).
8 Ibid., 1.1.1.5.
9 Ibid.
10 Ibid.

The discursive flexibility of the *theatrum mundi* metaphor in early modern England can be observed both in a synchronic and a diachronic perspective. If we focus on Shakespeare's own epoch, it is remarkable that the main alternative metaphor—that of life as a dream or sleep, which would become central to Calderón de la Barca's *La vida es sueño* (1635)—appears in just two significant passages in Shakespeare.[11] Crucially, it is modified in both cases, using sleep as the vehicle not for this life, but the next. The world-weary Hamlet famously muses: "To die, to sleep. / To sleep, perchance to dream. Ay, there's the rub, / For in that sleep of death what dreams may come / When we have shuffled off this mortal coil / Must give us pause" (III.1.67–70).[12] In *The Tempest* Prospero concedes that "[w]e are such stuff / As dreams are made on", but moves away from this emphasis on ephemerality to observe that "our little life / Is rounded with a sleep" (IV.1.156–158), i.e. preceded and followed by a lack of self-awareness and agency. Prospero, the humanist who regularly peruses his books—those "volumes that / I prize above my dukedom" (I.2.168–169)—is intellectually aware of the philosophical (and theological) position that death is not to be feared,[13] but as a practitioner of magic—emblem par excellence of human autonomy and the ability to control and shape one's environment—he is shaken by the thought that death might reduce him to a state of helplessness.

Unlike the sleep metaphor, the concept of *theatrum mundi* is suited to the negotiation of agency: awareness of the theatricality of life permits the regulation of one's behavior as well as instances of individual ingenuity. Early modern poetry is one domain in which the disparate interpretations of this image can be detected. In Walter Raleigh's poem "What Is Our Life", published in 1614 as part of his *History of the World*, the speaker construes human life as "a play of passion" (l.1).[14] He sustains this image

---

11 For a comparative analysis of the contemporaneous theater cultures in England and Spain, cf. the volume *Theatre Cultures within Globalising Empires: Looking at Early Modern England and Spain*, ed. J. Küpper and L. Pawlita, Berlin and Boston, MA 2018. Specifically on Shakespeare and Calderón, see L. Pawlita, "Dream and Doubt: Skepticism in Shakespeare's *Hamlet* and Calderón's *La vida es sueño*", in: *Theatre Cultures*, pp. 79–106.
12 Claudio, in *Measure for Measure*, labors the same point: "Death is a fearful thing" (III.1.116) and "The weariest and most loathèd worldly life / That age, ache, penury, and imprisonment / Can lay on nature is a paradise / To what we fear of death" (III.1.129–132).
13 Burton observes that the thought that "it is good to be here" is pervasive among his contemporaries even though it ought to be overcome: "Bonum est esse hic, they had rather be here" (*Anatomy*, 2.1.3.5). Michel de Montaigne contends with a similar sentiment in his essay "To Philosophize is to Learn How to Die".
14 Citations according to Walter Raleigh, "What Is Our Life", in: *English Poetry I: From Chaucer to Gray*, ed. Ch. W. Eliot, New York, NY 1909, §50.

throughout the text, equating the earth with the stage, God with a spectator "who sits and views whosoe'er doth act amiss" (6), and the grave with the "drawn curtains when the play is done" (8). The final couplet offers an arresting example of *memento mori*, shifting the focus from play to reality: "playing post we to our latest rest, / And then we die in earnest, not in jest" (9–10).

Raleigh's orthodox use of the *theatrum mundi* metaphor might be cited in support of the common critical assumption that this trope conveys "[a] sense of futility, of the vanity or folly of human ambition [...] characteristic of all meditative Elizabethan comparisons of the world to a stage".[15] It should be taken into account, however, that the poem places particular emphasis on the experience of heteronomy: everyone gets "dressed for life's short comedy" (4) even before birth, in the "tiring house" that is the mother's womb (3), only then to stand in God's constant judgement. It is therefore telling that Raleigh's attempt to celebrate death as a way to "hide us from the scorching sun" (7)—which can either be seen as a metaphor of God's or a monarch's wrath—is an example of prison literature: at the time of his writing, the courtier and explorer who had formerly led an expedition to South America and described it in a report entitled *The Discovery of the Large, Rich, and Beautiful Empire of Guiana* (1596) was being held in the Tower on charges of treason. His bleak interpretation of the *theatrum mundi* thus ties in with a mind-set that even among his contemporaries would have been psychologized as melancholy due to "loss of liberty, servitude, imprisonment", to quote the relevant chapter heading in Burton's book.[16]

By contrast, Shakespeare's Sonnet 15 approaches the trope in a starkly different way. Here, too, the speaker begins with the observation that the world is transitory; he puts this in familiar, theatrical terms, commenting "[t]hat this huge stage presenteth nought but shows / Whereon the stars in secret influence comment" (ll. 3–4). Instead of reinforcing the idea of vanity and predetermination, though (as the allusion to the stars might suggest), the sonnet's *volta* assures the addressee that the passage of time need not be suffered passively; the poet, for one, is self-empowered to resist transitoriness through his art: "And all in war with time for love of you, / As he takes from you, I engraft you new" (13–14).

---

15 A. Righter, *Shakespeare and the Idea of a Play*, London 1962, p. 148. Cf. J. Briggs, who links Righter's observation "to displays of scepticism, disaffection, or alienation in contemporary satire" (*This Stage-Play World: Texts and Contexts, 1580–1625*, 2nd ed., Oxford 1997, p. 294).
16 Cf. Burton, *Anatomy*, 1.2.4.5.

It is illuminating to complement this look at the *theatrum mundi* metaphor in Shakespeare's time with a brief consideration of its diachronic development. In 1705, a hundred years after Shakespeare, a rather obscure farcical play by the Huguenot immigrant Peter Motteux premiered at London's Theatre Royal in Drury Lane.[17] *Farewell Folly*, so its title, has recently attracted critical attention[18] due to a monologue that alludes to the motto that was supposedly on display above the Globe theater ("Totus mundus agit histrionem")—a motto whose actual use has long been in dispute. Motteux's play comments on the contemporary theatrical scene, confronting the audience with their own, possibly unconscious behavior. The protagonist, Mr Mimic, is an actor who observes that his audiences have become increasingly rowdy. Instead of paying attention to the action on stage, the spectators banter and joke among themselves, trying to make each other laugh. Mimic is initially offended by this show of disrespect for his profession—after all, he is the one who should entertain people with impersonations—but then he admits that he sometimes goes to the fair just to watch people interact and to pick up humorous mannerisms that he can bring to his roles on stage. Mimic the actor thus reveals himself to be a spectator of social role-play in the offstage world, gathering knowledge that he transfers to the portrayal of fictional characters. The ensuing feedback loop dissolves the supposed dichotomies between the actor and his impressionable audience, between the theatrical performance and real life, in the familiar metaphor of the world as a theater: "Sure all Mankind the Play'rs old Motto shares, / The Play'rs act all the World, and all the World the Play'rs. / Some have such Parts, they well may blush to own 'em: / Yet totus Mundus agit Histrionem. / We're all Comedians on the Stage of Life."[19]

It is remarkable that Mimic's argument is, first and foremost, metatheatrical rather than ethical. It does not present a moral exhortation about ideal conduct in an ephemeral, illusionary world; instead, it is concerned with the usefulness of theater, which is here presented—in alignment with theatricality as the modus operandi of the world—as a legitimate institutionalization of the human impulse to play-act. Forty years after the reopening of the London stages at the end of the Puritan

---

[17] Cf. W. J. Burling, *A Checklist of New Plays and Entertainments on the London Stage, 1700–1737*, Rutherford, NJ 1993, p. 39.
[18] Cf. R. Abrams, "Oldys, Motteux and 'the Play'rs old motto': the 'Totus Mundus' Conundrum Revisited", in: *Theatre Notebook*, vol. 61, 2007, pp. 121–130.
[19] Final speech of Act I, qtd. in: Abrams, "Conundrum Revisited", p. 121.

interregnum, such an insistence on the natural joy and social necessity of acting is not axiomatic. It is perhaps for this reason that Motteux's protagonist constructs a tradition that links his theatrical landscape to the heyday of the popular London stage before the civil war. "Totus mundus agit histrionem"—the whole world acts the player, or: acts in a play—has indeed long been believed to be the motto on display above the entrance of the Globe theater, in which Shakespeare held a share. However, this textual claim of mere continuation of an older theme is belied by the innovative farcical mode of *Farewell Folly*. Compared to the Middle Ages and the English Renaissance in the sixteenth century, Motteux's play has stripped away any Sceptic or Christian critique of the vanity of the world. There is no trace of an alarming experience of *desengaño*, that is, of the discovery of the transitoriness of the physical world and the subsequent disillusionment regarding its importance. Instead, the histrionic quality of day-to-day life is genially acknowledged as a form of bonding without which the social animal would cease to exist. Just as the members of Mimic's audience deliberately play the fool and communicate by provoking laughter, so Mimic himself will in the end agree to take part in a benevolent charade that unites in marriage his good friend and the friend's beloved.

Arguably, *Farewell Folly* illustrates a late stage in the early modern development of the *theatrum mundi* ideology, one in which social roleplay has been accepted as a feature of human life. It is only a comparatively small step from there to the dramaturgical analyses conducted in the social sciences, for example, by E. Goffman in his study of *The Presentation of Self in Everyday Life* (1956). Social play, Motteux's farce demonstrates, may be ridiculous at times, but the masquerade poses no threat to the self or soul (or whichever way inwardness may be conceived in a given case)—at least not as long as it is conducted in a state of reflexive self-awareness, with everybody knowing that everybody is playing. This sense of coming to terms with theatricality is common to several English texts of the eighteenth century; it is also emphasized in the following witty exchange between Shakespeare and Ben Jonson as imagined by the antiquarian William Oldys (fl. 1740):

Jonson. If, but stage actors, all the world displays,
Where shall we find spectators of their plays?

Shakespeare.   Little, or much, of what we see, we do;
We're all both actors and spectators too.[20]

With human beings assuming the roles of the actor and the spectator, i.e. the one traditionally ascribed to God, the idea that behavior can be both monitored and self-regulated comes to the fore. This positive self-consciousness distinguishes the eighteenth-century examples from the period when the words "Totus mundus agit histrionem" were allegedly visible above the entrance of the Globe: in Shakespeare's time, the discussion of the ethical implications of the *theatrum mundi* was still gaining momentum, and his plays show clear signs that this concept was a subject of controversial negotiations.[21]

S. Greenblatt has observed that

> [t]heatricality, in the sense of both disguise and histrionic self-representation, arose from conditions common to almost all Renaissance courts: a group of men and women alienated from the customary roles and revolving uneasily around a centre of power, a constant struggle for recognition and attention, and a virtually fetishistic emphasis upon manner. The manuals of court behaviour which became popular in the sixteenth century are essentially handbooks for actors, practical guides for a society whose members were nearly always on stage.[22]

In Shakespeare's fictional worlds, the characters' adaptation to this form of society is frequently painful: "[d]isguise and role-playing are often forced on the

---

[20] "Verses by Ben Jonson and Shakespeare, occasioned by the motto to the Globe Theatre—Totus mundus agit histrionem", attributed to Oldys in: G. Steevens, "Prolegomena", *The Works of Shakespeare with the Corrections and Illustrations of Various Commentators*, London 1773, s.p.

[21] To some extent, the religious variant of the *theatrum mundi* metaphor is counterintuitive because it must posit an autonomous and omnipotent being, God, as a spectator, and his heteronomous creatures, by contrast, as actors. As early as 1513, Thomas More's *History of Richard III* uses the trope in a more modern, quasi-sociological sense, differentiating between the powerful "actors", who know how to comport themselves in a given situation, and the passive "spectators": "And so they said that these matters 'be kings' games—as it were, stage plays—and for the more part played upon scaffolds. In which poor men be but the lookers-on. And they that wise be, will meddle no farther. For they that sometimes step up and play with them, when they cannot play their parts, they disorder the play and do themselves no good'" (*The History of King Richard III*, ed. M. Gottschalk, Dallas, TX 2012, p. 81. https://www.thomasmorestudies.org/docs/Richard_III_English_glossed.pdf, accessed 14 December 2018). While More's argument for social conservatism presents self-fashioning and social rituals as esoteric knowledge, his inversion of the orthodox world-as-theater metaphor, now with the "actors" as the powerful party, must have facilitated the diverging discussion in Shakespeare's time.

[22] *Renaissance Self-Fashioning: From More to Shakespeare*, Chicago, IL 1980, p. 162.

hero by his situation, but they are also a burden, a source of inner confusion and self-doubt."[23] As R. Weidle has argued, Shakespeare's history plays probe the difference between successful and less successful kings and link this investigation to the historical transition from the feudal code of honor and fealty to the paradigm of strategic interaction: successful kings are those who know "how to play", i.e. those who possess a psychological skill set that includes, in modern sociological terms, role distance and the ability to recognize the "frame" of a given situation.[24] Extending this interpretation to the tragedies, Weidle has likewise argued that the protagonists of Shakespeare's mature tragedies are tragic characters precisely because they are aware that they cannot adapt to the new code[25]; instead, they try in vain to navigate a changing social world by totalizing older concepts such as righteousness and trust.[26] Hamlet, who insists that weeping and dressing in black clothes cannot denote sadness for the simple reason that "they are actions that a man might play" (I.2.84), is a prime example: the force of his own argument leaves him virtually unable to have faith in anyone ever again. But *pace* Hamlet, social role-play constitutes an important aspect of the cultural trajectory that N. Elias called the civilizing process: only role distance (the awareness of one's own and other people's theatricality) allows the effective regulation and modification of one's own behavior, e.g. the control of violent impulses (which the psychologist S. Pinker has characterized as the greatest cultural advance since early modern times),[27] whilst at the same time permitting agents to perceive themselves as such: "we are not only aware of what we do, but we can also be aware that we are aware: consequently we can account for our actions and plan for them as well. This

---

[23] Briggs, *This Stage-Play World*, p. 267.
[24] R. Weidle, *Shakespeares dramaturgische Perspektive: Die theatrale Grammatik Erving Goffmans als Modell strategischer Interaktion in den Komödien und Historien*, Heidelberg 2002.
[25] R. Weidle, "'For They Are Actions that a Man Might Play': Role Play, Role Distance, Ego Identity and the Construction of Shakespearean Tragedy", in: *Arbeiten aus Anglistik und Amerikanistik*, vol. 29, 2004, pp. 173–197.
[26] The changeability of abstract concepts—and the question whether this is a liberating or destabilizing phenomenon—affected many domains of Renaissance culture. It can be observed in a dialogue from More's *Utopia* cited below, in which one party argues for universal truth, whereas the narrator aspires to a contextualized philosophy, one tailored to a specific monarch and society. Cf. P. Sokolov, who has explored the phenomenon of *paradiastole*—the rhetorical shift of concepts such as honor and courage—with a view to the consolidation of monarchical power in the early modern Netherlands: "Lucretia without Poniard: Pieter Corneliszoon Hooft's *Geeraerdt van Velsen* between Livy and Tacitus", in: *History and Drama: The Pan-European Tradition*, ed. J. Küpper, J. Mosch, and E. Penskaya, Berlin and Boston, MA 2019, pp. 72–85.
[27] S. Pinker, *The Better Angels of Our Nature: Why Violence Has Declined*, New York, NY 2011.

capacity for reflexive self-monitoring is a crucial constituent of human agency."[28]

The fact that, a hundred years after Shakespeare, plays like *Farewell Folly* could deal with the *theatrum mundi* metaphor in a farcical mode shows that Shakespeare was writing during a liminal phase when the orthodox meaning (and ethical evaluation) of the world as theater was already severely contested and the cultural advance of self-reflexive theatricality was taking hold.[29] In the following, I wish to elaborate the argument that the frequent occurrence of the *theatrum mundi* metaphor in Shakespeare's oeuvre does not reflect any particular vehemence on the playwright's part about its familiar implications

---

28 T. Nellhaus, *Theatre, Communication, Critical Realism*, New York, NY 2010, p. 150. Nellhaus argues for the existence of a nexus of theatricality, metatheater, and social ontology. Luigi Pirandello's novel *The Late Mattia Pascal* (1904) introduces a thought experiment that illustrates the link between theatrical awareness and the "pacification process" (Pinker) by reframing the characters of Sophocles' *Elektra* as puppets in a theater: "if at the climax of the play, just when the marionette who is playing Orestes is about to avenge his father's death and kill his mother and Aegisthus, suppose there were a little hole torn in the paper sky of the scenery. What would happen? [...] Orestes would still feel his desire for vengeance, he would still want passionately to achieve it, but his eyes, at that point, would go straight to that hole, from which every kind of evil influence would then crowd the stage, and Orestes would suddenly feel helpless. In other words, Orestes would become Hamlet. There's the whole difference between ancient tragedy and modern, Signor Meis—believe me—a hole torn in a paper sky" (*The Late Mattia Pascal*, tr. W. Weaver, New York, NY 2005, p. 139). Pirandello's example is astutely chosen, as *Hamlet* contains a similar case of hesitation before revenge, embedded in the First Player's recitation of the history of the Trojan War: "So, as a painted tyrant, Pyrrhus stood, / And, like a neutral to his will and matter, / Did nothing" (II.2.460–462). Pyrrhus, in this account, soon carries out his attack, and Hamlet is likewise unable to see anything positive about his questioning of his role as an avenger. Shakespeare, on the other hand, seems critical of characters that waste such opportunities for self-restraint—one might consider Macbeth before the murder: "If it were done when 'tis done, then 'twere well / It were done quickly" (I.7.1–2). Self-restraint as a form of agency is further explored in S. Greenblatt, *Shakespeare's Freedom*, Chicago, IL 2010, chap. 1.

29 Francis Bacon's essay "Of Simulation and Dissimulation" (1625) differentiates between people who fare better as "dissemblers", never letting others look into their hearts, and people who are able to "read" a situation (to recognize its frame, in Goffman's terminology) and hence may decide on a case-by-case basis which truths to divulge: "if a man have that penetration of judgment as he can discern what things are to be laid open, and what to be secreted, and what to be showed at half lights, and to whom and when (which indeed are arts of state and arts of life, as Tacitus well calleth them), to him a habit of dissimulation is a hinderance and a poorness. But if a man cannot obtain to that judgment, then it is left to him generally to be close, and a dissembler. For where a man cannot choose or vary in particulars, there it is good to take the safest and wariest way in general" (*Essays: Civil and Moral*, ed. Ch. W. Eliot, New York, NY 1909, §6).

regarding the vanity of the world, but rather speaks to its pluralized potential significance as a metaphysical and social comment. To this end, the next paragraphs will present a brief survey of the interpretations of the notion of *theatrum mundi* circulating during the English Renaissance, followed by an application of the findings to paradigmatic cases from the Shakespearean canon.

Even if the *theatrum mundi* metaphor is accepted as valid, the conclusions to be drawn from it are far from obvious. Should one interpret "theater" as "illusion" and "insignificance" and try to stay aloof (that is, be a spectator), or should one fulfill the role that one has apparently been handed by God, acting out the part as best one can? The first position was influentially articulated by the twelfth-century theologian John of Salisbury, who became Bishop of Chartres and wrote a mirror for princes entitled *Policraticus* (ca. 1159), which forms a likely immediate source for the sentence that became the Globe's motto. Building upon the metaphor of life as a play inherent in the first-century prose narrative *Satyricon* by Gaius Petronius, Salisbury asserts:

> Almost the entire world, according to the opinion of our friend Petronius, is seen to play the part of actor to perfection, the actors gazing as it were upon their own comedy and, what is worse, so absorbed in it that they are unable to return to reality when occasion demands. I have seen children imitate so long those afflicted with stuttering that even when they wished to they were unable to speak in the normal way; for usage, as someone has said, is difficult to unlearn, and habit becomes second nature.[30]

It is interesting to note that Salisbury takes care to include the word *fere*, "almost", emphasizing that most people—but not all—are engaged in the worldly play. Stressing that participation in the performance is not voluntary (in the sense that one cannot choose one's birth), but not entirely determined either (in the sense that some people manage to extract themselves from the play), Salisbury carries his qualification of the totalitarian theatricality of the world through the subsequent passages and then briefly abandons it in a surprising *correctio*, only to take it up again:

> It is surprising how nearly coextensive with the world is the stage on which this endless, marvellous, incomparable tragedy, or if you will comedy, can be played; its area is in fact that of the whole world. It is most difficult for anyone excluded to be admitted, or admitted to be excluded, as long as he wears this muddy vesture of decay.[31]

---

30 John of Salisbury, *Policraticus*, ed. and tr. C. Nederman, Cambridge 1990, p. 191.
31 Ibid., pp. 194–195.

This ambivalence is a recurrent aspect of Salisbury's text, which prevaricates in similar manner about the question whether life be best characterized as a tragedy or a comedy. The cleric first opines that "[t]he life of man appears to be a tragedy rather than a comedy in that the end is almost invariably sad; for all the sweetness of the world, however entrancing it may be, grows bitter, and mourning taketh hold of the end of joy."[32] Then, however, he introduces the Christian perspective that the whole cosmos is regulated by divine justice and that life is therefore more appropriately regarded as a comedy:

> None the less those departing hence have been kindly dealt with in that they are not taken from this drama of fortune to be cast into exterior darkness, where there shall be weeping and gnashing of teeth, nor do they have to pass from the snow waters which Job, the holy man, mentions to excessive heat. Kindly have they been dealt with in that they await their Elysian Fields, which the sun of justice illumines with his light.[33]

In conclusion, Salisbury shies away from scrutinizing, let alone criticizing, God's design of the world as a theater, but he has trouble negotiating the process of *desengaño*, which he seems to regard as simultaneously desirable and (almost) impossible.

Part of Salisbury's unease in handling his central metaphor may result from the fact that he encounters it in an ancient satirical text that does not fit seamlessly into a Christian perspective. The main part of the Petronian *Satyricon* tells of a feast that a freed slave, who has come into some money, gives for a number of rather vulgar friends and followers. The satirical thrust of the narrative is directed at the social role-play of an upstart whose pretense at wealth and education cannot hide his humble upbringing. This is a perspective that Salisbury largely ignores as he tries to incorporate the attractive play metaphor into a Christian worldview, that is, the performance that humankind delivers before the eyes of God.

By contrast, the aspect of role-play as a social technique became prevalent once again as the humanists opened up a different interpretation of the *theatrum mundi*, one that was concerned with playing one's worldly part to the best of one's ability. Erasmus of Rotterdam's *Praise of Folly* (1509) is one such text that uses the argument of social cohesion to give prudence precedence over *theoria*, or insight. The allegorical character of Folly presents a thought experiment in which "some wise man who has dropped from the sky"[34] tries to dispel

---

32 Ibid., p. 192.
33 Ibid.
34 Desiderius Erasmus, *Praise of Folly*, ed. and tr. C. Miller, New Haven, CT 1979, p. 38.

the illusion of the world. "What", Folly asks rhetorically, "would he get by it, except to be considered by everyone as insane and raving?"[35] She concludes that as "nothing is more foolish than wisdom out of place, so nothing is more imprudent than unseasonable prudence. [...] The part of a truly prudent man [... is to] pretend [with pleasure] not to notice anything, or affably and companionably be deceived [*vel connivere libenter, vel comiter errare*]."[36]

In *Utopia* (1516), Thomas More, Erasmus' friend and correspondent, uses the form of the fictional dialogue between himself and Raphael Hythloday, an experienced traveler, to make a similar case. Against Hythloday, who claims that he could never lie and implies that no philosopher should do so, the narrator argues that it is better to live peaceably in society than to be an outcast, however insightful one's position might be:

> [T]here is another philosophy more civil, which knoweth, as ye would say, her own stage, and thereafter, ordering and behaving herself in the play that she hath in hand, playeth her part accordingly with comeliness, uttering nothing out of due order and fashion. And this is the philosophy that you must use. Or else whiles a comedy of Plautus is playing, and the vile bondmen scoffing and trifling among themselves, if you should suddenly come upon the stage in a philosopher's apparel, and rehearse out of *Octavia* the place wherein Senece disputeth with Nero, had it not been better for you to have played the dumb person, than, by rehearsing that which served neither for the time nor place, to have made such a tragical comedy or gallimaufry? For by bringing in other stuff that nothing appertaineth to the present matter, you must needs mar and pervert the play that is in hand, though the stuff that you bring be much better. What part soever you have taken upon you, play that as well as you can and make the best of it. And do not therefore disturb and bring out of order the whole matter because that another which is merrier and better cometh to your remembrance.[37]

Shakespeare's mature tragedies are particularly concerned with the importance of such "companionable" role-play and the question how it might be distinguished from malevolent forms of deceit. The plots of *King Lear* and *Othello* both hinge upon the protagonists' inability to see through performances. Othello trusts his ensign's impersonation of an honest man, with devastating consequences; his failure to recognize Iago's deceitfulness aside, he erroneously believes that his freedom as a person is contingent upon his ability to arrive at his own decisions, rejecting external advice: "Were it my cue to fight, I should have

---

[35] Ibid. One may note in passing that Folly is, of course, using one of the lessons of Plato's Allegory of the Cave.
[36] Ibid., p. 48.
[37] Thomas More, *Utopia*, tr. R. Robinson, in: *Three Early Modern Utopias*, ed. S. Bruce, Oxford 2008, pp. 1–148, p. 41–42.

known it / Without a prompter" (I.2.84–85). Othello's negative impression of theatricality as a form of 'being told what to do' tallies with his naïve trust in an authentic core of his selfhood that is somehow closed off to his social environment—"that within which passeth show", as Hamlet would call it (I.2.85). Ironically, it is exactly this belief (and the concomitant lack of insight into the ways in which the presentation of selfhood can be strategically deployed) that makes Othello vulnerable to the manipulations of the "prompter" Iago.

Lear, in turn, gives his entire kingdom to the two daughters who flatter him whereas he punishes his third daughter, Cordelia, who sincerely tells him that he will have to share her love with her future husband. Lear, however, is not the only one to blame for the consequences. Arguably, there is something willfully stubborn about Cordelia's refusal to play-act, that is, her refusal to avow her love for her father the king in front of the assembled court. In the worlds of the play and of Elizabethan-Jacobean realpolitik, that inflexibility makes her an obsolete character, the literary equivalent of the Erasmian wise man from the sky who insists upon the righteousness of his position with an almost Kantian rigidity, oblivious to the results of his actions.

Macbeth offers a further interesting take on the *theatrum mundi* proposition because it features a morally tainted protagonist. As one might expect, the regicide is not a believer in the ascetic message of *theatrum mundi* at all—at any rate, he tries to change the divine script by putting himself in the position of king—but he does believe in the power of performance, telling his wife that "[we] must make our faces visors to our hearts, / Disguising what they are" (III.2.34–35). It is only when his plans go awry that Macbeth explicitly uses the world-as-theater metaphor, albeit in a nihilist variant, that is, without the Christian *encore* of the afterlife vouchsafed by God to his human players: "Life's but a walking shadow, a poor player / That struts and frets his hour upon the stage / And then is heard no more" (V.5.23–25). Here, Shakespeare approaches the ideology of vanity commonly ascribed to Calderón's plays, but the fact that Macbeth is so clearly disaffected with God—earlier in the play, he has vowed to "jump the life to come" (I.7.7), that is, to sacrifice the afterlife for success in this world—makes it impossible to interpret this drama as favoring the didactic power of the *theatrum mundi* metaphor.

This resistance to the reformative message of the trope is a recurrent phenomenon that can also be found in *Timon of Athens*, a tragedy that deals with the fall of a wealthy man who usually entertains many friends for dinner. When he falls on hard times, he discovers that he cannot rely on the support of his erstwhile friends and decides to shun humanity altogether. He dies a misanthrope, alone in the woods. The play does not explicitly employ the *theatrum mundi* metaphor, but Timon arrives at a conclusion that is shared by all

Shakespearean characters who do use it, viz. that it were better to be dead so as to send a scornful message to those who live their illusionary lives: "I am sick of this false world, and will love nought / But even the mere necessities upon't. / Then, Timon, presently prepare thy grave. / Lie where the light foam of the sea may beat / Thy gravestone daily. Make thine epitaph, / That death in me at others' lives may laugh" (IV.3.368–373). The decline of this benevolent person proves once again the Erasmian dictum that it is better to err happily—or at least to play along—than to seek the truth, or, as More's narrator puts it in *Utopia*, not to turn a comedy into a tragedy by willfully presenting the wrong scene. However, Timon, like Hamlet, does not direct his disgust at characters who are unconscious actors in God's theater of the world, but at role-players; he even showers a group of bandits with a treasure of gold because the thieves, in his eyes, are more honest than the merchants, jewelers, painters, and poets who used to flatter him: "Yet thanks I must you con / That you are thieves professed, that you work not / In holier shapes; for there is boundless theft / In limited professions. [*Giving gold*] Rascal thieves, / Here's gold" (IV.3.418–422).

Even if the negotiation of social role-play remains ambivalent throughout the Shakespearean canon, we can demonstrate that those characters who insist on the transitoriness of the world and belittle humankind by reducing it to the position of "mere players" are those who are either disappointed by a failure of their plans or who are melancholics by disposition. In addition to the aforementioned Jaques, the title-character of *The Merchant of Venice*, Antonio, numbers among those whose perception of the world is slanted by an imbalance of the bodily humors. In a dialogue with the exuberant and playful Graziano, Antonio claims the superior insight of the philosopher from the sky, arguing that "I hold the world but as the world, Graziano—/ A stage where every man must play a part, / And mine a sad one" (I.1.77–79). As Graziano observes, this is out of character: Antonio is "marvellously changed" (I.1.76). The observation is tantalizing because it allows the possibility that Antonio is indeed in a state of *desengaño*, seeing, as he suggests, the world as it really is. As we know from John of Salisbury, there is no going back. Bassanio, in any case, supports Antonio, telling his friend that he should pay no heed to Graziano's words (I.1.114). But Bassanio has good reason not to offend Antonio in this situation—he wants to borrow money—and the play in general, with its felicitous pairing of different couples in love who hear the music of the spheres of the divinely ordered cosmos, seems to confirm that Antonio's perspective is slanted. He is, after all, suffering from melancholy. His initial words "In sooth, I know not why I am so sad" (I.1.1) form the first line in the play and call the legitimacy of his later insights into doubt.

The obvious tension between Antonio's laments and his engagement in worldly enterprises, not least as a businessman, supports the assumption that he uses the philosophy of *desengaño* as a protective shield against the reality of his situation, which is characterized by constant fears of abandonment—in the course of the play, he stands to lose, in turn, his closest friend, his wealth, and his life. The psychological mechanism at play, then, is one that is already described in Aesop's *Fables*, specifically those devoted to the vice of self-delusion; a well-known version is the story about the fox who cannot reach the desired grapes and turns away, declaring that they are sour anyway. In an epimythium, Aesop interprets that fable as a lesson for "people who speak disparagingly of what they cannot attain".[38] In a comparable manner, Shakespeare's plays point out that *desengaño* is not a stance of disillusionment at all, but rather a different kind of illusion: characters like Hamlet or Antonio, who stand aloof and take pride in their *theoria*, have problems to cope with disappointments. Hamlet rationalizes his anti-social tendencies by taking recourse to philosophical speculations ("What a piece of work is man") rather than confront his grief for his father and his hurt pride that he did not become king. Antonio is similarly averse to social interactions that require a mask of friendliness; when Salerio excuses himself from a conversation, pointing out that Bassanio has arrived ("I would have stayed till I had made you merry / If worthier friends had not prevented me"), Antonio retorts bluntly: "I take it your own business calls on you, / And you embrace the occasion to depart" (I.1.60–61, 63–64). Here again it is plausible to assume that we are dealing with a protagonist who avoids the confrontation with the cause of his depression, trying instead to convince others and himself that sadness has turned him into "such as want-wit" that he has trouble "to know myself" and that "how I caught it, found it, or came by it, / What stuff 'tis made of, whereof it is born, / I am [yet] to learn" (I.1.6, 7, 3–5). The text implies that love is a likely reason; that the protagonist rejects this explanation—"Fie, fie" (I.1.46)—may well be a case of "protesting too much".[39]

If the middle period of Shakespeare's work is dedicated to two problems—can *desengaño* ever be a relevant ethical stance, and how can we distinguish between

---

[38] "The Fox and the Grapes", in: *Aesop's Fables*, tr. L. Gibbs, Oxford 2002, p. 125.
[39] It is remarkable, at any rate, that Antonio's greatest wish is that Bassanio will see him die: "Pray God Bassanio come / To see me pay his debt, and then I care not" (III.3.35–36). His desire to perish as some kind of secular martyr, who dies not for God, but for *philia* (or even *eros*), ties in with his belief that he has a certain part to play, but it also underlines the this-worldliness of his sorrow. A later scene, in which Antonio persuades his friend to give away a ring the latter has received from Portia, might even suggest that Antonio is trying to drive a wedge between Bassanio and his beloved: "My lord Bassanio, let him have the ring. / Let his deservings and my love withal / Be valued 'gainst your wife's commandëment" (IV.1.445–446).

morally superior and deceitful role-play?—it is a question worth further investigation what becomes of these concerns in Shakespeare's late plays. The so-called romances are tragicomedies in which, so it is usually maintained, Shakespeare revisits earlier themes and narratives, enriching them with supernatural and ostentatiously improbable elements. Thus, for example, *Othello* is an inquiry into the causes of jealousy, while *The Winter's Tale*, in which King Leontes decides from one second to the next that his pregnant wife must have been unfaithful to him, is an exploration of the results of jealousy and the ensuing losses. What saves *The Winter's Tale* from ending in tragedy is the empathetic decision by three characters to go "off script": a courtier warns Leontes' friend, whom the king suspects to be the seducer of his wife, so that he can flee in time; the queen is wrongly reported dead to the king and so saved from execution; her child is saved by a sympathetic courtier who persuades the king to abandon the girl to the kindness of strangers rather than have her killed. Thus, the characters relevant to the eventual reconciliation stay alive instead of dying an unjust death. There is a similar pattern in *Cymbeline*, another of the late romances, where a prudent apothecary sells a sleeping potion rather than poison to a murderous queen. The difference between an unhappy and a tragicomic ending is due to characters who have internalized the lesson that role-play and dissimulation are necessary social techniques, but that they can be used to a benevolent end. The companionable playing along of the social animal is paired with agency, with the awareness that even actors whose participation in the play is a given can have free will to decide how they discharge their lines. This may in fact be the most important lesson of the Erasmian conception of the *theatrum mundi*—that *connivere libenter*, to pretend gladly, that is, consciously, imbues actors with more freedom than the rival concept of *desengaño*.

This thesis is borne out by the play that offers what is arguably the most cogent test of the concept of *theatrum mundi*, *The Tempest*. Let us recall that it deals with a duke called Prospero who, due to his interest in magic rather than statecraft, ends up banished to an island. Fortune and magic leave the usurpers stranded on Prospero's island, where he scares and enchants them with all sorts of supernatural occurrences. In a religious perspective, Prospero, who stresses his godlike omnipotence—he can even raise the dead from their graves—, fulfills the role of the unseen creator. If we conceive of the island as a test for the shipwrecked characters, and thus as an allegory of the world, in which human beings must qualify for the afterlife, we can distinguish different groups. Some characters fail utterly: they think only of colonizing the island and remain in a constant state of illusion as to the reality of their situation. The most successful character, in this perspective, is Ferdinand, the young prince who has fallen in love with Prospero's daughter Miranda. Prospero orders him to perform menial tasks that are quite inappropriate for an aristocrat's son—chopping wood and carrying lumber—so that he will learn to value his eventual happiness. But although—or rather, precisely because—Ferdinand is aware of the theatrical nature of his task, he submits to it gladly and willingly, arguing: "Some kinds of baseness / Are nobly undergone, and most poor matters / Point to rich ends. This my mean task / Would be as heavy to me as odious, but / The mistress which I serve quickens what's dead / And makes my labours pleasures" (III.1.2–7). As we have come to expect, the play values neither illusion nor the form of *desengaño* that leads to flight from the world; instead, it favors the self-aware playing along that humanists like Erasmus and More demanded.

It is important to note that Prospero's character undergoes development too. In a religious perspective, his decision to forego his anger and to reconcile with his subjects is equivalent to the transition from wrath to love between the Old and New Testament. In a literal reading, Prospero's reform shows that the boundary between watching a play and acting in it is more permeable than he might have believed. Despite his intentions, the play that Prospero stages by using his enemies as unwilling, unaware actors, rekindles his capacity for empathy. Crucially, this change is concomitant with a reappraisal of theatrical awareness. Before his reform, the protagonist is critical of role-play. In Prospero's analysis, his brother, to whom he entrusted rule over his dukedom while studying his beloved books, was almost forced to usurp the dukedom because his self was swallowed up by the role. Thus, he "did believe / He was indeed the Duke. Out o'th' substitution, / And executing th'outward face of royalty / With all prerogative, hence his ambition growing" (I.2.103–106). The usurpation was an inevitable consequence of the brother's failure to distinguish between the role he played and his private person: "To have no screen between this part he played / And him he played it for, he needs will be / Absolute Milan" (I.2.108–110). Prospero here adheres to the anxiety about role-play, and instances of acting and pretending in general, that was frequently voiced in contemporary literature. Montaigne's essay "Of the Force of the Imagination", for example, cites the scholastic proverb according to which the power of the imagination can bring forth the thing itself.[40]

---

[40] Cf. N. Panichi, "'Fortis imaginatio generat casum': Montaigne and the 'power of the imagination'", in: *Rinascimento*, vol. 51, 2011, pp. 45–62.

At the beginning of the fourth act, Prospero channels his rage and disappointment into the *theatrum mundi* metaphor, a recurring pattern among Shakespeare's disaffected characters:

> Our revels now are ended. These our actors,
> As I foretold you, were all spirits, and
> Are melted into air, into thin air;
> And like the baseless fabric of this vision,
> The cloud-capped towers, the gorgeous palaces,
> The solemn temples, the great globe itself,
> Yea, all which it inherit, shall dissolve;
> And like this insubstantial pageant faded,
> Leave not a rack behind. We are such stuff
> As dreams are made on, and our little life
> Is rounded with a sleep. Sir, I am vexed.
> Bear with my weakness. My old brain is troubled.
> Be not disturbed with my infirmity.
> If you be pleased, retire into my cell
> And there repose. A turn or two I'll walk
> To still my beating mind. (IV.1.147–163)

Prospero's agitation highlights that he fully identifies with his feelings of anger and hatred; he continues with his fantasies of revenge on his servant Caliban and on the entire group:

> A devil, a born devil, on whose nature
> Nurture can never stick; on whom my pains,
> Humanely taken, all, all lost, quite lost,
> And, as with age his body uglier grows,
> So his mind cankers. I will plague them all,
> Even to roaring. (IV.1.188–193)

Prospero's subsequent reform comes about when Ariel, a spirit of the air, shows empathy and compassion for the prisoners:

> Ariel.   Your charm so strongly works 'em
>   That if you now beheld them your affections
>   Would become tender.
> Prospero.   Dost thou think so, spirit?
> Ariel.   Mine would, sir, were I human.
> Prospero.   And mine shall. (V.1.17–20)

The magician's change of heart seems sudden—indeed Shakespeare takes care to make it so, using four half-lines in which the characters' speeches complement each other without any pause. But the confluence of the sentences is part of the message: Prospero learns *through* theatricality, observing, then accepting and mirroring Ariel's feelings, and he also learns *about* theatricality, i.e. the substitution of the identification with an absolute (wrath, revenge, etc.) by self-consciousness, or role distance, which is necessary to be a moral agent in the full sense. Ariel's use of a hypothetical point of view (expressed in the subjunctive "*were* I human") enables Prospero to forego his total desire for revenge and replace it with a relative perspective. He still feels the pain of his brother's betrayal, but he is able to watch himself as a distant observer would and to make a moral choice: "Though with their high wrongs I am struck to th' quick / Yet with my nobler reason 'gainst my fury do I take part" (V.1.25–26).

Prospero's transition from *desengaño* (human lives as dreams) to identification (hatred and fantasies of torture) to role distance is a process of ethical maturation. The observation that "playing along" is necessary for agency matches the particular interest this play takes in characters who act outside their script. Explaining how he was able to survive his banishment in the first place, Prospero remembers how one would-be enemy resisted his "appointment" to a certain role in the scheme: "Some food we had, and some fresh water, that / A noble Neapolitan, Gonzalo, / Out of his charity—who being then appointed / Master of this design—did give us" (I.2.161–164). In a similar way, Ariel, who helps Prospero control his passions, has previously resisted acting, as the duke recalls: "And for thou wast a spirit too delicate / To act her earthy and abhorred commands, / Refusing her grand hests, she did confine thee / [...] / Into a cloven pine" (I.2.274–279). These passages, like the previously cited examples of the benevolent apothecary in *Cymbeline* or the sympathetic characters in *The Winter's Tale*, are also interesting because they do not, in a strict sense, pertain to situations of self-preservation, in which a form of politically astute dissimulation would have typically been advised by writers like Niccolò Machiavelli or, as quoted above, Francis Bacon. Instead, they link the new model of role awareness to an older discussion of the ethics of truthfulness, e.g. Thomas Aquinas' evaluation of different kinds of lies: "the sin of lying is diminished if it be directed to some good—either of pleasure and then it is a 'jocose' lie, or of usefulness, and then we have the 'officious' lie, whereby it is intended to help another person, or to save him from being injured."[41]

---

[41] Thomas Aquinas, *Summa theologiae: Latin text and English translation*, ed. Th. Gilby, London 1964, 2.2.Q110.

By way of conclusion, there is one related question worth addressing, which is the recurrence of metafictional jokes that betray the constructed nature of the literary texts throughout the Shakespearean canon, but particularly in the late plays. One example is Fabian's observation in *Twelfth Night* that the events are entirely unlikely: "If this were played upon a stage, now, I could condemn it as an improbable fiction" (III.4.114–115). Hamlet's remark "You hear this fellow in the cellarage" (I.5.153) is another instance of such communication on two levels, "*cellarage* being a term that reminds the audience that an actor is making noises down in the space beneath the stage".[42] *Cymbeline* even revels in the ostentatious unlikeliness of its plot. Discussing the abduction of two princes twenty years before, two gentlemen express doubts about this occurrence and invite the audience's ridicule regarding this important plot-point:

> Second Gentleman. That a king's children should be so conveyed,
> So slackly guarded, and the search so slow,
> That could not trace them!
> First Gentleman. Howsoe'er 'tis strange,
> Or that the negligence may well be laughed at,
> Yet is it true, sir. (I.1.64–68)

For several decades, the phenomenon of theater "about" theater—plays that call attention to their textual construction and the material and ideological conditions of their staging—has attracted considerable critical attention. Early studies included R. Nelson's *Play within a Play* (1958), which sought to establish self-reflexive drama as an "index to self-consciousness" and hence to "a given dramatist's controlling conception of the theater",[43] and L. Abel's *Metatheatre* (1963),[44] which considered metatheatrical plays as a subset of dramas that provided an alternative to the cathartic tragedy of ancient Greece. Metatheater, Abel contended, presents life "as already theatricalized"[45]: the protagonists are "aware of their own theatricality",[46] the hero is "conscious of the part he himself plays in constructing the drama that unfolds around him".[47]

---

42 M. Bell, *Shakespeare's Tragic Scepticism*, New Haven, CT 2002, p. 33.
43 R. J. Nelson, *Play within a Play: The Dramatist's Conception of His Art. Shakespeare to Anouilh*, New Haven, CT 1958, p. x.
44 L. Abel, *Metatheatre: A New View of Dramatic Form*, New York, NY 1963.
45 L. Abel, *Tragedy and Metatheatre: Essays on Dramatic Form*, ed. M. Puchner, New York, NY and London 2003, pp. 134.
46 Ibid., p. 135.
47 Ibid., p. 167.

As interest in modern and postmodern metatheater grew, Abel's theory did not fare well, with one critic noting that "Abel's contribution to the field has been of slight theoretical weight apart from his lexical addition."[48] Debates have ensued as to the general viability of the concept, with W. Egginton commenting that "there can be no theater that is not already a metatheater, in that in the instant a distinction is recognized between a real space and another, imaginary one that mirrors it, that very distinction becomes an element to be incorporated as another [...] work of mimesis."[49]

In addition, theorists of metatheater have sought to universalize the concept. A. Pérez-Simón has turned to R. Jakobson's functions of language to argue that we must assume an aesthetic function behind metatheatrical examples. J. Stephenson has relied on S. Świontek's work on two communicative systems in theater (the stage-stage axis, i.e. characters speaking to each other, and the stage-house axis, i.e. characters speaking for the audience) and has qualified metatheater as a form of deliberate alienation.[50] These linguistic or communication-centered approaches are supplemented by an interest in the psychological effects that metatheater produces. As S. Purcell has pointed out, Stephenson's approach presupposes a particular configuration of the theatrical performance (dark auditorium, quiet audience, proscenium stage) and therefore focuses on metatheatricality as a form of disruption.[51] He rightly contests the assumption that this was the historical norm and argues that metatheater is "more likely to produce delight than distancing" because it activates a specific potential of the human mind, or brain: that of perceiving a situation or idea in two frames of reference at the same time, an ability that A. Koestler called bisociation. Purcell's remains one of the most interesting approaches within a critical environment in which the discussion of the functions and effects of metatheater tends to fall short of an analysis of its "mechanics", that is, its conceptualization in terms of aesthetics and communication theory. As early as the 1990s,

---

[48] J. Stephenson, "Meta-enunciative Properties of Dramatic Dialogue: A New View of Metatheatre and the Work of Sławomir Świontek", in: *Journal of Dramatic Theory and Criticism*, vol. 21, 2006, pp. 115–128.
[49] W. Egginton, *How the World Became a Stage*, Albany, NY 2003, p. 74.
[50] S. Świontek, "Le dialogue dramatique et le métathéâtre", in: *Zagadnienia Rodzajów Literackich*, vol. 36, 1993, pp. 7–44.
[51] S. Purcell, "Are Shakespeare's Plays Always Metatheatrical?", in: *Shakespeare Bulletin*, vol. 36, 2018, pp. 19–35.

T. Kowzan pointed out that the study of metatheater ought to be historicized,[52] but, by and large, the ideological and epistemological value of metatheater has been sidelined in recent discussions.

As this essay has shown, the recovery of Abel's conceptualization of "consciousness" has the potential to inform future research into phenomena of theatricality in Shakespeare's plays. The plays use theatrical metaphors and metatheatrical pointers to achieve a number of purposes. Metatheater may indeed invite speculations about fiction and reality: "Rather than mimetically representing the 'real' world, metatheater calls into question accepted notions of that reality, stressing instead the world's theatricality."[53] But theatrical metaphors also serve to make situations plausible, e.g. in *Othello*, when the duke anticipates a diversionary maneuver and describes the Turkish fleet at Rhodes as "a pageant / To keep us in false gaze" (I.3.19–20). Similarly, the Duke of York, commenting on the deposition of Richard II, offers the explanation that the monarch lacked the charisma to gather enough support: "As in a theatre the eyes of men, / After a well-graced actor leaves the stage, / Are idly bent on him that enters next, / Thinking his prattle to be tedious, / Even so, or with much more contempt, men's eyes / Did scowl on gentle Richard" (*Richard II*, V.2.23–28). Importantly, though, the theatrical metaphors in Shakespeare possess an ethical dimension that must not be neglected. The analysis of which characters use them, in what mind-set, and to what purpose, shows that resistance to theatricality and role-play is either connected to an unhealthy despondency about the ephemerality of this world or to the inability to relativize concepts such as honor and revenge. Identification with absolutes, however, is shown to be an obstacle to moral agency. Shakespeare's plays offer theatricality as a remedy to heteronomy that is the consequence of obstinacy and single-mindedness. This point is often made ex negativo, as two final examples will illustrate. In *Antony and Cleopatra*, the Egyptian queen is anxious about becoming a character in a theatrical performance: "The quick comedians / Extemporally will stage us, and present / Our Alexandrian revels. Antony / Shall be brought drunken forth, and I shall see / Some squeaking Cleopatra boy my greatness / I'th' posture of a whore" (V.2.212–217). In *Troilus and Cressida*,

---

[52] "On peut invoquer, certainement, des raisons d'ordre philosophique, idéologique ou scientifique: impact de la théorie de la relativité, remise en question de certains principes, impact des grandes crises intellectuelles et politiques; là encore, l'analogie avec le siècle baroque s'impose" (T. Kowzan, "Théâtre dans le théâtre: signe des temps?", in: *Cahiers de l'Association internationale des études françaises*, vol. 46, 1994, pp. 155–168, p. 167).

[53] M. Frese Witt, *Metatheater and Modernity: Baroque and Neobaroque*, Madison, WI 2013, p. 14.

Ulysses (who tries to draw Achilles into the Trojan War and therefore wants to incite the Greek leaders against Achilles' companion Patroclus) appeals to a similar fear that greatness is lost if it becomes theatricalized: "With him [Achilles] Patroclus / Upon a lazy bed the livelong day / Breaks scurrile jests / And, with ridiculous and awkward action / Which, slanderer, he 'imitation' calls, / He pageants us. Sometime, great Agamemnon, / Thy topless deputation he puts on, / And like a strutting player [...] / He acts thy greatness in" (I.3.146–158).[54]

If greatness is the unmitigated readiness to fight, theatricality is indeed its opposite: the ability to tarry, to laugh, to change one's mind. Shakespeare's characters rarely recognize this as a positive development, but by problematizing the characters that resist theatricality, Shakespeare's plays support a cultural trajectory towards moral agency qua self-reflectiveness. By pointing out the artificial and unlikely qualities of his plays, Shakespeare provides a foil for the understanding of real life as equally contingent and yet—in the words of the first gentleman in *Cymbeline*—as true. The lesson particularly of the late plays, then, is not to seek *desengaño*, but to seek agency within the "script", the agency afforded by the possibility of consciously, sociably playing along.

---

[54] The unusual transitive phrase "to act something in" is structurally similar to the more common expression "to bind something in". The idea that power can turn into a form of megalomania that abhors any form of confinement is recurrent in Shakespeare; Macbeth, who—in the words of his wife—also strives to "be great" (I.5.16), despairs over the fact that even after the regicide he feels "cabined, cribbed, confined, bound in" (III.4.23). For an illuminating study of Shakespeare's bleak view of political leadership and its psychological cost, cf. also S. Greenblatt, *Tyrant: Shakespeare on Politics*, New York, NY 2018.

Joachim Küpper
The Conceptualization of the World as Stage in Calderón and Cervantes – Christian Didacticism and its Ironic Rebuttal

Calderón's *El gran teatro del mundo* (1630/1655), one of the two texts I will be dealing with in this paper, belongs to the core canon of world literature, a fact which is not least substantiated by its ongoing reception in modernity proper, the most important rewriting of the play being Hugo von Hofmannsthal's *Das große Welttheater* (1922). For this reason, I will keep my remarks concerning this drama rather brief.

El gran teatro del mundo is a one-act play, a so-called *auto sacramental*. This genre emerged at the end of the sixteenth century and flourished in Spain until the end of the seventeenth. The plays were performed on the Feast of Corpus Christi in the streets of Madrid, and attendance was free in order to reach a maximum number of spectators.[1] The intention of the plays was didactic: to propagate, once again, the basic truths of Catholicism as they had been reasserted by the Council of Trent (1545–1563). In a way, the *autos* constitute a continuation of the pan-European medieval tradition of religious drama—that is, morality plays and mystery plays—to which the Cervantine drama I will be dealing with in the second section of this paper is also linked, albeit in an oblique fashion. As to its generic form, one could characterize Calderón's drama and the numerous *autos sacramentales* conceived by playwrights such as Lope de Vega and Tirso de Molina as attempts to adapt medieval Christian drama to the demands of an age whose ideas of what constitutes a well-wrought play had been informed by humanism—in this case, by the reception of the classical tradition of dramatic production. The crucial difference displayed by *autos sacramentales* with respect to their medieval predecessors lies in their concision: while a standard *auto* consists of about 1,000–1,500 lines, morality plays and mystery plays comprised up to 60,000 lines during their final stage of generic evolution, that is, in the fifteenth century. The main device for concentrating

---

[1] For a more detailed account of the genre and of Calderón's oeuvre in general, see my *Discursive* Renovatio *in Lope de Vega and Calderón: Studies on Spanish Baroque Drama. With an Excursus on the Evolution of Discourse in the Middle Ages, the Renaissance, and Mannerism*, Berlin and Boston, MA 2017, esp. chap. 3.

Open Access. © 2019 Joachim Küpper, published by De Gruyter. This work is licensed under the Creative Commons Attribution-NonCommercial-NoDerivatives 4.0 License.
https://doi.org/10.1515/9783110622034-007

the teachings of Catholicism—the narrative of salvation history together with the axioms of moral theology—within no more than 1,500 lines (which means about 30 minutes of duration for the performance) was metaphor, namely in its extended version, the *metaphora continuata*, which is the standard definition of allegory in the contemporaneous manuals.² The *metaphora continuata* is a very apt device when it comes to highly concentrating a dramatic work's message; but, as demonstrated by the fifteenth-century morality plays—which had recourse to allegory but were nevertheless extremely long—such concentration is not the necessary consequence of the application of the device. Allegory functions as an enabling structure when it comes to the goal in question, and it is perhaps the most efficient one conceivable. But it is neither a sufficient nor a necessary condition.

Calderón's *El gran teatro del mundo* is presented here as a paradigm of the genre and even more so of the basic intention sustaining the genre. Thus, the interpretation of Cervantes's play as an ironic rebuttal of what is given expression in Calderón's *auto*—which might at first seem counterintuitive, given the respective dates of publication—is meant to convey that the former reacts to the general message and intention of the *auto* as genre.

Leaving aside any evaluation of its ideological profile, one has to say that Calderón's version of the concept of theater as a metaphor for human life in general³ is ingeniously conceived. It displays a maximum transparency of the metaphorical level as to its intended meaning as well as an exploitation of the semantic potential of the basic image that is rich and multifaceted to a degree which can hardly be characterized as otherwise than amazing. Although extremely simple as to its message, the play matches the highest standards of contemporary *conceptismo*—it should be mentioned that the personage named *Autor*, meaning God, explicitly articulates a corresponding claim when, during an interaction with *Mundo*, a personage representing the stage director, he calls the metaphor sustaining the play within the play "un *concepto* mío / la ejecución a tus aplausos fío" (p. 41, vv. 37f.; my italics).⁴

---

2 See, e.g., Emmanuele Tesauro, *Cannocchiale aristotelico*, Venice 1663, pp. 75 and 440.
3 As is well known, the metaphor as such has a long history, starting in pre-Christian antiquity; the main sources from classical times are Epictetus (*Encheiridion* § 17) and Plato (*Laws* 644D); all necessary details may be gathered from E. R. Curtius's chapter "Theatrical Metaphors" in his *European Literature and the Latin Middle Ages*, tr. W. Trask, Princeton, NJ 2013, pp. 138–144. Curtius has a tendency to neglect the reception of the metaphor under the auspices of the revival of Stoicism that is characteristic of pre-Counter-Reformation humanism (Erasmus of Rotterdam, Montaigne, Lipsius).
4 Citations according to: Pedro Calderón de la Barca, *El gran teatro del mundo*, in: Pedro Calderón de la Barca, *El gran teatro del mundo, El gran Mercado del mundo*, ed. E. Frutos Cortés,

The one and only act is divided into three sections. This structure constitutes, on the one hand, a resumption of basic Aristotelian principles (the prehistory, the story proper, and the end), and, on the other, an allusion to the dogmatic concept of the triune, of the configuration of three-in-one. The prehistory establishes the basic metaphor: the Christian God is presented as a sort of playwright (*El Autor*), while the World (*El Mundo*) is at the same time the stage and the stage director. There are a number of personifications or types of humans who are the actors of the play within the play: the King (*El Rey*), the Wise Man (*La Discreción*), who turns out to be a man of the Church, *Hermosura*, (female) Beauty,[5] the Rich Man (*El Rico*), the Peasant (*El Labrador*), the Poor Man (*El Pobre*), and, finally, a child (*Un Niño*), of whom spectators learn that it died in the process of being born or shortly after. In addition, Grace (*La Ley de Gracia*) plays a role—not that of an actor, however, but rather of a commentator. This is both a resumption of the classical concept of the chorus and an anticipation of devices familiar from modern, twentieth-century drama with its tendency towards the epic.

The actual stage is divided into two parts. On the upper part, God, the *Autor*, conceives the play within the play, which will take place on the "stage" below: he creates it, quite like a playwright, just by imagining it and subsequently articulating his imaginations, while emphasizing that the story it contains—that is, world history—is nothing but a short play,[6] a fictional episode (embedded in a more comprehensive reality) whose performance he will take delight in viewing (p. 41). As soon as the allegory of the World, the first personage appearing on the lower stage, has thus been created, it presents a brief account of salvation history with its three sections: *ante legem*, *sub lege*, and *sub gratia*, including an anticipation of the Apocalypse. Next, the *Autor* hires actors and assigns them the various roles already mentioned, following nothing other

---

Madrid 1983, pp. 39–89; English translations follow the version to be found in Pedro Calderón de la Barca, *The Great Theatre of the World*, in: Pedro Calderón de la Barca, *Four Great Plays of the Golden Age*, tr. R. Davis, Hanover, NH 2008, pp. 231–265; I do not provide direct translations of quotes whose content is sufficiently characterized in my own formulations.

5 *Discreción* as well as *Hermosura* seem to be "gendered" in the way made explicit above; but the religious person is also called "la religiosa" (p. 67, v. 845), and *Hermosura*, explicitly referred to as "la dama" at one point (p. 67, v. 841), represents, as the *Autor* says, *La Hermosura humana* (p. 51, v. 333f.)—that is, those humans (regardless of sex and gender) who take pride in their physical beauty.

6 The allegory of *Mundo* explicitly articulates this diagnosis ("¡Corta fue la comedia!"; p. 79, v. 1255); some lines later, the personage even makes use of the formulation "la farsa de la vida" (p. 80, v. 1290)—which might be considered an additional justification (if there is a need for one) of the comparison with the Cervantine *entremés*.

than his own discretion in the process of distribution. Those who ask for a "better" part, the actors hired to play the Peasant and the Poor Man, are told that the respective roles have to be filled in order for the play to be complete, and that there are no other parts available for them. It constitutes a slight breach of the perfectly devised allegory that these actors, in contrast to actors in the proper sense, do not have the liberty to turn down the offer of employment.[7] Their complaints are countered by the *Autor*, who says that at the end of the play they will receive their pay ("el salario"; p. 53, v. 424) not according to the hierarchical status of their roles, as is common in theater performances proper, but according to the quality of their individual performances. The measure of this quality is the degree of compliance with what may be called a preexistent role script, the imperative of *obrar bien*, that is, to act in the right way, i.e., according to the Christian commandment of love for one's neighbor. It needs to be emphasized that the play ("comedia") to be performed in the following, that is, the play within the play, bears exactly this title: "¿cómo [...] esta comedia[8] se llama?" / "what's the title of this famous play?" asks *Hermosura*; the *Autor* answers: "Obrar bien, que Dios es Dios" / "Do good, for God is God" (p. 54, v. 436–348 / p. 240).

Not least because of the extreme metaphorical condensation here at work, there is only one scene in the strict sense; the individual actors' compliance with the quality standard just mentioned is measured by way of this scene. It should be noted that the *Autor* emphasizes that all of the actors are endowed with free will ("[a]lbedrío"; p. 55, v. 482; *liberum arbitrium*), which enables them to perform well if they wish to do so. The actors' task is further facilitated

---

[7] —a logical inconsistency that translates the difficulty (or, rather, the impossibility) of harmonizing the assumption of free will on the part of humans and the dogma of divine *praescientia*: the play (within the play, that is, human existence) will take place in the way God "foresaw" it, whatever humans may decide. Nevertheless, the individuals have freedom of choice, but only within the limits of the specific role God has assigned them. The question of whether they would have "performed" better or worse within a different role than the one they are actually assigned remains open.

[8] For non-Hispanist readers of this essay, it should be mentioned that the term *comedia* is the general term for drama in Spanish Golden age usage. *Comedias* comprised tragedies, tragicomedies, and comedies (the latter in the Aristotelian sense of the term); as is apparent from the above quote, contemporary authors also subsumed the *autos sacramentales* under this generic term. Modern research, starting at the beginning of the nineteenth century, has introduced a strict differentiation between *comedias* and *autos* that seems not to have existed in the period of origin of the texts. This striking shift may be due to the fact that the degree of attention paid to issues of form in comparison to content and message is much greater in the case of modern literary studies than in the case of pre-nineteenth-century, esp. medieval and Baroque literature.

by the fact that the performance takes place under the auspices of *La Ley de Gracia*, who appears as a personage onstage. *La Ley* puts her auxiliary function into practice by repeating time and again, in a chorus-like fashion, the formula "Obrar bien, que Dios es Dios" (p. 65, v. 790; see also v. 808 and v. 942), that is, by reminding the actors what the play is about[9]; some amongst them, above all *El Rico*, consider this admonition to be boring ("¡Oh, cómo cansa esta voz!" / "Oh, how it tires me out!"; p. 66, v. 810 / p. 248).

At one point, the Poor Man asks the other actors to give him alms ("Dadme, por Dios, limosna"; p. 67, v. 860f.). The man of the Church immediately complies with this request, while all the others give nothing. Shortly afterwards, a voice (*Voz*) announces that the play is already approaching its end (pp. 71f.). The stage director divests the actors of their props (the King's crown, the Rich Man's gold and silver, etc.), and the latter leave the stage "desnud[os]" (p. 80, v. 1290), naked—which would not literally have been the case in contemporaneous performances.[10] The lower stage, governed by *El Mundo*, is closed, while the upper stage is opened once again. The *Autor* is having supper. He invites the Wise Man (the cleric) and *El Pobre* to join him, that is, to have wine and bread together with him. The King and *Hermosura*, the beautiful woman, who both performed badly, but apologized to the *Autor*—that is, repented before being divested of their roles[11]—are told that they will have to wait for a while, specifically in purgatory (p. 87, v. 1480), before they will be invited to participate in the meal. *El Labrador* also receives a finally benign verdict because he was in principle willing to give alms, but felt that charity might have a negative effect on the Poor Man's own efforts to escape from his misery by work—an argument that the *Autor*, that is God, seems neither to endorse nor unconditionally to reject. The rather benign treatment of the King, of Beauty, and of the Peasant is enhanced by the cleric's intervention, who asks the *Autor* for their waiting time to be reduced.

There is only one actor who receives an unqualifiedly negative evaluation: the Rich Man is not invited to supper, and the *Autor* states clearly that he will

---

9 At one point, the formula is expanded by adding an explicit reference to the Christian imperative of love for one's neighbor: "Ama al otro como a ti, y obrar bien, que Dios es Dios" (p. 70, vv. 947f.).
10 On the page specified above, the metaphorical usage of the term is even made explicit.
11 The King's last words are: "Si ya acabó mi papel, / supremo y divino Autor, / dad a mis yerros disculpa, / pues arrepentido estoy"; / "If my part's over, / Supreme and divine Author, / please forgive / My errors, because I'm truly repentant" (p. 72, vv. 1003–1006 / p. 252). The last words uttered by *Hermosura* before she exits the lower stage are: "Mucho me pesa no haber / hecho mi papel mejor" / "It grieves me greatly / That I didn't play my part more perfectly" (p. 74, vv. 1079f. / p. 253).

not be invited in the future. Instead of being paid, he will be punished by way of endless pains for having performed badly. In addition, the child who did not have any chance to perform either well or badly is denied access to the table, though without being punished; this harsh verdict is justified by the *Autor*, who tells him "en fin naces del pecado" (p. 87, v. 1507), a reference to original sin, which forms a crucial component of Christian dogma.[12] The relation between the two stages is specified in precise meta-language at the end of the *auto*: the *comedia* that took place on the stage of *El Mundo* was "el teatro [...] de las ficciones", while what takes place after its end, either the eternal supper with God or eternal damnation, is the "teatro [...] de las verdades" (p. 84, vv. 1387f.).

In recent decades, theoretical discussions revolving around the concepts of metaphor and more specifically of allegory have highlighted the arbitrariness characterizing the relation between *proprium* and *figuratum*. Such assumptions, based partly on certain highly abstract insights of Saussurian and post-Saussurian linguistics, partly on notoriously extreme statements by Nietzsche,[13] follow a rhetorical logic—in this case, the attempt at gaining attention by way of sensationalizing—much more than they constitute a sober assessment of basic semiotic mechanisms. Calderón did not have the power to impose metaphors constructed by him on the public according to his own discretion only; in order to be successful as a playwright, he hand to convince his audience, that is, to persuade them to "buy" his conceptualizing. The specifically Christian variant of the metaphor of the world as a stage which Calderón develops in the *auto* briefly analyzed gains its consistency by elaborating on two basic concepts

---

[12] If it were not the case that every human being is marred by sin, there would not have been a reason for God's self-sacrifice; it would have sufficed to propagate the idea of imitating morally exemplary individuals. Casting every human being as subject to sin leads by necessity to the postulate—somewhat absurd from an external perspective—that newborn children are sinners. Since they are endowed with a soul created by God in His likeness, they are full human beings, even already in their mothers' womb. A conceptualization that protects them against being killed before birth (abortion) or immediately afterwards, as is current practice within other cultural/religious contexts, also implies that they will never be able to access Paradise if they die before baptism. The problems caused by this dogmatically cogent clause became attenuated by the imperative practice to baptize newborn children immediately after birth (a sacramental act that frees them from the "stains" of original sin), and, in addition, by postulating a sort of neutral antechamber of hell, the *limbus*, which is certainly not a particularly pleasant place, but a place whose inmates are not subjected to pains. The *limbus* is the destiny assigned to those children (actually born or aborted, be it naturally or by human intervention) who died before baptism.

[13] I am thinking, of course, of Nietzsche's famous equation of truth and metaphor in *On Truth and Lies in an Extra-Moral Sense* (1873).

preexisting in the world-view of this religion, that is, concepts that were well-known to any spectator. The rhetorical impact of the play might not least be based on these external points of reference that secured—within the rather hermetic ideological context mentioned—a more than arbitrary dimension for what it presents: within a Christian frame, there is, indeed, an answer to the question that remains in suspense within the secular variants of the metaphor of the world as a stage (prominent since antiquity and present in Calderón's times in Shakespeare, amongst others), namely the question of where the corresponding concept: the non-stage, or, in other terms: reality, is to be sought.[14] As to content, the answer—in a world beyond this one—is nothing but dogma. But as to dramaturgical structure, there is, in Calderón, a contrasting "place" to "the world as a stage", whereas the secular variants exhibit nothing but a void.

No less than the one first mentioned, the second component that secures a highly compelling profile for Calderón's *concepto* has both a structural and a dogmatic dimension. Actors on a stage are not free to do what they want to do; they have to comply with what is called a script. Seen from this perspective, the metaphor of "the world as a stage" seems at first sight to be in contradiction to the *doxa* of "real life" as granting (free) choice to the individual, as well as to the dogma of *albedrío* (*liberum arbitrium*). In this *auto sacramental*, Calderón exploits to the fullest the meaning of "freedom of will" from a Christian, specifically a Counter-Reformation Catholic perspective: it consists in the decision to comply or not to comply with a preexisting role script that, as such, is by no means subject to human discretion. The "essence" of the life of a good Christian is basically *imitatio* (*mimesis*), specifically *imitatio Christi*—not necessarily to the extent of being ready to suffer martyrdom, but in any case to the extent of being prepared to deprive oneself of one's property, status, or well-being in order to "save" one's neighbor.

The Cervantine drama I will be dealing with is much less well known than Calderón's *auto*.[15] It bears the title *Entremés del retablo de las maravillas* and was first published in 1615. As is the case with all of the products of the author's attempt to gain access to the lucrative market of stage performances, the play was not very successful—for various reasons, Cervantes's theatrical

---

[14] The structure of the play, based on the device of the play-within-a-play, makes it possible to also present the cosmos of the "verdades" explicitly as "teatro", which allows the author to avoid attempts at spiriting away what is obvious, namely, that the "show" in its entirety is theater. The "teatro [...] de las ficciones" is, consequently, cast as an embedded episode within a stage performance representing "real reality".

[15] This part of my paper reproduces an analysis contained in my book *The Cultural Net: Early Modern Drama as a Paradigm*, Berlin and Boston, MA 2018.

oeuvre never attained to the immense success of his novels and novellas. As to this *entremés* in particular, it may also be that the author's ideological non-conformism, carefully veiled in the *Quijote* and the *Novelas ejemplares*, became all too obvious here for stage directors to be ready to risk a conflict with the Inquisition.

Entremés is a generic term. The French equivalent, *farce*, which is also used in English and German, may be more familiar, with the literal meaning of the terms being exactly the same: something that is placed between two other items. The original field of application of the term *farce* (deriving from the verb *farcir*) is the culinary sphere. It designates a mixture of meat and spices inserted into a larger piece of meat, usually poultry, in order to enhance the taste of the entire roast. In the case of drama, this whole into which the farce is inserted is a "serious" play divided into several acts, often with a didactic (in the age in question: religious) content. In the High Middle Ages, such didactic plays—mystery plays referring to Biblical history, mainly to Christ's birth or to the Passion; morality plays presenting allegories of virtues and vices fighting against each other—reached a length that caused their performances to last longer than one or two days. In order to provide some relief from such enormous quantities of doctrinal and moralizing material, dramatists inserted brief one-act plays, *entremeses* or farces, in between acts. The plots of these one-act plays were independent from those of the main plays, and their content was intended to be entertaining—that is, it was always comic, and in many cases also obscene. The reaction of contemporary audiences to these interludes seems to have been so positive that, from the thirteenth century onward, they developed into independent plays, typically performed by itinerant troupes on occasions such as festivals and fairs. The genre may be considered a paramount example of what M. Bakhtin calls the "carnivalesque", and its development is a no less paramount example of what he calls the evolution of the carnivalesque, taking place during the Renaissance, from a restricted to an emancipated cultural practice.[16]

The title proper of the Cervantine *entremés* is intentionally ambiguous: a "retablo" is primarily an altarpiece presenting religious paintings, including depictions of *maravillas*, meaning miracles (Christ's Ascension, for instance, or the descent of the Holy Spirit). But in Golden Age usage, "retablo" might also refer to a stage on which a show is performed.

The plot of the piece I will be discussing might be summarized as follows: a troupe of itinerant actors enters a village, sets up its stage (the *retablo*), and then performs various short scenes in order to entertain those villagers who are

---

16 See *Rabelais and His World*, tr. H. Iswolsky, Bloomington, IN 1984.

ready to pay a (modest) fee. We are thus dealing, once again, with a play within the play. The only link between these scenes is their sensational content: the biblical Samson tearing down the columns of a temple dedicated to an idol; a huge number of mice appearing on the stage and frightening in particular the female contingent of the audience; wild and dangerous beasts—such as bears and lions, or a bull who is said to have killed a man in Salamanca—running around on stage (etc.). However, there is in fact nothing to be seen on the stage. The actors behave and talk to each other as if the scenes mentioned were being performed, and the villagers enthusiastically agree, to the point of being seized by fear when the lions are allegedly prowling around on the stage. The reason for their readiness to accept the actors' pretentions as true is conveyed in a scene that takes place before the (non-)performances within the performance. The stage director tells the villagers that the contraption set up is named "the stage of miracles" because only people of legitimate birth (stemming from a couple who is united by the bond of sacramental marriage) and who are, in addition, so-called "old Christians" (*cristianos viejos*), that is, who are free from the suspicion of having Jewish ancestors, are able to perceive what is presented onstage.

The striking peculiarity of the Cervantine functionalization of a well-known motif (I shall come back to this point) is encoded in the ending. A quartermaster of the royal army suddenly appears. He announces that there are some dozen military men to be hosted, and asks the villagers to make the necessary preparations. These, however, or the bigger part of them, believe the quartermaster to be part of the stage action. They ask the stage director to present more entertaining scenes, and start hitting the quartermaster, as the latter does not show any readiness to leave the "stage". In those times, hosting military men from one's own country on their demand was, indeed, a legal obligation. If there was resistance to this law, the soldiers were entitled to take by physical force what was not conceded to them voluntarily. The military man reacts accordingly: he draws his sword and stabs a great number of the villagers. The play thus ends in a bloody disaster.

Put in a nutshell, one might say that there is a skeptical tenor—skeptical in the sense of the philosophical school—sustaining the entire construction. It is provided by the fact that the villagers really believe to be seeing what is only recounted to them; sensory perception might be biased by ideological commitments or societal constraints. The basic motif of the play is not unknown in European literary history. It cannot be excluded that Hans Christian Andersen based his fairytale *The Emperor's New Clothes* (1837) on a reading of Cervantes's *entremés*; but it may as well be the case that the two authors drew independently from corresponding material already available prior to Cervantes. The motif as such can be found in the *ejemplo 32* of the *Conde Lucanor* (1330–1335), a collection, written in Spanish, of entertaining as well as instructive short narratives that derive from the medieval oral tradition and may go back to autochthonous and/or to exogenous sources (Arab, Oriental). There is, however, a unique feature of Cervantes's usage of this motif. In the instances preceding and following it, the audience acquiesces to the veracity of what they have been told in order to avoid censure by the authorities. In Cervantes, by contrast, the bloody ending shows that many audience members really believe to see what, according to the deceivers, is "represented" onstage. What might be considered, in the case of the other texts that make use of the motif, an incrimination of conformism by way of ridicule, assumes in Cervantes the rank of a quasi-epistemological speculation: conformism might block cognition to the point of leading to disaster.

There is another point of divergence to be addressed. Of the two prerequisites for seeing what is allegedly happening onstage according to the tricksters of Cervantes's play, one finds only the first one in the *Conde Lucanor*, namely, the criterion of legitimate birth. The motif belongs to the traditional repertoire of the comic, since it refers to the body and its permanent resistance to the superimposition of those restrictive norms and laws we call civilizational, societal, or religious. As to what is known about the realities in premodern rural Europe, legitimate birth (as opposed to births out of wedlock) was more the exception than the rule—which is not astonishing, since such legitimacy is of relevance only in case there is something to inherit. For the lower classes, it is without any functionality. It is one of those many patterns of behavior that are constantly reasserted verbally while being more or less ignored practically.

Cervantes adds to this traditional comic motif an item he draws from a completely different discursive strand, the contemporary controversies revolving around the "right" religion and the "right" way to practice it. Highly intricate questions of orthodoxy in the literal sense are introduced into comedy and thematized in a way that would have been inconceivable in pragmatic and non-comic texts at that time. The concept of *limpieza de sangre* (purity of blood) refers to the first stages of racism in European history. Pressured by the increasingly successful Christian re-conquerors of the peninsula, many Spanish Jews had converted to Christianity in the fourteenth century. As delighted as the Iberian Christians might have been at first that so many Jews gave up their "stubborn"[17] resistance to

---

[17] "Stubbornness" (*obstinatio*), the willful rejection of what one is able to recognize as true but not ready to acknowledge, is the main "vice" ascribed by medieval Christian polemics to the "Synagogue" (the common metonymy for all people of Jewish faith).

acknowledging that Jesus was the Messiah announced in Scripture, they soon had to face the fact that these "new Christians" (*cristianos nuevos*) were not only sisters and brothers in Christ, but also became, on the grounds of the act of conversion, serious competitors in the worldly sphere. As Jews, they had been excluded from all of military and civil service, including the clergy and higher education. After baptism, these social spheres became accessible to them on equal grounds. With the skills and the adaptability their ancestors had to acquire during a long history of persecution, the *cristianos nuevos* performed well in these sectors formerly reserved for the "old Christians". The reaction to this evolution was a series of pogroms which exceeded in their violence what was known from previous European history. In order to cool the overheated atmosphere, the authorities promulgated the first statutes of *limpieza de sangre* in 1449, that is, rules that made all the aforementioned professions accessible only to those who were able to produce evidence that they were so-called *cristianos viejos*, that is, of non-Jewish lineage. Even without going into the details,[18] one might be able to imagine what the—perhaps even unintentional—consequences of these statutes were, namely, the general atmosphere of a witch-hunt that degenerated into a sort of proto-totalitarian racism in the year 1492, when all non-converted Jews and Muslims were exiled from Spain, and even more so in the course of and after the Counter-Reformation and the reinforcement of the Inquisition going along with the Catholic Church's attempt at regaining ideological control in the West. Being accused of illegitimate birth was nothing that would have had serious real-world consequences in the rural Spain of that time.[19] Being suspected of not being a *cristiano viejo*,

---

18 The seminal publication on the scenario briefly characterized above is D. Nirenberg's *Communities of Violence: Persecution of Minorities in the Middle Ages*, Princeton, NJ 1996.

19 As to the attitude of the Church, *fornicatio* (extra-marital intercourse with a view to gaining pleasure) was considered sinful; but, as questionable as the Church's positions may have been in those times in many other respects, the "products" of such sinful behavior, if there were any, that is, "illegitimate" children, were always accepted as equal members of the congregation. Within society at large, the patriarchal norms whose function is to guarantee the transmission of accumulated wealth from one generation to the next initially apply in the aristocratic milieu only. As early as in the late Middle Ages, the "new" class of the bourgeoisie adopted this code of conduct, called in Spanish *honor*, exactly for the reasons just mentioned: bourgeois people began casting themselves as "honorable" as soon as there was a relevant material possession they could leave to their (but not just any) children. In the countryside of all of Europe, sexual practices seem to have been quite promiscuous in premodern times. The Church tried to reconcile the realities with its dogma by creating the concept of *matrimonium in facie Dei*, which was nothing but a makeshift legitimization of a previous relationship between partners not united by marriage. The Council of Trent interdicted this practice. Only "regular" marriage in a church and in the presence of a priest legitimized by ordination to practice what was, from that time onward, a sacrament, was accepted. Innumerable Spanish Golden age texts from the period after the Council exploited the previous

in contrast, would, sooner or later. lead to a trial by the Inquisition. In case of a first trial, acquittal was the statistically prevalent outcome; in case of a second trial, the opposite was the case. In those days, being accused twice of not being of *sangre limpia*—the chief symptom being the secret abidance by Jewish ritualistic rules (avoiding the consumption of pork; taking a bath on Fridays rather than on Saturdays)—meant being subjected to torture in almost all cases and then burnt at the stake following upon an extorted confession.

It is thus extremely sensitive material that Cervantes touches upon in his *entremés*. By decidedly integrating comic material with highly intricate material revolving around the question of orthodoxy and, ultimately, of life and (violent) death, he re-functionalizes a genre whose task had been nothing more than to provide comic relief into an instrument of anti-totalitarian reflection. The pressure exerted by the *limpieza de sangre* statutes and the ensuing atmosphere of all-encompassing conformism is leading Spain into "seeing what is not there and not seeing what is there", into a complete loss of touch with reality—that is the message conveyed by this at first sight so harmless interlude.

An additional, albeit minor aspect which should be mentioned is that Cervantes made use of another ideologically relevant discursive material when he produced the play in question. The first noun of the title, "retablo", has, as already mentioned, two different semantic dimensions. Its primary meaning referred to in this specific context is: "a stage for puppet (or else dumb) shows". Its well-known secondary meaning—well-known because it is the standard meaning—is "decorative altarpiece". And there is a second word in the title referring to religion, namely, "maravillas". The primary reference of the term is the content of the play within the play, the "miraculous" onstage appearance of wild beasts from other continents. The secondary meaning—which, in this case as well, is the standard meaning—refers to supernatural phenomena that are supposed to be real.

The discussion revolving around the question of whether there are indeed miracles or whether these are delusions produced by the will to see them, or by deceivers who profit from making the populace believe that they are real—in this case: by God's ministers—belongs to the fiercest ideological controversies of early modern Europe. Protestantism as well as the more "enlightened" strands of Catholicism (Erasmianism) held that the Resurrection, the Ascension, and the concomitant supernatural events that occurred in that context were the last miracles before the end times, when there may be further ones.

(and, as one may assume, ongoing practice) of *matrimonium in facie Dei* in order to obliquely thematize practices which were considered to be sinful within the "official" discourse at that time.

Traditional Catholic dogma, and even more so the Church's ritual practices, were, however, firmly linked to the idea that miracles were an integral part of *contemporary* reality. Pilgrimages, devotion to saints, miracles occurring in such contexts, and the system of money collection linked to these practices were vital for Catholicism. During the deliberations at Trent, these practices, as well as the claim linked to them—namely, that they might help transgress the limits of regular, empirical reality—had been vigorously reasserted. Neither certain texts by Erasmus of Rotterdam (*Colloquia familiaria* [1518]), nor a literary text like the *Lazarillo de Tormes* (1552/1554), with its famous *buldero* chapter, would have been conceivable after the Council. But Cervantes ingeniously synthesizes this anti-Tridentine material with comic material of an—as it seems—completely harmless profile.

Erasmus' critique of miracles, as well as that of the anonymous author of the *Lazarillo*, also had recourse to comic devices (parody, satire) in order to treat a question which would not have been treatable on the peninsula in a "serious" way in those days. In his play, Cervantes reactivates this technique of "re-functionalization through assembly of the diverse" and thus succeeds at producing a decidedly anti-Tridentine text despite his status as an "official" and honored author of contemporary Spain. But his text is not an imitation of the precursors mentioned. What Cervantes introduces in order to secure this discursive and ideological margin in more difficult times than those of Erasmus and the *Lazarillo* is a change of register and an ensuing discursive diversity that is hardly conceivable for non-literary texts. It is not satire or parody—comic genres that have always been linked with more serious forms of ideological critique—but the, generically speaking, "lowest" variant of comedy, farce, that is here chosen in order to veil the ideological subversion conveyed by the text.

In conclusion, I will present some thoughts linked to the relation of the two dramas here discussed to the general topic of the conference from which the present volume emerged: theater as metaphor. I will not comment further on the specific aspect highlighted in the title of my paper, since it is evident from what I have said that the two plays stand in a relation of an assertion and its ironization. Cervantes does not try to convey that the Christian dogma is nonsensical or absurd. He just poses the question of whether an all too compliant, completely unreflecting, quasi-automatic stance towards this dogma and the ethical requirements linked to it might perhaps lead believers to fall prey to swindlers and deceivers. As is consistently the case in Cervantes's works, there is no thematization in the *entremés* of the dimension that Calderón refers to as the "teatro de las verdades"—that is, the dimension of life after death. Thus, from a logical perspective, one cannot exclude the possibility that the naïve villagers of Cervantes's play immediately go to paradise after being stabbed by the quartermaster—that is, if any such paradise exists. If there is nothing of the kind, however, the only "pay" the villagers receive for their ideological conformism is not an invitation to eternal supper in the presence of the Godhead, but, rather, ridicule and, finally, violent death. Is it all too speculative to assume that there is probably not much *eleos* (pity) to be expected of readers or viewers of the play or its performance when they are witnessing the final scene?

As to literary devices, the main difference between the Calderonian and the Cervantine versions of the basic motif consists in that there is an explicit allegorization of the motif in the *auto*, while there is none in the *entremés*. In Calderón, the stage (on the stage) is the world; the play ("comedia") performed on it is life; the actors are, in proper terms, real-world humans or types of humans; the playwright is God, who is in charge of the entire arrangement, while the actors have the liberty to perform well or badly, and are rewarded accordingly once the play is over; the reward consists in the most solid reality there is, at least from a Christian perspective: either hell or paradise.

In Cervantes, by contrast, the scenario in its entirety is mimetic in the Aristotelian sense. Although the statistical probability of such a scenario to be or become real is not very high, it is possible (*dynaton*) that similar events might have happened in sixteenth- or seventeenth-century rural Spain. The intention, however, is not documentary. On Cervantes's part, there is no ambition involved to provide a novella-like report on hardly believable but nonetheless "real" occurrences. The scenario on stage is, here no less than in Calderón's *auto*, a metaphor whose meaning refers to a sense (*sensus*) that differs from the proper meaning of the words (the *verba*, according to Quintilian's famous definition),[20] that is, from the text.

I would like to suggest conceiving of Cervantes's usage of the device of theater as metaphor as symbolic, whereas Calderón's usage is allegorical in the classical sense of the term. It does not make sense to assign a discrete metaphorical meaning to every single detail in Cervantes's play; by contrast, such a decoding does make sense in the case of Calderón's play. The Cervantine *entremés* is rather to be taken as a semioticized configuration that conveys a highly complex and comprehensive thesis concerning the interplay between the human mind and preestablished patterns of interpretation—preestablished, that is, by routine, custom, belief, or conformism. Ultimately, it is a thesis pertaining to the unreliability of the mind's assessment of sensorial perceptions.

---

20 See *Institutionis oratoriae libri XII*, here: 6:44.

The basic device at play in both texts—theater as metaphor—is accordingly to be seen as extremely versatile as to its semiotic functionalization. Its essence, or, to put it more modestly, the common denominator of its concrete instantiations—observable not only in the cases examined here, but also beyond—may reside in its engagement with a difficult question already raised in Aristotle's *Poetics*: what is play, imitation (*mimesis*), and what is real action (*pragmata*)?[21] And are there any strict criteria upon which we can rely in order to make a judgment in particular cases? Aristotle's answer to this latter question is, finally, negative: what is "theater" and what is "reality" depends on our personal attitude towards what occurs before our eyes. It is this attitude which determines whether we treat the corresponding scenes as bare facticity or as metaphor, meaning: as referring to something else which is not there, at least not *pro omaton*,[22] to quote the Stagirite.

---

21 See chaps. 1–4, spec. 4.
22 See *Poetics*, chap. 17.

Kirsten Dickhaut
The King as a "Maker" of Theater: *Le ballet de la nuit* and Louis XIV

Theater is often used as a metaphor in seventeenth-century France; the term covers, for instance, libraries, anatomical theater, and the *theatrum mundi*.[1] Moreover, it is used to illustrate the actions of states and of statesmen.[2] In the dramatic genre this particular metaphor is either—as in the case of Corneille's *Illusion comique*—presented as a play-within-a-play scenario, or the play itself represents in an allegorical way a specific, usually political idea.[3]

The Ballet of the Night, a courtly dance with text passages written by Isaac de Benserade, displays both variants of the metaphor—it contains a play within a play and has its own allegorical meaning. Both dimensions focus on the rising of the sun, which is presented in a literal as well as in a metaphorical way; this in turn reflects the way the King's power is shown. We are thus dealing with the interaction of a literal (in this case: meteorological) signification and a metaphorical meaning that conveys the political dimension of theater by way of a royal ballet that was danced by King Louis XIV himself in 1653.

To understand this particular ballet, we have to begin by considering its structure and symbolism and then proceed to examine the text which comprises the announcements, commentaries, and introductions to the dancing parts and presents the political program to be conveyed by the spectacle. The texts I refer to were published in four parts.[4] The *Ballet* is actually a collective work: Issac de Benserade wrote the verse, Giacomo Torelli[5] constructed the scenography and the costumes were probably designed by Beaubrun or Henri de Gissey (this is not clear). The choreography of the dance has not been documented. Many

---

[1] See the articles in the present volume. In the age in question, the idea of *theatrum mundi* is most prominently represented by Calderón de la Barca's *El gran teatro del mundo*.
[2] This starts with Baldassare Castiglione's characterization of his ideal courtier as an actor; see P. Burke, *The Fortunes of the Courtier: The European Reception of Castiglione's* Cortegiano, Malden, MA 1995; K. Dickhaut, "Fest-Spiele als höfische Gefüge: Castiglione, Versailles, *Les Plaisirs de l'île enchantée*, Paris und Molières *Tartuffe ou l'Imposteur*", in: *Soziale und ästhetische Praxis der höfischen (Fest-) Kultur im 16. und 17. Jahrhundert*, ed. K. Dickhaut, J. Steigerwald, and B. Wagner, Wiesbaden 2009, pp. 187–216.
[3] K. Dickhaut, "Magische(s) Gestalten in der frühneuzeitlichen Komödie: Ariostos *Il Negromante* und Corneilles *Illusion comique*", in: *Poetica*, vol. 48, 2016, pp. 59–80.
[4] "Bibliographic description, Rothschild B1/16/6", in: *Ballet de la Nuit: Rothschild B1/16/6*, ed. M. Burden and J. Thorp, Hillsdale, NY 2009, pp. 83–84.
[5] *Giacomo Torelli: L'invenzione scenica nell'Europa barocca*, ed. F. Milesi, Fano 2000.

Open Access. © 2019 Kirsten Dickhaut, published by De Gruyter. This work is licensed under the Creative Commons Attribution-NonCommercial-NoDerivatives 4.0 License.
https://doi.org/10.1515/9783110622034-008

composers were responsible for the music, among them the likes of Chambefort, Lambert, and Mollier. We thus have the verse (spoken text), the libretto (sung text), the colorful designs of the scenographical structure and of the costumes, and the list of the names of the courtiers who participated in the spectacle, as not only the King himself but the court, too, was involved in the staging. Five performances of the ballet are documented in the seventeenth century, all of them in 1653; every single performance was realized with the King as dancer.

In 2000, Gérard Corbiau released his Hollywood film *The King Dances*, and in 2017 the company of Dijon performed a modern version of the ballet—first in Dijon, then in Versailles. Before this, there had been no performance of the ballet for more than 350 years. Yet, what Corbiau's film suggests is not congruent, as far as quite a few details are concerned, with what the historical documents state[6]: Jean-Baptiste Lully and Molière were not involved in composing the score or the text; but, in fact, they participated in the ballet as dancers and comedians. Before presenting the structure of the performance and its metaphorical dimension I will briefly contextualize the ballet to provide insight into the event that is—mostly because of the King's costume (Fig. 1)—one of the best-known plays from that age, though it has been rarely studied.[7]

Early modern theater is focused on performance. The publication of the text is in many cases posterior to its performance on stage. The text may even be published for the first time after the playwright's death. The ephemeral moment of the staging was therefore of crucial importance. As a consequence, in the seventeenth century, the written text of a play did not have any other relevance than that of serving as a basis for the action on stage. What is decisive for theater is the actual performance of the play on stage, not the written text. Everything that was printed had a strategical or propagandistic function. In this way the *ballet de cour* and the opera were comparable to the genre of theater proper as all these artistic forms are mainly spectacles, although they are text-based; and all three could integrate music into their performances.[8]

Performances of the *Ballet of the Night* were very special, and not only because the King himself and the male members of the court danced on stage.[9] In

---

[6] A. Simonis, "Gérard Corbiau: Le Roi danse. Zur medialen Inszenierung des Phaëton-Mythos im Film", in: *Die verzaubernde Kunstwelt Ludwigs XIV.: Versailles als Gesamtkunstwerk*, ed. U. Jung-Kaiser und A. Simonis, Hildesheim 2015, pp. 249–270.
[7] Louis XIV as *Le Soleil*: BnF. Estampes, Hennin 41/3674.
[8] F. Böttger, *Die "Comédie-Ballets" von Molière-Lully*, Hildesheim 1979.
[9] J. Thorp, "Dances and Dancers in the *Ballet de la Nuit*", in: Burden and Thorp (eds.), *Ballet*, pp. 19–33.

Fig. 1: Louis XIV as *Le Soleil*, BnF, Estampes, Hennin 41/3674; copyright bpk 00051148, Paris 1653, RMN-Gp.

particular, the implied political symbolism marked the rise of the King to power at the moment that the Fronde, the revolt of the nobles, came to an end and the absolutist system experienced a restoration of its power. Mazarin was recalled to be prime minister in 1653, and in 1661 the young King himself effectively took over as monarch—until that year his mother had held the reins of the kingdom.[10] In this context, the ballet proposes a political strategy and represents at the same time the emergence of a new art form, one that will serve as a model for future court ballets. The King had danced for the first time in 1651 in the *Ballet de Cassandre*,[11] meaning that the *Ballet de la nuit* in 1653 was one of the earliest of the genre.

What has decisively marked the image of Louis in posterior times up to the present, the "staging" of his power in the Premier and Deuxième Versailles, was organized systematically only somewhat later in time, starting in 1661.[12] In 1653, he was still a very young, fourteen-year-old minor; at that point in time, one could watch the King making actual theater, as he was dancing on stage: the theatrical performance is meant to be an allegory of his concept of government. In order to promote the ballet, the King participated as a dancer, represented the allegory of the sun by embodying it, and had a booklet produced with a view to documenting the ballet's success.[13]

Structure and symbolism of the *Ballet de la nuit*

As the title partly suggests, the whole ballet is structured as a battle of the sun against the night; the light fights against the creatures of the darkness. Twelve dark hours represent chaos; allegorically, these "hours" of darkness hint at the Fronde that had just been defeated. As the symbolism of the sun is at its basis, it is evident that the ballet does not follow the strict formal rules of classicist theater. A three- or five-act scheme would necessarily lead to a configuration culminating in the ending, whereas it is the intention of the ballet to initiate and represent a beginning, namely: of the day (on the literal level) and of the rising King (on the allegorical level). Accordingly, the whole performance ends with the rise of the sun performed on the stage; it is divided into four parts with

---

10 P. Burke, *The Fabrication of Louis XIV*, London 1992.
11 M.-Th. Mourey, "Der König tanzt: Choreographierte Performanzen der Macht", in: Jung-Kaiser and Simonis (eds.), *Verzaubernde Kunstwelt*, pp. 193–215.
12 Burke, *Fabrication*, pp. 67–78.
13 Burden and Thorp (eds.), *Ballet*, pp. 90–117.

a climax at the end, when Aurora arrives and announces the sun. Day and night are metaphors for good and evil and they structure the play: Benserade's ballet has "as its central conceit the four Watches of the night, spanning a time period starting at 6 o'clock in the evening, and ending at 6 o'clock in the morning".[14] Every Watch lasts three hours. What is most surprising for a modern spectator or reader is the fact that the "performance time equaled (almost) the time of the piece",[15] which means that the audience viewed (or, rather, was obliged to view) about more than twelve hours of performance. Taking into account that some spectators did not hear or see anything during the performance as the stage of the Petit Bourbon was not conceived for such a wide-ranging theatrical performance with machines,[16] it is more than obvious that the King danced with selected members of the court mainly for themselves and less for the audience proper that was constituted by the "rest" of the court. The interaction on stage was a means of restoring ties between the relevant courtiers and the King.

The extreme length was certainly an important reason why the ballet was not performed that often. In addition, an event presenting the King as a dancer in a spectacle was quite rare. According to courtly etiquette, specific reasons had to be put forward to allow the King to perform on stage. Even if the spectacle helped stabilize the system of power, such a performance could only reach the intended effect if it was used as a strategy on special occasions. A king who is presented as being more interested in making theater than doing politics is not helpful if the aim is to reassert absolutism, even if the King-as-dancer and the King-as-ruler are merged by way of symbolism. The *Ballet de la nuit* might have eluded such a problematic because it yielded the opportunity to immediately transfer the "literal" action to the level of politics. Whereas the Fronde had tried to subvert the absolutist system, the ballet shows its restoration and presents its reinstatement as the affirmation of the universal natural order at the top of which there is the sun. The *Ballet de la nuit* finishes with an open ending, indicated by the sunrise. The sunrise gives no information about what the new day might bring. The same applies to the reign of Louis XIV. He has

---

14 M. Burden, "A Spectacle for the King", in: ibid., pp. 3–8, p. 3.
15 Ibid., p. 3.
16 Cf. ibid.: "The ballet [...] has as its central conceit the four Watches of the Night, spanning a time period starting at 6 o'clock in the evening, and ending at 6:00am the next morning: the first Watch lasted from 6:00pm (sunset) to 9:00pm; the second from 9:00pm to Midnight; the third from Midnight to 3:00am; and the fourth from 3:00am to 6:00am (sunrise). This 12-hour stage cycle took some 13 hours to perform according to Jean Loret, who on his first attendance spent that time trying in vain to see and to hear."

risen to power and beaten "darkness", i.e. the Fronde, for now, but it is impossible to foretell the future of his reign.

Why is theater and more precisely a dancing king a convincing strategy to reassert a hierarchy of power? Theater has a long tradition of symbolizing systems of power. Moreover, Louis liked to dance and he performed quite often (several times a year) from 1651 to at least 1664 as a dancer. This was an opportunity for him to present himself and to "appropriate" the power of the sun by actually performing as the solar star. But this was not the only aspect of the King that the court would see and admire. Even in the early phase represented by the *Ballet de la nuit*, Louis was performing in six different roles—only one of these was the sun.[17] Apparently, dancing was more important to the King than the specific role he was playing. This configuration fits nicely with E. Kantorowicz's idea that a prince has two bodies.[18] In the dance performance, the body politic was represented by the well-shaped physical body of Louis XIV. The gain in power intended by these performances was an effect of the merging of these two different bodies. Actually, Benserade merged all personae of the *Ballet of the Night* with the noble dancers' real lives. This means that the danced allegories (just as the other personae on stage) also represent the courtiers' biographies; the court does not only perceive what is represented, but also the person who is representing something. Thus, the court attains to a sort of self-reflection. Being the one and only king on the stage, even at a time when he was not yet able to rule independently, Louis conveyed that he already was the king. In order to present this idea convincingly, he made use of his outstanding physical qualities. A document from 1715 describes the King and his gifts as a dancer in the following way:

> [...] as the King knows Music perfectly well, and as he dances better than everybody at court, he commanded Lambert and Lully to write ballets, that were to be presented with machines at the Louvre in 1663 and were more spectacular than all the operas of Venice. We can say that the King's graceful dance performance eclipsed the best dancers of the Court.[19]

---

[17] Mourey, "Der König tanzt", pp. 193–215; A. Ausoni, "Ballet de la nuit", in: Milesi (ed.), *L'invenzione scenica*, pp. 242–256, p. 242.
[18] E. H. Kantorowicz, *The King's Two Bodies: A Study in Mediaeval Political Theology*, Princeton, NJ 1957; see also J.-M. Apostolidès, *Le prince sacrifié: Théâtre et politique au temps de Louis XIV*, Paris 1985.
[19] Jacques Bonnet, *Histoire de la musique, et de ses effets, depuis son origine jusqu'à present*, Paris 1715, p. 330; the translation is mine. See also R. Braun and D. Gugerli, *Macht des Tanzes— Tanz der Mächtigen: Hoffeste und Herrschaftszeremoniell. 1550–1914*, Munich 1993, p. 98.

This document is not linked to the *Ballet de la nuit* specifically. However, it still states that the King was almighty in a political sense and that he was also the best dancer. He had the best musical sense and the ability to perform better than others. He was in command on the battlefield as well as on the stage. We are not dealing with a spectacle that only aimed to entertain, but with one that allowed a kind of self-fashioning of the King. His theatrical performance was the metaphorical frame that allowed not just for comprehension of the idea that this twofold body was the best dancer and the best king, but also for that precise idea to be lived. The King dances not as the King but as an allegory; he represents sovereignty and incarnates the sun, just as the sun represents the King. The theatrical metaphor produces the interaction of sun and King as a sort of fusion, just like in an alchemical process. The sun and the King both represent themselves and the other; this is why the costume is bright and shining but the head of the performer is not covered with a mask: it shows Louis XIV's face, the face of power that is at the same time the face of the sun. Body politic and body physical merge.

In this way, the King merges with the symbol without being absorbed into it. Finally, the sun as a metaphor is naturalized. By wearing the costume, the King literally embodies the sun and—in a second step—he becomes the sun, thereby naturalizing the metaphor. P. Bourdieu explains this mechanism of power by stating that "the body learns something which is by no means a knowledge, it means just to become something."[20]

Let us have a look at the report on the performance of the ballet published by Théophraste Renaudot in 1653 in the *Gazette de France* which summarizes the event:

> On this day, the 23rd (February), the great *Ballet royal de la Nuit* was danced in the Petit Bourbon, for the first time, in the presence of the Queen, His Eminence and the entire Court, consisting of 43 *entrées*, all so sumptuous, both in the novelty of what was portrayed there and in the beauty of the *récits*, the magnificence of the machines, the superb splendor of the costumes and the grace of all the dancers, that the spectators were hard put to decide which of them was the most pleasing. Our young monarch was no less recognizable beneath his costume than the sun through the clouds that sometimes obscure the light yet cannot hide the unique character of shining majesty, which marked him out as different [...].
>
> But while, without question, he surpassed in grace who appeared time and again on stage, *Monsieur*, his only brother, was also without equal in his own right; and this nascent day star showed so easily who he really was, by the gentility and charming ways which are natural to him, that one could not doubt his rank [...]. You could see for yourself the

---

20 P. Bourdieu, *La domination masculine*, Paris 1987, p. 135.

contentment that the audience felt, notwithstanding the misfortune which seemed set to disrupt the event when fire took hold of one of the backdrops from the first *Entrée* and the first hour of this beautiful Night which was represented by the King; one could not but admire the thoughtfulness and courage of His Majesty who calmed the participants by his steadfastness, just as Cesar once put his trust in the helmsmen who piloted him [...]. So much so that this fire was happily extinguished, leaving spirits restored to their former tranquility, and that too was seen as a good omen.[21]

It is remarkable that the sun as a metaphor has been naturalized by the King's performance to the degree that the writer is able to use the sun as a metaphor to grasp the situation: "the sun seen through the clouds". The sun is here used as a metaphor to describe the King in his costume. In addition, the meteorological reference to the cloudy sky is congruent with the new understanding of the world. The Copernican turn[22] had produced the effect that astrology received a new role and that the sciences began discussing geography in a new manner, as shown, for instance, in the King's collection of globes established a few years later.[23]

If we take the Copernican turn into account, the process of naturalizing and embodying the sun acquires a new dimension. What weakened the Curia and the Pope actually strengthened the ideas of Louis XIV and also explains why his approach to using the sun was more effective than the symbolic practice of his father, who had already used the sun as a symbol for himself but not in such a consistent and naturalized way. When at the end of the ballet the King appears on stage as the sun, he not only embodies one celestial body amongst others; he also represents the idea that the entire world is rotating around France—thus, a robust claim to global power is implied. The King as allegory of the sun makes this claim explicit when he says in the 11th *Entrée* of the 4th Watch: "I pretend to signal my power and my fortune on Earth and on Water, I would scour all the four corners of the world to find my honor."[24] Contemporaneous spectators clearly grasped the meaning of the perfect matching of the sun to the King: "The high prince could not choose a better symbol nor

---

21 *Gazette de France*, quoted in: Burden, "Spectacle", p. 3.
22 H. Blumenberg, *Die Kopernikanische Wende*, Frankfurt/Main 1965.
23 http://www.bnf.fr/en/cultural_events/anx_exhibitions/f.globes_louis_xiv_eng.html, accessed 3 January 2019.
24 Burden and Thorp (eds.), *Ballet*, p. 47. See also the following quote: "Je n'ay que depuis peu roulé sur l'Horizon, Je suis jeune, & possible est-ce aussi la raison qui m'exempte des maux que la beauté nous cause (...) Sans doute j'appartiens au monde à qui je sers, je ne suis point à moy, je suis à l'Univers" (4th Watch, 10th *Entrée*, p. 116).

even a worthier one than the sun. This wonderful star is his true portrait."[25] Why is this match so evident? It is the uniqueness of the sun and of the King of France, but also their respective qualities which enabled the metaphor to be spontaneously accepted as well-conceived. The image of the sun is able to produce a portrait of the King in terms of ethics: the solar star is fair and equal as it gives light to everyone. It is thus conveyed as well that the King is constantly creating good things; both the sun and the King bestow life and joy while demonstrating their own work within their course.

Such a king is characterized by a specific competence, namely martial prowess and the ability to dance, as well as by a specific knowledge, namely, to know how things work (as he is able to make them happen). He "makes" theater, as it is he who makes the theatrical machines work, thus causing the audience to be amazed and overwhelmed. When the sun rises on the stage or the wagon brings in theatrical protagonists who produce specific effects, it seems quite logical that the King is not in the audience: he himself is the one from whom the amazement and the admiration of the spectators originate.

The political program of the *Ballet de la nuit*

As we have seen, the structure of the *Ballet de la nuit* consists of four Watches with altogether 43 scenes that show the dominion of the night which is finally ended by the rise of the sun, announced in the last scene by Aurora. The highlight of the entire performance is the appearance of Louis who dispels the darkness of the night. As the ballet was also a machine-play the scenography used technical instruments to create spectacular light effects.[26] Torelli's machinery provided lights that suggested burning fire and an even more intensive light as the King appeared. The procedure was explained in detail by Sabbattini, a well-known theater engineer (Fig.2):

> Lightning flashes were executed with a handheld device or by simply handling combustible material near a candle. In *Pratica di Fabricar Scene e Macchine ne' Teatri* (*Manual for Constructing Scenes and Machines in the Theater*), Sabbattini described a box with a handle and a lid that was perforated with small holes. A candle was attached to the top of the lid, and the box was filled with 'paint dust'. When the

---

25 Braun and Gugerli, *Macht des Tanzes*, p. 107.
26 M. Closson, "Scénographies nocturnes du baroque: L'exemple du ballet français (1582–1653)", in: *Penser la nuit (XVe–XVIIe siècle)*, ed. D. Bertrand, Paris 2004, pp. 425–448.

operator shook the box upward, the paint dust flew through the holes and ignited in the candle flame, making a bright flash.[27]

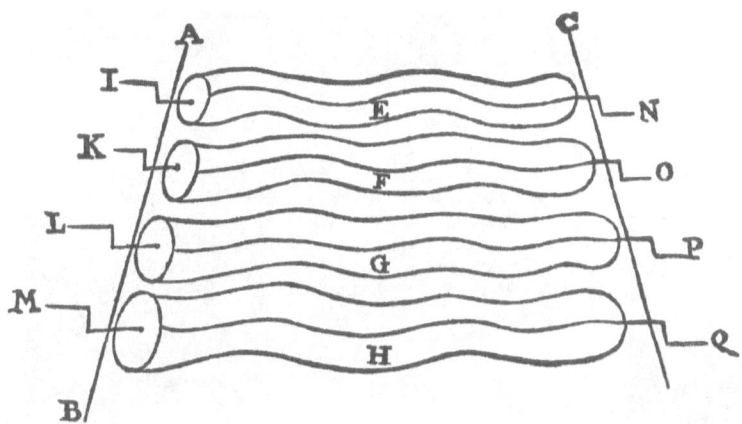

Fig. 2: Nicola Sabbattini, Wave Machine, *Pratique pour fabriquer scènes et machines de théâtre*, [tr. M. Maria and R. Canavaggia], Ravenna 1638, ch. 29, p. 114.

In the *Ballet*, the different phases of the night are presented as the time for comedies in the later evening (first phase), when there are actually two plays within the play, the time after midnight (second phase), when demons and witches appear (Fig. 3), and, finally, the preparation of the rise of daylight.[28] All the figures on stage have the same function, namely to represent the battle of good and evil and to introduce themselves in allegorical terms, just like a tableau of a psychomachia.[29] In this way, what happens is consistently tied to the political program to stabilize power

---

27 O. G. Brockett, M. Mitchell, and L. Hardberger, *Making the Scene: A History of Stage Design and Technology in Europe and the United States*, San Antonio, TX 2010, p. 117.
28 D. Parrott, "Art, Ceremony and Performance: Cardinal Mazarin and Cultural Patronage at the Court of Louis XIV", in: Burden and Thorp (ed.), *Ballet*, pp. 9–18, p. 9.
29 Starting with Prudentius we find this allegorical representation of a battle within the soul in all of pre-modern European literature; see U. Ebel, "Allegorisches Epos in der Tradition der Psychomachia", in: *Die italienische Literatur im Zeitalter Dantes und am Übergang vom Mittelalter zur Renaissance*, ed. A. Buck, vol. 2, Heidelberg 1989, pp. 166–167 and 322–330, pp. 166f; H. R. Jauss, "Form und Auffassung der Allegorie in der Tradition der Psychomachia (von Prudentius bis zum ersten Romanz de la Rose)", in: *Medium Aevum: Festschrift für Walter Bulst*, ed. H. R. Jauss and D. Schaller, Heidelberg 1960, pp. 179–206.

Fig. 3: Henri de Gissey (1621–1673): Scenery Design with Curieux Watching the Witches' Sabbath. 3rd Watch, 11th *Entrée, Ballet de la Nuit*, 1653.

against the enemies of the monarchy. For the King, this danger, which is represented by allegories, emanates from the Fronde.

Two years later, another ballet by Benserade would treat the same topic more explicitly. There we read the King pronouncing the following words:

> [...] J'ai vaincu ce Python qui désolait le monde,
> Ce terrible serpent que l'Enfer et la Fronde
> D'un venin dangereux avaient assaisonné:
> La Révolte, en un mot, ne me saurait pas nuire;
> Et j'ai mieux aimé la détruire
> Que de courir après Daphné [...]³⁰
>
> I conquered this Python that caused distress to the world,
> This terrible serpent that Hell and the Fronde
> Had "spiced up" by endowing it with a dangerous venom:

---

30 J.-P. Néraudau, *L'Olympe du Roi-Soleil: Mythologie et idéologie royale au Grand Siècle*, Paris 1986, p. 130. The translation is mine.

> The Revolt, to sum up, cannot harm me anymore;
> And I preferred to destroy it rather than to run after Daphne.

Here the King is presenting himself as a "new" and "better" Apollo who does not run after Daphne as was the case in the original myth; he rather wants to destroy his enemies. He prefers to do his duties as monarch over chasing after beautiful nymphs, that is, love.

In the *Ballet de la nuit*, the sun's / the King's enemies are not presented as venomous beasts, but rather as beggars, infectious people, demons, witches, and sorcerers (Fig. 3). They live in the darkness of the night, and when the sun rises, it tells them to retire. The King actually plays six different roles in the spectacle, the most important one of course being the allegorical representation of the sun. As to the further five roles, Benserade took care that Louis had a "good" part to play that allowed him to merge fiction and history: the King represents one hour of the twelve, but the most beautiful one (as the shining sun is considered most beautiful compared to the ugly creatures of the night).[31] In this part of the ballet, the King appears on the stage as an allegory of play ("jeu"), and he enters the stage directly after Venus, which is to convey that he is omnipresent in time, quite as the goddess who is at the same time the (brightest) morning star and the (brightest) evening star.

It is not astonishing that Venus characterizes the King as "a heroic man, severe, who likes bloody exploits and who already plans great deeds".[32] The young Louis is compared to Charlemagne[33] and it is said that the other kings have to fear him.[34]

At the end of the 3rd Watch, a Witches' Sabbath (cf. Fig. 3) is shown on stage along with three curious men who would like to view it; but before they are actually able to recognize what is happening, the Sabbath scene vanishes. The place where the Sabbath is set is a stage within the stage, since the two curious men in the front observe the action of the Sabbath as if they were the

---

31 "Voici la plus belle Heure & dans tous les cadrans. La première dessus les rangs [...]", qtd. in: H. Schulze, *Französischer Tanz und Tanzmusik in Europa zur Zeit Ludwigs XIV: Identität, Kosmologie und Ritual*, Hildesheim 2012, p. 109. The quotation does not figure in the Burden edition.
32 Burden and Thorp (eds.), *Ballet*, p. 23.
33 Ibid., p. 27.
34 *Ballet de la Nuit, divisé en quatre parties, ou quatre veilles: et dansé par Sa Majesté, le 23 février 1653*, Paris 1653, p. 36. This edition is available in *Gallica*: https://gallica.bnf.fr/ark:/12148/bpt6k724705, accessed 3 January 2019. The relevant passage is part of the 3rd Watch, *récit de la lune*.

audience of a play. One of these curious men is the King, who explains his ambition to emulate Apollo; as the ancient god, he wants to know and learn everything—the latter is meant in the literal sense ("rien n'échappe"); this is a claim to universal control which is a feature hardly to be found in classical myth:

> 3rd Watch, 11th *Entrée*:
> Je voudrois tout scavoir, je voudrois tout cognoitre,
> Rien n'échappe à mes yeux.[35]
>
> I would like to know everything, I would like to learn everything,
> Nothing escapes my eyes.

The intention of absolute control is clearly articulated; there is no attempt at rhetorically veiling it.

In order to control and dominate everything and everyone, the King has conceived a strategy which consists in self-control. As he is capable of controlling himself in any situation, he is sure of being able to triumph over his enemies:

> Je scaurai triompher de ma personne & d'elles [les passions]
> Ainsi que d'ennemis,
> Et me conter moy-mesme entre tous mes rebelles
> Combatus & soûmis.[36]
>
> I will know how to triumph over myself and them [the passions]
> As well as my enemies
> And I will count myself among all the rebels
> Beaten and submitted [by me].

As it is easy to shine even with a faint light in the night, the metaphor of day-and-night allows Benserade to integrate the King's brother into the play and to make the allusion to the concept of the great chain of being—from the Gods to the beggars—complete. Monsieur himself appears and demonstrates that this hierarchical order is not a mere construction. As he dances as a smaller star, namely the star of daybreak, he is compared to the King:

> Monsieur, frère unique du Roy, representant l'estoile du point du jour.
> Monsieur, sole brother of the King, representing the first star of the morning.
>
> Apres le grand Astre des Cieux
> Je suis l'Astre qui luis le mieux,

---

35 *Ballet de la Nuit*, 3rd Watch, 11th *Entrée*, p. 45.
36 Ibid., p. 46.

Il n'en est point qui me conteste,
Et mon éclat jeune & vermeil
Est beaucoup moins que le Soleil,
Et beaucoup plus que tout le reste.³⁷
[...]
Mon destin m'apprend que trop
Que je ne suis pas la première.
Mais je suis bien comme je suis,
C'est assez pour moy, si je puis
Percer les barreaux & les grilles,
Et d'un trait amoureux enfin
M'insinuer de grand matin
Dans la chambre où couchent les filles.
Je ne veux éclairer que là.
[...]
C'est mon emploi c'est mon affaire.³⁸

After the great star of the skies
I am the star that shines the brightest
There is none that is like I am
My young and ruby-red radiance
Is much less than [that of] the Sun, and much more than [that of] all the others.
[...]
My destiny teaches me very well that
I am not the first.
But I like what I am,
It is enough for me to pierce through bars and fences
And with an amorous touch to insinuate myself, when morning comes,
Into the rooms where girls sleep.
I want nothing more than to illuminate that.
[...]
That's my duty, that's my business.

There are three remarkable components in the speech of the King's brother: first, he says that he has received his position from destiny, meaning, in Christian terms, that it was providence that conferred it upon him. Second, he is of no danger to the King, as he is satisfied with his position, being better than everyone except the King; and third, ironically, his brightness is cut short as he shines most of all in the girls' rooms, which means that he is by no means a brave man or a fighter. His destiny is to enjoy himself by making love; he does not have any ambition to be in control of the country.

---

37 *Ballet de la Nuit*, 4th Watch, 9th *Entrée*, p. 64.
38 Ibid.

Finally, Aurora arrives and receives the urn with the dew, and the floor is open for the final "grand ballet". It starts with Aurora's *récit*:

> Récit de l'Aurore:
> Le soleil qui me suit c'est le jeune Louis.
> The sun that follows me is the young Louis.
>
> [After Aurora has said this, the sun rises and the King speaks, wearing the costume of the sun, and he announces what he will do—as sun, but also as King]:
>
> Le Roy, représentant le Soleil levant:
> Sur la cime des monts commençant d'éclairer
> Je commence déjà de me faire admirer,
> Et ne suis guerre avant dans ma vaste carriere,
> Je vien rendre aux objets la forme, & la couleur,
> Et qui ne voudroit pas avouer ma Lumiere
> Sentira ma chaleur.[39]
>
> The King representing the rising sun:
> Beginning to shine on the mountaintops
> I begin to make myself admired,
> And I am not yet much advanced in my course,
> When I come to give form and color to all things,
> And whoever does not want to acknowledge my Light,
> Will feel my heat.

The King of France begins his rule on the mountaintops, not down in the plains; he has a grand vision and wants to be admired because he sees himself as having an ethical role to play. He gives form and color to the objects of the natural world, meaning, he is God's deputy, representing him on Earth, and therefore almighty as far as the sublunary world is concerned. His shining will bring splendor to his country and glory to him. Whosoever dares to doubt his status as sun and King will feel his "heat", he says.[40] Here, the process of the naturalization of the metaphor has come to an end, as the King is not only

---

[39] Ibid., p. 66.
[40] "The king *had* to appear in the ballets, above all as a trump card to convince the courtiers that they had made the right decision in backing Mazarin's restoration. The king's participation in the ballet was part of a much larger policy, essential to Mazarin's chances of political survival, which depended upon convincing the political middle ground that Condé was not, as he claimed, pursuing a just struggle against the overweening power of an ambitious and self-interested first-minister. The key was to convince the political elites that Condé, his supporters and others in opposition to the First Minister were waging an illegitimate and treasonable war against the king of France" (D. Parrott, "Art, Ceremony and Performance", p. 17).

described as the solar star but also acts as the sun and therefore makes the universe feel his (strong and warming) power.

> Déja seul je conduy mes chevaux lumineux
> Qui traisnent la splendeur & l'éclat apres eux,
> Une divine main m'en a remis les resnes,
> Une grande Deesse a soûtenu mes drois,
> Nous avons mesme gloire, elle est l'Astre des Reines
> Je suis l'Astre des Rois.
>
> [...] Car enfin tout me void, j'éclaire toute chose,
> Et rien ne m'éblouyt.[41]
>
> Sans doute j'appartiens au monde à qui je sers,
> Je ne suis point à moy, je suis à l'Univers,
> Je luy dois les rayons qui couronne ma teste,
> C'est à moy de regler mon temps & mes saisons,
> Et l'ordre ne veut pas que mon Plaisir m'arreste
> Dans toutes mes Maisons.[42]
>
> I conduct my shining horses on my own
> That carry splendor and shine after them,
> A divine hand gave me the reins,
> A high goddess has supported my right,
> We even have the same glory, she is the star of the Queens
> I am the star of the Kings.
>
> [...] For everyone sees me, I bring light to everything
> And nothing is dazzling to me.
>
> With no doubt I belong to the world which I serve,
> I do not belong to myself, I belong to the Universe,
> I owe him the rays that cover my head,
> It is up to me to regulate my time and my seasons,
> And order does not allow for pleasure to make me tarry
> In any of my homes.

The King claims that he is capable of making the earth rotate; once again, the Copernican cosmological model is used with a view to conveying Louis's ideas concerning his role as King. Yet he also praises the universe to which, he says, he belongs. He is not acting for himself but for the world.

To summarize briefly: The King is a "maker" of theater in that he organizes a specific performance, the *Ballet of the Night*, in which he participates as an actor.

---

41 *Ballet de la Nuit*, 4th Watch, 9th *Entrée*, p. 67.
42 Ibid., p. 66.

He is the center of the spectacle and embodies, even naturalizes the metaphor of the sun, which is only possible within the context of theater. In this way, the theater itself somehow transcends its function, as the (Neo-)Aristotelian rules of the unity of action, time, and space are suspended. The participants are actors and spectators at the same time; the time of the play is almost equal to the represented time. The stage is not clearly defined; the long-lasting event necessarily calls for the participants to move on and off the stage. The sun as an ideological and political metaphor is used in the *Ballet* to show how the King and all the participants use the power of fiction to make the theatrical metaphor live.[43]

The idea of the dancing King was very attractive, but as convenient as it was when he was a young man, it became problematic later on in his reign. The genre of *Ballet de cour* flourished in the 1650s only: it needed the real presence of the King to be effective. What made the ballets so powerful at the time caused them to lose their appeal when the King stopped performing on stage as a dancer because his body was losing its youthful flexibility. Nevertheless, the success of the *Ballet of the Night* is still manifest today, as we still associate Louis XIV with the sun and most of all even with the costume depicted above, which seems to be his second skin.

---

[43] J. Nevile, *Dance, Spectacle, and the Body Politick, 1250–1750*, Bloomington, IN 2008.

Ekaterina Boltunova
War, Peace, and Territory in Late Eighteenth-Century Russian Outdoor Performances

In the historical narratives produced in present-day Russia, Catherine II (the Great) is largely associated with the conflict between the Russian and Ottoman Empires in the latter eighteenth century. Russia's victory culminated in its gaining the Black Sea provinces and the annexation of the Crimea.[1] Imagining the empress in such a way is radically different from earlier, late Imperial or Soviet interpretations. The latter see Catherine as more than just a figure associated with a successful foreign policy in the south, namely as a lawgiver on the throne, committed to the supremacy of law and shaping Russian legislation, and as an august patroness of the arts and sciences. The current emphasis on Catherine's foreign policy and its gains has undoubtedly been mandated by the need to set out a new historical narrative after the integration of the Crimea into Russia in 2014. The empress from the eighteenth century emerges as a potent factor in the legitimization of this step.

However, two and a half centuries ago, the empress herself found the search for symbolic forms to help appropriate the Black Sea provinces to be a much more difficult process. Looking back at the second half of the eighteenth century, modern scholars tend to focus on large-scale geopolitical designs such as the "Greek project" which aimed to restore the Byzantine Empire in some form.[2] The early stages of the quest for a new symbolic language are, by contrast, substantially less known. It began right after the Russian-Ottoman war of 1768–1774 was brought to an end by the Treaty of Kuchuk Kainarji (Küçük Kaynarca)—Russia emerged victorious from this war. This period reveals the first elements of the future geopolitical claims as well

---

[1] For example, this is how the empress is presented nowadays in the *Russia: My History* ("*Rossiia—moia istoria*") chain of new history parks that promote a pro-governmental interpretation of Russian history.

[2] A. Brikner, *Istoriya Ekateriny Vtoroy*, vol. 2, St. Petersburg 1885, pp. 390–498; S. Zhigarev, *Russkaya politika v vostochnom voprose (ee istoriya v 16–19 vekakh, kriticheskaya otsenka i budushchie zadachi): Istoriko-yuridicheskie ocherki*, vol. 1, Moscow 1896, pp. 203–223; A. Zorin, *Kormya dvuglavogo orla: literatura i gosudarstvennaya posledney treti 18—pervoy treti 19 vekov*, Moscow 2001, pp. 32–64.

as the metaphors and symbols through which Catherine II expressed her attitudes towards political events from the mid-1770s onward. When building the narrative of the Russian Black Sea and Crimea in later times, some of these were discarded as no longer necessary.

It is important to note that, in the first half of that decade, Russia was engaged in two, rather than one, war. In addition to the conflict with the Ottomans, Catherine's army appeared on the battlefields of the largest peasant revolt in Russia's history: Pugachov's rebellion (1773–1775). This revolt of various groups of peasants and Cossacks led by Yemelian Pugachov, who claimed to be the Emperor Peter III, can be seen as an act of resistance against the encroachment of the state on the lands and rights of the Yaik Cossacks who refused to comply with the duties imposed on them. The rebellion soon grew into a full-scale war in the Ural region and along the Volga river.

Having found her army challenged on both fronts, Catherine made a remarkable attempt at tracing a connection between the two. She even initiated an inquiry into possible French and Ottoman meddling in the internal affairs of Russia after Pugachov's rebellion had broken out. However, she soon discovered that her suspicions were groundless.[3]

Symbolically enough, victories on both fronts came in the same year (1774) and were remarkably interconnected, a configuration that can be seen in a timeline of events stretching from July 1774 to July 1775. On July 10, 1774, the Treaty of Kuchuk Kainarji between the Russian and Ottoman empires was signed at what is now Kaynardzha in Bulgaria. While the news had not yet reached the Russian capital (it reached St. Petersburg a fortnight after, on July 23) Catherine's government believed that at least with regard to the fight against the rebellion the imperial troops had already been victorious. The Pugachov Cossacks and peasants were thought to have been defeated and dispersed. However, the charismatic leader of the rebellion managed to escape to the Bashkir lands and rallied his supporters, raising a new army. From there, he proceeded back to the Volga and swiftly took the very important city of Kazan just a couple of days after the conclusion of the Kuchuk Kainarji Treaty (July 12). Frightened by the success of the insurgents, the Russian government dispatched the hero of the Turkish wars, Alexander Suvorov, to stop Pugachov's progress. In early September, Pugachov was arrested by his own Cossack colonels and handed over to the Imperial authorities. On November 4, he was transported to Moscow for trial; he was executed two months later. Two

---

[3] I. de Madariaga, *Rossiya v epokhu Ekateriny Velikoy*, Moscow 2002, pp. 431–432.

weeks after Pugachov was publicly decapitated in Moscow's Bolotnaya Square, Catherine II arrived in the city (January 25, 1775).[4]

The empress did not come to the old capital in order to attend the execution of Pugachov, as some scholars have suggested. [5] This said, it was indeed the military events revolving around Pugachov as well as the Turks that made her come to Moscow. There, Catherine intended to speak on peace (or rather the end of two wars). While in Moscow, she announced "The Manifesto on Signing the Peace Treaty with the Ottoman Porte" (March 17, 1775). She waited a long time to produce it, as the Manifesto appeared almost eight months after the news of the end of the Russian-Ottoman war was received in St. Petersburg.[6] On the same day, amnesty was granted to those who had engaged in the rebellion— death sentences were commuted to penal service, and some of the taxes due by peasants were waived. The amnesty was presented as an act of mercy on the occasion of the peace with the Ottoman Porte, thus establishing a connection between the two historical events, the internal revolt and the war against an external competitor.[7] Both wars found their symbolic ending in Moscow, the old capital, which in 1775 became the venue for both the execution of Yemelian Pugachov and the peace celebrations half a year later.

Having announced in her peace manifesto that the Lord "blessed us, after a longtime and toilsome war, with the desired peace", Catherine soon went on to organize and to personally oversee a grandiose festival in Moscow in celebration of the end of the war and the signing of the Treaty of Kuchuk Kainarji that took place July 21–23, 1775. The festival's culmination was a mass outdoor event on the Khodynska Field (*Khodynskoye pole*), located at some distance from the center of the city. The architect Vassily Bazhenov was commissioned to design a set that would explain the importance of the newly acquired lands north of the Black Sea to the Moscow crowd.

The centerpiece of the project was conceived in accordance with a plan developed by the empress herself. In a well-known letter to Baron von Grimm of April 7, 1775, Catherine explained her ideas:

> [At first], a plan of the festivities was drawn in the familiar manner: a temple of Janus, and a temple of Bacchus, and a temple of some other devil, all those stupid, intolerable allegories, and so huge, with an incredible desire to produce something meaningless. I was very angry about these plans, and on one fine morning I ordered

---

4 *Kamer-fur'erskiy tseremonial'nyy zhurnal* [1775], St. Petersburg 1878, p. 69.
5 V. Proskurina, *Mify imperii: Literatura i vlast' v epokhu Ekateriny II*, Moscow 2006, p. 197.
6 *Polnoe sobranie zakonov Rossiyskoy imperii*, vol. 20, St. Petersburg 1830, pp. 80–82, N° 14, 274.
7 Ibid., pp. 82–86, N° 14, 275.

my architect Bazhenov to me and said, 'Dear Bazhenov, there is a meadow three versts [3.2 km] away from the city. Let the meadow stand for the Black Sea; the two roads from the city will represent the Tanais [the river Don] and the Borysthenes [the river Dnieper]. At the mouth of the former you will build a refectory which you will name Azov, and at the mouth of the other, *a theater which you will name Kinburn* [my italics, EB]. You will also construct a Crimean peninsula out of sand and on it, you shall erect two ballrooms—Kerch and Enikale.[8] Left of the Tanais, a buffet will stand with wines and refreshments for the people; and in front of the Crimea, lights will signify both nations' joy at the signing of the peace treaty; on the other bank [...] fireworks will be set off, while the area representing the Black Sea will have scattered boats and ships which you will illuminate; the banks of the rivers, which are also roads, will feature scenery, mills, trees, houses in full illumination, and thus you will have a festival not overwrought, but probably still better than many others, and much simpler. I forgot to say that to the right of the Tanais, Taganrog[9] shall appear with a fair. You are prone to analyze everything, but is this not well-designed? Indeed, a sea on a piece of dry land is absurd, but please disregard this flaw and the rest will seem quite tolerable. The area is large, and the event will take place in the evening, and so it will pass off, at least, not worse than the ridiculous heathen temples, which so annoy me'.[10]

The geographical names in the empress's letter, which are mostly Greek, immediately stand out to the reader.[11] Each of the four coastal fortresses mentioned is matched with a recreational area—a ballroom, a refectory, a fair, or a theater. The extant drafts show that Bazhenov followed Catherine's vision almost to the letter: the Khodynka field was turned into a stylized version of the Black Sea, and four fortresses appeared on its "coast", matching those being integrated into the empire by the terms of the peace treaty—Kerch, Enikale, Azov, and Kinburn.[12]

The Khodynka field festivities were part of a larger event that was promised in the Manifesto of March 17.[13] It began with a solemn procession of the empress from the Kremlin to the Assumption Cathedral for a thanksgiving service and the gift-giving ceremony at the Faceted Chamber (*Granovitaya Palata*), the oldest throne hall of the Russian monarchs.[14]

---

[8] These are the names of two fortresses (which, accordingly, are represented by the ballrooms).
[9] Taganrog is a harbor city located on the shores of the Sea of Azov.
[10] "Pis'ma Ekateriny Vtoroy baronu Grimmu (1774–1796)", in: *Sbornik Russkogo istoricheskogo obshchestva*, vol. 23, St. Petersburg 1878, pp. 20–21.
[11] Such references will later be made in the "Greek project" that presented the new territorial acquisitions as the lands of (the Christian) Byzantine empire and of ancient Greece.
[12] Yu. Gerchuk (ed.), *Vasily Ivanovitch Bazhenov: Pis'ma. Poyasneniya k proektam. Svidetel'stva sovremennikov. Biograficheskie dokumenty*, Moscow 2001, p. 259.
[13] *Polnoe sobranie zakonov*, vol. 20, p. 82, № 14, 274.
[14] *Opisanie vseradostnogo torzhestvovaniya mira s Ottomanskoyu Portoyu, byvshago v Moskve 1775 goda iyulya 10 i posledovavshiya po tom chisla*, Moscow [1775], pp. 4–8 and 19–32.

During the latter, the empress sat on the throne with her imperial regalia displayed by her side.[15] The ceremony was also attended by the Grand Duke Pavel—the heir to the throne and, as some thought, its legitimate claimant (unlike the empress herself, who had acceded to it under a palace coup). He had already come of age and married in 1773. It is interesting to note that during the ceremony, the Grand Duke and his wife occupied seats typically reserved for females and children: they watched the ceremony through the window of the so-called Secret Room (*Tainik*) within the Faceted Chamber.[16] In the seventeenth century, this was the location where the tsarevny (imperial princesses) and underage tsareviches (imperial princes) stayed during important ceremonies taking place in the Chamber (audiences, embassy receptions, banquets, etc.).[17] In this way, the empress once again emphasized the existing hierarchy of power.

Upon the end of the official part, the public, popular festival started. Studying the 1775 festivities at the Khodynka field as they may be reconstructed from both textual and visual sources allows one to discern several levels of symbolism—from mental geography, which was in high demand in the political discourse of the period, to the use of theater as a powerful metaphor within the political practices of eighteenth-century Russia.

There is a longstanding belief among historians that Catherine II disliked Moscow. Indeed, during her reign, she paid only a few visits to the traditional capital of the Tsars (1762, 1767, 1775, 1787), and each of these was a highly symbolic one, marking respectively her coronation, the inauguration of the Legislative Commission (*Ulozhennaya Komissia*) that convened to give the country a modern law code, the victory in the war against the Ottoman Empire, and the celebration of her coronation's Silver Jubilee. Each had its own aspect of representing the empress—as a legitimate ruler, a lawgiver, or a victor. With time, the theatrical appeal of the "Russian tradition" also became part of Catherine's visits to Moscow: she would stay at the village of Kolomenskoye, a countryside residence of the Russian Tsars,[18] and would often wear what was then known as the

---

15 Ibid., p. 11.
16 Ibid.
17 E. Boltunova, "Imperial Throne Halls and Discourse of Power in the Topography of Early Modern Russia (late 17th–18th centuries)", in: *The Emperor's House: Palaces from Augustus to the Age of Absolutism*, ed. M. Featherstone, J.-M. Spieser, G. Tanman, and U. Wulf-Rheidt, Berlin 2015, pp. 341–352.
18 E. Gorokhova, "Prebyvanie Ekateriny II v Kolomenskom", in: *Kolomenskoe: Materialy i issledovaniya*, ed. L. Kopesnikova, vol. 13, Moscow 2011, pp. 145–162.

Russian attire (*russkoe plat'e*),[19] thus performing in some way as a sort of autochthonous ruler.

In this connection, the choice of the city in which to celebrate the victory over the Ottomans presents a most interesting link between Moscow and the Ottoman capital in the imperial discourse of the period. It is interesting to note that there were never any plans to host the victory celebration in the actual capital, St. Petersburg. Moscow was cast as a symbolic construct commensurate with Istanbul. The old Russian capital was Istanbul's true opposite. In terms of religious belief and the arts, it originated from Byzantium or Constantinople, that is, the city the Ottomans had transformed into Istanbul after having conquered the capital of the eastern Roman empire.

It is quite significant that historians of costume, in their discussions of how "the Russian attire" was introduced at the court in the 1770s, mention that one of the first occasions when the empress was wearing it was a public audience she gave to the ambassador of the Khan of Crimea, a vassal of the Ottoman Sultan in 1771. Four years later, all women at court were ordered to wear the traditional Russian dress on the occasion of the visit by the Ottoman ambassador.[20]

One might not be misled to put the festivities organized in Moscow on the occasion of the felicitous end of the two wars mentioned in a similar strategic-symbolic context: they were intended to establish a close link between the present and the Russian tradition, in this case by means of a festival for the people.

Such a speculation is all the more probable as there was a historical retrospection implied in the way the festival was arranged. By celebrating the victory over the Ottomans in Moscow, Catherine reminded her subjects of the age of Russia's first emperor, Peter I, and even of a slightly earlier period when the country's foreign policy was focused on wringing the fortress of Azov from the Ottomans. Thus, the empress underscored the continuity of Russia's foreign policy, painting the Russian-Ottoman war as a "Moscow war" rather than a St. Petersburg war, as a declaration of victory over a longtime historical adversary.

This is probably why the "Black Sea" designed by Bazhenov seems in fact to be more like the Sea of Azov under close scrutiny. In her letter to von Grimm, Catherine mentions two roads imagined as rivers under their Greek names, the Tanais and the Borysthene, which in Russian are known as the Don and the Dnieper. The empress directly connects those rivers to the Black Sea. However,

---

[19] An attire wherein the standard Western design was complemented by elements borrowed from seventeenth-century-style Russian dress (a specific type of sleeve, girdle, and floral ornament); cf. K. Borderiu, *Plat'e imperatritsy: Ekaterina II i evropeyskiy kostyum v Rossiyskoy imperii*, Moscow 2016, pp. 23–26.

[20] Ibid., p. 22.

the Don, with the fortress of Azov at its mouth, flows into the Sea of Azov. The poet Vassily Maykov (1728–1778) endorsed Catherine's view in his poem "Description of the Triumphal Buildings at the Khodynka Representing the Benefits of Peace". Attempting to decipher Catherine's allegorical language, he mentions that "the Don flows into the Black [sic!] Sea and improves the commerce therein", while the fortress of "Azov at the mouth of the Don" guards "the passage into the Black Sea".[21] Importantly, the sketches of the Bazhenov-designed festivities feature both geographic names—the Sea of Azov and the Black Sea. The observer is located on the "coast" of the former, between the fortresses of Azov and Taganrog[22]; the description of the territory is in contradiction with its visual "reading". Evidently, Catherine's fashioning of Russian victories intended to associate Azov, the area of the historical Russian-Ottoman conflict, directly with the Black Sea, without paying attention to the geographic facts.[23]

It is important to note the role the rivers Don and Dnieper play in this narrative of the Black Sea. Choosing the locations for the Khodynka performance, Catherine could have referred to other waterways, namely the rivers Larga and Kagul (Cahul), which were the locations of the Russian army's decisive victories in the Turkish wars. Yet, she preferred not to do that. Her choice was probably informed by the fact that the area where these battles had been won did not belong to Russia's territorial gains by the terms of the Treaty of Kuchuk Kainarji. But the preference for the Don and Dnieper, which played an extremely significant role in the Russian Empire's mental geography, might also have constituted an attempt to distract attention from another "river war": the geography of the Pugachov rebellion shows the rebels active by the rivers Volga and Yaik (which Catherine later renamed the Ural). Also significant in this context is Catherine's claim that she "creates sea on dry land", or, reversing the symbolism, she structures, that is, brings order to and controls the wild element of the sea (or rebellion).

The Don and the Dnieper, located by the Black Sea and matched to the geography of victory, are thus presented as the space of peace and prosperity. The Don-upon-Khodynka staged at the outskirts of Moscow becomes an

---

21 Vassily Maykov, "Opisanie Torzhestvennykh zdaniy na Khodynke, predstavlyayushchikh pol'zu mira", in: V. Maykov, *Izbrannye proizvedeniya* [Selected Works], ed. A. Zapadov, Moscow and Leningrad 1966, pp. 306–307.
22 "Plan ansamblya uvesilitel'nykh stroeniy na Khodynskom lugu v Moskve: Gravyura", Rossiyskiy gosudarstvennyy arkhiv drevnikh aktov (Russian State Archive/RGADA), f. 192, op. 1, d. 159.
23 In fact, the Sea of Azov is separated by the Taman peninsula from the Black Sea, though they are connected by the Kerch Strait.

allegory of plenty. Maykov explains that the "Azov on Don, where the refectory is, represents abundance brought about by peace".[24] The Dnieper (with the fortress of Kinburn at its mouth), situated "at the edge of [Russian] power", is turned into a space where "the resounding voices of the lyres are heard, singing how beneficial peace is to the monarchs".[25]

The festival field featured two theaters—one, meant for balancing acts, was erected on the Taman Peninsula,[26] and the other, as indicated by the empress in her letter to von Grimm, in the area representing the fortress Kinburn, now Russia's main outpost on the Black Sea. It is evidently this latter theater where Catherine watched a performance on July 23. In his book *Moscow of Old* (*Staraia Moskva*), M. Pyliayev states that two performances were given at the Khodynka Field: a French comedy and a Russian opera. Pyliayev reports that the empress, who was quite capable, if necessary, to evaluate European and Russian playwrights and performances in terms of their ability to communicate political messages,[27] did not attend the performance of the French play, but paid a visit to a piece titled *Ivan Tsarevich*, an opera whose libretto was in Russian.[28] The empress's choice of a performance in Russian on the set representing a former Ottoman fortress was hardly accidental. Celebrating the victory over the Ottoman Empire in the old capital of Russia, regarded as the seat of Orthodoxy and Russianness, the empress used theater as a kind of mediating power, an intermediary propagating symbolically her political strategy of appropriating the Black Sea provinces and converting them into genuinely Russian territory.[29]

The festivities at the Khodynka field, though outstanding and memorable, did not constitute the only symbolic interpretation suggested. The above-mentioned official ceremony at the Faceted Chamber included a speech given by the procurator general Alexander Vyazemsky, who addressed the empress herself and the

---

24 Maykov, "Opisanie", pp. 306–307.
25 Ibid.
26 See n. 23.
27 G. Ibneeva, "Ekaterina II i dvoryanstvo v tseremoniale imperatorskikh puteshestviy", in: *Romanovy v doroge: Puteshestviya i poezdki chlenov tsarskoy sem'i po Rossii i za granitsu*, ed. M. Leskinen and O. Khavanova, Moscow 2016, p. 38.
28 M. Pylyaev, *Staraya Moskva: Istoriya byloy zhizni pervoprestol'noy stolitsy*, St. Petersburg 1891.
29 The location of Kinburn at the mouth of the Dnieper was an additional hint at what was later called "Pan-Slavic" ideology. A. Zorin writes that "in Petrov's rhetoric [a late eighteenth-century poet, author of odes, EB] it is the Dnieper as the river uniting Great Russia, Little Russia and Poland that has come to symbolize the Russian empire itself and to prophesy the future Slavic brotherhood where Russia will play the leading role." (*Kormya dvuglavogo orla*, p. 151).

audience of courtiers, dignitaries, and military leaders. He glorified Catherine II's deeds and thanked her on behalf of the Senate and the people.[30]

Vyazemsky names the Russian empress the "wonder of the century"[31]; he then speaks on her achievements (the protection of Orthodoxy, the propagation of civil justice, the introduction of laws that encourage prosperity amongst the nobility as well as the merchants, the building of cities, etc.).[32] He goes back to the time of Peter the Great in order to recall the emperor's much less fortunate fight for the Black Sea, which enables him to describe Catherine (in a manner quite customary for the ideology of her rule) as the one who succeeded in achieving what Peter had intended to do. At one point, Vyazemsky mentions the Pugachov revolt, stating that Catherine "restored domestic peace shaken by evil disturbance in some region of the Fatherland".[33] By establishing this link, he obviously follows the same symbolic pattern presented by the 1775 festivities at the Khodynka field.

However, the dignitary suggests a meaningful alteration. He chooses to speak on the series of events of 1768–1774 by referring to a variety of locations and territories. The procurator general paints the picture of the whole world submitting to the will of the Russian empress—the fortresses of Khotin, Kagul (Cahul), and Bendery are conquered, the lands of Moldavia and Walachia "obey Catherine's scepter", the river Danube turns red with blood, the waters of the Bosporus strait run in "fear and despair" as the Russian fleet appears, the Dardanelles "tremble as they witness victories of the Russian navy", and even the Mediterranean Sea is "covered with [Catherine's] ships". He reports that Crimea, Russia's "source of countless scourges since ancient times" is now embracing "the empress' sincerity and generosity", and the people of the Peloponnese and the islands of the Greek archipelago "are stretching out their hands" to Catherine in search of protection. At the end of his speech, the dignitary states that "[Catherine's] trophies of glory rise almost to the gates of Adrianople"[34] and the empress's power makes Assyria and even the African lands tremble.[35] He focuses more on lands, seas, and adjoining straits than fortresses and rivers. Above all, he highlights the peoples of distant lands rather than those who populated the newly conquered territories. He is not restricting

---

30 The empress's short reply to it was delivered by the Imperial Vice Chancellor Ivan Osterman (*Opisanie vseradostnogo torzhestvovaniya mira*, p. 18–19).
31 Ibid., p. 18.
32 Ibid., p. 8 and pp. 16–17.
33 Ibid., p. 9.
34 The present-day Turkish city Edirne.
35 Ibid., pp. 10–12.

himself to the Russian achievements on the terms of the Treaty of Kuchuk Kainarji. Unlike the Khodynka field festivities, with their focus on the history of the Russian-Ottoman conflict and the need to communicate the idea of restored security inside the country, Vyazemsky's mental map knows no limits—his speech on Russian military power and expansion clearly reveals a geopolitical ambition. It is highly probable that he did not express this ambition on his own initiative only.

Interestingly enough, a detailed description of the Khodynka festivities and of the celebration at the Faceted Chamber (including the full version of Alexander Vyazemsky's speech) were published under one cover and were later sold by booksellers.[36] These interpretations of the historical events of the mid-1770s were equally usable for the discourse of power in Catherinian Russia.

---

36 Gerchuk (ed.), *Bazhenov*, p. 259.

Pavel V. Sokolov
Lucis an caliginis theatrum: Theatrical Metaphors in the Early Modern *historia literaria*

"Theater" can rightfully be called one of the metaphors early modern Europe "lived by": ranging from political writings to treatises on the art of memory, from philosophy (Descartes's famous "larvatus prodeo") to natural sciences, it "infected" nearly all the discourses of learned culture, including that of erudite self-reflection, that is, the text corpus called *historia literaria*, and in particular the subdiscipline of *notita auctorum*, i.e. the "science of unveiling true authorship". Very often, even the titles of the early modern treatises, aiming at detecting and unmasking anonymous and pseudonymous writers, included terms and expressions referring to theater or carnival: "Larva detracta", "Auteurs déguisés", "Visiera alzata", etc.[1] Behind this proliferation of theatrical vocabulary, there was something more than a mere accommodation of a fashionable metaphor suited to the needs of the "Wissenspolizei" in the Republic of Letters.[2] *Historia literaria* emerged at an intersection of multiple erudite discourses: historiography, ethics, jurisprudence, rhetoric, medicine, different political "idioms" (Tacitism, Aristotelianism, "Antimachiavellism"),[3] and therefore absorbed a large part of their conceptual equipment, inner tensions, and unresolved aporias. The omnipresence of the metaphor of the "republic" in the language of erudite self-description, dating back to Ermolao Barbaro and Erasmus of Rotterdam, led to the rapprochement of the imagery and conceptual frameworks of literary history and politics. In fact, this metaphor was one of the many used to

---

[1] For details, see M. Mulsow, "Praktiken der Deautorisierung: Die Entstehung von Anonymen- und Pseudonymen-Lexika im 17. Jahrhundert", pp. 1–21, p. 5. http://www.sfb-frueheneuzeit.uni-muenchen.de/archiv/2002/langtexte/mulsow.pdf, accessed 8 October 2018.
[2] Ibid., p. 6.
[3] See the manual *Die Diskurse der Gelehrtenkultur in der frühen Neuzeit*, ed. H. Jaumann, Berlin 2011, pp. 903–951.

Note: The research that is at the basis of this paper was conducted within the framework of the Basic Research Program at the National Research University Higher School of Economics (HSE) and supported within the framework of a subsidy granted to the HSE by the Government of the Russian Federation for the implementation of the Global Competitiveness Program.

Open Access. © 2019 Pavel V. Sokolov, published by De Gruyter. This work is licensed under the Creative Commons Attribution-NonCommercial-NoDerivatives 4.0 License.
https://doi.org/10.1515/9783110622034-010

designate learned society; the latter thus tended to be presented as a quasi-political body, crossing the borderlines of the emerging nation states.

This rapprochement elicited an intensive exchange of basic metaphors between the discourses of *historia literaria* and politics in the aforementioned variety of its idioms, Tacitism and "Antimachiavellism" first of all. One of the most remarkable examples of this rapprochement is the *Dissertatio accademica de republica literaria* by Johann Georg Pritz (Pritius, 1662–1732), a Lutheran philosopher and theologian from Leipzig and a passionate opponent of Pierre Bayle and Thomas Hobbes. His perhaps best-known work is titled *De damno atheismi in republica*, although his research interests went so far as to embrace the problem of the supremacy of men over woman and even questions such as *Moscowitischer oder rußischer Kirchenstaat*.[4] Pritz combines censure of the vices of erudite learning with that of the vices in matters political, as another polyhistor does in his *De historia literaria*, the "founding father" of scientific numismatics, Michael Lilienthal: "[...] almost all of what happens in the literary world corresponds to some part of the Republic, and can be referred either to its origin or to its citizens (because it does not recognize any head), form, orders, means of preservation, awards and punishments, diseases and ways of healing them, enemies, fates and so on".[5]

Actually, the language of (dis)simulation functioned as a "shared discourse" of politics, *historia literaria*, and drama. In his preface to Vincent Placcius's[6] tremendous volume, *Theatrum anonymorum et pseudonymorum*, containing some hundreds of unveiled pseudonyms and false identities,

---

[4] For details, see M. Czelinski-Uesbeck, *Der tugendhafte Atheist: Studien zur Vorgeschichte der Spinoza-Renaissance in Deutschland*, Würzburg 2007, pp. 116–117.

[5] "[...] nihil fere in re literaria occurrat, quod non partes Rei publicae subeat, & vel ad originem Rei pub. vel ad cives (caput enim non agnoscit) formam, ordines, media conservandi, praemia & poenas, morbos eorumque medelas, hostes, fata & hujusmodi quid referri valeat" (Michael Lilienthal, *De historia literaria certae cuiusdam gentis scribenda consultatio*, Lipsiae et Rostochi 1710, p. 8).

[6] Vincent Placcius (1642–1699) was a famous polymath, born in Hamburg; he graduated from the university of Leipzig as a legal specialist; later on, he taught as a professor of practical philosophy and rhetoric. He is particularly known (and in the last decades also very well-studied) in the scholarly literature for his poem on Christopher Columbus, but even more for his works dealing with "learned bookkeeping" and "moral medicine": *De arte excerpendi: Vom Gelahrten Buchhalten* (1689) and *De Scriptis et Scriptoribus anonymis atque pseudonymis Syntagma* (1708); see in particular: *Die Argonauten und Äneas in Amerika: Kommentierte Neuedition des Kolumbusepos Atlantis retecta von Vincentius Placcius*, ed. M. Scheer, Paderborn 2007; see also Mulsow, "Praktiken".

Matthias Dreyer,[7] the editor of the book, presents an extensive analogy between the theater of light and shadow (*lucis an caliginis theatrum*) and the unmasking of cryptonymous works:

> We leave to your free judgment, my generous reader, whether you should rather call a theater of light or shadow the work on anonymous and pseudonymous writers that we present to you. You will find there an immense and confused CHAOS of obscure names, masked appearances, variously fabricated of Anagrams and Schemes, and colored faces.[8]

The theater of masked erudite tricksters, illuminated by the light of *notita auctorum*, is involved in a kind of a *mise en abîme* of multiple theaters, with the theater of the world (*theatrum mundi*) and the theater of history (*theatrum historiae*) at the top. At the lowest level of this "golden chain", an individual—even a single human body—could be represented as a theatrical machine: the most famous representation of this kind is René Descartes's image of the passions as an *ensemble* of self-moving statues. Johann Burckhardt Mencke (1674–1732), a longtime editor of *Acta eruditorum* to whom the German language owes the word "Charlatan", begins the first of his two speeches titled *De charlataneria eruditorum* (1713, ed. 1716) with a comparison between the ancient and the contemporary theater of historical memory: according to Mencke, the "living picture of human things" degenerates into shameless flattery of the public.[9]

---

[7] Regarding the rather obscure figure of Matthias Dreyer (Dreier) (d. 1718), we have only very general information. According to Christian Gottlieb Jöcher's *Allgemeines Gelehrten-Lexicon*, he originated from Hamburg and served there as a canon; he was juris utriusque doctor and authored, together with a short introduction to Placcius' *Theatrum*, a juridical disputation titled *Disputatio inauguralis utrum exceptio restitutionis in integrum ex capite minorennitatis fit perpetua, an vero temporalis?* (cf. *Allgemeines Gelehrten-Lexicon, Darinne die Gelehrten aller Stände sowohl männ- als weiblichen Geschlechts, welche vom Anfange der Welt bis auf ietzige Zeit gelebt, und sich der gelehrten Welt bekannt gemacht, nach ihrer Geburt, Leben, merckwürdigen Geschichten, Absterben und Schrifften aus den glaubwürdigen Scribenten in alphabetischer Ordnung beschrieben werden*, vol. 2 [D–L], Leipzig 1750, p. 216).
[8] "Lucis an caliginis theatrum rectius dixeris, Benevole Lector, quod Tibi de Anonymis et Pseudonymis Scriptoribus hic sistimus, liberum penes te esto judicium. Immensum ac confusum CHAOS obscurorum nominum, larvatas species, ex Anagrammatis et Schematismis varie confictas, ac pigmenta prosopa ubique deprehendis" (Matthias Dreyerus, "Commentatio editoris de summa et scopo operis", in: Vincentius Placcius, *Theatrum anonymorum et pseudonymorum*, ed. Matthias Dreyerus, Hamburghi 1708, s.p.).
[9] "There was a very old tradition among Greeks and Romans, oh Listeners, to bring before the eyes of everybody in a theater all the events recorded in the memory of the times passed or provided by the contemporary epoch and the mode of the common life of men. This tradition was instituted in a way to be represented not only by speech and written text, but by gestures

The reflection on the vices of the erudite, the "charlataneria eruditorum", begins with rebuking the flaws of contemporary theater, in particular its way of eliciting affects; the corruption of *mimesis*—instead of bringing onstage the "customs" (*mores*) of nations, actors seek exclusively to amuse the spectators—thus reflects the ethical crisis of the whole world.[10]

The idea of the world as a corrupted theater is clearly stated also in the political discourse: we come across it, e.g., in the *Considérations politiques sur les Coups d'Etat* by Gabriel Naudé.[11] According to Naudé, this disordered space,

---

as well, as in a vivid picture of things, in order to incent mortals to behave virtuously. As time passed and the passion of greed became stronger, this tradition degenerated to such an extent, that mimes and drama actors do not reproduce impartially the morals of the people, but care exclusively about how to provoke laughter and loudness and ensure uproar and applause of the audience, or, if the matter is somehow more sad, to excite milder affects of the soul and bring tears to the eyes of spectators."—"Vetustissima inter Graecos Romanosque ac gentes alias consuetudo fuit, Auditores, ut omnium oculis repraesentarentur in theatro, quaecunque sive superiorum temporum memoria sive praesens aetas et communis hominum vivendi ratio, laeta aut tristia, suppeditaret. Quae cum initio ideo institute essent, ut, quaemadmodum sermone et scriptis, ita et gestu ipso velut in viva quadam rerum humanarum tabula ad virtutem amplectendam invitarentur mortales, successu temporis, cum lucri ingens cupiditas accessisset, ita degenerarunt, ut non aeque nunc mores populi spectent mimi et fabularum actores, verum id current tantummodo, qua ratione risus et cachinnos strepitusque ac plausus e spectatoribus elicere, aut si tristior fuerit materia, molliores animi affectus ciere oculisque lacrymas excutere valeant" (Iohann B. Mencke, *De charlataneria eruditorum declamationes duae*, Amstelodami 1716, pp. 1–2).

10 "But why should I dwell on these theaters, which had been instituted for deceiving a small number of people, coarse and foolish? The whole world is a theater, in which those, who zealously seek after fame, glory, and the universal applause of mortals, play the roles of actors."—"Sed quid moror haec theatra, quae ad fallendos paucos, eosque inficetos, & ineptos, excitata sunt? Ipse Orbis univerus theatrum est, in quo histrionum quodammodo partes sibi sumunt, qui famam, gloriamque, & communem mortalium plausum summa animi solicitudine sectantur" (ibid., p. 9).

11 Gabriel Naudé (1600–1653) was a famous early modern political scholar and a prominent specialist in the "art of establishing libraries"; he was also an important political figure—a physician to Louis XIII and a librarian to Cardinal Mazarin. Apart from the "art of establishing libraries", he contributed significantly to the history of seventeenth-century "Machiavellian" historiography and politics, paying particular attention to the categories of reason of state and coup d'état; a focus on the "mysterious" and "arcane" dimension of political prudence led him to explore various techniques of dissimulation and manipulation, including magic; see Fr. Meinecke, *Machiavellism: The Doctrine of Raison d'État and Its Place in Modern History*, tr. D. Scott, London and New Brunswick, NJ 1998, pp. 196–206; J.-P. Cavaillé, *Dis/simulations: Jules-César Vanini, François de La Mothe Le Vayer, Gabriel Naudé, Louis Machon et Torquato Accetto. Religion, morale et politique au XVIIIe siècle*, Paris 2002, pp. 199–265.

full of confusion, turns out to be the most appropriate arena for a confident political hero, searching to transcend ordinary human nature. With regard to the political sphere, the outstanding person is compared to a spectator, standing on the top of a high tower, eagerly awaiting an appropriate moment to appear onstage like a *Deus ex machina*.[12] This Machiavellian prince, intervening *in medias res* in the drama of the political world, finds his counterpart in the figure of a "literary Machiavellian", vividly depicted by Michael Lilienthal[13] in his famous treatise *De machiavellismo literario*. Here the behavior of the erudites is characterized as political behavior, the motives and goals of the learned are presented as identical to those of politicians, sharing the same values and objectives; politics and erudition manifest the same vices.[14]

---

12 "[...] 'what a pitiful thing is man, were it not that his soul was apt to soar above these human things!' That is to say that if he does not observe with a firm and sure eye, and as if he were in the keep of some high tower, the whole world, representing it as a theater quite badly arranged and full of confusion, in which some are playing comedies, others tragedies, and in which it is allowed to intervene like *Deus aliquis ex machina* whenever one has such a wish or various occasions convince one to do so." – "[...] 'o quam contempta res est homo, nisi supra humana se erexerit'. C'est-à-dire, s'il n'envisage pas d'un oeil ferme et assuré, et quasi comme étant sur le dongeon de quelque haute tour, tout ce Monde; se le représentant comme un théâtre assez mal ordonné et rempli de beaucoup de confusion, où les uns jouent des Comédies, les autres Tragédies, et où il lui est permis d'intervenir tamquam *Deus aliquis ex machina*, toutes-fois et quantes qu'il en aura la volonté ou que les diverses occasions lui pourront persuader de ce faire" (Gabriel Naudé, *Considérations politiques sur les Coups d'Etat*, [Amsterdam] 1667, p. 26).

13 Michael Lilienthal (1686–1750) was a Königsberg Lutheran theologian, historian, one of the founding fathers of scientific numismatics, and a remarkable theoretician of the ethics and politics of the Republic of Letters. *De machiavellismo* was not the only text Lilienthal dedicated to the problems of the literary Republic and historia literaria—three years previously, he published the treatise titled *De historia literaria* (1710).

14 "I. The first principle of political Machiavellianism: The rulers must consider their private interest as the highest goal, even if it has nothing to do with the common good. But literary Machiavellianism seeks not the public utility of the literary Republic, but only the increase of the author's own reputation by all means, even if obtaining it entails damaging and deceiving the literary world. II. Political Machiavellianism, having abandoned all the arts of a good prince and principate, turns exclusively to the wicked arts of domination and recommends them to the princes who are plotting in order to attain power. Similarly, literary Machiavellianism prescribes not the legitimate means to those who aspire at primacy in the Republic of Letters, but perverse and tyrannical ones. III. Political Machiavellianism recognizes it necessary for the princes only to have fictitious virtue and simulated religious faith. In the same way, literary Machiavellianism seeks to establish only a superficial erudition: because it teaches that for those who want to become famous in the literary world, it is enough to seem educated in the eyes of the plebe, even if in reality they are not. [...] IV. Political Machiavellianism, if you consider the practical aspect, has not begun with Machiavelli, but with the tyrants

As pointed out previously, in Mencke's discourses on "charlataneria" there are two different meanings of the term or concept of theater: on the one hand, theater is understood as the representation of memorable events of the past and of the "common principles of social life" (*communis hominum vivendi ratio*); on the other hand, it is a machine producing and manipulating affects (tears and laughter). The first type, a sort of "didactic theater", designed to educate the public and portrayed by Mencke in rather "republican" terms, finds its "monarchic" counterpart in Jesuit moral-political plays, as described, for instance, by Franz Lang.[15] In the latter's *Theatrum affectuum humanorum*, the Christian ethical message is easily discernible: "theatrical dialogues" are identified as "ascetic discourses" and "ethical exegesis".[16] In *Theatrum politicum* by Ambrosio

---

themselves: therefore, men learned the wickedness not from Machiavelli as their teacher, but they had practiced evil arts long before him." — "I. Machiavellismi politici primum principium est: Imperantibus commodum privatum pro supremo fine propositum esse debere, tametsi illud cum bono publico minime sit conjunctum. Sed Machiavellismus literatus non publicam Reipublicae literariae utilitatem quaerit, sed propriae solum existimationis incrementum quovis modo, etiam cum rei literariae damno ac deceptione, venari adlaborat. II. Machiavellismus politicus, relictis omnibus boni Principis et Principatus artibus, ad solas malas dominantium artes se convertit easdemque Principibus dominatui insidiantibus unice commendat. Pariter et Machiavellismus literarius primatum in Republ. literaria affectantibus non legitima media, quibus summum in illa fastigium adscendere queant, sed perversa nec nisi tyrannica praescribit. III. Machiavellismus politicus fictam tamen virtutem et religionem simulatam Principibus necessariam esse existimat. Ita quoque Machiavellismus literarius superficiariam stabilire conatur eruditionem: quandoquidem docet, satis esse hominibus, in orbe literario inclarescere cupientibus, dummodo vulgo videantur docti, licet re vera tales non sint. [...] IV. Machiavellismus politicus, si praxin inspicias, non cum Machiavello demum coepit, sed cum ipsis Tyrannis: non igitur Machiavello Magistro didicerunt nequitiam homines, sed vafras artes exercuerunt dudum ante Machiavellum" (Michael Lilienthal, *De machiavellismo literario, sive De perversis quorundam in Republica Literaria inclarescendi artibus dissertatio historico-moralis*, Regiomonti et Lipsiae 1713, pp. 6–10).

15 Franz Lang (1654–1725) was the longtime director of a Jesuit theater and a professor of rhetoric at the Jesuit *Gymnasium* in Munich, a playwright, and an author of several texts regarding the theory of affects, including theatrical affects (*Theatrum affectuum humanorum*) and stage action (*Dissertatio de actione scenica*). See R. G. Engle, "Lang's 'Discourse on Stage Movement'", in: *Educational Theatre Journal*, vol. 22, 1970, pp. 179–187; A. Rudin, *Franciscus Lang und die Bühne: Studien zur deutschen Theatergeschichte des 17. und 18. Jahrhunderts*, Emsdetten 1973.

16 "If you call it ascetic discourses, theatrical dialogues, scenic ethopeias, ethical exegesis or moral considerations, I will not disagree. I tried, as far as I could, to express the passions of human minds, their morals and affects, animated by vivid examples and ethical witnesses, and imitate them by action, in order to teach and to encourage the spectators to know themselves, to avoid vices, to adapt life to an exact criterion of truth and to the ultimate goal which is eternal happiness." — "Si Discursus Asceticos, si Dialogos theatrales, si Ethopaeias scenicas, si Exegeses

Marliano,[17] the prince is metaphorically presented as a mirror of virtues and vices, exposed to the whole world.[18] The author does not refrain from saying that the quasi-theatrical demonstration of moral exemplarity implies the risk of being exaggerated to the extent of coming close to the grotesque: King David, who had publicly shed tears in order to show his penitence concerning his past sins should have chosen, according to Marliano, the crocodile as his coat of arms; referring to Pliny's description of this animal, he thus conveys that the ethical exemplarity as presented in the *Theatrum politicum* may at times be nothing other than a *simulachrum* of morality.[19] "Theater" understood in this way plays a role similar to that of *specula principum*, demonstrating in a vivid form and based on historical examples *quid agendum est a principe* (Marliano).

Ethicas, si Considerationes Morales appellaveris, non refragabor dicenti. Ego humanarum mentium pathemata, mores & affectus, vivis rerum exemplis, & documentis moralibus animata, quantum sinebat mea tenuitas, ad artis, & naturae leges dictione exprimere, & actioni imitari studui, ut spectatores illorum intuit seipsos agnoscere, aversari vitia, vitam omnem ad honestatis, ac virtutis amussim componere, atque ad ultimum finem, qui aeterna felicitas est, dirigere discerent, vel monerentur" (Franciscus Lang, *Theatrum affectuum humanorum, sive Considerationes morales ad scaenam accommodatae*, Monachii 1717, s.p.).

17 Ambrosio Marliano (Ambrogio Marliani, 1562–1632) was a Pavian regular canon and a political and ecclesiastical writer whose *Theatrum politicum* was particularly popular not only in Western Europe, but among Greek and Romanian intellectuals as well; it was translated by Nicholas Mavrocordatos's secretary, Iohannes Abramios (Ιωάννης Αβράμιος), and published in Greek three times (in 1758, 1776, and 1802). Cf. A. Camariano-Cioran, "Traducerea greacă a 'Teatrului Politic' atribuită greşit lui Nicolae Mavrocordat şi versiunile româneşti", in: *Revista istorică română*, vols. 11–12, 1941–1942, pp. 216–258.

18 "They will attain it easily, if they approach justice, piety, and clemency, accompanied by other virtues, exposed like mirrors to the great Theater of the universe." — "Hoc autem facile praestabunt, si Justitia, Pietate, Clementia, ac caeteris virtutibus comitati incedant, tanquam specula amplissimo totius orbis Theatro exposita" (Ambrosius Marlianus, *Theatrum politicum, in quo quid agendum sit a Principe, et quid cavendum, accurate praescribitur*, Augustae Vindelicorum 1741, p. 23).

19 "This theater of sacred virtues, which constitute the prince as the elements of which he consists [...]. Certainly, I tried first of all to sprinkle here and there in the text the precepts of virtues so that they could easily flow down to the readers. This will happen without any doubt, if I propose my theater to the princes, in order to make their examples obtain the power of laws among others." — "Theatrum hoc sacrarum virtutum, quae optimum Principem tanquam elementa constituent [...] Certe hoc vel maxime studui, ut ibi virtutum praecepta inspergerem, unde ad omnes facile possent dimanare. Hoc autem procul dubio contingent, dum Theatrum hoc meum Principibus spectandum proponam, cum eorum exempla apud caeteros vim legis obtineant" (ibid., p. 20).

The "theaters" referred to in all these treatises are certainly rhetorical ones; the rhetoric is envisaged as a *techne*, explicitly presented as such and serving didactic purposes. But there was also another rhetoric which tried to hide its manipulative techniques ("celare artem"), a theater based on simulation and dissimulation. According to Mencke, the "paradigmatic" civil theater of virtues and vices is substituted by what we could call, using the terminology of such Baroque Aristotelian-Cartesian civil philosophers as Arnold Wesenfeld, a "pathological" one. Both the Baroque "civil pathology", i.e. the particular ethical-physical discipline dealing with the civil (social-political) effects of bodily motions,[20] and *historia literaria* are represented in terms of theatricality. Wesenfeld,[21] one of the most prominent theoreticians of civil pathology, defined the subject matter of his treatise as a "theater of the motions of the entirety of civil and military life" (*theatrum universalis motuum vitae civilis et militaris*). In this text, the entire fabric of civil life is interpreted in "kinetic" terms, regarded through the lens of a syncretic Aristotelian-Cartesian theory of motion: Wesenfeld's "theater of motion" embraces public life (customs, rules of conversation, education, imitation), private behavior (opinion, doubt, simulation and dissimulation, dissidence), and—last but not least—the vices and virtues (religion, freedom, superstition, novelty, originality, etc.) and their *simulacra*.[22] In Wesenfeld, as well as in Mencke, the "kinetic" rhetoric of affects is part of a larger problematic—namely of what N. Struever has

---

20 On this notion, see D. M. Gross, "Political Pathology", in: *Rhetoric and Medicine in Early Modern Europe*, ed. S. Pender and N. S. Struever, Surrey 2012, pp. 129–146.
21 Arnold Wesenfeld (1664–1727) was a professor of rational and moral philosophy in Frankfurt/Oder and an author of a number of logical, ethical and theological works, one of which is *Georgica animi et vitae*, which bears the name of one of the so-called Baconian *desiderata* (projecting further horizons of his "new world of sciences") and aims at "cultivating" the universe of the human affects. For more details on the Baconian *desiderata*, see: V. Keller, "The 'New World of Sciences': The Temporality of the Research Agenda and the Unending Ambitions of Science", in: *Isis*, vol. 103, 2012, pp. 727–734.
22 "[...] I bring to the eyes the force and the impression that things themselves and universal relations produce in individuals as well as their masses collected in a society. The strength and the efficacy of custom, practice, conversation, education, discipline, temperament, imitation. Then, the reason itself why praises, good deeds, humanity, gestures, and names move so differently. Further, various impressions of awards and punishments and motions, connected with opinion, doubt, simulation and dissimulation, trust and dissidence. Then, we have to show here virtues and vices and their images (*simulacra*), as well as those of religion, freedom, superstition, novelty, rarity, similitude, diversity of time and place and other commotions, originating from things, together with the modes of their combinations. For this reason, having disclosed the strategies of politicians as well as of the military [...], a lot of information concerning civil and military prudence can be added, if one considers very different motions of

called "a medical-rhetorical mindset".²³ If Mencke, partly ironically, partly seriously, defined the "charlataneria eruditorum" as a medical pathology, Scipione Chiaramonti²⁴ claimed in serious terms a close analogy between medicine and moral science: "medicine consists of five parts, which in Greek are called Physiology, Hygiene, Pathology, Semeiotic, and Therapy. The moral science includes the same parts."²⁵ In Mencke, the decay of theater, erudite vices, the degradation of the affective sphere, and the spread of medical pathologies are cast as going hand in hand.

Characteristically, Mencke was not alone to suggest the medical implications of "deviant" erudite behavior: in his *De plagio literario*, Johann Conrad Schwartz²⁶ drew a close connection between medicine—conceived by him according to humoral pathology—and the issue of plagiarism.²⁷ In Schwartz's opinion, the main task of any science consists in helping mankind (*commutare*

---

single objects and principles of their motions in conjunction with each other." — "[...] vim ac impressionem, quam res ac relationes universae, tum in singulos homines, tum plures in unam societatem collectos faciunt, ob oculos ponam. Vis et efficacia Consuetudinis, Exercitationis, Conversationis, Educationis, Disciplinae, Temperamenti, Imitationis. Ipsa ratio, quomodo Laudes, Beneficia, Humanitas, Gestus, Nomina tam diverse commoveant. Porro Praemiorum et Poenarum variae impressiones; ut cum Opinione, Dubitatione, Simulatione et Dissimulatione, Fiducia, Dissidentia conjuncti motus. Tum etiam a Virtutibus ac Vitiis eorumque simulacris, nec non Religione, Libertate, Superstitione, Novitate, Raritate, Similitudine, Temporis ac Loci diversitate, plurimisque ejus generis a rebus dipendentes commotiones simul cum modis se comparandi, ob oculos ponendi hic essent. Qua ratione, nudatis Stratagematum tum Politicorum tum Militarium fundamentis [...] multum ad Prudentiam Civilem ac Militarem adjici posset, si motus tam diversi singulorum objectorum, motuumque horum rationes in una compage spectarentur" (Arnold Wesenfeld, *Georgica animi et vitae, seu Pathologia practica, moralis nempe et civilis*, Francofurti ad Viadrum 1696, Praefatio, s.p.).

23 See S. Pender, "Between Medicine and Rhetoric", in: Pender and Struever (eds.), *Rhetoric and Medicine*, pp. 37–61, p. 40.

24 A fervent opponent of both Galileo and Tycho Brahe, Scipione Chiaramonti (1565–1652), apart from astronomical and mathematical writings, authored a treatise titled *De coniectandis cuiusque moribus et agitantibus animi affectibus libri decem* (1665).

25 "Quinque partes Medicina continet, quae Graecis vocibus dicuntur, Physiologia, Hygiina, Pathologia, Simiotica, Therapeutica. Eas omnes Moralis quoque includit" (Scipio Claramontius, *De coniectandis cuiusque moribus et agitantibus animi affectibus libri decem*, Helmstedt 1665, p. 5).

26 Johann Conrad Schwartz (Schwarz, 1677–1747) was an eighteenth-century German polyhistor with an extraordinarily broad spectrum of scientific interests, ranging from Latin grammar to the necromancy of the Witch of Endor. The treatise on plagiarism was one of his earliest writings (published for the first time under the title *Tentaminis de plagio litterario Dissertatio I* in Halle in 1701, second edition in 1706).

27 Johann Conrad Schwartz, *De plagio literario liber unus*, Lipsiae 1706.

generi humano), the soul and the body alike. Given that scholars are especially prone to suffer from melancholy, literary production should primarily aim at remedying "the misery of Melancholics". But a broad array of literary genres and activities, including very respectable ones—fables, enigmas and emblems, investigations of ancient inscriptions, *picturae loquentes*—are perfectly useless and even harmful in this respect, because they cause an increase in black bile (*augent miserias Melancholicorum, non auferunt*). Within this model suggested by Schwartz, the literary thief is defined as a choleric; his strivings aim at exciting the admiration of others. Yet neither does this type of "one-sided and subtle" knowledge aid the plagiarist himself.[28] Finally, Schwartz also rejects the "elitist" attitude, because the subtleties of the sharp mind are understandable only to a small minority (*acumina inutilia magni faciamus propter paucitatem eorum, qui ista procreant*). According to Schwartz, the "truthful and genuine wisdom" can be reduced to four disciplines—physics, mathematics, moral philosophy, and theology—and the learned can consequently be categorized either as "wise men", or as people offering nothing but "trifles" or "obscure subtleties" (*vel sapientes, vel nugivenduli et argutatores umbratiles*).[29]

But within the contemporary debates, the *homo eruditus* is not only conceived as a *homo histrio*, subject to various humoral pathologies, he is also presented as a *homo proteus*. And again, this metaphor is common to the discourses of politics, *historia literaria*, and "theatrical rhetoric". The conception of an actor/orator as a "delightful Proteus" has been studied by H. F. Plett[30]; although not mentioned by Plett, the "learned Machiavellian" is also portrayed as a "rival of Proteus" by the aforementioned Dreyer,[31] as well as the "prudent politician" in Gabriel Naudé's reasoning on the "coup d'état":

> [...] this political prudence is rather similar to Proteus, of whom we are only able to have any certain knowledge after having descended in *secreta senis* and contemplated with a

---

28 "Linguarum subtilior et supervacanea consideratio, notitia plerarumque inscriptionum, antiquitates et historiolae quaedam, Geomantiae et Astrologiae defensiones vaferrimae, similiesque artes solivagae augent miserias Melancholicorum, non auferunt" (ibid., 86).
29 Ibid., p. 96.
30 H. F. Plett, "Theatrum Rhetoricum: Schauspiel—Dichtung—Politik", in: *Renaissance-Rhetorik / Renaissance Rhetoric*, ed. H. F. Plett, Berlin 1993, pp. 328–368, p. 335.
31 "An empty man, perfidious, Proteus' rival,—what could he worship but a matchmaker of crimes and vices, a frivolous dissimulator? [...] The lust of lying had blackened the masked Demon to such an extent, that almost all fear the odious name of Devil." — "Homo vanus, sublesta fide, Protei aemulus, quid nisi scelerum ac vitiorum pronubum ac frivolum dissimulatorem indigitare poterit? [...] Larvatum ex orco Daemonem ipsa mentiendi libido tantopere denigravit, ut odiosum Diaboli nomen fere omnes exhorrescant" (Dreyerus, "Commentatio", s.p.).

fixed and assured eye all the diversity of movements, figures and metamorphoses by means of which *Fit subito sus horridus, atraque Tigris, / Squamosusque Drago, et fulva cervica Leaena* (Virgil. in Georg. IV).³²

Making use of problematic or illegitimate rhetorical means with a view to influencing the emotional "kinetics" of the citizens of the "Respublica literaria", Lilienthal's literary Machiavellian or Mencke's pathological "charlatan" perform a political act, playing the role of a "tyrant" in the Republic of Letters. Theatrical behavior in this Republic menaced its particular political form of a "shared sovereignty", exalted by Pierre Bayle in famous words anticipating both Rousseau's paradisiacal "state of nature" and the revolutionary slogan of "liberté, égalité, fraternité"; from Bayle's perspective, even the right to conduct a quasi-Hobbesian *bellum omnium contra omnes* at times becomes a privilege and is not a danger under the auspices of this Republic.³³ The use of theatrical imagery in the discourse of self-description of the *orbis literatorum* was not confined to the needs of the "police of erudition": it also dealt with the utopia of the *homo eruditus* as a would-be citizen of a "Republic of Letters" conceived as a nucleus of the future Europe, an international political entity able to substitute the medieval myth of "Res publica Christiana", discredited by the period of the religious wars and the subsequent emergence of the

---

32 "[...] plutôt cette Prudence Politique est semblable au Prothée, duquel il nous est impossible d'avoir aucune connoissance certaine, qu'après être descendus in *secreta senis*, et avoir contemplé d'un oeil fixe et assuré, tous ses divers mouvements, figures et Métamorphoses, au moien desquelles, *Fit subito sus horridus, atraque Tigris, / Squamosusque Drago, et fulva cervica Leaena* (Virgil. in Georg. IV)" (Naudé, *Considérations*, pp. 8–9).

33 "This Republic is absolutely free. Only the empire of Truth and Reason is recognized there, and under their aegis it is permitted to wage war innocently against whomsoever. Friends must be in guard against friends, fathers—against their children, fathers-in-law against their sons-in-law: it is like in the Iron Age: *Non hospes ab hospite tutus, / Non socer a genero*. Each man here is simultaneously a sovereign and a subject to the jurisdiction of another. The Laws of the Society did not harm the independence of the state of Nature as far as error and ignorance are concerned: all individuals have the right of the sword in this respect and can exercise it without asking the permission of those who rule." – "Cette République est un Etat extrêmement libre. On n'y reconnaît que l'empire de la Vérité et de la Raison, et sous leurs auspices on fait la guerre innocemment à qui que ce soit. Les amis s'y doivent tenir en garde contre leurs amis, les pères contre leurs enfants, les beaux-pères contre leurs gendres: c'est comme au siècle de fer: *Non hospes ab hospite tutus, / Non socer a genero*. Chacun y est tout ensemble Souverain, et justiciable de chacun. Les Lois de la Société n'ont pas fait de préjudice à l'indépendance de l'état de Nature, par rapport à l'erreur et à l'ignorance: tous les particuliers ont à cet égard le droit du glaive, et le peuvent exercer sans en demander la permission à ceux qui gouvernent" (Pierre Bayle, *Dictionnaire historique et critique*, vol. 4, Paris 1820, p. 584).

nation states.³⁴ In this respect, one may cite a famous formulation from Giambattista Vico's *New Science*, in which the "academies" are presented as the highest stage of the evolution of civilization: "This was the order of human things: first the forests, after that the huts, thence the villages, next the cities and finally the academies".³⁵

Literary Machiavellism, armed with theatrical-rhetorical "stratagemata", continued to pose a challenge to the pre-Enlightenment alternative to Baroque politics propagated by Vico as well as by Bayle, who gave expression to it in an almost ecstatic way: "[…] les Savants se doivent regarder comme frères, ou comme d'aussi bonne maison les uns que les autres. Ils doivent dire, *Nous sommes tous égaux / Nous sommes tous parents / Comme enfants d'Apollon*".³⁶ Paradoxically, a behavior contrary to that described by Bayle and aiming at unmasking the *arcana domitionis* and introducing the ethics of transparency into the *orbis literatorum* was accused to be an instance of literary tyranny itself: the literary attack on the erudite masquerade that M. Mulsow interpreted in terms of J. Habermas's conception of the passage from the Baroque policy of dissimulation to the "Enlightenment" idea of the public sphere (*Öffentlichkeit*) exposed the citizens of the Republic of Letters to the censorship of the "real" political bodies, both secular and ecclesiastic. As Theodor Ludwig Lau,³⁷ one of the victims of this "symbolic violence", claimed, censorship "smells like literary tyranny" and causes a number of disasters, being similar to tyranny in the proper sense of the term.³⁸ This is why such theoreticians of the learned sphere as Jakob Thomasius suggested the

---

34 On this point, see D. Goodman, *The Republic of Letters: A Cultural History of the French Enlightenment*, London and Ithaca, NY 1994, pp. 12–52.

35 *The New Science of Giambattista Vico: Unabridged Translation of the Third Edition (1744) with the Addition of "Practic of the New Science"*, tr. Th. G. Bergin and M. H. Fisch, Ithaca, NY 1976, p. 70.

36 Pierre Bayle, *Nouvelles de la République des Lettres (mois de Mars 1684)*, Amsterdam 1684, Préface, s.p.

37 Theodor Ludwig Lau (1670–1740) was a noted figure of the "Radical Enlightenment": a freethinker, jurist, and political writer; his reflections combined the interest towards politics in general (*Entwurf einer wohl eingerichteten Polizey*, 1717) and politics in the Republic of letters in particular. For more details on Lau, see the recent monograph by E. Donnert, *Theodor Ludwig Lau (1670–1740): Religionsphilosoph und Freidenker der Frühen Neuzeit*, Frankfurt/Main 2011.

38 "It smells like literary tyranny. It promotes ignorance and errors. It impedes solid erudition. It is contrary to reason and truth. Then, it also harms the Authors: still, those who suffer quasi-punishments do not burn in the sign of ignominy and infamy. The books suffer glorious martyrdom. The authors, illustrious for truthfulness and reasonableness, become martyrs." – "Tyrannidem sapit literariam. Ignorantiam promovet et errores. Solidam impedit eruditionem. Rationi adversatur et veritati. Autoribus interim: tales qui patiuntur quasi-Poenas: nullum ignominiae vel infamiae inurunt Notam. Libri: gloriosum sustinent martyrium. Autores: illustres pro veritate

introduction of a sort of autonomous "erudite court" and tried to promote a specific juridical category—*crimen extrajudiciale*—for dealing with the cases of dissimulation in the Republic of Letters without the intervention of the common judiciary.[39] The aforementioned Johann Schwartz rather wished to rely on the notions of sociability (*socialitas*) and natural right: he considers plagiarism a moral turpitude (*turpitudo*), and draws a comparison between the conduct of a plagiarist and a person violating basic social norms: "if someone walks naked in a public place, he behaves indecently and would face a heavy punishment"; but still, he does not violate the natural law, "because he does not do any harm to the general rules of sociability".[40] These and similar "Enlightenment" discourses will progressively substitute the Baroque rhetoric of theatricality as a language governing the (self-)description of the Republic of Letters until the Kantian idea of the "public court of reason" will transfer the whole discussion onto new ground.

---

et ratione, martyres fiunt" (qtd. in Mulsow, "Praktiken", p. 15; for further details see Mulsow's article).

[39] On the category of *plagium extrajudiciale* in Tommasius, see H. Jaumann, "Öffentlichkeit und Verlegenheit: Frühe Spuren eines Konzepts öffentlicher Kritik in der Theorie des *plagium extrajudiciale* von Jakob Thomasius (1673)", in: *Strukturen der deutschen Frühaufklärung, 1680–1720*, ed. H. E. Bödeker, Göttingen 2008, pp. 99–118.

[40] "If someone walked naked in a crowded forum, he or she would behave shamefully and would be worthy of the gravest punishment, but he or she would not violate the law of nature in this way, because sociability would not be injured either by this walk, or by a [distorted] Greek sentence. For sociability is like a rule, to which also the items governed by natural law should be adapted. Some cases of plagiarism contradict the natural law, others the principles of humanity, and still others the principles of decorum." — "Si quis in celebritate fori nudus ambularet, inhoneste ageret & gravissima poena dignus esset, sed jus naturae non violaret. Socialitas enim nec illo incessu, nec graeca hac sententia conturbatur. Socialitas autem est tanquam regula, ad quam res juris naturalis exigi solent & debent. Nonnulla plagia juri naturae, quaedam officiis humanitatis, alia decoro, adversari" (Schwartz, *De plagio literario*, p. 76).

II: **The Romantic Turn**

Petr Rezvykh
Theater, World History, and Mythology: Theatrical Metaphors in Schelling's Philosophy

This paper deals with the evolution of the theatrical metaphor in Schelling's philosophical oeuvre. Like other key figures of German idealism, Schelling made ample use of dramatic and theatrical concepts as basic metaphors underpinning his transcendental-philosophical, anthropological, metaphysical, and religious-philosophical thought. As I shall try to demonstrate, the use of theatrical metaphors was not only a rhetorical accessory for Schelling, but one of the fundamental components of his philosophy. The privileged position that theatrical imagery holds in Schelling's work is due to the specific character of his thought, in which the dialectic of the one and the many functions as an interpretative key to the historical process.

Already in the earliest of Schelling's major texts, the pivotal issue of philosophy as such was considered as being intimately connected with the structural peculiarity of one particular dramatic genre, namely ancient tragedy. In his *Philosophical Letters on Dogmatism and Criticism* (1795), written in Tübingen, the contradiction between subject and object and, consequently, between freedom and necessity was considered as a starting point, making possible the very existence of philosophy. Every philosophy's primary aim is to discover a means of conceiving the absolute principle of being, bringing together and mediating between freedom and necessity, that is, theorizing the identity of subject and object.

There are two possible contradictory ways of conceiving such a principle, and thus two major philosophical systems: dogmatism, which relies on the absolute object (for Schelling this is represented by Spinoza's ethics), or criticism, which relies on the absolute subject (here Schelling is referring particularly to Fichte's *Wissenschaftslehre*). Kant's philosophy is viewed not as a distinct philosophy, but as a meta-philosophical construct which explores the conditions of possibility of the above-mentioned contradictory positions. The main task of the *Philosophical Letters* is to explicate various philosophical implications of the two systems, which give contrary answers to the same question: "How do I ever come to egress from the absolute, and to progress toward an opposite?"[1]

---

1 Friedrich Wilhelm Joseph Schelling, *The Unconditional in Human Knowledge: Four Earlier Essays (1794–1796)*, tr. F. Marti, London 1980, p.164.

Open Access. © 2019 Petr Rezvykh, published by De Gruyter. This work is licensed under the Creative Commons Attribution-NonCommercial-NoDerivatives 4.0 License.
https://doi.org/10.1515/9783110622034-011

For Schelling, the absolute cannot be expressed in philosophical language otherwise than through these two contradictory idioms.

But in the concluding tenth letter, having examined the metaphysical and ethical implications of both systems, Schelling suddenly declares that the solution of the contradiction between dogmatism and criticism can exclusively be expressed in artistic form:

> You are right, one thing remains, to *know* that there is an objective power which threatens our freedom with annihilation, and, with this firm and certain conviction in our heart to fight *against* it exerting our whole freedom, and thus to go down. You are doubly right, my friend, because this possibility must be preserved for art even after having vanished in the light of reason; it must be preserved for the highest in art.[2]

According to Schelling, this highest artistic form is ancient tragedy, representing in action the struggle between the hero and fate:

> A mortal, destined by fate to become malefactor and himself fighting against this fate, is nevertheless appallingly punished for the crime, although it was the deed of destiny! The ground of this contradiction, that which made the contradiction bearable, lay deeper than one would seek it. It lay in the contest between human freedom and the power of the objective world in which the mortal must succumb necessarily if that power is absolutely superior, if it is fate. And yet he must be punished for succumbing because he did not succumb without a struggle. That the malefactor who succumbed under the power of fate was punished, this tragic fact was the recognition of human freedom; it was the honor due to freedom. Greek tragedy honored human freedom, letting its hero fight against the superior power of fate. In order not to go beyond the limits of art, the tragedy had to let him succumb. Nevertheless, in order to make restitution for this humiliation of human freedom extorted by art, it had to let him atone even for the crime committed by fate. As long as he is still free, he holds out against the power of destiny. As soon as he succumbs he ceases to be free. Succumbing, he still accuses fate for the loss of his freedom. Even Greek tragedy could not reconcile freedom and failure. Only a being deprived of freedom could succumb under fate. It was a sublime thought to suffer punishment willingly even for an inevitable crime, and so to prove one's freedom by the very loss of this freedom, and to go down with a declaration of free will.[3]

Here the structure of the tragic action turns out to be the only means of expressing the inexpressible—the absolute identity of necessity and freedom. Schelling interprets ancient Greek tragedy as a very special artistic form of performance that is able to make visible the deepest root of the most fundamental philosophical question (which is impossible to access by means of discursive philosophical thinking) and in this way turns out to be an aesthetic analogue to Kant's

---

2 Ibid., p. 192.
3 Ibid., pp. 192–193.

transcendental philosophy. What has become its *ground* in the critical philosophy of Kant finds its *presentation* and *performance*, and the only possible one, in classical Greek tragedy. It is remarkable that Schelling's explanation of the philosophical relevance of tragedy is based on a gradual reduction: art is reduced to the dramatic form, the dramatic form to the schema of tragedy, and the schema of tragedy to a singular tragic plot, namely to the Oedipus myth. The Oedipus model also serves as a paradigm for the interpretation of modern tragedies; it is obviously not by chance that Schelling makes a direct allusion to Shakespeare's *Hamlet*, the paradigmatic modern tragedy, at the end of the following passage:

> It is the highest interest of philosophy to awaken reason from its slumber, by means of that unchangeable alternative which dogmatism offers to its confessors. If reason can no longer be awakened by this means, then at least one can be sure of having tried the utmost. The trial is all the easier, since that alternative proves to be the simplest, most intelligible, most genuine antithesis of all philosophizing reason, when we try to render to ourselves an account of the last foundations of our knowledge. Reason must renounce either an objective intelligible world, or a subjective personality; either an absolute object, or an absolute subject, freedom of will. This antithesis once definitely established, the interest of reason demands also that we watch with the utmost care that it be not obscured again by the sophistries of moral indolence, in a veil which would deceive humanity. It is our duty to uncover the whole deception, and to show that any attempt at making it acceptable to reason can succeed only through new deceptions which keep reason in constant ignorance and hide from it in the last abyss into which dogmatism must inevitably fall as soon as it proceeds to the last great question, which is, to be or not to be.[4]

In the "System of Transcendental Idealism", Schelling's first systematically conceived treatise, the remarkable link between theatrical imagery and the problem of the identity of necessity and freedom reemerges; this time, however, the metaphors are no longer based on the structure of the dramatic narrative, but rather on the form of the scenic representation itself. The contrariety of necessity and freedom, interpreted here as an intersubjective development of the opposition between unconscious and conscious activity that forms the basis of self-consciousness, is, according to the principles of transcendental idealism, a keystone of world history. In the context of this idea, Schelling refers to the traditional metaphor of world history as a Theater of the World: individuals endowed with freedom of will behave like actors, performing their roles as best as they can. But Schelling modifies this metaphor in an unexpected way: a free play of individuals appears here as a processual manifestation of the

---

4 Ibid., p. 194.

unique author of the play, of which single performers are no more than fragments:

> If we think of history as a play[5] in which everyone involved performs his part quite freely and as he pleases, a rational development of this muddled drama is conceivable only if there be a single spirit who speaks in everyone, and if the playwright, whose mere fragments (disjecta membra poetae) are the individual actors, has already so harmonized beforehand the objective outcome of the whole with the free play of every participant, that something rational must indeed emerge at the end of it. But now if the playwright were to exist independently of his drama, we should be merely the actors who speak the lines he has written. If he does not exist independently of us, but reveals and discloses himself successively only, through the very play of our own freedom, so that without this freedom even he himself would not be, then we are collaborators of the whole and have ourselves invented the particular roles we play.[6]

In this passage, it is not a specific dramatic genre, but the very form of the theatrical performance that is used as a paradigmatic metaphor for the manifestation of the non-objectifiable unity through a dynamic manifoldness. It is very important that Schelling denotes the specificity of such a manifestation with the theologically loaded term "revelation":

> Now it can straightway be inferred from the foregoing, which view of history is the only true one. History as a whole is a progressive, gradually self-disclosing revelation of the absolute. Hence one can never point out in history the particular places where the mark of providence, or God Himself, is as it were visible. For God never *exists*, if the existent is that which presents itself in the objective world; if He *existed* thus, then *we* should not; but He continually *reveals* Himself. Man, through his history, provides a continuous demonstration of God's presence, a demonstration, however, which only the whole of history can render complete.[7]

It is not only remarkable that Schelling refers to the form of the extempore play[8] in which the actors have the freedom to improvise their parts as a model of the historical process. The theatrical metaphor allows the author to substantively re-accentuate the idea of world history as a gradual revelation of God, which was already contained in Lessing's essays on the philosophy of history. Schelling

---

[5] Schelling uses the German word *Schauspiel*, which refers not to any kind of play but specifically to a theatrical show.
[6] Friedrich Wilhelm Joseph Schelling, *System of Transcendental Idealism*, tr. P. Heath, intr. M. Vater, Charlottesville, VA 1978, p. 210.
[7] Ibid., p. 211.
[8] See H. Zeltner, "Das große Welttheater: Zu Schellings Geschichtsphilosophie", in: *Schelling-Studien: Festgabe für Manfred Schröter zum 85. Geburtstag*, ed. A. M. Koktanek, Munich and Vienna 1965, pp. 113–130.

differentiates the idea of God's revelation through world history from the Enlightenment idea of an "Education of the Human Race". There are no privileged moments in the history of mankind when the revelation anticipates the evolution of human reason in order to indicate the direction of historical development, but, rather, history as a whole is a continuous disclosure of God becoming Himself. What is revealed is not a metaphysical divine essence but the transcendental "ultimate ground of the harmony between freedom and the objective (or lawful)"[9] and, as conveyed by what Schelling expresses in the previous quote, the revelation cannot be understood as a singular event within history. Schelling thus transforms the traditional topos of *theatrum mundi* in a very radical way. World history is a Theater of the World, but neither an author nor a strictly defined set of roles for the various actors performing in the play exists.

The same theatrical metaphor will also be used by the later Schelling in the "Philosophy of Revelation", where the image of theatrical performance becomes an important component not of his philosophy of history, but of his theological reflections. The decisive role here is played by two recurrent motives featuring in all versions of Schelling's text: "divine irony" and "divine hypocrisy", terms he introduces in his theory of the mythological process with a view to his explanation of creation and his interpretation of ancient mysteries.

Schelling's theory of creation is centered on the doctrine of the so-called potencies, uncreated intra-divine demiurgic forces that act in the process of creation as God's instruments. Through the theory of potencies, Schelling tries to eliminate the main defect of the traditional models of creation, namely the strong opposition between the being of the creator and the being of the creature. The three potencies are three various but at the same time deeply inter-connected modes of being of God as the unifying spirit. They express various aspects of His attitude towards His own being. Hence they are thought of as ontological modalities, namely as the possibility to be (Seinkönnen), the necessity to be (Seinmüssen), and the duty to be (Seinsollen). In order to have the potencies appear to Him, God must separate or distinguish them from Himself. This, however, is impossible as long as He exists as absolute; in an absolute being, there is no difference between "can", "must", and "ought". So God's self-revelation can only begin if He as it were suspends the act of His existence and thus enables the potencies to manifest their difference. Only then do they appear to Him, now just as potencies, i.e. possibilities not of His own being, but of another dimension of being, distinct from God, in which He can manifest Himself.

---

[9] Schelling, *System*, p. 210.

In the act of revelation, God, to use Schelling's own expression, "puts potencies in tension" and stimulates them to mutual activity. Thanks to this tension of the potencies, the primary impetus to the process is given, in which the potencies take different positions and generate in God different possible creatures. The process aims at restoring or rather generating the divine being. In this respect, the fact of the tension between the potencies is paradoxical: creation is an inversion of relations which in their original function are constitutive of God Himself. Schelling indicates this inversion with the term *universio* (created by an etymological derivation from *uni-versum*, meaning: the reversed unity) and provocatively characterizes it as "divine irony" and "divine hypocrisy".

In his "Philosophy of Mythology" Schelling writes:

> Die Potenzen in ihrer gegenseitigen Ausschließung und ihrer gegeneinander verkehrten Stellung sind nur der durch die göttliche Ironie äußerlich verstellte Gott; sie sind der verkehrte Eine, inwiefern, dem Schein nach, das was verborgen, nicht wirkend seyn sollte, offenbar und wirkend, das was positiv, offenbar seyn sollte, negirt und in Potenz-Zustand gesetzt wird.[10]

> Potencies in their mutual exclusion and inverse relation to each other are God, externally pretending to be other than Himself by means of divine irony; they are the one, but inverted, because that which should be hidden, inactive, becomes explicit and active, while that which should be positive, explicit, is negated and reduced to the state of a potency.

But it is highly remarkable that in one of the early versions of this construction, in the lecture course "Foundation of Positive Philosophy" (1827), Schelling refers to the theatrical imagery again, in this case in order to characterize God's way of being the world creator:

> Eben Gott [...] ziemt es, jenes Sein durch Auseinandersetzung *begreiflich* zu machen, es zu einem Schauspiel zu machen, das er intellectuellen Naturen gewähren könnte, in denen er sich die Zeugen dieses Vorganges selbst erzog. Nichts verhindert ihn, diesen natürlichen Willen nun umgekehrt zum Verhüllenden seiner Gottheit zu machen.[11]

> It is right for God to make that being comprehensible through an altercation, to transform it into a play that He could grant to the intellectual natures, in which He Himself educated

---

[10] Friedrich Wilhelm Joseph Schelling, *Sämtliche Werke*, ed. K. F. A. Schelling, sect. 2, vol. 2, Stuttgart and Augsburg 1856–1861, p. 90.

[11] Friedrich Wilhelm Joseph Schelling, *Grundlegung der positiven Philosophie: Münchner Vorlesung, Wintersemester 1832/33 und Sommersemester 1833*, ed. H. Fuhrmans, Turin 1972, pp. 353–354.

the witnesses of this process. Conversely, nothing prevents Him from transforming this natural will into that which hides His divinity.

Through the act of divine irony God thus becomes able to "transform His being into a play" (Schauspiel). Schelling emphasizes that the idea of an ironic hypocrisy of God is the only possible key to the entire Christian worldview and makes the following remark in this context:

> Die Rationalisten können freilich nach ihren Begriffen die Handlungsweise eines Gottes nicht sehr vernünftig finden, der wie ein Virtuos die Schwierigkeiten sich erschafft, um sie zu überwinden. Man könnte aber diesen Rationalisten—mit Hamann—die Frage entgegenhalten, ob sie noch immer nicht gemerkt haben, dass Gott ein Genie sei, welches sich wenig darum kümmert, was sie für vernünftig halten.[12]

> The rationalists can't find it rational if a God acts in such a way that He, as a virtuoso, produces difficulties for Himself in order to overcome them. One could counter such rationalists by asking, with Hamann, if they have not yet realized that God is a genius who does not care too much about what they take to be rational.

The reference to Hamann is a very clear indication that Schelling sees an aesthetic dimension in the act of *universio*. It is not only the traditional theological idea of the divine economy, but an attempt to think the process of creation by means of a paradigmatic analogy with theatrical performance. Obviously, theatrical performance also serves as an archetypical image of the revelation of the one through the dynamic many. But if in the "System of Transcendental Idealism" God's revelation in history took place in the absence of the spectator, the "divine hypocrisy" in the creation takes "future intellectual creatures" into account: the main result of the action is the creation of the spectator. In the same lecture course, Schelling says:

> Nicht für sich bedurfte Gott dieser Bewegung; er hat nicht nötig, sich gleichsam einen Spiegel zu verschaffen, worin er sich selbst beschaue; denn er ist sich selbst von Ewigkeit bekannt. Er muss den wirklichen Vorgang um eines anderen willen wollen, alles um eines zukünftigen Willens; und so ist allerdings der Entschluss zu jener Umkehrung nur denkbar im Hinaussehen auf künftige intellektuelle Geschöpfe.[13]

> God does not need this movement for His own sake; He has no need to create a mirror in which He could look at Himself, for He knows Himself from eternity. He must will this real event for the sake of the other, everything is for the sake of a future will; so the decision for that inversion is only conceivable in His looking forward towards future intellectual creatures.

---

12 Ibid., p. 355.
13 Ibid.

In Schelling's theory of the mythological process, theatrical metaphors reveal new aspects of signification. Since the process of creation, based on "divine hypocrisy", is nothing but the process of restoring the broken equilibrium of potencies, it ends up in the created being, in which the potencies, having exhausted all possible positions, return to unity and quiet. Of course, this being is *man* as he was originally created. In the first man as the last integral result of creation, the demiurgic forces are balanced; but it is precisely this state of affairs that enables him to break the equilibrium anew and put it in motion. With this new tension of potencies, the freedom of the first man and the immediacy of his relation to God are lost; he "falls away" from the absolute and is caught up in the motion of potencies that he himself initiated and that separate him from God. This is how human consciousness emerges, for which the content of being is mediated and represented by the emergence of the same potentials which had manifested themselves in the creation. This entering of the potentials into the consciousness of man and their necessary motion is a mythological process, a "transcendental theogony".

Schelling characterizes this process in a very specific way:

> Als ein bloß im menschlichen Bewußtseyn sich ereignender, kann dieser Proceß natürlich nur durch Vorstellungen oder Erzeugung von Vorstellungen sich ankündigen und äußern. Diese Vorstellungen—die mythologischen—lassen sich [...] nicht als erfundene, nicht als erdichtete [...], sie lassen sich vielmehr nur denken als nothwendige Erzeugnisse des unter die Gewalt der Potenzen, die in ihrer Spannung nicht mehr göttliche, sondern nur noch kosmische Bedeutung haben, gefallenen menschlichen Bewußtseyns.[14]

> This process which takes place in man's consciousness can evidently announce itself only through representations or through the production of representations. These representations, as mythological ones, can be regarded neither as invented, nor as fictional [...], they can only be seen as necessary products of the human consciousness which has fallen under the dominance of the potencies which in their tension are no more of a divine but only of a cosmic significance.

In the mythological process, consciousness itself (the spectator, created as a result of the *universio*) turns to a stage on which struggling potencies are moving, represented in the form of pagan gods. The free art of the divine hypocrisy appears here in its higher form, as an intrinsically necessary process of the gradual de-substantialization of images. The process of world-creation was one of the division of the forces whose restored equilibrium had become the ground for a finite human consciousness, so that the play was played for the sake of the future spectator. The mythological process, on the other hand, is one in

---

14 Schelling, *Sämtliche Werke*, sect. II, vol. 3, p. 378.

which the spectator is identical with the stage and sees its inner life as being played within him. Unlike the act of creation, the mythological process seems to be more cinematographic or oneiric than theatrical in its structure. Nevertheless, it is based on the same pattern of a reversal in the relationship between unity and manifoldness that can be observed in Schelling's earlier applications of the theatrical metaphor. The potencies appear in their mutual tension as various mythological persons who dominate human consciousness in various ways at the various moments of the process; the diversity of the potencies is to be overcome through the whole process. It is quite remarkable that according to Schelling's theory, mythology ends with the mysteries, in which consciousness is freed from the necessity of the mythological process, truly experiencing in images its whole history, and feeling in the end an ecstatic unity with forces that had previously been alien to it. Here the entirety of mythology is conceived as a process of the interplay of three potencies, and the potencies themselves appear as aspects of the same god, Dionysus (Zagreus, Bacchus, and Iakhus). According to Schelling's reconstruction, the constitutive trait of the mysteries, which produces this liberating effect, is the "theatrical performance" ("scenische Darstellung")[15] of the past mythological process in its true significance and at the same time as its ecstatic end. We can thus conclude that in Schelling's interpretation of mythology, theatrical imagery also plays a key role in understanding the link between mythology and (Christian) revelation. The liberating and healing (or even salvational) potential of the theatrical performance is of great importance to Schelling: only through a theatrical performance can human consciousness confront itself with its own substantial ground, with its reality, and gain the real freedom which finds its realization in the religious experience.

To conclude: we can see that the theatrical metaphor plays a paradigmatic role in the philosophy of Schelling, from the very beginning up to the latest versions of his metaphysics. The image of the theatrical play serves as the main pattern for the conceptualization of every process in which freedom and necessity are mediated through each other—of thinking as such, of world history as a whole, of the very genesis of the world, and of the history of human consciousness.

---

15 Ibid., p. 460.

Elena Penskaya
The Philosophical Narrative as a Semiotic Laboratory of Theatrical Language: The Case of Jean Paul in the Context of the Russian Reception

"Theater" and "drama": this familiar but invariably troublesome distinction requires a word of explanation, since it has important consequences with regard to the objects and issues at stake. "Theater" is taken to refer here to the complex of phenomena associated with the performer-audience transaction: that is, with the production and communication of meaning in the performance itself and with the systems underlying it. By "drama", on the other hand, is meant that mode of fiction designed for stage representation and constructed according to particular ("dramatic") conventions. The epithet "theatrical", then, is limited to what takes place between and among performers and spectators, while the epithet "dramatic" indicates the network of factors relating to the represented fiction. This differentiation demarcates discrete levels of a unified cultural phenomenon for purposes of analysis. A related distinction arises concerning the actual object of the semiotician's labors in this area; that is to say, the kinds of text which he is to take as his analytic corpus. Unlike the literary semiotician or the analyst of myth or of the plastic arts, the researcher of theater and drama is faced with two quite dissimilar—although intimately related—types of textual material: that produced in the theater and that composed for the theater. To put the question differently: is it possible to re-found in semiotic terms an exhaustive poetics of the Aristotelian kind, concerned with all the communicational, representational, logical, fictional, linguistic, and structural principles of theater and drama?[1] This is one of the central motivating questions behind this article.

I

The study of metaphor is becoming increasingly intensive, penetrating the most diverse domains of knowledge, such as philosophy, logic, psychology, psychoanalysis, hermeneutics, literary studies, literary criticism, the theory of fine arts, semiotics, rhetoric, linguistics, philosophy, etc.

---

[1] T. Hawkes, *The Semiotics of Theatre and Drama*, London 1987, p. 9.

Of all the numerous theories of metaphor, this study focuses on two trends, the semantic and pragmatic ones. The reason for this is that, even though the cognitive efficiency of metaphorical conceptualization is well recognized, the jury is still out on the peculiar phenomenon of metaphorical truth. For instance, adherents of the semantic school believe that metaphor effects consist in shaping a new meaning by creating some kind of a screen filter[2] and thus approach the phenomenon of metaphor as a tool for the construction of meaning. Their conception of metaphor creates a peculiar optics, where the tenor is revealed *through* metaphorical expression, or, to put it in other words, the tenor is "projected" onto the vehicle's semantic field, and a unified integral system of characteristics is used to filter or organize the interpretation of another system. Interactions imply demonstrating one system of characteristics using the other one in order to build a new conception of or a fresh perspective cast on the object.[3]

Treating metaphor as a form of thought became possible with the emergence of broader views on thinking, which was now understood not only as a domain of formal logic but also as a creative process. This approach contributed much to undermining the conventional theories of the mind and defying the existing stereotypes.[4] Such theories were named *interactive metaphor models*—a prevalent approach in the theory of metaphor in the twentieth century, which interpreted metaphor as an interaction of ideas,[5] the meaning of metaphor thus being regarded as the outcome of a special kind of interaction among various contexts.[6]

The idea of metaphor representing a special form of thought was discussed in terms of various interaction theories that studied the mechanism of metaphor.[7] One of the strongest conclusions was that the intellectual activity behind metaphor is essentially *imaginative thinking* interpreted in terms of Ludwig Wittgenstein's aspect perception. Aspect perception manifests itself in that the same conception can first be seen as one thing and then as another. Wittgenstein understood this type of mental activity as involving a flight of fancy.

The antagonistic pragmatic school reduces the effects of metaphorization to metaphor's aesthetic role and denies the possibility of creating a new

---

2 M. Black, *Models and Metaphors: Studies in Language and Philosophy*, Ithaca, NY 1962.
3 M. Black, *The Labyrinth of Language*, New York, NY and Toronto 1968.
4 M. Beardsley, "Metaphorical Senses", in: *Nous*, vol. 12, 1978, pp. 3–16.
5 C. Bazzanella, "Metaphor and Context: Some Issues", in: *Langage et référence: Mélanges in Honour of Kerstin Jonasson*, ed. H. Kronning, C. Norén, B. Novén, G. Ransbo, L.-G. Sundell, and B. Svane, Uppsala 2001.
6 I. A. Richards, *The Philosophy of Rhetoric*, 2nd ed., Oxford 1967.
7 R. Harris, M. Lahey, and F. Marsalek, "Metaphors and Images: Rating, Reporting and Remembering", in: *Cognition and Figurative Language*, ed. R. Honeck and R. Hoffman, Hillsdale, NJ 1980, pp. 163–181.

meaning within a metaphorical framework. Advocates of the pragmatic school do not differentiate between the content of metaphor and the literal meanings it is based on. The phenomenon of metaphorization is thus associated with novelty produced by overlapping heterogeneous meanings.[8]

The past decades have seen the focus of metaphor research shift from philology (rhetoric, stylistics, literary criticism), where the analysis and evaluation of the poetic metaphor prevail, to spoken language and the domains synthesizing styles, traditions, and genres; in particular, the theatrical metaphor has become a subject of research interest in the humanities.[9] Metaphor is now being analyzed as closely interrelated with mental processes as well as in terms of articulating certain epistemological and even metaphysical problems. Researchers interpret metaphor as the backbone of the processes of thinking and of creating not only culture-specific worldviews but also the universal vision of the world. The growing theoretical interest in metaphor was inspired by the expansion of metaphor into various types of discourse and the increased frequency of usage in diverse texts, from poetry and journalism to languages of different scientific domains.[10] Since the Middle Ages, the versatility and ubiquity of metaphor in multiple genres of literary, everyday, and scientific speech have made researchers concentrate not so much on its aesthetic value as on its application advantages,[11] which implies genre-specific functional limitations[12] and results in diluting the very concept of metaphor, which has come to denote any form of indirect figurative reference in the literary or visual arts.[13]

Widely recognized as a literary device, metaphor becomes scientifically legitimized and treated as a valid mental mechanism. While it used to be understood as a comparison between two static semantic forms, now metaphor is represented as the outcome of interaction between meanings and thus becomes an integral part of the constantly developing language system. The functions of metaphor go well beyond producing a linguistic setting to frame new facts. Metaphor also serves to express a special way of conceptualizing those facts based on the principle of the imaginary, which makes it possible to acknowledge the heterogeneity between

---

[8] H. G. Coenen, *Analogie und Metapher: Grundlegung einer Theorie der bildlichen Rede*, Berlin and New York, NY 2002.
[9] W. Shibes, *Metaphor: An Annotated Bibliography and History*, Whitewater, WI 1971.
[10] *Theorie der Metapher*, ed. A. Havercamp, Darmstadt 1983.
[11] R. Hoffman, "Some Implications of Metaphor for Philosophy and Psychology of Science", in: *The Ubiquity of Metaphor: Metaphor in Language and Thought*, ed. W. Paprotté and R. Dirven, Amsterdam 1985, pp. 327–380.
[12] Ibid.
[13] J. P. Aarts and J. Colbert, *Metaphor and Non-Metaphor*, Tübingen 1979.

image and meaning.[14] By enriching philosophical vocabularies, metaphors produce polysemantic terms, which result in the overlapping of semantic fields and their distinctive features. The semantic scope of metaphors is defined intuitively, as term/content compatibility is assessed through linguistic intuitions, which vary across individuals and situations.[15] Metaphorization, which is ultimately eradicating metaphor as such, results in categories of linguistic semantics.[16]

The mechanisms of metaphor in different texts and the transformations it has gone through since ancient times have been analyzed at the interface of historical and cultural processes, leading to conventionalization of meaning.[17] P. Ricoeur was the first to apply a hermeneutic approach in the theory of metaphor. He offered a corresponding model of metaphor which drew on the ideas of philosophical hermeneutics and associated metaphor with the deepest worldview level concealed by everyday life. Ricoeur argues that there cannot be an adequate theory of metaphor that does not take imagination and perception into account, yet he insists on interpreting these two processes in terms of semantics rather than psychology. He believes that images and imagination form a special kind of medium similar to flowing imagery, in and through which similarities can be seen; in addition, images help bring different concepts closer together and change logical distances between them. According to Ricoeur, imagination is about exposing relationships through images. He demonstrates that it is imagery that brings the process of metaphorization to its specific maturity.[18]

Modern metaphor analysis also draws on the hypothesis proposed by G. Lakoff and M. Johnson, which holds that metaphor embraces the principle of theatricalization, theatrical optics, and play, as it serves to conceptualize a phenomenon using terminology that is normally used to describe other phenomena.[19]

The past quarter-century has yielded definitive studies which explore the origin of metaphor as a phenomenon using tools that range from describing the overall mechanism of metaphor[20] to analyzing its specific applications in texts of different types (scientific, literary, political, etc.).[21] It should be noted, however, that along with scientific (linguistic, neuropsychological) metaphor

---

14 P. de Man, "The Epistemology of Metaphor", in: *Critical Inquiry*, vol. 5, 1978, pp. 13–30.
15 M. Mühling-Schlapkohl, "Metapher: Schlüssel des Verstehens?", in: *Theologie und Philosophie*, vol. 79, 2004, pp. 189–199.
16 *Aspects of Metaphor*, ed. J. Hintikka, Dordrecht, London, and Boston, MA 1994.
17 A. Biese, *Die Philosophie des Metaphorischen*, Hamburg and Leipzig 1893.
18 P. Ricoeur, *The Rule of Metaphor: Multi-Disciplinary Studies of the Creation of Meaning in Language*, tr. R. Czerny with K. McLaughlin and J. Costello, London 1978.
19 G. Lakoff and M. Johnson, *Metaphors We Live By*, Chicago, IL 2003.
20 A. Goatly, *The Language of Metaphors*, London and New York, NY 1997.
21 R. Gibbs, *The Poetics of Mind*, Cambridge 1994.

analysis and related research in linguistic philosophy, metaphor has also been approached as a fundamental property of any language, philosophical or scientific, that has a specific set of metaphorical matrices.[22]

Disputes over metaphor as a phenomenon also reveal the modern trend of utilizing its epistemological potential. Although the idea of metaphorical conceptualization being related to cognition dates as far back as the philosophy of Romanticism, the way metaphor is associated with cognitive processes today is something different. While the abundance of metaphors in the language of philosophical Romanticism had to do with the urge to validate the principle of imagination and spontaneity in cognition, modern philosophy regards metaphor as a means of reflection of a special type. Metaphor allows for the synthesis of different layers of knowledge and for the fusion of hypotheses and assumptions on the one hand and verified knowledge on the other into one connected whole.[23] Metaphor's ability to unite different meanings into integrated wholes implies a mechanism for adjusting facts. This mechanism is triggered by the very principle of fictitiousness and assumed likeness. The modus of likening enables metaphor to equate different phenomena and integrate the unknown into the structure of existing knowledge.[24]

The modus of fictitiousness typical of metaphorical conceptualization provides an insight into seemingly ambiguous verbal expressions as well as logically and linguistically unregulated structures, breaking the patterns of logical organization in texts and lifting the restraints on a recombination of their components. The introduction of metaphor thus makes it possible to bring together objects that are extremely remote from one another.[25] The combination of the known and the unknown in semantic meaning transfers is always the result of conventions, and metaphor is an effective tool to provide such a dialogical development of content.[26]

II

Jean Paul (Johann Paul Friedrich Richter, 1763–1825), one of the most unorthodox German writers, eludes classification under the titles of Romanticism,

---

[22] J. Derrida, *Margins of Philosophy*, tr. A. Bass, Chicago, IL 1982.
[23] H. Kubczak, "Begriffliche Inkompatibilität als konstitutives Prinzip der Metapher", in: *Sprachwissenschaft*, vol. 10, 1994, pp. 22–39.
[24] J. D. Sapir, "The Anatomy of Metaphor", in: *The Social Use of Metaphor: Essays on the Anthropology of Rhetoric*, ed. J. C. Crocker and J. D. Sapir, Pittsburgh, PA 1977, pp. 3–32.
[25] J. Vervaeke and J. M. Kennedy, "Conceptual Metaphor and Abstract Thought", in: *Metaphor and Symbol*, vol. 19, 2004, pp. 213–231.
[26] F. G. Droste, "Metaphor as a Paradigmatic Function", in: *Poetics*, vol. 11, 1982, pp. 203–211.

classicism, neo-baroque, or sentimentalism, his oeuvre embodying the cultural project of the transitional period of the turn of the nineteenth century. His texts, dubbed a "dreadful monster" by Thomas Carlyle and considered "unbelievably mature" by Goethe, seem to comprise multiple incongruous layers, aesthetic techniques, literary styles, cultures and identities, drawing the reader into a phantasmagoric space, astoundingly ordinary and yet surreal at the same time. This study seeks to demonstrate this creative (contrapuntal and ironical) multi-layeredness and identify Jean Paul's mechanisms of creating literary works and essays in philosophical aesthetics, which, on the one hand, fit into the cultural context of the "end of the age of rhetoric", and on the other, anticipate the challenges of the upcoming age of modernist art. A large-scale symposium held several years ago in Moscow discussed the comparative issues associated with the reception of Jean Paul's works in various national contexts where his ideas, images, techniques, and strategies have been employed for local cultural and literary needs.[27] The reception of Jean Paul in Russian literature has been intense, with the 2010s seeing another climax in interpretation of his oeuvre.

Jean Paul's role, influence, and literary charm are as great as the extent to which he was disregarded, at least among Russian-speaking readers, throughout the twentieth century and the very beginning of the twenty-first century. The label "the German Laurence Sterne" suggests a very inaccurate analogy, which can only give the most superficial and tentative idea of the writer's hierarchies, contexts, and narrative style. The degree of inaccuracy is directly proportionate to the differences in sentimentalism and pre-Romanticism between England and Germany. German literary culture of that period features much more elements of the Baroque, mannerism, and (*avant la lettre*) expressionism than is the case in texts from the British Isles; the description of German novels of the eighteenth century as "frantic encyclopedias"[28] is a perfectly appropriate term to define the genre and style of Jean Paul's works. Jean Paul was on everyone's lips and minds in nineteenth-century Russia. It might suffice to recall that Vissarion Belinsky, a famous Russian literary critic, demanded that this writer's influence should be restricted.[29]

---

27 "Tvorchestvo Zhan Polya: na granitse kul'tur i stiley" [Jean Paul's Oeuvre: At the Interface of Cultures and Styles]. Report presented at the international conference held by the Gorky Institute of World Literature, Russian Academy of Sciences (17 June 2014, Moscow).
28 J. W. Smeed, "Thomas Carlyle and Jean Paul Richter", in: *Comparative Literature*, vol. 16, 1964, pp. 226–253.
29 Vissarion Belinsky, "Retsenziya na 'Antologiyu iz Zhan-Pol' Rikhtera'" [Review of *Anthology of Jean Paul Richter*], in: Vissarion Belinsky, *Polnoe sobranie sochineniy: V 13 t.* [Complete Works in 13 vols.], vol. 8, Moscow 1955, p. 59. A work on Jean Paul was published in Russia in 1844. It was an anthology that not only failed to shed light on the author, but even distorted the very concept of him: sentences pulled out from different works were presented as

The composer Robert Schumann was referred to as "Jean Paul in music",[30] a "translator of Richter's verbal metaphors and images into the language of sounds, a skillful interpreter of the Baroque phonological structure of his figures of speech".[31]

The case of Jean Paul is unique, indeed. The nature of his narration is polysynthetic and based on his own philosophy of theatrical language, the origins of which are discovered at the interface of theater, literature, and dramaturgy. In his novels and literary works, the researcher will find a hybrid combination of various genres and forms, which allows him to regard theater as a space for cultural transformation.[32] In such a dynamic environment, metaphor plays a pivotal role in Jean Paul's literary system and intellectual pursuits. According to Jean Paul, metaphor extends the potential of speech.

This paper provides insight into the specific aspects of theatrical space in non-theatrical works by Jean Paul (as well as some of his quasi-theatrical plots) connected with his reception within Russian culture and literature.[33] We will dwell on the structure of his works and his theatrical perspective, which had a latent yet considerable influence on the subsequent culture of Europe, including Russia. The urgency of this endeavor originates from the fact that Jean Paul is barely known to present-day Russian readers; his works are rarely published and little studied.[34]

---

anecdotes, no more than that. Belinsky produced a very awkward article on this account, which boiled down to a recommendation not to fall for the eccentric Jean Paul too much.

30 S. Goddard, "[Review of] *Der Einfluss Jean Pauls auf Robert Schumann* by Hans Kötz", in: *Music & Letters*, vol. 15, 1934, p. 177.

31 J. Daverio, "Reading Schumann by way of Jean Paul and His Contemporaries", in: *College Music Symposium*, vol. 30, 1990, pp. 28–45.

32 The bibliography of Richter's works as well as of scholarly studies devoted to his oeuvre is extensive. See E. Berend, *Jean Paul-Bibliographie*, Berlin and Munich 1925; E. Berend, *Prolegomena zur historisch-kritischen Gesamtausgabe von Jean Pauls Werken*, Berlin 1927; E. Berend, *Jean Paul-Bibliographie*, Stuttgart 1963; T. Schestag, "Bibliographie für Jean Paul", in: *MLN* (German Issue), vol. 113, 1998, pp. 465–523.

33 Twelve volumes had been published by July 1934. Richter's works were translated into Russian mostly in journals of the first half of the nineteenth century: *Mnemozina* (1824, vol. I); *Moskovskiy Telegraf* (1827); *Moskovskiy Vestnik* (1827, vols. I–III; 1830, vol. IV); *Sovremennik* (1838, vol. XII; 1841, vol. XXII), *Moskovskiy Nablyudatel* (1839, vol. I), etc. Independent publications: *Antologiya iz Zhan-Polya Rikhtera* [Anthology of Jean Paul Richter], St. Petersburg 1844; *Tsvety, plody i shipy, ili brachnaya zhizn', smert' i svad'ba advokata bednykh Zibenkeyza* [Flower, Fruit, and Thorn Pieces, or The Wedded Life, Death, and Marriage of Firmian Stanislaus Siebenkäs, Parish Advocate in the Burgh of Kuhschnappel], tr. Ye. Barteneva, St. Petersburg 1937; *Zibenkez* [Siebenkäs], Leningrad 1937.

34 A. Sidorov's translation of Jean Paul's novel *The Life of the Little Schoolmaster Maria Wuz in Auental* was prepared for publication by Academia in 1922, yet it was never finalized. An edited typescript is stored in the Academia Fund of the Russian State Archive of Literature and

One major reason for this situation is the fact that he is incredibly hard to translate (which did not pose a problem in the nineteenth century, when reading knowledge of German was common among the educated in Russia). Only one of Jean Paul's novels has been translated into Russian so far—*Siebenkäs*, by A. Kardashinsky in 1937.[35] The translation leaves out large passages, namely all of the "digressions" that are so typical of Jean Paul.

The Russian translation of *The Awkward Age* was published by the German publisher Otto Reichl, who has opened a branch in Moscow and divulges, among other things, classical German literary works that are unexplored in Russia.[36]

A new surge of interest in Jean Paul's artistic heritage has been observable in Germany since the mid-1990s.[37] Theatrical dimensions, by the way, are mentioned in each of the relevant studies. The titles of these books represent highly

---

Art (RGALI) (fund 629, series 1, archival unit 1393). Academia was a publishing house of the Petrograd University Philosophy Community, which existed in 1921–1937 in the RSFSR and later in the USSR. The publishing house is famous for high-quality classical literature publications and illustrations as well as for employing a number of well-known translators and artists. Sidorov (1891–1978) was a Soviet art historian, bibliophile, collector, expert in bibliography and history of drawing, Doctor of Sciences in Art History (1936), corresponding member of the Academy of Sciences of the Soviet Union (1946), Honored Art Worker of the RSFSR (1947), author of works on individual issues of Western European art of the Renaissance and Modernism, the research papers *The Graphic Language of Rembrandt, The Art of Beardsley*, and others. Sidorov was recruited by the Joint State Political Directorate in 1928 under the codename of *Stary* ("Old") to conduct secret surveillance of the Moscow artistic intelligentsia. Investigating the case of the Moscow-based artist and political prisoner Leonid Nikitin, his son Andrey wrote in his book *Mystics, Rosicrucianists and Templars in Soviet Russia*: "A. Sidorov, who owned the largest collection of books and manuscripts on occultism in Moscow, a Templar, a Rosicrucianist and a high-ranking Mason—as reported by informed contemporaries—remained intact amidst that purge. He kept taking interest in mysticism, discussed it enthusiastically with his acquaintances and sometimes even lent them books on occultism and theosophy. While many of those people ended up in prison and forced labor camps, he survived through the horrendous years successfully." Sidorov went on translating Jean Paul Richter's works and commenting on them. His manuscripts remained unpublished and are now kept in the Russian State Archive of Literature and Art (RGALI) (fund 632, series 4, archival unit 305).

35 *Siebenkäs* was published by the publishing house Khudozhestvennaya in the thick of the Great Purge in Leningrad in 1937.

36 *Zhan Pol': Grubiyanskie gody. Biografiya. V 2 tomakh* [Jean Paul: The Awkward Age. Biography. In 2 vols.], Moscow 2017. The book includes extensive commentaries based on German academic publications and was largely improved by the translator T. Baskakova. The afterword contains a detailed analysis of *The Awkward Age* (in the context of Jean Paul's work) and touches upon Jean Paul's influence on modern Western literature.

37 H. Kaiser, *Jean Paul lesen: Versuch über seine poetische Anthropologie des Ich*, Würzburg 1995; U. Hagel, *Elliptische Zeiträume des Erzählens: Jean Paul und die Aporien der Idylle*, Würzburg 2003; S. Eickenrodt, *Augen-Spiel: Jean Pauls optische Metaphorik der Unsterblichkeit*, Göttingen 2006.

relevant problems that open up new paths of interpretation; however, the time for a comprehensive understanding of Jean Paul's texts is obviously yet to come.

Jean Paul's place in the history of German and European literature is hard to determine, as very few studies go deep into at least one of his novels, which appears strange. Russian researchers of Jean Paul consistently analyze poetic devices but never summarize (or interpret) the content of any specific novel.[38]

There are reasons for reckoning Jean Paul among the pre-Romantics, partially because he pays a lot of attention to humor and irony in his theoretical work *Introduction to Aesthetics*. However, the ways in which he constructs and ironically presents his plots are based on visual—theatrical—collisions. They are extremely controversial and often involve nearly palpable forms, intrigue and conflict, i.e. everything the reader needs to feel like a spectator. The instantaneous switching between narratives creates a powerful optical illusion in which readers/spectators find themselves submerged. For instance, Jean Paul applies irony when opposing routine life (mediocre and sometimes hilarious) to an eternal perspective on this routine and human life as such.

This is where it comes to a crucial characteristic of his textual production. Jean Paul impregnates many of his works, whether philosophical, autobiographical, or fictional, with visionary images of outer space. They are full of theatrical metaphors: *The Awkward Age* (an autobiographical novel), for example, ends with a visionary picture of the evolution of the human language, which is presented as a scene with a drop curtain and linguistic elements appearing as characters in a mystery play.

The theatrical dimension of Jean Paul's metaphors reveals his connection to an earlier literary tradition. This "ancient pedigree" of his can be observed in his theatrical symbols and emblems as well as in the allegorical structure of his narratives. Emblems do not play a great role among other Romantic writers. Jean Paul uses his theatrical ciphers that pass from text to text and live a life of their own, combining and forming individual internal plotlines within the narrative. For instance, there is a scene in *The Awkward Age* where a man wearing a mask offers money to people in a tavern for throwing eggs out of an open window. No one can succeed because the window is enchanted. This reads as a comical scene, but broken eggs are compared to the "unhatched" intentions and hopes of young writers in another work of Jean Paul's, *Life of Fibel*. A man

---

[38] V. Admoni, *Zhan-Pol' Rikhter: Rannii burzhuazny realism* [Jean Paul Richter: Early Bourgeois Realism], Leningrad 1936; M. Trotskaya, *Zhan-Pol' Rikhter v Rossii* [Jean Paul Richter in Russia], Moscow and Leningrad 1937.

in a mask appears, and then another one, compared to a puppeteer. The same episodes, if only more extended, can be encountered in *Introduction to Aesthetics* and *Titan*. A description of a puppet theater occurs three times in *Introduction to Aesthetics*. The roles in these puppet plays are played by Jean Paul's literary teachers, such as Cervantes, Shakespeare, Swift, and Sterne.

It is well established that Jean Paul borrowed quite a lot from Laurence Sterne, including the plot of *The Awkward Age* revolving around a mysterious heritage (this storyline is presented in Sterne's *Sentimental Journey*, in the chapter "The Fragment. Paris"). However, Jean Paul embellished Sterne's plot with a multitude of important details—theatrical, tellingly—creating a much more interesting book, to my mind, yet intentionally leaving the reference to Sterne in his text. He incorporates entire passages from *Introduction to Aesthetics*, in which Sterne is present as a character in a puppet play. Both Sterne and Jean Paul can be regarded as the founding fathers of the meta-novel or the meta-play, i.e. a novel that recounts how a novel is written and going deep into the nature of a literary or theatrical text.

Ludwig Börne, a younger contemporary of Jean Paul, said in his *Speech on Jean Paul*, commemorating the writer's death in 1825:

> He did not live for everyone! But the time will come when he will be born for everyone, and everyone will lament his death. He is simply standing patiently by the gate to the twentieth century and waiting with a smile on his face for the slow people he is a part of to catch up with him.[39]

Börne wishes to convey that Jean Paul was far ahead of his readers, and this is perfectly true. Back in the nineteenth century, what was valued most was the way Jean Paul described the life of the so-called humble man. Altogether, Jean Paul found little understanding in the nineteenth century. He was rediscovered in Germany at the turn of the twentieth century by the poet Stefan George and his circle of disciples. It was, indeed, George who most profoundly delineated the significance of Jean Paul. In a eulogy from 1896, George reunited Jean Paul and Goethe and declared Jean Paul Germany's second greatest poet after Goethe. As to the historical facts, Goethe was disposed positively towards Jean Paul in the beginning, but when Jean Paul came to Weimar to meet him, both Goethe and Schiller found him frenetic or somewhat strange. Perhaps they felt irritated by the abundance of baroque metaphors in his works that was beyond

---

[39] Ludwig Börne, "Denkrede auf Jean Paul Friedr. Richter", in: Ludwig Börne, *Sämtliche Schriften*, ed. I. and P. Rippmann, vol. 1, Düsseldorf 1964, pp. 787–799, p. 798.

all reasonable limits. Neither of them allowed themselves such extravagances as references to the Gothic novel or the creation of fantastic fiction.

George intended a radical revision of the German literary tradition, insisting on the two centers of gravity within it—the one occupied by Goethe, the other by Jean Paul. If Goethe is a great observer, the master of clarity, precision, and balanced construction, then Jean Paul, the dreamer, provides the objects' aura, colors, metaphors, hues, and tones. For George, Goethe is the architect of the German language, while Jean Paul is its musician and theater producer.[40]

George published an anthology of fragments from Jean Paul's works in 1900, focusing on things that differed strikingly from what mesmerized readers in the nineteenth century: the anthology included descriptions of dreams and bright, surrealistic theatrical metaphors. George referred to this anthology as "the surrealistic theater".[41] "Jean Paul's theatrical darkness"—this is how his biographer Börne described his style.[42]

In one of his letters, Jean Paul explains that in *The Awkward Age* he depicts himself as two twin brothers with different tempers. The brothers compose and stage various scenes and plays all the time, and all those scenes and plays evolve into a "garden of forking paths", just like that of Borges.

However, the story of the protagonists themselves turns out to be even more captivating. The novel begins with a scene in which a rich man's last will is read aloud. The man leaves all his property to a poor rural boy, provided that he will do a series of—at first sight—rather meaningless tasks. In addition, the will demands that a writer be found to document the boy's actions day by day. The drafts describe eleven versions of those tasks—their number is reduced in the print-version—which refer to quests as familiar from medieval literary texts. A writer is found, and his name is Johann Paul Richter. As we can see, *The Awkward Age* is created by Jean Paul (whose real name is Johann Paul Richter) himself, but as a literary character created by the "real" Jean Paul. Moreover, the will says that the deceased man's name used to be J. P. Richter, and the poor young boy will inherit this name together with all the property in case he succeeds. There are also seven other claimants, who are to receive some part of the inheritance for every mistake the boy commits. The register of mistakes is described as plots of plays revolving around *qui pro quo* situations. Five of them

---

[40] P. Fleming, "June 10, 1796: An Alien Fallen from the Moon", in: *The New History of German Literature*, ed. D. Wellbery, J. Ryan, H. U. Gumbrecht, A. Kaes, J. L. Koerner, and D. E. von Mücke, Cambridge, MA 2004, pp. 465–470; E. Förster, "1796–1797: A New Program for the Aesthetic Education of Mankind?", in: ibid., pp. 470–474.
[41] Stefan George, "Jean Paul", in: Stefan George, *Tage und Taten*, Berlin 1927, p. 61.
[42] Börne, "Denkrede", p. 790.

are purely comical, vaudeville-like. The "potential heirs" probably impersonate some dubious personal traits of the protagonist—otherwise speaking, they point to temptations that the boy will have to cope with in his further life. The novel is teeming with riddles and symbols, so the reader had better be extremely attentive not to get lost or confused. This results in a very perceptible theatrical mishmash, which turns the novel into a sort of immersive theater.

In order to understand Jean Paul, one needs to pay attention to details. All characters in the novel are parts—or partial reflections—of the author's personality. One of the most intricate problems related to this work has to do with its title. It translates from German as "age of transition", or "awkward age", but the protagonist is 24 years old, far past the "awkward age" (meaning: adolescence). Some reliable dictionaries claim that the very notion of *Flegeljahre*, i.e. the awkward age, appeared only after Jean Paul's novel was published, hence was coined by this text. The German word *Flegel* has a variety of meanings, including "threshing flail" and "rude fellow". For an ultimate understanding, it is important to take into account the "rude literature" trend that was popular among German writers at that time. Adherents of this philosophy presented themselves as illiterate rednecks and behaved rudely to those with refined taste. This latter meaning seems to be decisive to me. In the end, the novel describes the period during which the two brothers gradually evolve into writers. They venture into different forms, jointly create a novel called *Kogel Mogel, or Heart*; the draft versions of the text contain seventeen namesake plays. The years of discipleship are awkward for the brothers, who live in poverty, with nothing coming easily to them. At the same time, they are rude rebels themselves (the avant-garde, using contemporary language) and they create a sort of rude theater. *Introduction to Aesthetics* features Jean Paul's philosophical argument about what rude theater looks like. Curiously, Antonin Artaud would reproduce this philosophical argument almost entirely when explaining the principles of his Theater of Cruelty.

Theatricality gets concentrated in those fragments of Jean Paul's works which describe events that are very similar to nightmares. The same plot travels from text to text: action takes place at night, a man wearing a mask appears, etc.

A separate work of his is devoted uniquely to dreaming. When Jean Paul was nominated an honorable member of the Frankfurt association *Museum*, he felt obliged to "work off" his title and wrote his book *Museum*, published in 1815, which is a collection of essays of various kinds, including his text about dreaming.

One of the most obsessive dreams is the one about puppets, including mechanical ones, and scenes from a puppet theater with the puppeteer wearing a mask. The piece about dreaming, *A Glance Thrown into Dreaming*, turned out to be a very profound one. Jean Paul is trying to show how dreams are born, arguing that they are created by "co-workers", which include "brain" (an accumulator of sensual impressions), the mind (the "thinking I"), "the power of the subconscious", and the "outside world".

According to Jean Paul, theater is where the imagination, which is in charge of dreaming, is triggered. Traces of such stagings can be found in *The Awkward Age*. The very idea of the novel—to show a few characters in one—originates from here, too. At times, Jean Paul's narrative seems visually convincing—"as if one could see the story played out on stage", according to his attentive reader and biographer Börne.

For instance, Jean Paul uses only a few sentences to describe a scene where a man sneaks back to the village where his mother lives. The details are nearly photographically precise: what his mother is wearing (a sleeveless jacket tailored for males), the way she is dumping out bad and defective lettuce leaves from a bowl, and the fact that she "didn't have a single word [with her husband], which is so typical of rural families". Jean Paul was a man of endless literary experiments.

Jean Paul explains that the relationship between the book and the reader is analogous to that between the stage and the spectator. He believed that books and stages were basically the same things. Books are capable of creating powerful optical illusions, too. This is manifested, for example, in the way Jean Paul provides some trustworthy information about himself, despite all the fantastic nature of *The Awkward Age*. The narrator suddenly mentions having moved to another city and even specifies his new address and describes the view to be seen from the window. All of this miraculously matches the events in Jean Paul's "real" life at the time of writing this chapter. However, the new address is immediately followed by the phrase: "my shelter (which is also what my body is)".

Jean Paul's theatrical fantasies manifest themselves on the level of the plot, in his metaphors, in sentence structures, and in the way space and time are organized. For instance, a character is walking along a road on a fall day. Out of the blue, he finds himself in a valley "in the midst of spring": flowers are blooming, nightingales are singing, etc. He soon gets back to the road, which is followed by the phrase: "[...] *fall* birds were squawking in the woods of the river valley left behind".

Jean Paul's texts are similar to linguistic labyrinths, moving through which is a separate storyline with a scenario and drama of its own. In particular, they feature an abundance of Latin words and titles of various books, e.g. law lists of those times.

Jean Paul had a penniless youth and could not afford to buy books. Whenever a novel title caught his attention, he would imagine a book it might fit. Then he started writing out passages from books. He accumulated thousands of notes on most diverse subjects: witchcraft, kinds of birds, etc. Later on, while working on yet another novel, he would use those notes as a basis for his refined metaphors. The twentieth-century German writer Arno Schmidt also produced note cards first and then knitted them together into his novels—I believe he learned the method from Jean Paul. The University of Würzburg has uploaded all of Jean Paul's notes onto their website. There are myriads of them, but keyword research tools are very helpful. This project helps reconstruct the theatrical aspects of Jean Paul's language.

Intricate syntax is another aspect of his theatrical perspective and yet another useful tool for creating and preserving theatrical space. In *The Awkward Age*, Jean Paul as a character obtains rewards for every chapter written. Rewards are objects from the testator's *Kunstkammer*, and each chapter is entitled after the respective object. The difficulty lies in the fact that it is not always clear what exactly those objects are, e.g. a rare shell, a "mammoth bone from near Astrakhan", etc. The titles are also a sort of author's comment on what is going on in the chapter. For example, gemstones can be genuine or fake, expensive or cheap, and all of them assign specific color accents to the chapters. This information is embedded in the titles in German but lost when translated into Russian. One of the chapters translates as "red hawk", while the calque translation would be "scissor tail". Scissors in *The Awkward Age* and other Jean Paul novels are a metaphor for the writer's and playwright's "styling" efforts. Jean Paul approaches the content of a literary work and its stylistics, or form, separately, which is why he depicts himself as two twin brothers.

Jean Paul became an iconic figure for modernist authors. For instance, Paul Celan was his admirer and would frequently cite his words. The first book that Celan bought when he moved to France in 1948 was a multivolume collection of Jean Paul's oeuvres. Hans Henny Jahnn's novel trilogy *River without Banks* is full of Jean Paul's theatrical metaphors and references to the writer. Jahnn depicts the protagonist as several characters, namely as the crew and passengers of a "wooden ship". Jean Paul had already introduced this device, as we can see in *The Awkward Age*.

III

In conclusion, I would like to come back to the three essential yet non-researched cases of the reception of Jean Paul in Russian culture in the second half of the nineteenth century, which provide insight into the theatrical metaphorics of Jean Paul's literary discourse and its subsequent interpretations.

The theatrical semantics of images pervades Jean Paul's most significant works, which have traditionally been associated with the fundamentals of nihilism at its climaxes in the early nineteenth century, in the 1860s, and at the turn of the twentieth century.[43] It should be recalled that an extended debate was caused by the way nihilism was interpreted by Friedrich Heinrich Jacobi, to whom the term allegedly owns its popularity. Jacobi used the word "nihilism" to describe the theoretical philosophy of Immanuel Kant and the idealism of Johann Gottlieb Fichte (whom he considered to be a convinced Kantian). "Jacobi invented the notion of nihilism, and that was [...] a seminal discovery of his."[44]

Nihilism in Russia had its ideological roots in the German and French interpretations of the notions of "nihilism" and "nihilist". However, the theoretical origins alone cannot explain exactly why the movement was so widespread in Russia in the 1850s–1860s. It is commonly believed to have spread due to the newly emerged milieu of *raznochinets intelligentsia* (intellectuals of various social classes). Having appeared suddenly and in large numbers, *raznochintsy* dissociated themselves from their social roots, shaping the image and worldview of outcasts who broke with their family and social class traditions but never found new ones. At the same time, the fascination with nihilism was a way of fighting for personal identity. Russian critics of the nineteenth century considered Jean Paul to be a pioneer of European nihilism. For example, Belinsky used the word "nihilism" as a synonym of "idealism" when referring to Jean Paul. N. Dobrolyubov in his critical analysis of an 1858 book by Bervi interpreted nihilism as "negation of any real existence" and as a sort of revival of skepticism.

In his article *From the History of "Nihilism"*, the present-day Russian researcher A. Mikhaylov names two of Jean Paul's works among the sources of this intellectual movement, namely *Speech of the Dead Christ from the Universe that There Is No God*, which is a section of his novel *Siebenkäs*, and *Introduction to Aesthetics*, where Jean Paul describes Romantic poetry as "nihilistic". Jean Paul's writing style is very concise in these texts, and his discourse is palpable, rhetorically convincing and suitable for being performed on stage.[45]

---

[43] W. Mueller-Lauter, "Nihilismus", in: *Historisches Wörterbuch der Philosophie*, ed. J. Ritter and K.-F. Gründer, vol. 6, Basel and Stuttgart 1984, pp. 846–853; K. Risenhuber, "Nichts", in: *Handbuch philosophischer Grundbegriffe*, Munich 1973, pp. 991–1008; *Le Petit Robert*, Paris 2001, p. 1152.

[44] A. Mikhaylov, *Jean Paul: Vorschule der Aesthetik*, Moscow 1981, p. 21.

[45] A. Mikhaylov, "Iz istorii 'nigilizma'" [From the History of "Nihilism"], in: A. Mikhaylov, *Obratny perevod* [Reverse Translation], Moscow 2000, pp. 537–627.

Jean Paul's influence on later literature and, in particular, on the ideology of nihilism is unquestionable. However, his ideas were rarely transformed beyond recognition when being transplanted into different literary periods.[46] An unpublished essay, *Jean Paul Richter* by the Russian writer Vsevolod Krestovsky, has been recently discovered in state archives.[47] Krestovsky (1839–1895) was a writer, poet, and literary critic. He is most famous for his novel *The Slums of Saint Petersburg* (1864–1867). Krestovsky was among the first to address criminal issues and the lowest social strata, which he exposed in his novel dramatically in most diverse manifestations, including the ties of the Russian elite of that time with organized crime. This novel about the seemingly refined life of Petersburg and its covert but true life concealed from the public eye constitutes a social portrait of the whole of Russian society. Contemporaries would read the novel avidly, recognizing familiar locations and characters. Reader interest and broad discussion were stimulated by a caper storyline, psychological and realistic accuracy of character description, familiar localities, and convincing sketches of life typical of various social strata.

In his essay *Jean Paul Richter*, written in 1863, Krestovsky investigates *Speech of the Dead Christ from the Universe that There Is No God* to trace optical and acoustic metaphors in Jean Paul's text; the whole scene passionately describing Christ's travel around the universe is interpreted as a polyphony of music and light, a majestic theatrical performance.

> Now a sublime noble figure, bearing an imperishable sorrow, sank down from on high to the altar, and the dead all cried: "Christ! is there no God?"
> He replied: "There is none."
> Each whole shadow of the dead, not only their breasts alone, shook, and one by one they were ripped apart by their quaking.
> Christ went on: "I traversed the worlds, I ascended into the suns, and soared with the Milky Ways through the wastes of heaven; but there is no God. I descended to the last reaches of the shadows of Being, and I looked into the chasm and cried: 'Father, where art thou?' But I heard only the eternal storm ruled by none, and the shimmering rainbow of essence stood without sun to create it, trickling above the abyss. And when I raised my eyes to the boundless world for the divine eye, it stared at me from an empty bottomless

---

[46] N. Kovalev, "Zhan-Pol' i yevropeyskiy nigilizm XIX–XX vekov" [Jean Paul and European Nihilism of the 19th–20th Centuries], in: *Romano-germanskaya filologiya: Konteksty kul'tury i literaturnye svyazi. mezhdunar. sb. nauch. st.* [Romance and Germanic Philology: Cultural Contexts and Literary Connections. International Research Paper Collection], Novopolotsk, pp. 143–145.

[47] V. Krestovsky, *Zhan Pol' Rikhter* [Jean Paul Richter], Russian State Archive of Literature and Art (RGALI), fund 341, series 1, archival unit 514, pp. 1–7 (autograph).

socket; and Eternity lay on Chaos and gnawed it and ruminated itself.—Shriek on, discords, rend the shadows; for He is not!"[48]

This universal drama depicted by Jean Paul is epistemologically described by Krestovsky as the cradle of nihilism, assuming the role of a social masquerade in the Russian and European contexts of that time. Nihilism as theatrical performance, as a theater of masks, can also be observed in the feuilleton chapters of *The Slums of Saint Petersburg*. Thus, Krestovsky's essay devoted to Jean Paul and the study of his theatrical metaphors became a laboratory of thought and imagery for his own novel.

It has been established that Jean Paul's novel *The Awkward Age* has a number of draft versions. These drafts, incidentally, are kept in the archive of the Russian playwright Aleksandr Sukhovo-Kobylin (1817–1903),[49] author of the trilogy *Scenes from the Past*, who considered himself a Russian Hegel. He devoted his life to translating Hegel's works into Russian and later developed a philosophical system of his own. Sukhovo-Kobylin studied in Heidelberg in the 1840s and obtained Jean Paul's documents from Hegel's disciples. He looked up to Jean Paul as his literary mentor and even imitated some of his works in his younger days, especially the novel *Titan* (Sukhovo-Kobylin's drama *Cleon*, a text that remained unpublished, imitated the plot of *Titan*).

N. Minin, the first biographer of Sukhovo-Kobylin, mentions the edition of *Titan* with the playwright's margin notes that he kept in his library.[50]

Sukhovo-Kobylin would refer to Jean Paul's works, especially his novel *Titan*, as his own "preparatory school for aesthetics".[51] No early works of Sukhovo-Kobylin have survived, but his drafts and diaries allow for the reconstruction of his consistent interest in Jean Paul as well as Jean Paul's influence on his

---

[48] The text is an excerpt from *Speech of the Dead Christ from the Universe that There Is No God* (1796), a section from Jean Paul's *Siebenkäs*. This "dream" passage was celebrated throughout Europe at one time, especially when Madame de Staël translated it into French. This translation by E. Casey comes from the anthology *Jean Paul: A Reader*, ed. T. Casey, Baltimore, MD 1992. It is the only English translation of Jean Paul besides the early ones by Thomas Carlyle and others.

[49] Aleksandr Sukhovo-Kobylin, *Nabroski. Chernoviki. Filosofskie sochineniya* [Sketches. Drafts. Philosophical Essays], Russian State Archive of Literature and Art (RGALI), fund 438, series 1, archival unit 1, pp. 2–49.

[50] N. Minin, *Katalog biblioteki Aleksandra Sukhovo-Kobylina* [Catalog of Aleksandr Sukhovo-Kobylin's Library], Manuscript section of the Institute of Russian Literature, fund 186, archival unit 14, p. 47. Sukhovo-Kobylin owned the following edition: Jean Paul [i.e. Paul Friedrich Richter], *Titan*, 4 vols., and *Komischer Anhang zum* Titan, Berlin 1800–1803.

[51] Aleksandr Sukhovo-Kobylin, *Dnevnik: 14 aprelya 1867* [Diary: April 14, 1867], Russian State Archive of Literature and Art (RGALI), fund 438, series 2, archival unit 14, p. 12.

literary and intellectual life. *Titan* and its intrinsic theatrical metaphorics play an exceptionally important role in Sukhovo-Kobylin's reflections. In his margin notes, the playwright points to the abundance of hyperbolae, comparisons, personifications, and similes in Jean Paul's baroque language. Whenever Sukhovo-Kobylin mentions Jean Paul's aesthetics and novels in philosophical, journalistic, or epistolary contexts, he regards him as the "creator of metaphors", invariably using the authentic Greek term μεταφορά in its original Aristotelian meaning, which implies understanding art as imitation, or mimesis, of nature.

Sukhovo-Kobylin describes *Titan* as a "dramatic novel" whose synthetic structure is a melting pot for an array of epochs, from classical antiquity, Renaissance, and the Baroque to the Enlightenment and Romanticism. This conception is captured in his *Vsemir (All-World) Doctrine*, the manuscript of which contains verbatim fragments of *Titan*.[52] Sukhovo-Kobylin's diaries contain various translations of Jean Paul's story *Biographical Recreations under the Brainpan of a Giantess* (1795), which was an important phase in shaping the key masked characters of *Titan*. These translated fragments are used in the drafts of the last play of Sukhovo-Kobylin's trilogy, *The Death of Tarelkin*, as well as in his philosophical utopia *The Vsemir Doctrine*. The story's protagonist, Count Lismore, originally was named Albano (which is the name of Sukhovo-Kobylin's character who presents Jean Paul himself to the Russian reader, bringing his shadow from behind the scenes). Count Lismore, the prototype of the *Titan* character, is represented by Sukhovo-Kobylin as being biographically close to himself, which is manifested in his disgust for the enjoyments of social life.

Another aspect worth attention has to do with the fact that Jean Paul realized more and more that the end of the century meant saying goodbye to the Enlightenment era. That was when he began to develop two new trends in his works, reflecting on the departing year and critically re-evaluating the present and the future. Both trends are embodied in the concept of *Säkulum* (end of century), which acts as a literary code encompassing historical, philosophical, moral, and religious issues of the turning point in history in both retrospective and prospective dimensions. The ideas of "the end of the age", "the end of the world", and the Apocalypse as Judgment Day are developed by Sukhovo-Kobylin in his philosophical sketches and his dramatic trilogy *Scenes from the Past*, particularly the second and third parts, i.e. the plays *The Case* and *The Death of Tarelkin*.

---

52 Aleksandr Sukhovo-Kobylin, *Negelism. Uchenie Vsemira. II tom. Materialy k teme: "Vsemir i ego formula"* [Nihilism. The Vsemir (All-World) Doctrine. Materials on the Topic: Vsemir and Its Formula], Russian State Archive of Literature and Art (RGALI), fund 438, series 1, archival unit 80, p. 27.

Sukhovo-Kobylin felt attached to Jean Paul's aesthetic theory. His drafts of *The Case* contain excerpts from *Preparatory School for Aesthetics* and *Preface* to *Titan*. He literally uses the pieces where Jean Paul talks about form, composition, and narratives. For instance, he introduces a metaphor of theatrical play to the discussion of the principles of creating characters in a novel: "Theatrical mask in my works is not a Greek comedy mask manufactured on the model of someone ridiculed; instead, it is the Nero mask, which resembled his lover when he played a goddess and himself when he played a god."[53] Like Jean Paul, Sukhovo-Kobylin attached great importance to the historical and biographical background of his works. Like Jean Paul, he perceived himself as the "guide", his readers as being "guided", and his works as "the world's free ball".

Dwelling on the problem of discriminating between "historiography" and novel in *Preparatory School for Aesthetics*, Jean Paul reflects on the ratio of truth to fiction in "historiographic" and poetic texts. The writer makes reference to the historiographer Voltaire, "the great poet of the world theater", who called for writing "history by the rules of drama" and articulated his aesthetic postulate accordingly. Since truth is available to neither historian nor novelist, for different reasons, both have to create their own literary truth by means of aesthetic deception. "This truth", wrote Jean Paul, "is a romantic story corresponding to a historical novel". His "true-to-life" portrayal of the contemporary historic processes in the novel format is similar in its structure, disposition of characters, and conflicts to the classicist aesthetics of Enlightenment drama, which brings it close to Voltaire's "historiography". Later, in *Preparatory School for Aesthetics*, Jean Paul would refer to historiography as a type of "dramatic novel". "In the focus of drama", a narrative work is organized as a historical one. As Jean Paul says in *Preface*, in each of his "historical chapters", dubbed *Jobelperioden*, he would like to "provide the reader [...] with multiple ideas— they are the length and mass of time [...], so that short time periods seem long, as the chapter implies".[54] The "mandatory pages" in *Titan*—the satirical excursuses—must be integrated in the novel's plotline, providing the background to

---

[53] Ibid., p. 29.
[54] Sukhovo-Kobylin's drafts and fragments from *Titan* were compared using the following edition: Jean Paul, *Sämtliche Werke: Historisch-kritische Ausgabe*, ed. E. Berend, Weimar 1927ff. and Berlin 1952ff.; Abteilung I: Zu Lebzeiten des Dichters erschienene Werke, Abteilung II: Nachlass, Abteilung III: Briefe. This collection of Jean Paul's complete works was commissioned by the Preussische Akademie der Wissenschaften and carried on, in 1952, by the Deutsche Akademie der Wissenschaften and, later, the Berlin-Brandenburgische Akademie der Wissenschaften. Section ("Abteilung") I, in 19 vols., contains the works published in the poet's lifetime; section II, in 5 vols., is dedicated to the writings Jean Paul left behind unpublished; section III, in 9 vols., collects the letters by Jean Paul. (A fourth section, dedicated to the letters

highlight the main events. Instead of being intricate digressions to readers, those pages must help their understanding of the novel's events through their qualities of freedom and judgment.

> The mandatory pages tell about people who are almost unrelated to my characters; it is not only the extravagant blister of satirical digressions that should be visible on those pages but also the soulful reader and the lector, who walk freely and consciously among historic figures in a courtyard warehouse or in a manège, surrounded by armies, laborious miners and Jews, [...] theater companies, and nevertheless feel undersatisfied.

This fragment was excerpted by the Russian playwright and inserted into his *The Vsemir Doctrine* drafts. Sukhovo-Kobylin's commentary may be boiled down to the following statements:

(i) "Titanism" is one of the pivotal symbolic images in the novel. This borrowing from ancient mythology embodies Jean Paul's paramount idea, which is the main reason for creating this grandiose architectural structure—the idea of synthesis. However, all kinds of interpretations and evaluations are possible, be they elevated, ironical, or harshly satirical.

(ii) The titanic characters form a "carousel", twirling around and reflecting one another like mirrors, destroying one another in a system of mutual annihilation.

   (a) The first "titan" is Gaspard de Cesara, Albano's mentor. The teacher is the most important figure. And, while teaching, he demands a practical approach to the world from his disciple. Gaspard's ambitious aspirations turn to dust, and he ends up as a deceived deceiver run over by the wheel of reality that he had wanted to control.

   (b) Another "titanic" character is that of the librarian Schoppe. Jean Paul sees him as a philosopher and humorist, who annihilates the elevated with his humor. The writer decomposes the "normal", familiar understanding of the world, people, and things, discovering new relations among them, unexpected similarities and analogies between antithetical objects. Jean Paul perceived the world not as harmonious but as chaotic, seeing the abnormal and bizarre as the truth about the mad world, where the "beau-idéal" is nothing but an abstract norm.[55]

   (c) In his letter to Albano, Schoppe imposes a cruel sentence on his age and contemporaries:

---

written *to* Jean Paul, was prepared later; 9 vols. were published from 2003 to 2017). In the following, Roman numerals denote sections, Arabic ones indicate volumes and pages.

55 This character is biographical to some extent (for both Jean Paul and Sukhovo-Kobylin), being an earthbound man full of pungent criticism.

> But, honestly speaking, old pal, this poses the question, what is left for someone (in terms of prospects as well as desires) whose life has been oversalted [...] by the outgoing century, [...] who is equally distressed by everyone's flat hypocrisy, the glittery polish of preserved wood, the disgusting immorality of the German theater of life, the Pontine Marshes of Kotzebue's spoiled and careless sentimentality, which even the Holy Father could not make dry and solid, and the dead pride that neighbors living vanity? That is why the only thing I can observe for hours is children and animals at play, as I am convinced that their love is real and not flirtatious. What, I am asking for the last time, is left for someone who is sick of life, first of all because it is too difficult to make it better and too easy to make it worse? Even the best people make you believe in the evil—with all their elevated ambitions [...], they have to balance between money and honor [...]. What is then left for a human being in an era where black is made, well, not white, but gray and where [...] no feelings can arise except hatred towards the tyrants and slaves at the same time and anger at ill-treatment? And how is someone so tormented by their life supposed to react?[56]

The lonely Schoppe—Sukhovo-Kobylin notes, drawing parallels with his own life—is drawn into the vortex of an intrigue centering around Albano. This scandal drives him mad. He suffers from guilt imposed by society. It is no coincidence, as Sukhovo-Kobylin remarks, that Fichte's mask appears—Fichte's philosophical system was detested by the playwright. He quotes Jean Paul:

> "My Lord", Schoppe said to his friend Albano, "whoever often reads Fichte and his main vicar and servant Schelling from boredom, as I do, finally understands all the gravity. The *I* organizes itself and the rest, referred by many as the world. When philosophers create something, e.g. an idea or themselves, they look like that drunk pal who, having peed into a well, spends a night before that well, waiting for the sound of urine landing to cease and, consequently, takes credit for everything that he hears. The *I* thinks itself, which makes it a pseudo-subject and at the same time the place for storing both the empirical and pure *I*'s. The last thing that mad Swift said shortly before his death was, "*I* is me, philosophically enough!"[57]

Schoppe's reflections on alienating human beings from their human self and turning from alive to dead may be considered the chief motif in the historiosophy and theatrical world of Sukhovo-Kobylin, which is evidenced in the fragment that the playwright purposefully wrote out and translated:

> I look at the epoch from all the sides and I smile. I have nothing to say: people are folded as a napkin on a plate into the most diverse and whimsical shapes—a nightcap, a pyramid, [...]. And the outcome, old pal? Oh Lord, the outcome? I have nothing to say, dang me...

---

56 Jean Paul, *Sämtliche Werke*, I, 5, p. 235.
57 Sukhovo-Kobylin, *Nabroski. Chernoviki. Filosofskie sochineniya*, p. 19.

(d) The most significant character for Sukhovo-Kobylin is Roquelaure, whose name is transcribed as a reference to the travel raincoat invented by Henry IV, one of the favorite clothing items of the playwright, who left Russia almost for good after 1862. Commenting on the play *A Tragic* written by Roquelaure, Sukhovo-Kobylin spots parallels with his own grotesque character Tarelkin, who also deliberately plays his own death on stage. The end of Roquelaure in the structure of the "dramatic novel" is double, both in the novel and in the play. While the macrostructure of his five-act drama reproduces the key elements of the novel—Jean Paul's grand master plan of making his novel a collision of life and art—the last act depicts the death of Roquelaure himself. Wearing the mask of Albano, he must seduce Linda, who suffers from night-blindness. "That would easily come to my mind in a poetic work, but never in real life!" he says. "Yes, this is brilliant, only a great tragic actor can do it [...]," he said [...] Tarelkin, for his part, wears the mask of a deceased functionary to find out dark secrets, bring discredit upon his boss and get the money.

The novel's reality, aesthetically transposed to *A Tragic*, reveals its contradictory aspects just as the distorting mirror of art reflects the lives of Roquelaure and other characters in the novel and Sukhovo-Kobylin's trilogy reflects his own life.

In *Preparatory School for Aesthetics*, Jean Paul describes the form of his novels as "dramatic", the structure of narration and the disposition of characters and conflicts being largely determined by the classicist method of Enlightenment drama, which brings it close to the historiography of Voltaire, who urged historians to create "history by the rules of drama". Jean Paul tried to cement the "disconnected prose" with a "certain rigor of form". "Such a form", he explains, "lends passionate maturity to scenes, a modern touch to words, an agonizing suspense and poignancy to characters and the motive, power to the intrigue, etc.". Sukhovo-Kobylin considered his trilogy *Scenes form the Past* to be a dramatic novel.

Finally, the last thing to mention is that the Russian theatrical producer Vsevolod Meyerhold translated Jean Paul's works, *The Awkward Age* and *Siebenkäs* in particular, but those translations have never been published. Some of his draft essays on Jean Paul's poetics have survived, in which he points to the theatrical imagery of his writing style and the special expressive ability of the "dark spots". As is known, Meyerhold staged a constructivist-biomechanical version of Sukhovo-Kobylin's tragical farce *The Death of Tarelkin* in 1922, in which he intended to use fragments from Jean Paul's novels *Die unsichtbare*

Loge (1793), *Hesperus oder 45 Hundsposttage*, and *Titan*, translated by Meyerhold himself and mentioned in Sukhovo-Kobylin's diaries.[58]

As we can see, the theatrical metaphorics of Jean Paul Richter's philosophical and literary works have made their way into other genres as well as other historical and cultural contexts.

---

58 Sukhovo-Kobylin's play *The Death of Tarelkin* was staged by Meyerhold at the GITIS Meyerhold Workshop; see Russian State Archive of Literature and Art (RGALI), fund 998, series I, archival unit 146.

Tatiana Smoliarova
Theatrical Metaphor and the Discourse of History: Nikolai Karamzin

Of the various examples provided by dictionaries to illustrate the notion of metaphor, the two that come up most often are both related to theater: the indispensable Shakespeare's "all the world's a stage" and the anonymous poeticism "the curtain of night fell upon us." As observed by R. Tronstad in her small, yet wonderfully rich and subtle article "Could the World Become a Stage? Theatricality and Metaphorical Structures", theater as a form of art and metaphor as a figure of speech share at least one important feature: they each require both similarity and difference, identity and non-identity at the same time. Neither theater nor metaphor exists without a gap—between the two meanings merged in a third one in the case of metaphor, or between the real and imaginary world in the case of theater.[1] This may explain, if only in part, a certain affinity between the two.

Boris Pasternak's "Remarks on Translations from Shakespeare" (1956) contains one of the best definitions of metaphor ever given:

> The use of metaphor is a natural consequence of the shortness of man's life and the vastness of his tasks planned for a long time ahead. Because of this discrepancy he is obliged to look at things with eagle-eyed keenness and to explain himself in momentary, instantly understandable flashes of illumination. This is what poetry *is*. The use of metaphor is the stenography of a great personality, the shorthand of the spirit. The tempestuous vitality of Rembrandt's, Michelangelo's, Titian's brush is not the result of deliberate choice. Assailed, each one of them, by a stormy, insatiable thirst to draw the entire universe, they had no time for other kinds of drawing.[2]

It is no coincidence that Pasternak came up with this definition so late in life, when his own sense of the discrepancy between "the shortness of man's life and the vastness of his tasks" was particularly acute. It is also no coincidence that this rare, if not unique, theoretical reflection on metaphor in Pasternak's (thoroughly metaphorical) oeuvre emerged as a "remark on translation" from Shakespeare, namely his reflections on translating *Hamlet* (1941) and *Macbeth* (1951).

---

[1] R. Tronstad, "Could the World Become a Stage? Theatricality and Metaphorical Structures", in: *Substance*, vol. 31, Special Issue: Theatricality, 2002, pp. 216–224.
[2] Boris Pasternak, "Remarks on Translations from Shakespeare", in: *The Marsh of Gold: Pasternak's Writings on Inspiration and Creation*, ed. and tr. A. Livingstone, Boston, MA 2008, p. 90.

Shakespeare's "all the world's a stage" belongs to the "absolute metaphors", in H. Blumenberg's terminology, or to the "metaphors we live by", in G. Lakoff and M. Johnson's.[3] It is one of the metaphors that seem "so natural and so persuasive in our thought that they are usually taken as self-evident".[4] A little less evident and hence less abused, although also nearly embedded in everyday language and thinking, is the metaphor of life as a walking shadow from the fifth act of *Macbeth* ("Out, out, brief candle! / Life's but a walking shadow, a poor player / That struts and frets his hour upon the stage / And then is heard no more" [V.5.23–26]). Most likely, this image goes back to the last surviving ode by Pindar, *Pythian 8*, composed and performed shortly before the poet's death: "Man's life is a day. What is he? / What is he not? A shadow in a dream / Is man" (ll. 95–98).

We will return to the distant echoes of both Pindar and Shakespeare, shadows of shadows, soon. For now, the general question that arises concerns the oscillating relevance of theatrical metaphors. The world's always a stage, yet the acuity and freshness of the perception that it is one varies from one era to the next. When and why do we need theatrical metaphors? Can we trace the logic and rhythm in their *entrances* and *exits* (to remain in the same metaphorical field)? Which forms, types, and genres of theater come to the forefront as *vehicles* for the same (or, possibly different) *tenors*, to use the terms coined by I. A. Richards in *The Philosophy of Rhetoric* (1936)?[5] For it is obvious that Aristotelian tragedy, observing the unities of space, time, and place, will not serve the same metaphorical goals as Shakespearean drama, or the various forms of theater based on the aesthetics of *tableaux*, in which one stage-picture follows another with little attempt to connect them.[6]

"Narration is created by conceptual thought", wrote O. Freidenberg, Pasternak's cousin and lifetime correspondent, in her posthumously published book *Image and Concept: Mythopoetic Roots of Literature*. "Conceptual thought leads to the proposition of goal, cause, condition, which move the plot forward and fill it with connections to real processes, presents dependence and leads to certain results. A 'picture' cannot portray the ideas 'if,'

---

3 H. Blumenberg, *Paradigms for a Metaphorology*, tr. R. Savage, Ithaca, NY 2010; G. Lakoff and M. Johnson, *Metaphors We Live By*, Chicago, IL 1980.
4 Lakoff and Johnson, *Metaphors*, p. 28.
5 I. A. Richards, *Philosophy of Rhetoric*, New York, NY 1936.
6 On the general shift towards the aesthetics of tableaux in the European theater in the late eighteenth century see: P. Frants, *L'esthétique du tableau dans le théâtre du XVIIIe siècle*, Paris 1998.

'when,' 'so that,' 'because,' etc.; speech, however, creates with these expressions a logically developed story."[7]

I would suggest that the turns of centuries, with their sudden disturbances in the hundreds or the thousand columns, with their distinctive anxieties, from the medieval anticipation of the end of the world to the unforgettable Y2K (the virtual end of the computer world expected in the year 2000, whose failure to materialize links it with other millennial apocalypses) seem to be particularly welcoming circumstances for the use of theatrical metaphors. The turn of the century weakens "conceptual thought"; history moves away from complex and compound sentences to sentences without conjunctions. The sense of discontinuity in time, the tenuous quality of the fabric of life, and the unreliability of the world require a correspondingly fragmented form of expression. For this reason, at the turn of centuries and in times of social upheaval the "metaphoric weight" falls on what in other times are marginal, secondary theatrical genres, such as melodrama, the puppet-theater, or optical shows like the magic lantern or shadow plays.

This is why we are not surprised to find distant echoes of both Pindar's and Shakespeare's lines in John O'Keefe's comic opera *The Dead Alive, or the Double Funeral*, composed in the momentous year 1789, just across the Channel from Revolutionary France. Looking at his (allegedly) dead mistress, a servant first speaks—and then begins to sing—the following lines:

> The world is all nonsense and noise.
> Fantoccini or Ombres Chinoises,
> Mere pantomime mummery;
> Puppet-show flummery:
> A magical lanthorn confounding the sight.—
> Like players or puppets we move,
> On the wires of ambition and love,
> The poets write wittily,
> Maidens look prettily,
> Till death drops the curtain—all's over—good night.[8]

---

[7] O. Freidenberg, *Image and Concept: Mythopoetic Roots of Literature*, tr. K. Moss, ed. N. Braginskaia, Amsterdam 1997, p. 90. An eminent classical philologist, Freidenberg (1890–1955) was persecuted by the Soviet authorities. A great deal of her abundant scholarly heritage, in many ways foreshadowing later developments in Cultural Studies, was discovered, studied, and published by N. Braginskaia. Her theory of mythopoetical thinking largely revolves around the notion of a movement from image to concept, from myth to metaphor.

[8] John O'Keefe, *The Dead Alive: or The Double Funeral. A comic opera. In two acts. With additions and alterations. As performed by the Old American Company*, in New-York: with universal applause, New-York 1789.

All the performances catalogued in O'Keefe's lines—Chinese shadows and magic lanterns, Fantoccini silhouettes and wire-controlled marionettes—seem to share the same principle of discontinuity, the same lack of "if, when, so that, and because", in Freidenberg's words. Of course, the succession of pictures in an optical or puppet show may be subject to a certain narrative sequence, but may just as well be completely unmotivated and brought together solely by the "Et voici, et voilà" exclamations of their masters—puppeteers, lanternists, and other itinerant "Savoyards". At most of these shows, one is unable to predict what will come next.

The unprecedented dissemination of magic lanterns during the French Revolution furthered the wide-ranging scope of the shows and developed their satirical and propagandistic tendencies. These tendencies gave rise to the appearance in France in the early 1790s of works of a particular, paraliterary genre, whose roots can be traced to both literary and oral traditions—that is, the "printed lanterns", political satires, and pamphlets of the revolutionary and post-revolutionary years. Presented in the form of magic lantern libretti, they either told the story of the revolution as a whole or concentrated on its significant episodes and figures—as if they were to be read by magic lantern operators, explaining the content of the show to the audience. The title of each brochure carried the obligatory phrase "magic lantern" in connection with an attributive (*La lanterne magique de* ...) and almost always the subtitle "pièce curieuse". Some of these "amusing pieces" may indeed have been coupled with images in an actual magic lantern show, but the majority of the so-called scenarios were actually literary or, to be more precise, journalistic works. In them, the conceit of the "magic lantern" was used to motivate a suspension of the usual principles of literary composition, replacing the expected emphasis on cause and effect or coordination and subordination with the random arrangement of images typical of the optical show.

This association of magic lanterns with the French Revolution was famously canonized by Edmund Burke in his *Reflections on the Revolution in France* (1790) and developed almost half a century later into the idea of *phantasmagoria*—one of the key concepts of Thomas Carlyle's *The French Revolution: A History* (1837). According to Louis— Sébastien Mercier, we owe the very word *fantasmagoria* (originally spelled with an "f"), the optical show that it describes, and the philosophical and historical ideas associated with it, to Etienne-Gaspard Robert, better known as E.-G. Robertson.[9] A former professor of

---

9 Mercier writes the following in *Néologie*, his wonderful dictionary of the "new words of the new century": "Fantasmagoria is an optical game that presents to our gaze the battle

Optics and Physics from Liège, Robertson conquered the Revolutionary "tout Paris" with his optical shows, an important step in the history of the "pre-cinema".[10]

It is precisely at this phantasmagoric moment that Nikolai Karamzin, the future author of the first full-fledged history of Russia, then a twenty-four-year-old traveler, avid learner, and a "young Scythian", as he liked to call himself, spent four months in Paris. Important as it was for a Russian traveler in general and for Karamzin in particular, the French capital was not supposed to become either the main destination of his *Grand Tour* or the emotional focus of the *Letters of a Russian Traveler,* the literary account of the trip, but history altered his plans.

Karamzin's "active observation" of the French Revolution, his shifting views of it (shared with so many, and consisting of initial enthusiasm, subsequent consternation and despair, and ultimate ambivalence); the significant cuts and changes to the thirty-three letters dedicated to Paris in the *Letters of a Russian Traveler* between 1791 and 1801—these topics have been thoroughly studied, and we are not going to address them now.[11] What is important for us, though, is how theatrical metaphors, which acquired the status of *topoi* in the Age of Revolution, shaped Karamzin's thoughts about history as he was conceiving and composing the texts that preceded, foreshadowed, or accompanied his magnum opus, *The History of the Russian State* (1803–26).

---

between life and shadow, at the same time dethroning the old tricks of the priests. [...] These illusions created by masters of phantoms amuse the ignorant and cause the philosopher to fall to thinking [...] O specter! O illusoriness! Who are you? What are you?" (*Néologie; ou, Vocabulaire de mots nouveaux, à renouveler, ou pris dans des acceptions nouvelles,* Paris 1801, pp. 259–60). On the metaphorical sense of the word and its history, see T. Castle, "Phantasmagoria: Spectral Technology and the Metaphorics of Modern Reverie", in: *Critical Inquiry,* vol. 15, 1988, pp. 26–61.

10 The striking figure of E.-G. Robertson has become ever better known and studied in recent years. The spectral images of fantasmagoria occupy the chief place among the "turn-of-the-century" theatrical metaphors. I refer the reader to M. Heard, *Phantasmagoria: The Secret Life of the Magic Lantern,* Hastings 2006, and the chapter on Robertson, his lanterns, and their reception in Russia in my book *Three Metaphors for Life: Derzhavin's Late Poetry,* Brighton, MA 2018.

11 According to Yu. Lotman, of all the Russians who happened to be in Paris in 1789–1790, Karamzin was the one most frequently present at the Assembléé Nationale, the Convent, and other major revolutionary "stages" (*Sotvorenie Karamzina,* Moscow 1987). Cf. also I. Serman, "Kul'tura i svoboda v 'Pis'makh Russkogo Puteshestvennika' Karmazina", in: *La Revue russe,* vol. 12, 1997, pp. 19–28; L. Kisljagina, "The Question of the Development of N. M. Karamzin's Social Political Views in the Nineties of the Eighteenth Century: N. M. Karamzin and the Great French Bourgeois Revolution", in: *Essays on Karamzin: Russian Man of Letters, Political Thinker, Historian, 1766–1826,* ed. J. L. Black, The Hague and Paris 1975, pp. 91–104.

Letters of a Russian Traveler first appeared serially in the *Moscow Journal*, the periodical Karamzin published for about two years upon his return from Europe, until the burden of serving as its sole editor wore him out. At the point when the *Moscow Journal* folded, the letters that deal with revolutionary Paris had not yet been published.[12] As a separate edition, the *Letters* appeared in two "portions"— in 1797 and in 1801. Here is what the final version of letter 98 says about the Revolution:

> Do not think, however, that the entire nation has been participating in the tragedy that is now being played out in France. Hardly a hundredth part is active: all the others watch, judge, argue, weep or laugh, clap or whistle, as in the theatre [...] This story has not ended yet.[13]

We find another variation on the theatrical theme in Karamzin's famous (nominally anonymous) note, known as "A Word on Russian Literature" ("Un mot sur la littérature russe"), written in French for the Hamburg émigré periodical *Spectateur du Nord*, and also published in 1797:

> The French Revolution belongs to that type of manifestation which decides the fate of humanity for many centuries to come. A new epoch is beginning. I see this, and Rousseau foresaw it [...] One event replaces another, like waves of a stormy sea; and people want to view the Revolution as already completed. No, no. We will see many astonishing phenomena. [...] But now I draw the curtain. ["Non! Non! On verra encore bien de choses étonnantes [...] Je tire le rideau."][14]

"It was there that he met History", Yu. Lotman wrote about Karamzin's 1790 sojourn in Paris.[15] In Lotman's otherwise unembellished writing style, which carefully skirts the loquacious and the pathetic, this phrase stands out as overtly metaphorical, not so different from "all the world's a stage". Moreover, these two metaphors could be merged together, for what Karamzin was exposed to in May–June 1790 (according to the *Letters'* ambiguous, somewhat distorted chronology) was both the *Stage of the World*, stirred up by revolutionary turmoil, and the

---

12 The last letter published in the *Moscow Journal* was dated 27 March 1790 and "sent" from Paris.
13 Nikolai Karamzin, *Letters of a Russian Traveller: A Translation with an Essay on Karamzin's Discourses of Enlightenment*, tr. and ed. A. Kahn, Oxford 2003, p. 264.
14 Nikolai Karamzin, "A Few Words about Russian Literature" [A Letter to the *Spectateur du Nord* about Russian Literature]", in: *The Literature of Eighteenth-Century Russia*, ed. H. B. Segel, vol. 1, New York, NY 1967, p. 438.
15 Yu. Lotman, "Kolumb Rossijskoi Istorii", in: Nikolai Karamzin, *Istorija Gosudarstva Rossiiskogo*, vol. 4, Moscow 1988, p. 5.

overwhelming *World of the Stage*—the countless Parisian theaters, a detailed account of which the *Russian Traveller* gives in letter 100, one of the longest in the book:

> Since my arrival in Paris I had spent every evening without exception at the theater and had yet to observe twilight [...] A whole month spent daily at the theater! And still not to have had my fill either of Thalia's laugh or the Melpomene's tears... And to enjoy these delights with a new sensation every time. Surprising, and yet true [...] the theatres here are perfect, each in its own way, and [...] every aspect of performance forms a lovely harmony, which affects the heart of the viewer in the most pleasant way possible.[16]

If someone goes to the theater every single night for several months in a row, this cannot help but permeate his language and affect the way he perceives the world. Hence it is no wonder that theatergoing becomes the framework into which the historical events that Karamzin's narrator witnessed were inevitably set. Theater and politics form an "equilateral" metaphor of sorts, continually trading off the roles of tenor and vehicle.[17]

In his vast panorama of the theatrical life of Paris in *Letter 100*, the Russian Traveler fails to mention one theater, the shows of which, according to Lotman's comprehensive commentary, Karamzin almost certainly attended: the Theater of Chinese Shadows (*Théâtre des Ombres Chinoises*). Founded and made famous by François Séraphin in the early 1780s, first located in Versailles and then in the Palais-Royal, in 1790 the Theater of Chinese Shadows moved to the Boulevard du Temple. Lotman suggests that Karamzin's silence on this point may merely confirm the symbolic status of the shadow in his depiction of the world: the author's experience became so thoroughly internalized that a vivid impression was transformed into a recurrent metaphor, "one of Karamzin's favorites in both his thinking and language". We find it, among other places, in the closing lines of the *Letters'* final version (1801):

> And you, my dears, quickly ready for me a tidy little cottage where I will be free to amuse myself with the *Chinese shadows* of my imagination, to let my heart grieve and to find comfort in friends! [italics in the original, TS]

---

16 Karamzin, *Letters of a Russian Traveler*, p. 268. This letter first appeared in the almanac *Aglaia*, published by Karamzin, in 1795.

17 On Karamzin's theatergoing at the time of the Revolution and its metaphorical potential see M. Stemberger, "Karamzine dans les théâtres de France: théâtre, théâtralité et révolution dans les *Lettres d'un voyageur russe*", in: *Karamzine en France: L'image de la France dans les "Lettres d'un voyageur russe"*, ed. R. Baudin, Paris 2014, pp. 174–191.

As has been observed and discussed by several scholars, Karamzin's frequent use of the optical metaphor of the "Chinese Shadows" in the writings of the 1790s was largely inspired by his interest in Socratic and Platonic philosophy and connected with Plato's *Allegory of the Cave*, the "hyper image" of European Culture (to use W. T. Mitchell's expression).[18] Yet it seems that there is another, less evident connection between Plato's *Republic* and our present subject.

Let us go back several pages in *The Republic*, towards the end of book 6. It is here that Plato lays out his theory of sight, where a crucial role is (quite naturally) allotted to sunlight. It is the Sun that makes sight possible and elicits the intelligible from the visible; it is sunlight that lets us approach—perhaps even grasp—the Forms. We find a variation of this theory in Karamzin's article "Something about the Sciences, Art, and Enlightenment" (1793), devoted to polemics with the postrevolutionary defamation of knowledge (and in particular with certain views of Jean-Jacques Rousseau). Karamzin argues that man

> collects endless ideas or notions that are nothing but the immediate reflections of objects and which rush into his soul with no order, but soon a magic force emerges, which we call Reason, and which was only awaiting the sensuous impressions to begin its own action. Like a radiant Sun, it illuminates the chaos of ideas, divides and combines them, finds similarities and differences between them, relationships, the particular and the general, and produces the abstract ideas that comprise Knowledge.[19]

This reinterpretation of John Locke's epistemology leads to the main question that confronted Karamzin throughout the last decade of the eighteenth century, as he pondered the chief project of his life (Karamzin declared his intention to consecrate himself to the *History* in 1793, when the article on Sciences and Art was written, i.e., ten years before Alexander I appointed him court historian). How was he going to organize the tableaux of Russian history, "floating in disarray before his mind's eye" (as he admitted in one of the letters to his friend and correspondent Ivan Dmitriev)?[20] How to connect these "moving

---

18 A. Cross, *N. M. Karamzin: A Study of His Literary Career, 1783–1803*, Carbondale, IL 1971, p. 17; T. Page, "Karamzin's Immoralist Count NN or Three Hermeneutical Games of 'Chinese Shadows'", in: *The Slavic and East European Journal*, vol. 29, 1985, pp. 144–156.
19 Nikolai Karamzin, "Nechto o naukah, iskusstvah i Prosveshenii", in: Nikolai Karamzin, *Izbrannye Sochinenia v dvukh tomakh* [Selected Works in 2 vols.], vol. 2, Moscow and Leningrad 1964, pp. 132f. The article was first published in the first issue of the almanac *Aglaia* (1794).
20 In a similar way, publishing his prose fragment "Tale" in 1929 (the original title of which was "Revolution" [!]), Pasternak wrote: "Fragments of this story have been flashing before me for ten years, and at the beginning of the Revolution, some of them made it into print. [...] [B]etween the

images"? How could he simultaneously observe and avoid chronology? What might take the place of the simple linear sequence of a chronicle?

Even in 1802, just a year before being appointed at court, Karamzin represents Russian history as a defile of isolated images in his note "On Events and Characters in Russian History that are Possible Subjects of Art: A Letter to NN". Published the same year in the *Messenger of Europe*, "Events and Characters" was originally addressed to and compiled at the request of Count Alexander Stroganov, the new president of the Academy of Fine Arts.[21] In 1801 Stroganov amended the existing Statute of the Academy with a supplement suggesting that the students of the Academy should be offered a number of "patriotic" subjects for their paintings. Karamzin was the first to respond to this initiative.

> If a historical character is presented strikingly on canvas or in marble, it makes even the chronicles more interesting for us: we are curious to find out from which source the artist got his inspiration, and with great attention we read the description of the man's deeds, recalling what a lively impression he has made on us.[22]

The moments suggested by Karamzin as "lending themselves as subjects of artistic representation" are fully in line with the definition of the "historical statement" that R. Barthes formulated in his highly influential article "The Discourse of History" ("Le Discours de l'histoire" [1967]):

> The historical statement must lend itself to a figuration destined to produce units of content, which we can subsequently classify. These units of content represent what history *speaks about*; as signifiers, they are neither pure referent nor complete discourse: their totality is constituted by the referent discerned, named, already intelligible, but not yet subjected to a syntax.[23] [author's italics]

---

novel in verse known as *Spektorsky*, which was begun later, and this prose there will be no disparity: it's all the same life."
21 Nikolai Karamzin, "On Events and Characters in Russian History that are Possible Subjects of Art", in: Segel (ed.), *Literature of Eighteenth-Century Russia*, vol. 1, pp. 459–469. The text was first published in the *Messenger of Europe*, no. 24, 1802.
22 Ibid., p. 459.
23 R. Barthes, "The Discourse of History", in: R. Barthes, *The Rustle of Language*, tr. R. Howard, New York, NY 1989, pp. 127–140, p. 133. In the French original this phrase provides slightly different visual associations. Barthes talks about the "découpage destiné à produire des unités du contenu". The affinities between "The Discourse of History" and Karamzin's *Foreword* to his *History of the Russian State* (*Istorija Gosudarstva Rossiiskogo*)—an English translation of which is available, for example, in *Russian Intellectual History: An Anthology*, ed. M. Raeff, New York, NY 1966, pp. 117–124—are amazing. Not only do both authors distinguish among three kinds of historical discourse (and these classifications, made one hundred

Selecting these units is the first, analytical step, to be followed by various synthetic—and syntactic—operations. It seems that Karamzin responded to Stroganov's request so enthusiastically because in the early 1800s the proper "discourse of history" and especially its *syntax* were still to be defined. Before a suitable organizing principle is found, the "pictorial units" are arranged according to the "Magic Lantern principle"—like slides pulled from a wooden box by the skillful hand of the Master of the Show. This very arrangement bears a metaphorical meaning.[24]

The (partly feigned) randomness of the connections between the "slides" of the "Events and Characters" is somewhat undermined by associations and symbolic equations projecting one epoch onto another (to give just one example, Karamzin calls the Kievan Prince Sviatoslav [942–972], known for his well-planned military campaigns, "the ancient Suvorov"). The same principle of distant echoes, situation rhymes, and other forms of poetic parallelism among the epochs would become one of the unifying tropes of the *History*. Here is what Karamzin writes in the *Foreword*, his *profession de foi*, begun as early as 1803, not published until 1818 (when the first eight volumes of the *History* were, as Karamzin put it, "served out"), and dated 7 December 1815:

> The reader will notice that I do not describe events one at a time, by years and days, but combine them so that they may be more readily imprinted on the memory. The historian is not a chronicler. The latter considers only chronology, whereas the former is concerned with the nature of events and their interrelations; he may make mistakes in the allocation of space, but he should allocate its proper place to everything.[25]

Needless to say, Karamzin's choice of the "Events and Characters" is in fact quite consistent. The staginess and intense dramatic quality of all the *tableaux*

---

fifty years apart, are essentially the same); sometimes their statements coincide almost verbatim: "Like natural history, human history does not tolerate fictions; it presents only what is or was, but not what *might have been*" (ibid., p.121); "[...] the status of historical discourse is uniformly assertive, constative; historical fact is linguistically linked to a privilege of being: one recounts what has been, not what has not been or what has been questionable" (p. 135).

24 Commenting on the role of the magic lantern in the narrative structure of Marcel Proust's *À la recherche du temps perdu*, M. Riffaterre writes, "The magic lantern [...] belongs in the grammar [of the narrative]. [...] [It] displays no image that appears immediately metaphorical per se. Instead, the magic lantern signifies a function, the projection of the self onto the other. It signifies [...] *as syntax signifies*" ("On Narrative Subtexts: Proust's Magic Lantern", in: *Style*, vol. 22, 1988, pp. 450–466, p. 453).

25 Karamzin, *Foreword*, pp. 122–123.

stand out: each "performance" is chosen to show a certain historical scene at a moment when the heat of passion is at its highest.²⁶ Nothing irreversible has happened yet, but it is just about to take place. This, for instance, is how he renders one of the most emblematic scenes in Old Russian history—the death of the tenth-century Russian ruler Prince Oleg of Novgorod, from a snakebite:

> Oleg, the conqueror of the Greeks, with his historic character, can inspire the imagination of a painter [...] I would portray Oleg at the moment he kicks the skull, an expression of scorn on his face; the snake sticks his head out, but has *not yet* stung him: the expression of pain in a heroic face is unpleasant. Behind him stand soldiers with Greek trophies as a sign of their conquest. At a certain distance one could present the old wizard, who looks at Oleg meaningfully.²⁷

In avoiding "the expression of pain in a heroic face" and choosing open-ended ("not yet") situations, Karamzin seems to be in keeping with the precepts of Gotthold Ephraim Lessing, whose *Laokoon Revisited,* one of the pivotal texts in the history of European aesthetics, appeared in 1766, the year of Karamzin's birth.

For Lessing, a choice of a single moment that should "metonymically" stand in for the rest of the story is the only way to reconcile the contradiction between verbal and visual mediums:

> Since the artist can use but a single moment of ever-changing nature, and the painter must further confine his study of this one moment to a single point of view, while their works are made not simply to be looked at, but to be contemplated long and often, evidently the most fruitful moment (*der prägnanteste Augenblick*) and the most fruitful aspect of that moment must be chosen. Not that only is fruitful which allows free play to the imagination. The more we see the more we must be able to imagine; and the more we imagine, the more we must think we see. But no moment in the whole course of an action is so disadvantageous in this respect as that of its culmination. There is nothing beyond, and to present the uttermost to the eye is to bind the wings of Fancy.²⁸

"Pregnant moments" have the potential of being resolved in many different ways. Karamzin is all the more sensitive to Lessing's theory that it lets him restore to history, if only in part, the subjunctive mood allegedly so foreign to it.²⁹ The very "expositions" that he chooses for the *Events and Characters* are

---

26 The dramatic composition of the scenes described by Karamzin becomes particularly striking when juxtaposed with the static, monumental nature of Mikhail Lomonosov's selection of "Ideas for Artistic Scenes from Russian History" (1764), a much earlier work pursuing a similar goal.
27 Karamzin, "Events in Russian History", p. 461.
28 Gotthold Ephraim Lessing, *Laokoon Revisited*, 2005, pp. 16–17.
29 Karamzin, "Events and Characters", pp. 459–469.

metaphors of sorts, where the "pregnant moments" serve as vehicles and the tenor is history viewed as an array of both realized and non-realized possibilities, a series of cruxes, of roads taken and not.[30]

Lessing then proceeds to discuss specific examples from antiquity and focuses on the art of Timomachus, who, among the old painters, "seems to have been the one most fond of choosing extremes for his subject":

> He did not paint Medea at the moment of her actually murdering her children, but just before, when motherly love is still struggling with jealousy. We anticipate the result and tremble at the idea of soon seeing Medea in her unmitigated ferocity, our imagination far outstripping anything the painter could have shown us of that terrible moment. For that reason her prolonged indecision, so far from displeasing us, makes us wish it had been continued in reality. We wish this conflict of passions had never been decided or had lasted at least till time and reflection had weakened her fury and secured the victory to the maternal sentiments.

Even if we have much less pity for Prince Vladimir, about to be killed by Rogneda (also known as Goreslava, 962–1002), the wife he first raped and then abandoned, than for Medea's poor children, Karamzin's suggestions on how to tell this famous story and to represent Rogneda's "prolonged indecision" seem to follow Lessing's advice quite straightforwardly:

> For the last time he visits her and falls asleep in her chamber: Rogneda takes the knife— but delays—and the prince, awaking, tears the deadly weapon from her trembling hands [...] I see the unfortunate Goreslava inclined by her heart, her night clothing in disarray, and hair disheveled. The room is illuminated by a night lamp, one can see only the plainest decorations and the carved image of Perun standing in a corner. Vladimir has risen from his bed and holds in his hand the knife...[31]

---

30 In his very last work, "The Truth as Lie" (known as "On Gogol's Realism" in Russian), dictated to his colleagues several months before his death, Yu. Lotman discusses the "three-dimensionality" of the literary space in Gogol: "Life never developed in a linear direction for Gogol. It was, as it were, an endless bundle of possible probabilities. The more closely Gogol tried to approach reality (at that time, 'reality' [*deistivtel'nost'*] was a new word that had just come into fashion), the more the potential variety of its unrealized possibilities would unfold before him; each of these possibilities was just as 'real' as those that happened in life itself [...] It is as if Gogol's thinking is three-dimensional; it always entails the proposition, 'But what if things happened another way...?' In general, this 'what if' is the basis of what is usually called 'fantasy' in Gogol's work" ("The Truth as Lie", in: *Gogol: Exploring Absence*, ed. S. Spieker, Bloomington, IN 2000, pp. 35–36). This thought can be extrapolated to Karamzin—the lifetime "protagonist" of Lotman's thinking and writing—for his dynamic, "three-dimensional" vision of history, a compressed preview of which is given in the "Events and Characters", can also be described as an "endless bundle of possible probabilities".

31 Karamzin, "Events and Characters", p. 464.

The Caravaggesque presentation of Rogneda's room, the very chiaroscuro suggested to potential artists, can be seen as a realization of one of the key metaphors of Karamzin's "historical emotion" (to use B. Eikhenbaum's expression).[32] Explaining his preference for *remote* history, Karamzin repeatedly talks about twilight, about the play of light and shadow:

> Not allowing myself any invention, I have sought for expression in my own mind, but for ideas only in the sources [...] I wished to unify what has been handed down to us by centuries into a system clear and coherent in the harmonious correlation of its parts [...] Making an exhaustive study of the materials on the remotest history of Russia, I was cheered by the thought that there is some inexplicable fascination for our imagination in a narrative about distant times—there are the sources of poetry! Contemplating open space, does not our glance usually dart past everything that is near and clear, to the horizon's end, where the shadows grow thick and dark and the impenetrable begins?[33]

In 1815, the same year to which the *Foreword* is dated, Karamzin wrote a letter to Grand Duchess Ekaterina Pavlovna, who had always been one of his main supporters and who suggested that Karamzin should also address and explore recent history: "History, modest and solemn, loves the silence of passions and tombs, remoteness and twilight, and of all the grammatical tenses it is most of all the past perfect that beseems it. The rapid movement and noise of the present, the closeness of the subjects and too bright a light tend to embarrass her."[34]

In his book *Spatial History* (2013) M. Iampolsky claims that it was, among other things, the theory of chiaroscuro, developed by Roger de Piles at the turn of the seventeenth and eighteenth centuries, that marked the emancipation of painting from the centuries-old bondage of *Ut Pictura Poesis*, a rejection of the rhetorically constructed argument, and a move towards the self-sufficient rhetoric of the image (and *coloris* as its utmost manifestation). The mastery of chiaroscuro allows the artist (Rubens was de Piles' favorite example) to transform a multiplicity of objects into a single one, marks the shift from the chronological sequence, unfolding in time, to the whole, unfolding in space. This is somewhat similar to the process of "aestheticization" that

---

[32] B. Eikhenbaum, "Karamzin", in: B. Eikhenbaum, *Skvoz' Literaturu*, Leningrad 1924, pp. 37–49. This essay, first published in 1916, written in commemoration of the 150th anniversary of Karamzin's birth, is one of three major articles by Eikhenbaum (the other two were dedicated to the poets Gavrila Derzhavin and Feodor Tiutchev) that explore the particular kind of *artistic knowledge* possessed by each author.
[33] Karamzin, *Foreword*, p. 122.
[34] Karamzin, *Neizdannyje Sochinenija i perepiska*, vol. 1, St. Petersburg 1862, p. 119.

history undergoes in the eighteenth century: it changes from *Historie* into *Geschichte*, from a verbal sequence to a painterly (and, hence, theatrically organized) space.[35] In this way we may say that chiaroscuro is not just one of the "stage effects" of Karamzin's theater of history, but also a necessary condition of his historical vision, moving from continuity to contiguity, from metonymy to metaphor.

It is only this "synthetic" vision that lets a historian reconcile "the ordinary citizen" "to the imperfections of the manifest order of things". Karamzin sees such "reconciliation" as his mission:

> Rulers and legislators act according to what history teaches, and consult its pages as a navigator consults his charts. Human wisdom needs experience, and life is short [...] But the ordinary citizen, too, should read history. *It reconciles him to the imperfections of the manifest order of things*, as something usual in all ages. It consoles him when the state suffers calamities, by bearing witness that in bygone times similar events—and even more terrible ones—occurred [...] History feeds moral feelings and by its righteous verdict disposes the soul to a justice which assures our good and the harmony of society. So much for its usefulness. But how many pleasures for the heart and the mind! [italics are mine, TS.]

What Karamzin does in his *Foreword* can serve as the perfect illustration to Barthes' observation in "The Discourse of History":

> [T]he presence, in historical narration, of explicit speech-act signs tends to "de-chronologize" the historical "thread" and to restore, if only as a reminiscence or a nostalgia, a complex, parametric, non-linear time whose deep space recalls the mythic time of the ancient cosmogonies, it too linked by essence to the speech of the poet or the soothsayer.[36]

Karamzin did not think of himself as a soothsayer. But even when consecrating himself to the *History* ("taking the [monastic] vows of a historian", as Prince Viazemsky put it), he remained a poet.

***

After expressing the idea that metaphor is a shorthand forced upon us by life's brevity (a remedy of sorts), in his "Remarks on Translations from Shakespeare", with which we opened these notes, Boris Pasternak moves on to the crucial role played by rhythm in Shakespeare's poetry:

---

35 Cf. R. Koselleck, *Futures Past: On the Semantics of Historical Time*, New York, NY 2004, pp. 32–35.
36 Barthes, "Discourse", pp. 130–131.

> The fundamental principle of Shakespeare's poetry is rhythm [...] Rhythm is at the basis of his texts, rather than being their final framework [...] In his dialogues the driving force of rhythm defines the sequence of questions and answers, the speed of their alternation; in his monologues it defines the length or brevity of sentences [...] This is the rhythm of a free historical personality which erects no idol for itself and is thus sincere and sparing of words.

In Pasternak's understanding, while rhythm lies at the basis of all of Shakespeare's plays, it is of particular importance in *Hamlet*. Rhythm may be the only thing that can enable us to come to terms with a time that is "out of joint"—not really "setting it right", but creating a kind of harmony within cacophony, mitigating the anguish of uncertainty with the anticipation that some expectations will be met, if only in matters of form.

> This music consists in a measured alternation of the solemn and the anxious. Through it the work's atmosphere is condensed and made extremely compact [...] The rhythmic principle compacts and makes tangible this general tone of the play. Yet it is not its sole application. The rhythm has a modifying effect on a certain harshness which would be unthinkable without its harmonious effect.

For Karamzin as well, poetic rhythm was a manifestation of theodicy, and he too translated Shakespeare. It is to him that we owe the first translation of *Julius Caesar* into Russian, published, albeit anonymously, as early as in 1787. Prefacing the publication of *Julius Caesar* with his own "remarks on translations" and explaining the urge to "lay a foundation in this way for the Russian public's familiarity with this great poet", Karamzin wrote:

> That Shakespeare did not adhere to the rules of the theater is true. The real reason for this, I think, was his ardent imagination, which would not be bound by any prescriptions. His spirit soared as an eagle and was not able to measure its soaring as the sparrows measure their flights. He did not want to observe the so-called "unities" which our present dramatic authors so meticulously maintain: he did not want to impose limits to his imagination [...] His dramas, like the immeasurable theater of nature, are full of variety; taken together, they form a complete whole.[37]

It is common knowledge that the "complete whole" of Shakespeare's dramas was designed for and could only be realized in the complex space of the Globe Theatre, with its several levels, jutting into audience space, making possible the overlapping scenes of action and corners of intimacy from which he constructed his plays. It is this stage that Shakespeare had in mind when talking about "all the world"— not the arena stage of the ancient theater or the flat, deep box of the proscenium

---

[37] Nikolai Karamzin, "On Shakespeare and His Tragedy *Julius Caesar*", in: *Selected Prose of N. M. Karamzin*, tr. H. M. Nebel, Jr., Evanston, IL 1969.

stage of neoclassical tragedy. It has also been observed that it is in the spirit of this Elizabethan "thrust" (or "apron") stage that Pushkin conceived his *Boris Godunov*, probably the most important Russian historical drama ever written, dedicated to the memory of Karamzin.[38] What makes this association between Karamzin and Shakespeare's theater even more curious is F. Yates' discovery of a link between the art of ancient and medieval mnemonics—the inscribing of "images" into "places"—and the spatial structure of the Globe. Yates suggested that the very distortion of its stage was that of "a memory room". Karamzin's art was first and foremost the art of memory, which is why he was particularly passionate about the remote past. Curiously, *The Art of Memory,* Yates's groundbreaking study, so fundamental to twentieth century intellectual history, first appeared in 1966, as if to commemorate Karamzin's bicentennial. He would have appreciated this diachronic rhyme.

---

[38] C. Emerson, "Tragedy, Comedy, and History on Stage", in: *The Uncensored Boris Godunov: The Case for Pushkin's Original Comedy*, ed. Ch. Dunning, Madison, WI 2006, p. 159.

Olga Kuptsova
Theater as Metaphor in the Drama of Alexander Ostrovsky

Theatrical metaphors in Alexander Ostrovsky's dramatic work can be found first of all in his meta-theatrical plays (*The Forest, Guilty Without Fault, Talents and Admirers*) as well as in plays with inserted theatrical fragments, references to dramatic art, and recurrent dramatic motifs (*Poverty Is No Vice, The Deep, An Ardent Heart*, and others). Theatrical metaphorics may also be observed in his plays describing the theatrical behavior of characters who play roles and disguise themselves in real life, being deceitful and underhanded (*Enough Stupidity in Every Wise Man, The Marriage of Belugin, Money to Burn*, and others).

Ostrovsky, who may be considered the father of Russia's national theatrical repertoire, occupies a place between Mikhail Lermontov (*Masquerade*) and Anton Chekhov (*The Seagull*) in Russian meta-theater of the nineteenth century.

In Lermontov's *Masquerade*, theatrical metaphors can be found according to the following dichotomies: life–play/masquerade, face–mask, natural–unnatural, true–false. In addition, "play" is closely connected in this drama to card games (games of chance or fortune). Some curious things come to the surface when we compare Lermontov's early play *A Strange Man*, its protagonist being the first Arbenin or a sort of proto-Arbenin, to *Masquerade*. In *A Strange Man*, characters' lines are demonstratively packed full with mentions of theater (various types of theater being mentioned for no apparent reason: home theaters of the nobility in their two versions—with children and adults acting, French theater companies, etc.), but all of them, while attesting to some mandatory theatrical quality of social life in general, nonetheless keep away from metaphorical generalization. Already the very title of *Masquerade* implies theatricality (unnatural, wrong, and deceitful behavior, in Lermontov's perception) as the main key to understanding the events in the play, namely the development of the plot and the characters' behaviors. In this regard, it is also noteworthy that certain authors highlight the dramatic nature of Lermontov's narrator, making him akin to the main character of his dramas and, importantly, of his prose as well, thus turning the whole literary world of Lermontov into a metaphorical theater of passions, fatal choices, tragic mistakes, and so on.[1]

---

[1] See, for instance, S. Savinkov, "Dramatis personae lermontovskoy dushi" [The *Dramatis Personae* of Lermontov's Soul], in: *Filologicheskie zapiski*, vol. 7, 1996, pp. 35–45.

At the other pole of theatrical metaphorics, we find Chekhov's *The Seagull*, written as a prophecy, a premonition of "director's theater", which the Russian stage had not yet seen. *The Seagull* would later be staged in the Alexandrinsky Theater (without a director in the modern sense of the word), and then in the psychologically oriented Moscow Art Theater by Konstantin Stanislavski; Vsevolod Meyerhold turned out to be a natural for the role of Konstantin Treplev, which he eventually performed in the Moscow Art Theater. When compared to Romantic drama of the early nineteenth century, the symbolic and metaphysical play, written by a debutant playwright and staged by him at an amateur countryside theater, employed a different kind of theatrical metaphorics, with a demiurge director, creation of the world, and the concept of the world-as-a-theater (already not only in a social, but in a universal sense).

Otherwise speaking, we are dealing with one interpretation of William Shakespeare's famous formula—"All the world's a stage"—in the case of Lermontov and a different, diametrically opposed one—theater as the world (in a broad, cosmic sense)—in the case of Chekhov.

Ostrovsky's theatrical metaphorics has a somewhat different dimension, although it can be regarded as a bridge between Lermontov and Chekhov. Ostrovsky's early play *Poverty Is No Vice*, which was extremely popular among his Slavophile friends, is set in an idyllic patriarchal *uyezd* town. It tells the story of Lyubim Tortsov, an impoverished alcoholic with a noble heart, who flees from his native town to Moscow after his father's death. In this city of sin, this new Babylon, Tortsov wastes all of his inheritance on public houses and—theater. It becomes obvious from Lyubim's lines that he regularly goes to the theater to watch the most famous tragedian of Russian Romanticism, Pavel Mochalov, performing onstage. Theater has a narcotic effect on him, taking him to a different reality, making him experience strong feelings, and tantalizing him with vivid imagery. Unable to find anything resembling that in real life, Lyubim turns to wine as a substitute for the theater drug. Ostrovsky uses the story of this character (and some other characters from his earlier plays) to articulate a bitter and dramatic résumé of the obsession with theater among his generation of "men of the forties". Inspired by Vissarion Belinsky's articles on theater as a "magical world" and the image of a genius actor exercising a magnetic and irrational effect on the crowd, students of the 1840s looked up to Mochalov as the incarnation of that "magician" of the scene. They eventually created a cult of his personality, which was in no small part accountable for the transformation of Mochalov's roles into behavioral models, above all the so-called "kitchen-sink Hamletism".

During the 1870s–1880s, Ostrovsky wrote three meta-theatrical plays: *The Forest, Guilty Without Fault,* and *Talents and Admirers*. They share the specific feature of the protagonists being actors. However, the actors are never described acting on a theater stage—instead, they act on the stage of life.

The comedy *The Forest* is the most curious example in terms of theatrical metaphorics, as the reader can distinguish several layers, interconnected and autonomous at the same time. Ostrovsky wrote *The Forest* in the middle of his career, in a sense summarizing it, being disillusioned with the former theatrical ideals and worried about the future of the Russian theater. As a result, throughout the following decade, he would assume responsibility for that future, contribute to theater reforms, engage in theatrical translation, consider changing his occupation, and delve into history and the history of theater in particular.

The first theatrical-metaphorical layer in *The Forest* is about the actor being recognized as an artist. In the wake of Belinsky, who presented Mochalov as an artist equal to Shakespeare in his famous article *Shakespeare's "Hamlet": Mochalov as Hamlet*, Ostrovsky presents two provincial actors, Grigory Neschastlivtsev and Arkashka Schastlivtsev, whose dramatic talents are doubtful and whose everyday behaviors are flawed, as far superior to and more noble than the residents of the Penki Estate (the shabby-genteel nobility and the emerging ravenous entrepreneurs). It is interesting (from a historical perspective, too) in this regard to observe the successive set of the actors' self-characterizations in the play, their gradual evolution from skomorokh (the nomadic type—"unmounted travelers"), court jester, actor—to noble artist.

The generation of the forties witnessed a growth of self-awareness in the theatrical milieu. An imperial edict of 1839 granted the right to obtain the hereditary Freedom of the City to first-class actors of imperial theaters upon twenty years of service. "Before that, the title of Imperial Court Artist did not imply any specific social standing. As such actors and their descendants did not belong to the tax-paying class, they did not benefit from any civil rights", recalls Pyotr Karatygin.[2] Changes in actors' civil rights brought about changes in their self-perception and in the social attitudes toward them. The developing system of benefit performances required actors to get involved in selecting plays for such performances, among other things. Actors had to take up the task of writing (translations, theatrical adaptations, vaudevilles—anything the theater would need), but they were also becoming—in this case, voluntarily—part of the corpus of Russian literature with their poems, prose, memoirs, and reflections on the art of acting.

Writing actors were getting to know the literary and university milieus, joining literary cliques, and attending salons, especially in Moscow, where spectators called the Maly Theater "the second university"—that is, a

---

[2] *Zapiski:* Ch. 2 [Notes: Part 2], Leningrad 1930, p. 12.

full-fledged competitor to the Moscow State University—as early as in the 1840s. Mikhail Shchepkin, one of the most famous actors of that age who had been born as the son of a serf, was friends with Alexander Pushkin, Nikolai Gogol, Alexander Herzen, and other outstanding writers; another famous actor, Alexander Martynov, befriended Ostrovsky, Ivan Turgenev, Nikolay Nekrasov and *Sovremennik*-associated literary men. These friendships drew the actors from their closed theatrical circles, integrating them into the common habitat of Russian art. Over time, this tendency spread to provincial actors as well.

The second layer has to do with actors' self-representation. The roles they play in life correspond to the characters they play on stage, Neschastlivtsev being a tragic, Schastlivtsev a comedic actor. The Romantic repertoire of the Russian (and European) theater of the 1840s–1850s was built around the emblematic playwright Shakespeare. *Hamlet* was a must for Romantic tragic actors, a proof of their commitment to the stock character. For Ostrovsky, one of the paramount themes in *Hamlet* was the problem of boundaries and possibilities in acting and theater as such. It is not only *The Mousetrap* but also Hamlet's instructions for actors on *how* to act in the play within the play that made sense to the Russian playwright. Shakespeare's scene describing the arrival of the comedians to Elsinore, for instance, is comparable to the encounter of two actors on horseback in *The Forest* in terms of their narratives. However, Hamlet opposes himself to a comedian as he welcomes the actors, while Neschastlivtsev "tries on" the role of Hamlet and greets his colleague Schastlivtsev from the elevated perspective of the Prince of Denmark. All of the quotes from Shakespeare's tragedy pronounced by Neschastlivtsev (whether appropriately or not, whether they be small or very important fragments of the role) in *The Forest* "rhyme" the story of Penki residents with that of the Prince of Denmark. In both cases, deception, hypocrisy, and crime are discovered with the help of comedians.

In the end, Hamlet from Penki (this is the name of the estate, owned by the widow Gurmyzhskaya, where the actors arrived) is not destined to be realized. There is no fertile soil for Hamletism there. The crowd prevents Hamlet from playing out his role. This unfinished role of Hamlet is comical, the great enthusiasm being totally wasted. Having started as Hamlet, Neschastlivtsev is forced to finish his stay at Penki playing two other theatrical roles, which are textually intertwined.

In the final part, one of the two dramas in the prompter Arkashka Schastlivtsev's parcel turns out to be the five-act *The Robbers* by Friedrich Schiller, whose influence on Russian Romantic theater was at least as significant as that of Shakespeare. The robbers theme is represented in *The Forest* in two parallel dimensions. On the one hand, the social perception of skomorokhs/actors and robbers is very much identical. On the other hand, the theme of "noble robbers" is of central importance in the Romantic repertoire. Therefore, the forest fellowship of "noble robbers" and the guild fellowship of "noble artists" act as contextual synonyms, forming a unique theatrical metaphor.

The thick Bohemian forest with its owls and eagle owls resonates well with the forest surrounding the Penki Estate, "where any fugitive and any beggar will find shelter". Neschastlivtsev himself tells Schastlivtsev that they are "similar to robbers". Schastlivtsev, in his turn, describes the tragic actor as follows: "His manners are all robber-like, a sheer Pugachev!" In the scene where the widow Gurmyzhskaya is robbed of her money, Neschastlivtsev fiddles with a fake handgun, pulling it out, putting it onto the table, and putting it back after getting the money—all of this being part of the theatrical "Robin Hood toolkit" as well.

The simple fact that Ostrovsky ranks his characters together with those of Shakespeare and Schiller is very telling. The monologue quoted in *The Forest* is spoken by Karl Moor in the second scene of the first act of *The Robbers* (that is, compositionally it refers to the set-up), and its misanthropic narrative explains every move that Moor makes afterwards, having entered on the path of robbery, revenge (albeit of a noble sort), and, eventually, crime. Neschastlivtsev, pronouncing the same lines, also leaves the widow's estate at the height of his personal and professional success.

Another plotline is presented by the comic actor Schastlivtsev. In the third act of *The Forest*, Schastlivtsev surrenders very reluctantly to the tragic Gennady Neschastlivtsev's request to play a servant—a role well suited to his theatrical skills as a comic figure—not onstage but in a real-life situation (in Gurmyzhskaya's Penki Estate) and presents himself to Karp, another domestic servant of Gurmyzhskaya, as Sganarelle. From that point on and up to the moment when the actor stops performing as a servant, Ostrovsky creates the image of Arkashka Schastlivtsev based on the "flickering" outlined in this short dialogue—between the character-specific traits (recognizable, Molierian, typical of the original Sganarelle) and the generalized characteristics of an "alien" comical mask of the European theater.

Arkashka-Sganarelle, representing the comical theatrical plotline, plays his role within one of the consistent and central scenarios of the preceding European comedy tradition of folklore and literary theater (Roman, Spanish, Italian, French, English). Arkashka Schastlivtsev is a "foreigner" indeed; unlike Neschastlivtsev, he does not build his historical and theatrical reminiscences around Russian archetypes. This Schastlivtsev–Sganarelle plotline can be conventionally referred to as the Harlequin plotline and Arkashka's behavioral model may be seen as Harlequinade, the Harlequin character being understood broadly, as it was later interpreted in the Silver Age of Russian culture. Alternatively, it may be said, in the terms of Vsevolod Meyerhold, that Schastlivtsev playing Sganarelle demonstrates the possibilities of the "trickster" stock character.[3]

In *The Forest*, Arkashka Schastlivtsev is not completely equated with Sganarelle and his behavioral patterns. He simply resembles a Molière-style trickster servant, so he plays this role easily. However, the play has two segments—before accepting the role and after throwing off the mask—in which Arkashka is not identified with his scenic stock characters. The romantic finale of Ostrovsky's comedy, where actors who lose financially turn out to be winners in terms of personal freedom and human dignity, is a hymn to acting as an altruistic game. Yet, Neschastlivtsev and Schastlivtsev fulfill their scenic function in real life at the same time by helping, as servants are supposed to do in the *commedia dell'arte*, the enamored couple Aksyusha and Pyotr (even though these latter two do not belong to "the nobility").

There is another curious, historically authentic detail that contributes to the play's theatrical metaphorics, which is contained in the list of cities that appear in the actors' dialogues and monologues when they are talking about where they have performed in the past. The tragic character's (i.e., Neschastlivtsev's) list of locations is longer than that of the comic character (Schastlivtsev): Arkhangelsk, Astrakhan, Kishinev, Irkutsk, Poltava, Pyatigorsk, Kerch, Kremenchug, Lebedyan, Crimean Karasubazar (it is unlikely that this town had a theater, but Neschastlivtsev has been there somehow), Tiflis, Novocherkassk, Yekaterinburg. Neschastlivtsev also says that he could perform in Kostroma, Yaroslavl, Vologda, and Tver in the future. In fact, the play shows him on a journey from Kerch to Vologda. He has traveled a longer distance than Schastlivtsev, whose theatrical locations are rather limited (Arkhangelsk, Kremenchug, and Kursk) and who travels in the opposite direction, from Vologda to Kerch.

It is tempting to attempt an analysis of this geography, e.g. by comparing the actors' locations to their prototypes' places of work. Such an approach definitely makes sense. However, there could be a different perspective on this extensive geography of the actors' travels, which covers nearly the whole of the European part of the Russian Empire. It may be the case that it is not about the nomadic lifestyle of provincial actors, but about the universal nature of the art of acting—an element not referring to a singular case, but with universal applicability.

---

[3] Ivan Aksenov, Valery Bebutov, and Vsevolod Meyerhold, *Amplua aktera* [Actor's Stock Characters], Moscow 1922, p. 6.

Nomadism (freedom), the basis of the actor's profession since the era of wandering troupes (skomorokhs), is emphasized in the finale, the two actors symbolizing the theater of the Romantic, virtually bygone era, literally "vanishing scenery". Wandering actors vanish into nowhere. The tragic actor Neschastlivtsev does not appear anywhere else; tragic figures of the Mochalov type are a thing of the past. Appearing as a Robinson, a voluntary "court jester" of Paratov in the play *Without a Dowry*, Arkashka Schastlivtsev lowers his standards as a comic.

The third layer in *The Forest* is represented by theater/acting in real life, namely the bigotry of Gurmyzhskaya and the hypocrisy of Bulanov. It also includes the initial situation of the actors' plotline, i.e. the deceitful behavior of Neschastlivtsev and Schastlivtsev who conceal their occupation from the Penki Estate residents. Neschastlivtsev pretends to be a military retiree, passing Schastlivtsev off as his servant. However, this self-interested deception is gradually transformed as the intrigue evolves. The art that the actors serve transforms and frees them, revealing the best of their qualities and encouraging them to perform noble actions. For Ostrovsky, Neschastlivtsev, and Schastlivtsev embody a farewell to the Romantic philosophy that ranked any artist (including actors) above "philistines" and "non-creators" (regardless of social class) by default. *The Forest* is a hymn to Romanticism and a sober recognition of its problematic effects at the same time.

The Forest became a reference point for two subsequent meta-theatrical plays by Ostrovsky. The drama *Guilty Without Fault* raises the question of two types of acting ("to be" or "to seem"), which reminds the reader of the discussion of *The Paradox of the Actor* by Denis Diderot. This text had just been translated into Russian at the time Ostrovsky's play was written. The very name of the drama *Talents and Admirers* points to the importance of the spectator for theater, the mutual influence of the stage and the audience. In *Talents and Admirers*, Ostrovsky definitively says goodbye to the Romantic philosophy of a proud-hearted and independent, free artist.

However, Ostrovky's late theatrical-metaphorical phraseology requires further in-depth analysis, which is beyond the scope of the present article.

III: Twentieth-Century Experimentations and Theoretical Explorations

Juana Christina von Stein
The Theater of the Absurd and the Absurdity of Theater: The Early Plays of Beckett and Ionesco

The *theatrum mundi* metaphor can clearly be detected in all non-dramatic texts that refer to theater—while no theater per se is in sight. However, when we are confronted with the metaphor of theater in drama itself, it must be decided upon whether this is a metaphor of theater or, possibly, an instance of meta-theater. Due to the fact that the metaphor of theater is bidirectional in that it can be used to represent the world itself as theater, and vice versa, that theater can represent the world,[1] the metaphor is tremendously flexible. Indeed, this double possibility of representation might encourage critics to see the Great Theater of the World when what they are actually confronted with is an example of meta-theater.

This essay will examine this issue by looking at the theater of the absurd. Furthermore, it will seek to demonstrate how the early theater of the absurd attempts, at times, to show the absurdity of theatrical conventions to a much greater extent than it attempts to show the absurdities of the world in which we live. In addition, this paper will show to what degree meta-theatricality in the early plays of the theater of the absurd also served to question the functioning of the *theatrum mundi* metaphor, and it will examine how meta-theatricality and theater as a metaphor could mutually reinforce one another, making the stages of the post-war world a place to rethink and to highlight the limits of the age-old idea of the *theatrum mundi* which dates back to Antiquity.[2] Moreover, this paper seeks to convey the degree to which Ionesco and Beckett abandoned meta-theatricality in the course of their careers, in favor of an analogy between the stage and the world, in order to proclaim the absurdity of the world, which

---

[1] See B. Quiring's insightful introduction to the volume *Theatrum Mundi: Die Metapher des Welttheaters von Shakespeare bis Beckett*, ed. B. Quiring, Berlin 2012, pp. 7–29, p. 7.
[2] A general survey of the history of the metaphor can be found in E. R. Curtius's book *Europäische Literatur und lateinisches Mittelalter*, 7th ed., Bern 1969, pp. 148–154. Regarding the changes the *theatrum mundi* metaphor underwent in the twentieth century, see especially M. Harries, "Das Ende einer Trope für die Welt", in: Quiring (ed.), *Theatrum Mundi*, pp. 191–217; see in particular pp. 205ff.

Open Access. © 2019 Juana Christina von Stein, published by De Gruyter. This work is licensed under the Creative Commons Attribution-NonCommercial-NoDerivatives 4.0 License.
https://doi.org/10.1515/9783110622034-015

is precisely what absurdist theater is known for. The plays of Ionesco and Beckett developed from initially providing poetological reflections on drama on stage to using the stage first and foremost to instruct the audience on the human condition. Moreover, both playwrights may well have altered their plays in response to the observations made by critics right from the very beginning of their dramatic attempts.

Even though they struggled with the label "absurd",[3] theater critics and literary scholars have always agreed on the fact that the theater of the absurd was about the absurdity of the world rather than about the absurdity of theater.[4] Since the very beginning of its scholarly reception, the absurdity of the theatrical situation has scarcely been discussed. For instance, the first article on Beckett's *Waiting for Godot*, written by L. Spitzer's student E. Kern in 1954,[5] refers to the "[...] vivid dramatization of the paradox of the condition of man, whose intellect makes him aware of the universe's slighting of reason and makes him long for a state where reason shall be conferred upon this universe [...]".[6] M. Esslin's pioneering book *The Theatre of the Absurd* from 1961, now in its eighth edition, has had a significant impact on the genre it tried to define, and it may well have not only changed the academic and public reception, but also influenced the very nature of absurdist theater itself.[7] According to Esslin, the theater of the absurd can be defined by the philosophical meaning its authors intend to convey, which he claims to consist in the assumption that

---

[3] See M. Y. Bennett, *The Cambridge Introduction to Theatre and Literature of the Absurd*, Cambridge 2015, pp. 6f. If the nineteenth century was the century of epochs, the twentieth century was the century of labelling. Nevertheless, there has been no type of label that has not been controversial, which is why the debate about the criteria of the theater of the absurd seems to tell us more about the practice of labelling than about the actual plays.

[4] The first to criticize pigeonholing of the theater of the absurd (especially Esslin's categorization) was L. Abel in his work *Metatheatre: A New View of Dramatic Form*, New York, NY 1963; the most recent criticism was that of M. Y. Bennett in *Reassessing the Theatre of the Absurd: Camus, Beckett, Ionesco, Genet, and Pinter*, New York, NY 2011.

[5] See also Bennett, *Cambridge Introduction*, p. 128.

[6] E. Kern, "Drama Stripped for Inaction: Beckett's *Godot*", in: *Yale French Studies*, vol. 14, 1954, pp. 41–47, p. 47. Kern remarks that *Waiting for Godot* is not a play by all traditional standards, as it entirely lacks the Aristotelian plot lines (p. 41). However, she does not make this feature the subject of discussion.

[7] See Ch. Innes, "The Canon: The Theatre of the Absurd. By Martin Esslin", in: *Times Higher Education Supplement*, June 18, 2009, qtd. in: Bennett, *Cambridge Introduction*, p. 3.

human existence is essentially absurd, and that modern man is in the midst of a spiritual crisis.[8]

All of the relevant concepts remained attached to these thoughts, defining the theater of the absurd as theater that first and foremost exposes the absurdity of the human condition, defining the plays as having "in common the basic belief that man's life is essentially without meaning or purpose and that human beings cannot communicate".[9] Encyclopedias such as *Britannica* define the genre as the works of playwrights who expressed a "postwar mood of disillusionment and scepticism [...] in bizarre terms" and of authors who "shared a belief that human life was essentially without meaning or purpose and that valid communication was no longer possible. The human condition, they felt, had sunk to a state of absurdity [...]."[10] Furthermore, the theater of the absurd is also seen as a literary response to World War II and the Shoa,[11] to "the modern world shaken in its traditional beliefs and in grave doubt as to the meaning of existence and the possibility of communication between men [...]".[12] In Germany, where the reception of absurdist plays was particularly strong, scholars—although they highlighted Beckett's and Ionesco's rupture

---

8 See M. Esslin, *The Theatre of the Absurd*, Harmondworth 1972, especially the preface and the introduction.

9 *The Concise Oxford Companion to the Theatre*, ed. Ph. Hartnoll, Oxford and New York, NY 1972, p. 548.

10 "Theatre of the Absurd", in: *The New Encyclopædia Britannica*, vol. 28, p. 556.

11 Nevertheless, it can be questioned whether it is at all plausible to maintain that dramatists of the theater of the absurd argue implicitly—immediately after the horrors of World War II and the absolute loss of order—that the audience needed to be taught in theater that the world and the values mankind claims to follow are absurd. Apart from this, the precursors of Beckett's and Ionesco's theater of the absurd, such as Alfred Jarry, are to be found at a time when the two world wars were not in sight. One could resolve this issue by claiming that Jarry was a forefather of the theater of the absurd because he exposed not the absurdity of the world, but rather the absurdity of theater. In this sense, *Ubu Roi* has to be primarily regarded as a parody of conventional theater, which is altogether possible and has in fact occasionally been suggested (see: J. Grimm, *Das avantgardistische Theater Frankreichs: 1895–1930*, Munich 1987, here chapter III: "Das Theater Alfred Jarrys: Die Zerstörung der theaterästhetischen Konventionen"; H. Beauchamp, "*Ubu Roi*, ou *Macbeth-Guignol*: un retournement fondateur de la parodie dramatique moderne", in: *Poétiques de la parodie et du pastiche de 1850 à nos jours*, ed. C. Dousteyssier-Khoze and F. Place-Verghnes, Oxford and Bern 2006, pp. 203–213; R. Morse, "Monsieur Macbeth: From Jarry to Ionesco", in: *Macbeth and its Afterlife*, ed. P. Holland, Cambridge 2004, pp. 112–125).

12 *A Handbook of Contemporary Drama*, ed. M. Andersen, J. Guicharnaud, K. Marrison, J. Zipes, et al., London 1971, p. 2. One might, of course, object that the literary absurd is much older than modern theater itself (see, for instance, N. Cornwell's study on *The Absurd in Literature*, Manchester and New York, NY 2006).

with traditional forms of theater—even explicitly mentioned in their compendia that the expression "absurdes Theater" was wrong in terms of the logic of language, because the claim is not that it is theater that is absurd, but rather the plot embodying the "metaphysical homelessness" and the "social alienation of mankind".[13] Whenever the lack of theatrical logic and conventional structure in the plays was noticed, critics used to argue that the form was above all absurd in order to support the absurd content.[14] The absurd dramatic form seemed to be nothing more than the appropriate form for the representation of the absurdity of the world. The "concept of *homo absurdus*"[15] has always been and still is at the center of every definition or interpretation of these plays.

---

13 See, for instance, R. Hess's definition of "Theater des Absurden" in *Literaturwissenschaftliche Grundbegriffe für Romanisten*, ed. R. Hess, G. Siebenmann, and T. Stegmann, 4th ed., Tübingen and Basel 2003, pp. 332–334, p. 332. See also G. von Wilpert, who defines "Absurdes Drama, absurdes Theater, Theater des Absurden" as an avant-garde form of drama, "die aus Protest gegen bürgerl. Scheinsicherheit, unechte Lebensführung und lebensfernen Intellektualismus in provozierender Abkehr vom konventionellen Theater das Gewohnte in Frage stellt, Raum für die absurde Logik einer sinnentleerten Welt schafft und das Sinnlose oder Sinnwidrige zur Grundlage dramat. Gestaltung nimmt" (*Sachwörterbuch der Literatur*, 8th ed., Stuttgart 2001, p. 4).

14 See, for instance, Esslin's introduction to *The Theatre of the Absurd* ("The absurdity of the Absurd"), as well as *The Penguin Dictionary of Literary Terms and Literary Theory*, ed. J. A. Cuddon, 4th ed., London 1999, p. 912, or Hess, "Theater des Absurden", pp. 332f. See also the entire *Erlanger Rede*, held by Wolfgang Hildesheimer in 1960, where Hildesheimer attempts to prove that the theater of the absurd is not about the absurdity of theater, but rather the absurdity of the world. Commencing with a psychological sleight-of-hand ("Das absurde Theater dient der Konfrontation des Publikums mit dem Absurden, indem es ihm seine eigene Absurdität vor Augen führt. Da jedoch das Publikum im allgemeinen nicht ohne weiteres gewillt ist, die Philosophie des Absurden hinzunehmen, geschweige denn, auf sich selbst zu beziehen und sich selbst als absurd zu betrachten, so betrachtet es die Konfrontation auf dem Theater als absurd" ["Über das absurde Theater", in: Wolfgang Hildesheimer, *Theaterstücke: Über das absurde Theater*, Frankfurt/Main 1976, pp. 169f.]), he states that the theater of the absurd was "weniger eine Rebellion gegen eine hergebrachte Form des Theaters als gegen eine hergebrachte Form der Weltsicht, wie sie sich des Theaters bedient und sich auf ihm manifestiert" (p. 171), and that its playwrights were clearly not interested in "burning questions" of theater, as well as being indifferent towards the question of whether theater as an institution was to have a future or not (p. 180), which is extremely doubtful, as Beckett's play *Eleutheria* or Ionesco's plays *Victime du devoir* or *L'impromptu de Versailles* deal—even explicitly—with these issues.

15 *Penguin Dictionary*, p. 911.

K. W. Hempfer was the first to conjecture that the theater of the absurd needed to be defined by more characteristics than its exposure of the metaphysics of absurdity.[16] In particular, it is Ionesco's and Beckett's problematization of language in their plays—pointed out extensively by critics—which Hempfer considers to be not only a concomitant feature, but a hallmark that is conducive to defining the very essence of the theater of the absurd.

This essay endeavors to demonstrate to what degree the theater of the absurd not only encapsulates the absurdity of the world in which we live or the absurdity of language itself, but also the absurdity of language in theater, and hence the absurdity of theatrical conventions.

Meta-theatricality is a crucial aspect of absurdist theater, which has long been neglected by critics who have favored a more didactical reading right from the outset. In particular, the early plays of Ionesco and Beckett seem to present a much greater sample of meta-theatrical references than is typically assumed in the relevant scholarship. At the beginning of their dramatic careers, both playwrights were rather sceptical towards theater itself. Beckett thought of play-writing as a form of recreation from his novelistic work.[17] Ionesco, who had studied and taught French literature, did not like the medium at all, rarely going to view plays and feeling quite uncomfortable in the theater. In 1958, he described in a most entertaining article titled "Expérience du théâtre" to what degree he "hated" theater:

---

16 See K. W. Hempfer, who demonstrates that the breaking of the rules of presupposition constitutes another hallmark of absurdist theater ("Die Theorie der Präsuppositionen und die Analyse des Dialogs im 'Absurden Theater' (am Beispiel von Ionescos *La cantatrice chauve*)", in: *Zeitschrift für französische Sprache und Literatur*, suppl. no. 4, 1977, pp. 33–70). Bennett was the last one who attempted to define the genre not in terms of the possible *meaning* of the plays (i.e. "the world is absurd"), but in terms of techniques and aesthetic forms preferred by a certain group of authors, an approach that seems to prevent reductionist labelling (*Cambridge Introduction*, p. 8). However, Bennett does not focus on the meta-theatricality of the plays either—indeed, the contrary sometimes appears to be the case: "However, Pirandello and (even more so) Brecht were experimenting with the *meta-theatrical*, with Brecht breaking the 'fourth wall' of theater. The theatrical absurd with the exception of mostly two plays (Genet's *The Blacks: A Clown Show* and Jack Gelber's *The Connection* [...]) is neither meta-theatrical nor does it make any attempt to 'break the fourth wall' of theatrical realism. In this way, Pirandello and Brecht exert essentially no influence upon the playwrights associated with the Theatre of the Absurd" (p. 14).
17 See S. E. Gontarski, "The Body in the Body in Beckett's Theatre", in: *Samuel Beckett: Endlessness in the Year 2000*, ed. A. Moorjani and C. Veit, Amsterdam and New York, NY 2001, pp. 169–177, p. 170.

> Il me semble parfois que je me suis mis à écrire du théâtre parce que je le détestais. [...] Je n'y goûtais aucun plaisir, je n'y participais pas. Le jeu des comédiens me gênait: j'étais gêné pour eux. Les situations me paraissaient arbitraires. Il y avait quelque chose de faux, me semblait-il, dans tout cela. La représentation théâtrale n'avait pas de magie pour moi. Tout me paraissait un peu ridicule, un peu pénible.[18]

Eight years earlier, Ionesco had written his very first play, *La cantatrice chauve* (*The Bald Soprano* or *The Bald Prima Donna*). The subtitle of the play is "Anti-pièce", which already hints at its parodistic character. The beginning of the play, which is also the "beginning" of the beginning of Ionesco's dramatic career, starts with the following stage direction:

> *Intérieur bourgeois anglais, avec des fauteuils anglais. Soirée anglaise. M. Smith, anglais, dans son fauteuil et ses pantoufles anglais, fume sa pipe anglaise et lit un journal anglais, près d'un feu anglais. Il a des lunettes anglaises, une petite moustache grise, anglaise. A côté de lui, dans un autre fauteuil anglais, Mme Smith, anglaise, raccommode des chaussettes anglaises. Un long moment de silence anglais. La pendule anglaise frappe dix-sept coups anglais.*[19]

The more detailed the stage direction, the harder it becomes to represent: A middle-class English interior, with English armchairs and an English evening (maybe the actors are having tea)—these might be feasible. An Englishman, seated in his English armchair and wearing English slippers, is smoking his English pipe and reading an English newspaper—this sounds rather ridiculous, but not as absurd as an "English fire" or "A long moment of English silence"; the latter descriptions are neither imaginable nor representable on stage. However, the most absurd element of the stage direction is the English clock, which strikes "17 English strokes", as a clock cannot strike "English" strokes and no hall clock could go beyond 12 strokes.[20] Also, why does it have to be exactly 17 strokes, and not 16 or 18? One does not know, and one is not going to find out because this is irrelevant for the plot. All one can do is guess that this stage

---

[18] Eugène Ionesco, "Expérience du théâtre", in: *La Nouvelle Revue Française*, vol. 62, 1958, pp. 247–270, p. 247. See also Esslin, *The Theatre of the Absurd*, p. 134.

[19] Eugène Ionesco, *La cantatrice chauve*, in: Eugène Ionesco, *Théâtre complet*, ed. E. Jacquart, Paris 1991, pp. 7–42, p. 9. [*A middle-class English interior, with English armchairs. An English evening. Mr. Smith, an Englishman, seated in his English armchair and wearing English slippers, is smoking his English pipe and reading an English newspaper, near an English fire. He is wearing English spectacles and a small gray English mustache. Beside him, in another English armchair, Mrs. Smith, an Englishwoman, is darning some English socks. A long moment of English silence. The English clock strikes 17 English strokes* (translation by D. M. Allen).]

[20] Before naming the play *La cantatrice chauve*, Ionesco titled it *L'Anglais sans peine* and *L'Heure anglaise*.

direction contains an empty precision, leading absolutely nowhere, just like the stage directions at the very beginning of Beckett's *Fin de partie*, where Clov's running around is detailed meticulously, and even the exact number of steps he has to take is indicated.[21] Indeed, in the case of Beckett's play, one is not able to discern why the author is forcing the actor to take exactly this number of steps. Yet, as this is the question we immediately ask ourselves when reading the text, Beckett and Ionesco seem to be playing with the recipient's impulse to interpret everything, to look out for the sense behind things, to see symbols everywhere, especially in absurdist theater, in a decidedly non-realistic theater, where (so it seems) everything that happens on stage has categorically been construed as figurative, as a metaphor for something concerning the real world. Ionesco and Beckett seem to be parodying the approach that the ideal recipient of theater[22] is always inferring that everything is a symbol and has some deeper and hidden meaning that needs to be revealed. Beckett even raises the issue explicitly on stage with the famous line where his characters ask themselves: "On n'est pas en train de … de … signifier quelque chose ?"[23]

However, unlike most of Beckett's stage directions, the aforementioned directions of Ionesco are not even possible to enact. Therefore, they cannot be written for the actor or the spectator, but merely for the reader. This supposition is confirmed by a stage direction we find two pages later in *La cantatrice chauve*:

Un autre moment de silence. La pendule sonne sept fois. Silence. La pendule sonne trois fois. Silence. La pendule ne sonne aucune fois.[24]

---

21 "*Il* [Clov] *descend de l'escabeau, fait six pas vers la fenêtre à droite, retourne prendre l'escabeau, l'installe sous la fenêtre à droite, monte dessus, tire le rideau. Il descend de l'escabeau, fait trois pas vers la fenêtre à gauche, retourne prendre l'escabeau, monte dessus, regarde pas la fenêtre. Rire bref. Il descend de l'escabeau, fait un pas vers la fenêtre à droite, retourne prendre l'escabeau, l'installe sous la fenêtre à droite, monte dessus, regarde par la fenêtre*" (Samuel Beckett, *Fin de partie*, Paris 1957, p. 14). [*He gets down, takes six steps (for example) towards window right, goes back for ladder, carries it over and sets it down under window right, gets up on it, draws back curtain. He gets down, takes three steps towards window left, goes back for ladder, carries it over and sets it down under window left, gets up on it, looks out of the window. Brief laugh. He gets down, takes one step towards window right, goes back for ladder, carries it over and sets it down under window right, gets up on it, looks out of window* (translations are Beckett's own).]
22 See also M. Pfister, *Das Drama*, 11th ed., Munich 2001, p. 222.
23 Beckett, *Fin de partie*, p. 49. ["We're not beginning to … to … mean something?"]
24 Ionesco, *La cantatrice chauve*, p. 12. [*Another moment of silence. The clock strikes seven times. Silence. The clock strikes three times. Silence. The clock doesn't strike.*]

Again, we find very precise indications, mentioning the exact number of strokes, seven times, three times, and then we have to deal with the hilarious instruction of "*La pendule ne sonne aucune fois*"; later on in the play, one encounters the following stage directions:

> *Un assez long moment de silence... La pendule sonne vingt-neuf fois*[25]

and

> *La pendule sonne tant qu'elle veut. Après de nombreux instants, M. et Mme Martin se séparent* [...].[26]

"*The clock strikes as much as it likes*". What does the clock like to do? How many are "*nombreux instants*", and can we count those moments of silence? "*Nombreux*" seems to be more precise than *quelques* moments, but one cannot talk about numerous moments of silence, as several consecutive moments would just be one long moment. Hence, the more precise the instruction, the less realizable it becomes. The absurd stage directions regarding the clock are less due to the fact that the clock indicates the opposite of the correct time "in a spirit of contradiction", as Esslin asserts together with Monsieur Martin,[27] but they are first and foremost a parody of stage directions in general. What follows the "seventeen English strokes" is Madame Smith saying "Tiens, il est neuf heures", and obviously, there is a lack of logic, as 17 strokes do not mean that it is nine o'clock.[28] What comes next is something that Hempfer has pointed out as being a sheer violation of the basic rules of presupposition, here: pragmatic presupposition.[29]

> Mme SMITH. Tiens, il est 9 heures. Nous avons mangé de la soupe, du poisson, des pommes de terre au lard, de la salade anglaise. Les enfants ont bu de l'eau anglaise. Nous avons bien mangé, ce soir. C'est parce que nous habitons dans les environs de Londres et que notre nom est Smith.[30]

---

25 Ibid., p. 19. [*A rather long moment of silence. The clock strikes 29 times.*]
26 Ibid., p. 21. [*The clock strikes as much as it likes. After several seconds, Mr. and Mrs. Smith separate (...).*] There are similar stage directions in scene VIII: "*Il embrasse ou il n'embrasse pas Mme Smith*" [*He either kisses or does not kiss Mrs. Smith*] (p. 33), and "*Mme Smith, tombe à ses genoux, en sanglotant, ou ne le fait pas*" [*falls on her knees sobbing, or else she does not do this*] (ibid.).
27 Esslin, *The Theatre of the Absurd*, p. 139.
28 The spectator is not necessarily going to notice this logical error at all, because he will probably not count the strikes right from the first strike, nor will he notice the eight strikes to be missing.
29 Hempfer, "Die Theorie der Präsuppositionen", pp. 53–60.
30 Ionesco, *La cantatrice chauve*, p. 9. ["There, it's nine o'clock. We've drunk the soup, and eaten the fish and chips, and the English salad. The children have drunk English water. We've

It is commonly known that Ionesco picked up the idea of breaking those rules of presupposition from his English language textbook, where people constantly repeat what others already know. However, it is clear that Ionesco's aim is not to mock study books, but to question the use of language, namely the language of the theater, because first of all, parodying stage directions refers to nothing but theater, as this is the only place where they exist. The meta-linguistic commentaries within Madame Smith's comment have to be regarded as meta-theatrical commentaries, not least because no one would ever talk in that way—well, almost no one: a protagonist in a poorly made theater play could do so, especially in the exposition of the play, which has been, since the beginning of theater, a crucial element of the well-wrought play according to accepted theatrical techniques.[31] An artful announcement of the plot line, the smooth introduction of the *dramatis personae* and the situation, is commonly considered to be indispensable for a successful play. Ionesco's expository scene is far too explicit, and he seems to be doing everything but endeavoring to use any form of technique. The playwright's first theatrical attempt starts with a parody of a classical *scène d'expositon*, which is, by all means, not always eminently subtle or realistic either—this is what Ionesco could have meant when he said in "Expérience du théâtre" that "Les situations me paraissaient arbitraires. Il y avait quelque chose de faux [...]. Tout me paraissait un peu ridicule, un peu pénible."

As one delves further into the *Bald Soprano*, one discovers further parodies of typical elements of classical theater, and of the knowledge one acquires in school. Given that Ionesco was a teacher of French literature, he was most likely to have been teaching theatrical techniques and conventions to his students. There are, for example, Monsieur and Madame Smith's guests, a couple called Monsieur and Madame Martin, who realize already in the first half of the play, little by little, and after a long chat, that they actually are husband and wife and live together in the same apartment with their pretty

---

eaten well this evening. That's because we live in the suburbs of London and because our name is Smith."]

31 See also Bennett, who claims that "Ionesco is exposing how unrealistic theatrical realism actually is. The characters Mr. and Mrs. Smith must awkwardly and unnaturally talk about themselves, what is going on, and provide context for themselves and their actions" (*Cambridge Introduction*, p. 83).

little "white-eyed and red-eyed" daughter. This "revelation" is obviously nothing more than a ludicrous parody of an anagnorisis:

> Alors, chère Madame, je crois qu'il n'y a pas de doute, nous nous sommes déjà vus et vous êtes ma propre épouse... Élisabeth, je t'ai retrouvée !
> [...]
> *Ils s'assoient dans le même fauteuil, se tiennent embrassés et s'endorment.*[32]

Apart from this scene, we find an extremely short love story in the play, but it is a love story without a story: Towards the end of the play, a clandestine couple is revealed, but no other character is really interested in learning more about their relationship.

Finally, *La cantatrice chauve* ends how it started, precisely like Beckett's *Endgame* a few years later.[33] It might have been that the French, more than any other nation, were used to a quite rational development of the action, to a clear beginning, a clear climax, and a clear ending, following *les règles du théâtre classique* and Aristotelian plot lines.[34] As Ionesco appears to be parodying these expectations, he is calling theatrical conventions into doubt right from the beginning of his first play.

In his early career as a dramatist, Ionesco wrote a series of poetological plays, which were not particularly successful. *Victimes du devoir* (*Victims of Duty*), written in 1953, was one of Ionesco's favorites.[35] It has a real—an absurd—plot, but as a "Pseudo-Drama" (the subtitle of the play), it is essentially a long disquisition on drama (from antiquity to the twentieth century), which starts with a facetiously clumsy dialogue between a husband and his wife, both sitting in their living room. The wife is darning socks when the husband asks her, out of the blue, about her conceptions of contemporary theater: "Que penses-tu du

---

[32] Ionesco, *La cantatrice chauve*, p. 18f. ["Then, dear lady, I believe that there can be no doubt about it, we have seen each other before and you are my own wife ... Elizabeth, I have found you again!" (...) *They sit together in the same armchair, their arms around each other, and fall asleep.*]

[33] On the various forms of repetition that can be found in Beckett's work, see P. Brunel, "Autour de Samuel Beckett: Devanciers, épigones et hérétiques", in: *La mort de Godot: Attente et évanescence au théâtre*, ed. P. Brunel, Paris 1970, pp. 9–39, in particular pp. 31f.

[34] M. Kesting was the first to draw attention to this point (*Das epische Theater: Eine Untersuchung zum Formproblem des modernen Dramas*, Munich 1957, especially pp. 159f.); see also H. Seipel's critique in: *Untersuchungen zum experimentellen Theater von Beckett und Ionsesco*, Bonn 1963, in particular pp. 67ff., and P. Ronge, *Polemik, Parodie und Satire bei Ionesco: Elemente einer Theatertheorie und Formen des Theaters über das Theater*, Bad Homburg vor der Höhe 1967, pp. 41ff.

[35] Esslin, *The Theatre of the Absurd*, p. 152f.

théâtre d'aujourd'hui, quelles sont tes conceptions théâtrales ?"[36] At the end of the play, a character named Nicolas d'Eu concludes that in theater, one should no longer separate the tragic and the comic.[37] Yet Nicholas does not wish to be a writer as he claims: "Nous avons Ionesco et Ionesco, cela suffit !"[38]

L'impromptu de l'Alma ou le caméléon du berger, written in 1955, clearly implies a reference to Molière's *L'impromptu de Versailles*,[39] where the author/director/actor Molière discusses the rehearsal of a play with his actors and reflects on the contemporary state of theater and on the art of theater in general. Ionesco's *L'impromptu de l'Alma* is likewise an entirely poetological play; the main actor plays the author, Ionesco, and critics appear on stage, asking the author to be more instructive and to write a play that has an ideological message:

> IONESCO, *qui a repris un peu le courage.*
> > Messieurs, peut-être, le théâtre est-il, simplement, le drame, une action, une action dans un temps et un lieu donnés...
>
> [...]
> BARTHOLOMÉUS I.
> > Le théâtre, Monsieur, est une leçon sur un événement instructif, un événement plein d'enseignement...[40]

Indeed, *Victimes du devoir* and *L'impromptu de l'Alma* have mostly been forgotten, unlike Ionesco's plays which have a moral lesson, such as *La leçon* (*The Lesson*) and *Rhinocéros* (*Rhinoceros*), where meta-theatricality is rare or not to be found at all. *La leçon* is not only a parody of authoritarian French education in general, but above all it is a (not particularly subtle) critique of all sorts of totalitarianism, and the brassard *"portant un insigne, peut-être la svastika nazie"* at the end of the play is an explicit reference to very recent history.[41] *La leçon* may be regarded as anticipating the flagship play of absurdist theater, *Rhinocéros*, which Ionesco wrote four years later. In this play, which was eminently successful in Germany, the population of a typically French village turns, one after the other, into rhinoceroses, until only one human is left to fight the raucous animals. The story can be dissected quite

---

36 Eugène Ionesco, *Victimes du devoir*, in: Ionesco, *Théâtre complet*, pp. 203–250, p. 207.
37 Ibid., p. 243. See also Ionesco, "Expérience du théâtre", p. 269, in order to assess to what degree the character is repeating the author's own vision of theater.
38 Ionesco, *Victimes du devoir*, p. 246.
39 Molière himself is the subject of discussion in Ionesco's play—see *L'impromptu de l'Alma ou le caméléon du berger*, in: Ionesco, *Théâtre complet*, pp. 423–466, pp. 435ff.
40 Ionesco, *L'impromptu de l'Alma*, p. 439.
41 Eugène Ionesco, *La Leçon*, in: Ionesco, *Théâtre complet*, pp. 43–75, p. 74.

easily: The village is the world in which we live, the hero is the average Frenchman with the average French name Béranger, and the moral lesson we learn is clear: we should not become rhinoceroses like the others, that is, we should neither become *collaborateurs* of the Nazis nor adherents of (Stalinist) communist totalitarianism. The plot is absurd, but it has a real message, indeed quite a concrete moral message; since the beginning of its reception, the play has rightly been regarded as more of a parable than an instance of absurdist theater.

Taking into account the degree to which Ionesco's early plays differ from his later ones, critics have tried to categorize his work into different phases[42]: his earlier plays were either said to focus first and foremost on the malfunctioning of language,[43] or on the exposure of the "total absurdity of the world".[44] However, one might doubt that a sentence like "C'est parce que nous habitons dans les environs de Londres et que notre nom est Smith" constitutes a satirical parody of language, and that the formulation "La pendule ne sonne aucune fois" genuinely instructs us on the total absurdity of the world.

In view of the fact that the analysis of the possibilities and limits of theater was crucial for Ionesco (see his *Notes et contre-notes* from 1962),[45] the failure of communication and the absurdity of the action taking place on stage can equally be considered to constitute a parody of theater itself. Not least because Ionesco claimed to feel uncomfortable in the theater—namely in any theater, not only when attending performances of Boulevard Theater or existentialist plays—his parodistic early plays appear to amount to a problematization of theater in general.

---

[42] See also K. Schoell's overview in his essay "Eugène Ionesco, *Rhinocéros* (1959)", in: *20. Jahrhundert: Theater*, ed. K. Schoell, Tübingen 2006, pp. 239–278, pp. 242–244.
[43] See, for instance, H. Hanstein, who published a study on the evolution of Ionesco's theater, calling the language in the early plays "alienated language" ("entfremdete Sprache") (*Studien zur Entwicklung von Ionescos Theater*, Heidelberg 1971, esp. chapter II: "'Entfremdete Sprache' und das Phänomen der Aggression in den frühen Stücken"), or Seipel, *Untersuchungen*. See also S. Sontag's original objection to the reading focusing on a critique of language: "[It] misses the important fact that in much of modern art one can no longer really speak of subject-matter in the old sense. Rather the subject-matter is the technique. What Ionesco did—no mean feat—was to appropriate for the theater one of the great technical discoveries of modern poetry: that all language can be considered from the outside, as by a stranger. [...] His early plays are not about 'meaninglessness'. They are attempts to use meaninglessness theatrically." ("Ionesco", in: S. Sontag, *Against Interpretation*, New York, NY 1966, pp. 115–123, p. 119).
[44] R. Daus, *Das Theater des Absurden in Frankreich*, Stuttgart 1977, esp. pp. 44f. and pp. 49f.
[45] See, in particular, Ronge, *Polemik, Parodie und Satire bei Ionesco*.

Eleutheria is the title of Samuel Beckett's first completed dramatic attempt, undertaken in 1947. However, Beckett never wanted it to be released, and it therefore remained unpublished until 1995, six years after his death. Beckett's biographer and friend, James Knowlson, reports that Beckett thought the play was "overexplicit",[46] and there is no need to contradict Beckett's assessment. Nevertheless, it is far from clear what, indeed, is overexplicit in this play. There are not many scholarly studies of *Eleutheria*; however, one point most of them have commented on are the explicit references to Arthur Schopenhauer's philosophy, which are still to be found in Beckett's later plays, as many critics have pointed out.[47] In addition, what I consider first and foremost to be overexplicit is the play's meta-theatricality and its questioning of the medium of theater, which raises the issue of the limits of the *theatrum mundi* metaphor.

A short summary of the plot might be helpful at this point: The play deals with a promising young author named Victor who has a pretty fiancée and wealthy parents, but who claims to lack freedom (*eleutheria*), which is why he has left his family and lives the life of a hermit in a studio apartment, basically staying in bed all day long. His overt aim is to get rid of his body, and to watch himself slowly dying. We find very clear references to Schopenhauer's concept of self-effacement, where real freedom is not the freedom *of* the will, but the freedom *from* the will, and the will is, in all cases, the will of the body. Following the main character of the play, Victor (or Schopenhauer), this leads to two sorts of possibilities: either asceticism, or the enjoyment of art, which, however, turns out to be a merely temporary solution (Victor tries all forms of art, but all are in vain). Interestingly, these ideas are not only extremely close to Schopenhauer, but also remind us of Kierkegaard's concept of the aestheticization of life. In light of this, it might not be accidental that the main protagonist is named Victor—as the latter lives the life of a hermit, the name echoes the pseudonym

---

[46] James Knowlson, *Damned to Fame*, London 1996, p. 363. The fact that *En attendant Godot* was completed so shortly after *Eleutheria* (and would have been offered for production almost at the same time) might have been the initial reason for Beckett's withholding it; see also M. J. Sidnell's essay on Beckett's early dramatic attempts: "Beckett's Discovery of Theater: *Human Wishes* and the Dramaturgical Contexts of *Eleutheria*", in: *The South Carolina Review*, vol. 43, 2010, p. 36–49, esp. p. 41.
[47] Regarding Beckett's general interest in Schopenhauer, see in particular U. Pothast, *Die eigentliche metaphysische Tätigkeit: Über Schopenhauers Ästhetik und ihre Anwendung durch Samuel Beckett*, Frankfurt/Main 1982. S. Schneider has shown to what degree Beckett illustrates Schopenhauer's philosophy in *Eleutheria* ("Samuel Becketts *Eleutheria*: Die menschliche Freiheit als Schopenhauersche Tragikomödie", in: *Germanisch-Romanische Monatsschrift*, vol. 50, 2000, pp. 361–377).

under which Kierkegaard published *Either—Or*, namely Victor Eremita. Hence, Beckett does not only seem to be referring to Schopenhauer, but also to Kierkegaard. Therefore, Theodor W. Adorno's dictum of "Kulturmüll"—"cultural trash", as he calls the quoted discourses in *Endgame*—appears to be applicable to *Eleutheria* as well.[48] Nonetheless, it is remarkable that in *Eleutheria*—a play which raises the issue of the *theatrum mundi*, as we will see—Beckett refers so extensively to Schopenhauer, a philosopher who availed himself frequently of the metaphor of *Welttheater*.[49]

In the following, I will focus on the aforementioned meta-theatricality of the play. Right in the first scene of *Eleutheria*, Victor's father, Monsieur Krap, states, "Au point de vue dramatique, l'absence de ma femme ne sert à rien",[50] which already hints at the potential self-awareness apparent in this character. A few lines later, when the strange Dr. Piouk enters, we are confronted with the following dialogue:

M. Krap.   Je me demande à quoi vous allez servir dans cette comédie.
Dr. Piouk, *ayant mûrement réfléchi*.
           J'espère que je pourrai être utile.
Mme Meck, *inquiète*.
           Je ne comprends pas.
Dr. Piouk. Et vous, cher monsieur, votre rôle est-il bien déterminé ?
M. Krap.   Il est terminé.
Dr. Piouk. Vous restez pourtant en scène.
M. Krap.   On dirait.[51]

---

[48] "Was Beckett an Philosophie aufbietet, depraviert er selber zum Kulturmüll, nicht anders als die ungezählten Anspielungen auf Bildungsfermente [...]" ("Versuch, das Endspiel zu verstehen", in: Theodor W. Adorno, *Versuch, das Endspiel zu verstehen: Aufsätze zur Literatur des 20. Jahrhunderts I*, Frankfurt/Main 1973, pp. 167–214, p. 167). See also E. Fischer-Lichte, who identified an impressively large number of literary quotes in *Endgame* (*Geschichte des Dramas. Band 2: Von der Romantik bis zur Gegenwart*, Tübingen 1990, pp. 245–248).

[49] On the other hand, one has to consider that Schopenhauer was simply *the* philosopher of twentieth-century artists, probably not least because he claims that art can lead to metaphysical insight. On Schopenhauer's *Welttheater*, see *Die Welt als Wille und Vorstellung*, ed. W. Frhr. von Löhneysen, Stuttgart and Frankfurt/Main 1976, vol. II, especially ch. 31: "Vom Genie" (p. 498). The most recent and remarkably popular examination of Schopenhauer's "Welttheater" was undertaken by Michel Houellebecq in *En présence de Schopenhauer*, Paris 2017, especially ch. 4: "Le théâtre du monde".

[50] Samuel Beckett, *Eleutheria*, Paris 1995, p. 33. ["Dramatically speaking, my wife's absence serves no purpose" (translation by M. Brodsky).]

[51] Ibid., p. 40. [M. Krap: "I'm wondering of what use you're going to be in the farce." Dr. Piouk: (*Upon mature reflection*) "I hope that I will be able to be useful." Mme. Meck: (*Worried*) "I don't understand." Dr. Piouk: "And your role, my dear sir, is it very clear-cut?" M. Krap: "It is being

In Act II, the meta-theatricality gains momentum as well as an interesting twist, which leads us back to our main interest: namely the intertwining of meta-theatricality and theater as metaphor. When Victor's family and a glazier are in Victor's room and Victor is not seen, the dialogue is as follows:

> Mme Meck. Où est-il ?
> Vitrier. Il est sous le lit, madame, comme du temps de Molière.
> (*Victor sort de sous le lit*) Il fallait y rester.
> Mme Meck. A quoi rime cette comédie ?
> Vitrier. C'est dans un but de délassement et de divertissement publics, madame.[52]

In this dialogue, the characters themselves are merging meta-theatricality and theater as a metaphor. Madame Meck calls the ridiculous situation a comedy, referring to the *theatrum mundi* as "the world as a stage". The glazier is obviously referring to the history of theater, to Molière, and is talking about the sense and purpose of theater itself, with the stage representing the world. This linkage between the two meanings of the metaphor intensifies as the play continues.

What started as more or less explicit allusions to the characters' meta-theatrical self-awareness becomes open criticism of theater itself:

> Vitrier. Ne voyez-vous pas que nous sommes tous en train de tourner autour de quelque chose qui n'a pas de sens ? Il faut lui trouver un sens, sinon il n'y a qu'à baisser le rideau.
> Dr. Piouk. Et après ? Je ne vois aucun inconvénient à ce qu'on baisse le rideau sur mon non-sens; c'est d'ailleurs ce qui arrive le plus souvent.[53]

However, it is in the third and final act where we find Beckett's most explicit breaking of the fourth wall,[54] and a highly exceptional form of meta-theatrical

---

cut." Dr. Piouk: "Yet you are on stage." M. Krap: "So it appears".] See also remarks like Madame Meck's: "Ça tourne au mélo" (p. 98) or the glazier, who ascertains: "Le temps qu'on perd avec les figurants !" (p. 101).
52 Ibid., p. 74. [Glazier: "He is under the bed, Madame, as in Molière's days. (*Victor comes out from under the bed*) You should have stayed there." Mme. Meck: "Where is the method to this madness?" Glazier: "It is with a view to public entertainment and refreshment, Madame."]
53 Ibid., p. 111. [Glazier: "Don't you see that we are all busy focusing over and over on something that has no meaning? A meaning for it must be found, otherwise we might as well ring down the curtain." Dr. Piouk: "So what? I have no objection to the curtain's being rung down on something senseless, besides, that's what most often happens."]
54 On Beckett's use of breaking the fourth wall, see N. Davis, "'Not a Soul in Sight!': Beckett's Fourth Wall", in: *Journal of Modern Literature*, vol. 38, 2015, pp. 86–103, esp. p. 91.

self-awareness: At one moment in *Eleutheria* the play stagnates, and a spectator leaves the auditorium and climbs onto the stage in order to criticize the plot, its author, and the actors. The spectator claims to be a representative of the audience: "Car je ne suis pas un, mais mille spectateurs, tous légèrement différents les uns des autres."[55] "Audience member" and "actors", as well as a "stage-box voice" discuss the script extensively, but nonetheless, the controversy does not lead anywhere.[56] The "spectator" goes on asking Victor to shape the narration of his life so as to result in an acceptable story, threatening him with his "Chinese torturer":

> Spectateur.   [...] Sortez un peu de vos généralités, je vous en prie. C'est votre cas qui nous préoccupe, pas celui du genre humain.
> Victor.   Mais ils sont solidaires.
> Spectateur.   Comment ? Balivernes ! [...][57]

Victor, who is forced to tell his individual story, claims it to be possible for the audience to transfer his particular case to life in general—but the spectator considers this thought to be sheer "balderdash". Hence, the question raised here is whether one particular case can be translated into a point concerning the human condition. Is it at all possible to link these levels? At this moment in the play, the answer is anything but evident. Victor continues to tell the "story" of

---

55 Beckett, *Eleutheria*, p. 127. ["For I am not one audience member, but a thousand, all slightly different from each other".]

56 Interestingly, already in Beckett's earliest play, the "spectator" compares the play to a chess game—and a chess game of the lowest level—to explain his discomfort while attending the play: "C'est comme lorsqu'on assiste à une partie d'échecs entre joueurs de dernière catégorie. Il y a trois quarts d'heure qu'ils n'ont pas touché à une pièce, ils sont là comme deux couillons à bâiller sur l'échiquier, et vous aussi vous êtes là, encore plus couillon qu'eux, cloué sur place, dégoûté, ennuyé, fatigué, émerveillé par tant de bêtise. Jusqu'au moment où vous n'y tenez plus. Alors, vous leur dites, mais faites ça, faites ça, qu'est-ce que vous attendez ? Faites ça et c'est fini, nous pourrons aller nous coucher" (ibid., p. 133). ["It's like when you watch a chess game between players of the lowest class. For three quarters of an hour they haven't touched a single piece. They sit there gaping at the board like two horses' asses and you're also there, even more of a horse's ass than they are, nailed to the spot, disgusted, bored, worn-out, filled with wonder at so much stupidity. Up until the moment when you can't take it anymore. Then you tell them, So do that, do that, what are you waiting for, do that and it's all over, we can go to bed"]. It is commonly known that Beckett was intrigued by chess (see for instance *Murphy* or *Endgame*); see P. Brockmeier, *Samuel Beckett*, Stuttgart 2001, pp. 154f.

57 Beckett, *Eleutheria*, p. 144. [Spectator: "Get out a bit from under these generalities, if you please. We're preoccupied with your case, not with that of the human race." Victor: "But they are of a piece." Spectator: "What? Twaddle!"]

his life, which the "spectator", before leaving the stage,[58] surprisingly states to be "pas mal du tout, [...] un peu longue, un peu ennuyeuse, un peu... bête, mais pas mal, pas mal du tout, jolie même par endroits, à condition de ne pas y regarder de trop près, chose que nous ne faisons jamais".[59] For the *spectateur*, a badly constructed story appears to be better than no story at all.

The end of the play is announced with Victor renouncing his quest for "true freedom", concluding:

> Victor. [...] On ne peut pas se voir mort. C'est du théâtre. Je ne...[60]

One last time, we have to make the choice: is it the play to which he is referring, or is it life in its entirety, which is, after all, just a play?

The final stage direction in *Eleutheria* reads as follows:

> *Puis il* [Victor] *se couche, le maigre dos tourné à l'humanité.*[61]

Why did Beckett choose the lofty word "mankind" and not just "the audience"? This can be taken to be a thoroughly optimistic understanding of theater as a metaphor; with this stage direction, the author himself is finally accepting the spectators as representatives of humankind. Hence, he considers it to be possible to take one particular case and extrapolate from it a statement about the human condition.

The intertwining of meta-theatricality and theater as a metaphor reaches its apex in Beckett's *Endgame*. The play abounds with meta-theatrical elements, as well as invocations of the topos of *Welttheater* that scholars have already pointed out extensively, emphasizing first and foremost the prevalence of plays within the play.[62]

---

58 See the insightful analysis in Davis's essay "'Not a Soul in Sight!'", esp. p. 96.
59 Beckett, *Eleutheria*, p. 149f. ["It wasn't bad at all, your story, a bit long, a bit boring, a bit silly, but not bad, not bad at all, even pretty-sounding in spots, on condition that one isn't too particular, something we never are."]
60 Ibid., p. 150. ["One cannot see oneself dead. It's theatrics. I no—".]
61 Ibid., p. 167. [*Then he gets into bed, his scrawny back turned on mankind.*]
62 See Fischer-Lichte, *Geschichte des Dramas*, particularly the chapter "Zerstückelung und Wiedergeburt", pp. 240–289. See also K. Dorney's approach that reads *Endgame* as a meta-linguistic and meta-theatrical commentary ("Hamming it up in *Endgame*: A Theatrical Reading", in: *Samuel Beckett's* Endgame, ed. M. S. Byron, Amsterdam and New York, NY 2007, pp. 227–252).

Endgame opens with the famous line: "Fini, c'est fini, ça va finir, ça va peut-être finir."[63] Beckett is hereby immediately raising the question of whether it is the play or the world that is finished. Both readings are possible, as he could be representing on stage a post-apocalyptic scene dealing with the end of the world or he could be mocking our Aristotelian plot expectations by starting the play with saying that it is all over. This double reading, put forward by the playwright right at the beginning, is maintained throughout the entire play; Clov, for instance, remarks towards the end of the play: "C'est ce que nous appelons gagner la sortie".[64] This meta-theatricality is similar to the question posed by Nell and Clov: "Pourquoi cette comédie, tous les jours?"[65]—the characters might be aware of their own theatricality[66] and questioning their job as actors, or they might be questioning the senselessness of their life by referring to a theatrical metaphor.

On the one hand, the characters in *Endgame* explicitly invoke the idea of the stage as a place that represents the world:

> Hamm. Fais-moi faire un petit tour. (*Clov se met derrière le fauteuil et le fait avancer.*) Pas trop vite ! (*Clov fait avancer le fauteuil.*) Fais-moi faire le tour du monde ! (*Clov fait avancer le fauteuil.*) Rase les murs. Puis ramène-moi au centre.[67]

When Clov starts to observe the world beyond the stage through his telescope, Hamm does not want him to look at anything special, but to "[r]egarde la terre",[68] to see "rien que le tout",[69] and a "[n]oir clair" is the predominant color of "tout l'univers".[70] Hence, Clov is supposed to look at the world outside the stage in the same manner one would look at a stage representing the world. In other words: in this famous teichoscopy, the actors themselves are

---

63 Beckett, *Fin de partie*, p. 15. ["Finished, it's finished, nearly finished, it must be nearly finished."]
64 Ibid., p. 109. ["This is what we call making an exit."]
65 Ibid., p. 29 and p. 49. ["Why this farce, day after day?"]
66 See George Tabori, who staged *Fin de partie* in 1998 at the Akademietheater of the Vienna Burgtheater as a rehearsal.
67 Beckett, *Fin de partie*, p. 41. ["Take me for a little turn. (*Clov goes behind the chair and pushes it forward.*) Not too fast! (*Clov pushes chair.*) Right round the world! (*Clov pushes chair.*) Hug the walls, then back to the center again."] Fischer-Lichte interprets Hamm as a tragic hero who, like any other dramatic hero, constantly needs to be (in) the center of attention/the world (*Geschichte des Dramas*, p. 247f.).
68 Beckett, *Fin de partie*, p. 43. ["Look at the earth."]
69 Ibid., p. 97. ["merely the whole thing".]
70 Ibid., p. 48. ["Light black. From pole to pole".]

looking at the Great Theater of the World.[71] However, the most interesting point here is that at the same moment, the limits of the exposed world are explicitly commented on by Hamm, as he knocks at the walls and ascertains that they consist of theater mock up:

> Hamm. Tu entends ? (*Il frappe le mur avec son doigt replié. Un temps.*) Tu entends ? Des briques creuses. (*Il frappe encore.*) Tout ça c'est creux ![72]

To a certain degree, all of Beckett's characters in his earlier plays are aware of the fact that they are part of a play being performed on stage, questioning their own performance and function and exposing the limits of the concept of the *theatrum mundi*. This has been especially pointed out with regard to *Fin de partie*,[73] but it applies to *Waiting for Godot* as well, where Vladimir and Estragon perform exercises similar to acting exercises,[74] or, additionally, anticipate the audience's reaction, talking about this "[c]harmante soirée" where "on se croirait au spectacle",[75] or claiming: "Voilà notre fin de soirée assurée".[76] This meta-theatricality gains momentum when Vladimir complains: "Je commence à en avoir assez de ce motif".[77] We also find stage directions, at least in the original French version, which are as unusual as Ionesco's, as they appear to be mocking the very essence of stage directions: "*Estragon agite son pied, en faisant jouer les orteils, afin que l'air y circule mieux.*"[78] Beckett not only indicates *what* the characters should do, but *why* they should do so, and his nonsensical explanation does not make things clearer. When Vladimir and Estragon start to look for a path to escape from their situation, they define the limits of the

---

71 On this point see M. J. Schäfer, who pursues the theme of the *theatrum mundi* metaphor in *Endgame* in his essay "Samuel Becketts Reduktion des Welttheaters im *Endspiel*", in: *Null, Nichts und Negation: Becketts No-Thing*, ed. A. v. Schäfer and K. Kröger, Bielefeld 2016, pp. 117–141, especially p. 122.
72 Beckett, *Fin de partie*, p. 42. ["Do you hear? (*He strikes the wall with his knuckles.*) Do you hear? Hollow bricks! (*He strikes again.*) All that's hollow!"] See also Schäfer, "Reduktion", p. 125.
73 M. Foucré was the first to point out the degree to which the characters in the play are aware of the fact of being on stage (*Le geste et la parole dans le théâtre de Samuel Beckett*, Paris 1970).
74 Samuel Beckett, *En attendant Godot*, Paris 1952, p. 107.
75 Ibid., p. 47. ["Charming evening we're having", "It's worse than being at the theatre" (here and in the following translated by Samuel Beckett).]
76 Ibid., p. 109. ["Now we're sure to see the evening out."]
77 Ibid., p. 117. ["I begin to weary of this motif."]
78 Ibid., p. 13. The stage direction means: "Estragon moves his foot, playing with his toes in order to improve the circulation of the air between his toes." In Beckett's English version of *Fin de Partie*, the stage direction is much shorter and less odd: "*Estragon pulling at his toes*".

exposed world on stage, as they desperately try to leave the stage. While they look around, they realize "Nous sommes cernés !",[79] "Il n'y a pas d'issue par là",[80] and Vladimir pushes Estragon towards the auditorium (*Vladimir va le relever, l'amène vers la rampe. Geste vers l'auditore*) and says, "Sauve-toi par là. Allez." However, Estragon flinches in horror, whereupon Vladimir cracks the hoary theater joke: "Tu ne veux pas ? Ma foi, ça se comprend."[81]

The level of the characters' self-awareness distinguishes Beckett's earlier plays from his posterior ones.[82] The most famous of all is probably *Happy Days*, the first play written after Beckett had taken a break from theater. The play is primarily a long soliloquy of the female protagonist, whose body is slowly sinking into the ground, and who constantly exclaims "This is a happy day!" She appears to have no idea she is part of a play, nor does she recognize the bizarre nature of her situation.[83] *Happy Days* forms a world in itself, an absurd, unrealistic, and probably metaphorical world, but a world as a whole, where the human being is sinking deeper and deeper into the ground, and incessantly calling out that "this is a happy day". Beckett's late characters are, just like Ionesco's late characters, unable to reflect on the entirely absurd situation and their own absurd actions. They do not wonder why they are sinking into the ground or why people are transforming into rhinoceroses; they do not question the absurd situation and they know even less about their being part of a play. Ionesco and Beckett confront the audience with a more than strange situation,

---

79 Ibid., p. 104. ["We're surrounded!"]

80 Ibid. ["There's no way out there". (*He takes Estragon by the arm and drags him towards front. Gesture towards auditorium.*)]

81 Ibid. ["You won't? Well, I can understand that."] On the stage as a "claustrophobic space, surrounded at all sides, to which the character is condemned: an infernal space from which there is no real escape", see Davis, "'Not a Soul in Sight!'", p. 98.

82 See Bennett, who makes a similar statement for *Godot, Endgame*, and *Act without Words I* (*Cambridge Introduction*, p. 57; see also p. 82 on Ionesco's *Rhinocéros*). Davis claims that—from *Eleutheria* to *Endgame*—"Beckett moves away from his initial experimentation with explicit fourth-wall breaks—which can be seen as part of an unsuccessful first attempt at establishing his personal theatrical model [...]" ("'Not a Soul in Sight!'", p. 101). One might object that breaking the fourth wall is a genuinely meta-theatrical effect, and over the course of his career Beckett simply reduced every form of meta-theatrical effect.

83 See Bennett, *Cambridge Introduction*, p. 57. The only potentially ambiguous moment could be the beginning of act two when Winnie exclaims: "Someone is looking at me." She could mean some divine being, or the spectator. This latter interpretation would seem to be supported by the slightly meta-theatrical remark she makes immediately afterwards: "What is that unforgettable line?" (*Happy Days*, London and Boston, MA 2010, p. 160). On the interdependency between the subject and its perceiver in Beckett's work, see Fischer-Lichte, *Geschichte des Dramas*, p. 252, as well as Sh. Levy, *Samuel Beckett's Self-Referential Drama: The Three I's*, Basingstoke 1990.

which can only be resolved if it is accepted as an allegorical plot—constituting a world in itself and allowing the recipient to conceive of the stage as a place where it is possible to make statements about the real world. In their early absurdist plays, one still has to decide whether the dialogue or the commentary are intended as meta-theatrical references or rather refer to the *theatrum mundi*, whereas in the playwrights' later plays, this question is not even raised.

As has become clear, part of the absurdity presented on stage in the earliest plays of Beckett and Ionesco is the absurdity of theatrical conventions, expressed primarily in meta-theatrical remarks. The staged plot is, of course, absurd—yet this is not the only, nor the basic feature of the theater of the absurd. Another crucial point is the absurdity on the meta-theatrical and self-referential level, which has been neglected by critics, who, in order to emphasize a didactic interpretation right from the beginning, have preferred to cling to general assumptions about the world. This essay, however, has sought to draw attention to the early plays of Ionesco and Beckett in order to illustrate their range of meta-theatricality and to demonstrate how this meta-theatricality served to expose the limits of the *theatrum mundi* metaphor. Hence, it is necessary to speculate on the reasons why, at the beginning of their careers, the playwrights attempted to make this metaphor a subject of discussion. As mentioned at the beginning of this essay, the metaphor of the Great Theater of the World functions in both directions insofar as the world can be seen and understood as a stage and the stage can be seen as representing the world. Indeed, generalizability is a necessary condition for every form of representation. Therefore, the actual question raised by Ionesco and Beckett appears to be whether this completely broken post-war world is still *generalizable* and thus suitable for representation to the degree that the stage could represent the world.

Susanne Zepp
Chico Buarque's *Gota d'água, uma tragédia carioca*: Theater as Metaphor in Brazil during the Military Dictatorship, 1964–1985

The piece titled *Gota d'água, uma tragédia carioca* by Chico Buarque and Paulo Pontes, created in 1975, marks a pivotal chapter in the rich history of the reception of the Medea myth by authors since Euripides' first elaboration of the plot. This play uses Euripides' *Medea* as a model with regard to both content and form. *Gota d'água* is particularly concerned with the status of theater as a performance medium and with the complex interrelation between art and life that is reflected in the onstage activity. The intention of this article is not to provide a (new) interpretation of the play, for which purpose we may refer to the existing research, which has investigated these questions in an impressive manner.[1] Rather, this paper argues that Chico Buarque's 1975 play is mainly interested in indicating the limits of "theater as metaphor"; for that reason, it is especially relevant for the discussions conducted in this volume.

---

[1] See for example G. R. Lind, "Uma nova versão brasileira do mito de Medéia: *Gota d'água* de Chico Buarque de Holanda e Paulo Pontes", in: *Cadernos de Lit.*, vol. 15, 1983, pp. 26–38, and M. I. Guimarães, "A *Gota d'água* de Chico Buarque e Paulo Pontes: Palavra poética como ação dramática e denúncia", in: *Estudos Brasileiros*, vol. 8, 1982, pp. 40–82, but also more recently L. C. Barros, "Tragédia social em *Gota d'água*, de Chico Buarque e Paulo Pontes: Aspectos hipertextuais e intermediais", in: *Espéculo: Revista de Estudios Literarios*, vol. 31, 2005, s.p.; D. J. M. Toneto, "Jasão e a eterna busca do velocino de ouro: Uma leitura a partir do estabelecimento de contratos Fiduciários/Jasão and the everlasting search for the golden velocin: A reading based on the establishment of fiduciary contracts", in: *Estudos Lingüísticos*, vol. 32, 2003, s.p.; D. J. M. Toneto, "Breves considerações sobre figurativização em *Gota d'água*: Ideologia e lugar social", in: *Itinerários: Revista de Literatura*, vol. 20, pp 23–32; F. Marques, "O banquete da meia dúzia: Fontes e estruturas de *Gota d'água*", in: *Estudos de Literatura Brasileira Contemporânea*, vol. 8, 2000, pp. 3–14; E. S. Rocha, "A arte de narrar e de resistir em *Gota d'água*", in: *Itinerários: Revista de Literatura*, vol. 10, 1996, pp. 193–201; M. H. M. Neves, "*Medéia* (uma tragédia grega) e *Gota d'água*", in: *Rev. de Letras: Sér. Lit.*, vol. 25, 1985, pp. 97–101; R. Roux, "*Gota d'água*: Une tragédie brésilienne? ou, l'ambigüité de la 'classe moyenne'", in: *Cahiers d'études romanes*, vol. 10, pp. 251–254; D. Mimoso-Ruiz, "La *Médée* d'Euripide et *Gota d'água* de Paulo Pontes et Chico Buarque", in: *Théâtre et société*, ed. E. Konigson and R. Marienstras, Paris 1980, pp. 97–110.

First, I will recall the historical context, as Chico Buarque's 1975 play can only be understood against the backdrop of the political realities of the period of military dictatorship in Brazil. As a second step, there will be a close reading of the play's programmatic preface in order to develop the argument; finally, this preface will be considered synoptically, comparing it to a paradigmatic passage from the drama proper.

I

When, in 1964, the elected government of Brazil was overthrown in a *coup d'état*, an authoritarian regime was established that was controlled by the armed forces; the period of dictatorial rule lasted until 1985.[2] In a global context, the coup may be regarded in light of the major impact of the Cold War on Brazilian politics and society, as the military justified their action as a rescue and protection of the Brazilian nation from the "communist threat".[3] The move towards authoritarian rule, however, had a long pre-history; as M. Napolitano put it, "domestically, the coup was the result of an authoritarian, exclusionary, and conservative political culture disseminated among the civilian and military elite since the establishment of the republic in 1889".[4] The Brazilian armed forces sought to control the state and civil society.[5] Any political leaders were required to submit to the national objectives that the military defined.[6]

---

[2] For a concise analysis of the coup in a global context, see the brilliant article by M. Napolitano, "The Brazilian Military Regime, 1964–1985" (2018), in the online version of the *Oxford Research Encyclopedia of Latin American History*, to be found here: http://oxfordre.com/latinamericanhistory/view/10.1093/acrefore/9780199366439.001.0001/acrefore-9780199366439-e-413, accessed 15 January 2019.
[3] See H. S. Klein and F. Vidal Luna, *Brazil, 1964–1985: The Military Regimes of Latin America in the Cold War*, New Haven, CT 2017. The book offers an analysis of the politics of the military dictatorship in Brazil against the backdrop of the Cold War and the history of Latin America in its entirety.
[4] Napolitano, "The Brazilian Military Regime". Klein and Vidal Luna make a strong case for the assumption that Getúlio Vargas's regime laid the ground for the military regimes of Brazil.
[5] See F. D. McCann, *Soldiers of the Pátria: A History of the Brazilian Army, 1889–1937*, Stanford, CA 2003.
[6] F. D. McCann has pointed out that after playing the decisive role in overthrowing the Brazilian Empire (1822–1889), "the army was the strong-arm of the Republic defending and extending its authority. [...] The army, indeed the three armed services, historically has been largely autonomous [...]" ("Brasil: Acima de Tudo!! The Brazilian Armed Forces: Remodeling for a New Era", in: *Diálogos: Revista do Departamento de História e do Programa de Pós-Graduação em História*, vol. 21, 2017, pp. 57–95, p. 59.

From the end of 1968 onward, that is, starting in the third year of rule, censorship of the press and of all artistic activities became more rigorously enforced.[7] The reason was that the authoritarian regime, although well-established, did not remain uncontested; as Napolitano formulated:

> One of the distinctive elements in the history of the Brazilian military regime was the formation of a vigorous social, cultural, and, to a lesser extent, partisan opposition, which took shape [...] shortly after the military seized power. Although it had considerable support, particularly among conservative sectors of the middle class, the regime ultimately lacked a durable social base of support.[8]

Very soon after the *coup d'état*, even the conservatives who had initially supported the regime became conscious of the fact that the military had its own agenda. An essential point within this agenda was a drastic restriction of freedom of speech and artistic expression. Students and workers formed opposition movements, and some sections of the left joined the armed struggle. The attempt to bring this resistance movement against the regime into the public sphere was prevented by a legislative reform. Napolitano characterized the new law concerning freedom of speech as follows:

> Amid the turmoil, the relative freedom of expression that remained in Brazil was buried by Institutional Act No. 5, the hallmark of an era of intense repression that would last until the end of 1978. Institutional Act No. 5 further strengthened the president's power over the other branches of government and suspended *habeas corpus* for political prisoners, among other harsh measures. [...] It is important to stress that the Institutional Acts were not merely a "legalistic façade" for the regime, as if its actual power emanated solely from arms and violence. The Institutional Acts were essential for the strategy of avoiding the personalization of political power and guaranteeing some normative rules for political life.[9]

The legal framework of the "institutional acts" enabled the most violent and extra-legal period of political repression, in which every form of opposition was fought with utter brutality. By combining restrictive domestic measures

---

[7] See O. Fernandez, "Censorship and the Brazilian Theatre", in: *Educational Theatre Journal*, vol. 25, 1973, pp. 285–298; see also L. Souza Pinto, "Cinema brasileiro e censura durante a ditatura militar/Cinéma brésilien et censure pendant la dictature militaire", in: *Cinémas d'Amérique Latine*, vol. 9, 2001, pp. 157–164.
[8] Napolitano, "The Brazilian Military Regime". T. J. Power differentiates three factions of opposition to the military rule: firstly, the intellectual wing, then the social movement wing, and, finally, the armed resistance (cf. "The Brazilian Military Regime of 1964–1985: Legacies for Contemporary Democracy", in: *Iberoamericana*, vol. 16, 2016, pp. 13–26, p. 14).
[9] Napolitano, "The Brazilian Military Regime".

suggesting relative political stability and a promotion of industrial development, the Brazilian economy began to prosper, also as a result of international capital investment. It was primarily the military and the elites of the authoritarian regime rather than the general population that benefited from this boom. Yet the economic upswing calmed many sections of society and made it difficult for the opposition to gain support. In the cultural and artistic fields, however, the opposition to the military regime was constantly growing. In fact, many conservatives also reacted negatively to reports of torture and censorship. The result of the emergence of a quantitatively restricted but multifaceted opposition allowed for the creation of a limited sphere where a critical culture that sought to articulate dissident content in an encrypted form of expression was able to unfold.

Chico Buarque's artistic work is closely linked to this specific political and cultural configuration. Chico Buarque is the pen name of Francisco Buarque de Hollanda, who was born in Rio de Janeiro in 1944. To this day, Chico Buarque is rightfully regarded as one of Brazil's most renowned contemporary artists. His socio-critical songs, which have indeed become veritable classics of contemporary Brazilian pop music, are also well known beyond Brazil. In fact, these songs constitute the major part of his artistic work. But Chico Buarque also wrote narrative, essayistic, and dramatic texts or was involved in the stage performance of the latter. His song texts are poems that have become a sort of lyrical conscience of an entire nation.

In the period of dictatorship, Chico Buarque's oeuvre was consistently subject to censorship, especially with regard to his songs, but also with regard to his involvement in dramatic productions. Frequently, there was a link between these two strands of his activities; the songs were often composed for plays that became more or less rigorously censored.

When, in 1975, Chico Buarque decided to write, together with Paulo Pontes, *Gota d'água, uma tragédia carioca*, they elaborated on the concept of a versified recreation of Euripides' tragedy *Medea*, accompanied by music, that was set in the context of the contemporaneous suburbs of Rio de Janeiro.

Before dealing with the text proper, I would like to briefly analyze the preface to the dramatic work, in which the authors outline the three "fundamental preoccupations" that their play is trying to reflect. The first preoccupation reads as follows:

> Gota d'água, a tragédia, é uma reflexão [...] insuficiente, simplificadora, ainda perplexa, não tão substantiva quanto é necessário, pois o quadro é muito complexo e só agora emerge das sombras do processo social para se constituir no traço dominante do perfil da vida brasileira atual. De tão significativo, o quadro está a exigir a atenção das melhores energias da cultura brasileira; necessita não de uma peça, mas de uma dramaturgia

> inteira. Procuramos, pelo menos, diante de todas as limitações, olhar a tragédia de frente, enfrentar a sua concretude, não escamotear a complexidade da situação com a adjetivação raivosa e vã.[10]

This first "fundamental preoccupation" that the preface formulates has been read in research as a reference to the consolidation of the prevalent socio-economic model in Brazil during the "last few years" (i.e. those of the military dictatorship). But when we focus on the semantic horizon of the concepts of "tragedy", "theater", and "play" in this quote, a slightly different interpretation seems to suggest itself. Chico Buarque and Paulo Pontes establish in this preface a substantial differentiation that is played out in the course of the entire tragedy; this differentiation focuses on the idea that the degree of responsibility for our behavior offstage is fundamentally different from any behavior onstage. In the sphere of art, the quality of the artistic activity is to be judged only by the quality of the art-product produced—meaning, in the case of theater, by the actual performance. The ethical quality of everyday activity is determined only by the quality of that activity itself, i.e., it should be judged on the basis of the state of mind of the individual, in particular according to the question of whether he or she intended to do good just for the sake of goodness. Ethical judgment means to posit that everybody is responsible for her or his behavior, the consequences and parameters of which cannot be confined. From my point of view, Chico Buarque and Paulo Pontes' preface to *Gota d'água* makes evident that the tragedy contained in the play stands for the tragedy of Brazil as a nation; at the same time, the preface highlights the differences between the two poles of this relation—a relation that the authors explicitly do not want to understand as metaphoric only.

The authors' second concern as referred to in the preface relates the question of an adequate representation of Brazil's cultural reality through art to another argument:

---

10 Edition qtd.: Rio de Janeiro 1977, pp. XI – XX. – *Drop of Water*, the tragedy, is a reflection that is [...] insufficient, simplistic, still perplexed, not as substantive as necessary, because the situation is very complex, and it only now emerges from the shadows of the social dynamics to constitute itself in the dominant trait of the profile of Brazilian contemporary life. The situation is so momentous that it is demanding the attention of the best energies of Brazilian culture; it needs not only a play, but a whole dramaturgy. Considering all limitations, we attempt to at least look at the tragedy directly and face its concreteness, not concealing the situation's complexity with angry and vain adjectives. [My translation.]

> A segunda preocupação do nosso trabalho é com um problema cultural, cuja formulação ajuda a compreender o que foi dito acima: o povo sumiu da cultura produzida no Brasil—dos jornais, dos filmes, das peças, da TV, da literatura, etc. Isolado, seccionado, sem ter onde nem como exprimir seus interesses, desaparecido da vida política, o povo brasileiro deixou de ser o centro da cultura brasileira. Ficou reduzido às estatísticas e às manchetes dos jornais de crime. Povo, só como exótico, pitoresco ou marginal. Chegou uma hora em que até a palavra povo saiu de circulação. Nossa produção cultural, claro, não ganhou com o sumiço. [...] Esta deve ser uma luta, de modo particular, do teatro brasileiro. É preciso, de todas as maneiras, tentar fazer voltar o nosso povo ao nosso palco. Do jeito que estiver ao alcance de cada criador: com o *show*, a comédia de costumes, o esquete, a revista, com a dramaturgia mais ambiciosa, como se puder. O fundamental é que a vida brasileira possa, novamente, ser devolvida, nos palcos, ao público brasileiro. Esta é a segunda preocupação de Gota d'água. Nossa tragédia é uma tragédia da vida brasileira.[11]

Stating that the *Brazilian people* disappeared from the national cultural production seems, at first sight, to be a nod to a Marxist conception of history: The people who do not own the means of production will always struggle against those who do own them. However, there is another aspect implied in the quote referred to above which seems to be much more important and which is marked by the concept of the people. Chico Buaque and Paulo Pontes refer very insistently to the idea of a supposed Brazilian "national identity". The passage problematizes the relationship that has developed between left-wing artists, the media, and the state in Brazil under the military dictatorship. The preface not only criticizes the fact that the military regime contributed to the emergence of the idea of an "authentic Brazilian identity"—it also cautions other artists against contributing to this ideology by "folklorizing" their artworks. The culture industry, and above all television in Brazil under the military dictatorship, succeeded in trivializing the works of even the most critical artists by putting

---

[11] The second concern of our work is with a cultural problem whose formulation helps to understand the above-mentioned: the people have disappeared from the cultural production of Brazil—from newspapers, films, plays, TV, literature, etc. Isolated, cut off, without having either a place or a means to express their interests, they disappeared from political life; the Brazilian people is no longer the center of Brazilian culture. It has been reduced to statistics and crime headlines in the newspapers. Depicted just as exotic, picturesque, or marginal. Eventually even the word people went out of circulation. Our cultural production, of course, did not gain with the disappearance. [...] The Brazilian theater must in a specific way embrace this struggle. It is by all means necessary to try to bring our people back to our stage. Any way within the reach of each creator: with the musical performance, the comedy of manners, the skit, the magazine, with the more ambitious playwright, in any possible way. The key to a solution of the problem is how to manage to give back, on the stage, Brazilian life to the Brazilian public. This is the second concern of *Drop of Water*. Our tragedy is a tragedy of Brazilian life. [My translation.]

them in the context of samba, football, and telenovelas. The military had a clear agenda to promote a new national culture that would create an artificially harmonized, folkloric image of Brazilian art beyond class and cultural struggles. In such precarious times, art is not a luxury. Either it is part of the codes, symbols, and signs of the ruling system—or it is not. The piece by Chico Buarque and Paulo Pontes distinctly exploits the autonomy of classical tragedy in order to distance itself from the concept of artistic production as being explicitly linked to political movements: in a period when the "official" discourse propagated economic progress in a euphoric manner, *Gota d'água* succeeds in artistically depicting the existential experience of a young woman, determined by violence, indifference, and oppression, in a way that eludes in a most sophisticated manner being sanctioned negatively by censorship. From my perspective, the piece is an example of what aesthetic resistance can mean in contemporary literature. The final sentence "Nossa tragédia é uma tragédia da vida brasileira" is aimed at these cultural realities imposed by the military.

The third issue Pontes and Buarque raise, relating form to content, is the need to emphasize communication over spectacle in the theater. They aim to promote a critical spirit of inquiry through theater:

> A nossa terceira e última grande preocupação está refletida na forma da peça. [...] A palavra, portanto, tem que ser trazida de volta, tem que voltar a ser nossa aliada. Nós escrevemos a peça em versos, intensificando poeticamente um diálogo que podia ser realista, um pouco porque a poesia exprime melhor a densidade de sentimentos que move os personagens, mas quisemos, sobretudo, com os versos, tentar revalorizar a palavra. Porque um teatro que ambiciona readquirir sua capacidade de compreender, tem que entregar, novamente, à múltipla eloquência da palavra, o centro do fenômeno dramático.[12]

In my opinion, this focus on the importance of language is crucial for understanding the whole play. Buarque and Pontes demonstrate that the term "the people" has lost its meaning—through the appropriation of the term by the military as well as the depoliticization of art on the part of the cultural left through folklorization. Chico Buarque and Paulo Pontes wish to re-valorize poetry as a form that draws the recipients' attention to the multifaceted meaning of the

---

[12] Our third and last major concern is reflected in the form of the play. [...] The word, therefore, must be brought back, it must become our ally again. We wrote the play in verses, thus poetically intensifying dialogues that could be understood as realist; we did that because poetic language better expresses the density of the emotions that moves the characters, but above all because we tried to re-valorize the word by the device of versification. A theater that strives to regain its ability to understand [i.e. the world], must, once again, give expression to the multiple eloquence of the word which is at the center of the phenomenon of drama. [My translation.]

words—and to the fact that the latter can easily be ideologized and abused. In this respect, the hybridization of music and versification on the one hand and of colloquial language and dialect on the other should be understood as an objection to the concept of art as expressing a homogeneous national identity; the hybridity of registers of expression creates effects of defamiliarization (*ostranenie*). What Chico Buarque and Paulo Pontes say in their preface—in fact, this is an analysis of contemporaneous Brazilian culture in one of the toughest periods of the military dictatorship—amounts to the claim that the regime's cultural policy of the time had the intention of temporarily comforting the underprivileged with folklore.

Gota d'água was awarded the Premio Molière for best drama of the year. Pontes and Buarque deserve distinction for not having accepted the prize; they rather took advantage of the honor offered to them with a view to the opportunity to repeat their positions, as expressed in the foreword, in public.

In order to round off the remarks concerning the preface with a (selective) reading of the drama proper, the plot may be briefly summarized: The protagonist, Jason/Jasão by name, is a young composer of samba songs who has already had some success—particularly with a song titled "Gota d'água". In the wake of this success, Jasão forsakes his wife Joana and his two children to marry the daughter of the rich Creon/Creonte, whom he expects to support him in his further social advancement. Creonte owns the house where Joana lives and exploits the tenants with excessive rent demands.

Jason is presented as a personage who embodies the conflicts and the weaknesses of an artist under the given political circumstances. He actually belongs to the camp of the cultural left, but tries to ascend. To justify his actions, Jason argues that he will be able to help his people better by working in the camp whose main figure is Creonte. But when Creonte physically and emotionally maneuvers him into a position of power, Jason helps Creonte to drive Joana out of her apartment. The fact that Jason agrees to Creonte's corresponding request is a clear sign of his fundamental weakness, and it is the reason why Joana, abandoned by Jason, tries to take revenge. The central question is how Joana will achieve her revenge.

The second part of *Gota d'água* is more closely based on the model of tragedy. Creonte summons Joana to demand her to immediately move out of the apartment he owns. The scene is composed as an echo of the storyline known from Euripides, in particular when Creonte admits his fear of Joana and bends to her plea for an extra day of mercy with regard to her small children. The plot's culminating scene consists in Joana's decision to use her children for her revenge. She enumerates all the injustices that have befallen her—and realizes that all this has happened without any reason. She has done nothing to deserve such a fate. She then gives her ignorant children poisoned cakes to eat with the remark that it is better to die than to experience a daily tragedy for which neither the children nor herself are responsible. Joana finally also takes the poison and dies with her children (whereas in Euripides, Medea is able to flee to Athens and to ask for asylum at the court of King Aegeus).

Regarding the transformations to which Chico Buarque and Paulo Pontes subjected the tragedy of Euripides, one might hypothesize that there is an implicit problematization in the play of the tendency to understand theater and art in general as metaphors for social and political criticism. In his article on the political allegory *La muerte no entrará en palacio* by the Puerto Rican playwright René Marqués, D. L. Shaw has pointed out the difficulties of integrating social protest into the form of tragedy. He observes that

> tragedy and straight social or political protest are intrinsically incompatible, for tragedy, in so far as it is a protest at all, is a protest against the human condition and not against specific social or political conditions. Though it is possible to envisage a tragedy which includes social or political criticism, this can only be indirect and balanced against some other force which is not in itself morally superior.[13]

Chico Buarque and Paulo Pontes' play can be interpreted as conveying that tragedy—and maybe art as a whole—has its primary role in portraying fundamental human conditions and conflicts. Especially regarding the preface discussed previously, the play can be understood as a plea for autonomous literary creation, since in systems of oppression only the latter can unfold a critical potential. Politically engaged art requires an independent subject that can act freely. But from Chico Buarque and Paulo Pontes' point of view, this freedom is non-existent, at least at the time of the composition of their play. The dilemma of politically engaged literature is that, intentionally or not, it still conveys meaningfulness even in the most extreme situations. But this meaning was forfeited in Brazil after 1964. The piece is thus reminiscent of Theodor W. Adorno's critique of culture, arguing that the inner contradiction of culture is that it contains a promise of humanity on the basis of an inhuman, repressive social system—and ultimately denies itself when, by becoming what he calls a cultural industry, it is completely subject to the rules of the mass production of commodities.

The reference to the tragedy of Euripides can also be understood as a piercing critique of the fact that art often remains part of the system that it superficially seeks to criticize, thus supporting the system instead of helping to overthrow it.

---

[13] D. L. Shaw, "René Marques' *La muerte no entrará en palacio*: An Analysis", in: *Latin American Theatre Review*, vol. 2, 1968, pp. 31–38, p. 33.

Nevertheless, Chico Buarque and Paulo Pontes are not trying to abandon art. They are concerned with a genuine aesthetic resistance that may only emerge from artistic autonomy.

With their play, Chico Buarque and Paulo Pontes figuratively convey a concept that is contained in Adorno's idea of autonomous art: It is only through autonomy that literature can refuse its economic exploitability and resist becoming a part of the existing system.[14]

The versified form of the play itself becomes the strongest marker of artistic autonomy.[15] In their focus on the limits of "theater as metaphor", Chico Buarque and Paulo Pontes draw attention to the pitfalls of the concept of committed literature, theater, and art.[16]

With the fate of the character of Jason, the successful Samba composer who becomes part of the oppressive system, Chico Buarque and Paulo Pontes remind their audience that metaphoric representations of political reality run the risk of being exploited by politics for its own purposes. Their play rejects the notion of art as an a priori commitment to a particular political ideal. The form of tragedy and the poetic diction shift the play's focus from a sentimental, *telenovela*-like story to develop a different confrontation with Brazilian realities. Jason is a character representing the danger that an artist can become part of the oppressive system, and he may be seen as a reminder of the view that art and literature have to develop their own, specific devices for making a meaningful contribution to political discussions. The military dictatorship had managed to lure more and more creative people into a cultural system that made the artist an integral part of the system itself. Chico Buarque and Paulo Pontes were committed to freeing art, theater, Samba, and literature from this logic.

---

[14] Theodor W. Adorno, "Engagement", in: Theodor W. Adorno, *Gesammelte Schriften 11: Noten zur Literatur*, Frankfurt/Main 1974, pp. 409–430.

[15] In his lecture on poetry and society, Adorno highlighted the fact that poetry is already in its form a mode of resistance that refuses the rules of speaking obtaining in capitalist societies ("Rede über Lyrik und Gesellschaft", in: ibid., pp. 49–68).

[16] Yet, their insights on commitment and autonomy have moved a long way from Jean-Paul Sartre's defense of committed literature in his famous essay of 1948, *Qu'est-ce que la littérature*? When replying to Sartre, and even more urgently to Brecht, in his 1962 article "Commitment" Adorno reworked the central argument of his 1958 essay "Trying to Understand *Endgame*", in which Beckett's negativity was seen as offering the only acceptable consolation in the face of general disintegration.

II

As previously stated, this paper is not intended as a new comprehensive analysis of the piece *Gota d'água*. However, I would like to illustrate the thesis developed on the basis of a reading of the preface by examining an extract from the play itself. This excerpt is taken from the central dialogue between Joana and Jason in the second act of the drama that is followed by an altercation between Creonte and Joana leading to the final scene:[17]

JOANA — Pára, Jasão, pára! Assim já é demais... Você tem cara pra vir aqui e me botar pra fora?	JOANA— Stop, Jason, stop! That's enough. You got the nerve to come here and kick me out?
JASÃO — Não é assim, Joana...	JASON — It's not like that, Joana...
JOANA — Nossa Senhora!	JOANA— Mother of God!
JASÃO — Vim aqui na melhor das intenções pra cumprir com minhas obrigações de pai...	JASON — I came here with the best of intentions to fulfill my duty as a father...
JOANA — Pai? Porra, que pai!... Essa não!	JOANA— Father? Damn, father!... Come on!
JASÃO — Não grita!... Eu vim buscar a solução ideal, acredite se quiser, um jeito pra que nem você, mulher, nem os meninos passem privação Pode mudar, sem preocupação Hoje mesmo, pode ir se mudando que eu te garanto, eu fico te pagando todo mês uma pensão... Bem, seria uma espécie de aposentadoria	JASON — Don't yell!... I came looking for the ideal solution, believe it or not, a way in which neither you, woman, nor the kids have to endure hardship You can move, no worries Today already, you can start moving that I guarantee you, I'll keep on paying you a pension every month... Well, it would be a kind of retirement payment
JOANA — Eu não quero dinheiro de Creonte	JOANA— I don't want money from Creon
JASÃO — O dinheiro é meu!...	JASON — The money is mine!...
JOANA — É? Qual é a fonte de renda? Violão?...	JOANA— Really? What's the source of the income? Guitar?...
JASÃO — Isso não importa	JASON — It doesn't matter
[...]	[...]

---

17 Pp. 119 – 168.

(continued)

JOANA — Será verdade o que eu estou ouvindo? Que cinismo! Meu Deus, mas que cinismo!... Jasão, menino, você está agindo não sei como, só sendo hipnotismo Ou você é coisa de pau e corda que Creonte vem e toca. Jasão, acorda, menino, Jasão, acorda Sou eu que estou aqui, limpa a visão Sou a Joana, te conheci criança, lembra? Mas qual, você não lembra nada	JOANA— Is it true what I am hearing? How cynical! My God, how cynical!... Jason, boy, the way you're acting I don't know how, you must be under hypnosis Or you're a wood-and-string thing that Creon comes and plays. Jason, wake up boy, Jason, wake up I'm the one who's here, clear up your eyes It's me Joana, I've known you as a child, remember? Surely not, you don't remember anything
Me deixou com frio, sem esperança, dois filhos sem pai, toda esculhambada, vem um velho safado e me escorraça	You left me cold, hopeless, two children without a father, all screwed up, then comes an outrageous old man and kicks me out
e o Jasão, essa criança que eu fiz homem, não me protege, pior, passa pro lado de lá? Que força infeliz tem o mundo de Creonte, meu Deus, que fez com que Jasão virasse isso?	and you Jason, the child whom I made a man, doesn't protect me, worse, goes over to the other side? What a disgraceful force has the world of Creon, my God, that made Jason turn into this?
JASÃO — Agora você vai ouvir os meus argumentos sem fazer rebuliço Falo calmo e o mais claro que puder Tudo o que eu fiz ou vou fazer da vida devo a mim mesmo, ao meu modo de ser Talento não se faz sob medida De barro ruim não sai boa panela	JASON — Now you're going to listen to my arguments without making a fuss I speak calmly and as clear as I can Everything I've done or will do with my life is thanks to myself, to my character Talent is not tailor-made Out of bad clay one cannot make a good pot
[...]	[...]
JASÃO — Essa é a verdade, esse é o motivo da separação, só quero sossego e tranqüilidade JOANA — [...]	JASON — That's the truth, that's the reason for the breakup, I just want peace and tranquility JOANA— [...]

(continued)

(continued)

Mas, Jasão,	But Jason,
já lhe digo o que vai acontecer:	I'll tell you what's going to happen.
tem u'a coisa que você vai perder,	there's something you're going to lose,
é a ligação que você tem com sua	it's the connection you have with your
gente, o cheiro dela, o cheiro da rua,	people, their smell, the smell of the street,
você pode dar banquetes, Jasão,	you can have banquets, Jason,
mas samba é que você não faz mais não,	but you won't be making any more samba,
não faz e aí é que você se atocha	you won't, and that's where you're fooling yourself
Porque vai tentar e sai samba brocha,	Because you're going to try and make only limp-dick samba,
samba escroto, essa é a minha maldição	screwed-up samba, that's my curse
"Gota d'água", nunca mais, seu Jasão	"Drop of water" never again, mister Jason
Samba, aqui, ó...	Samba, here, oh...
JASÃO — Tá bem. Tem razão, Joana	JASON — All right. You're right, Joana
JOANA — Nunca...	JOANA— Never...
JASÃO — Muito bem...	JASON — Very well...
JOANA — Você não engana ninguém...	JOANA— You can't fool anybody...
[...]	[...]
JOANA — Creonte... Por que um homem onipotente	JOANA— Creon... Why would an all-mighty man
assim, poderoso assim, precisa jogar	like you, powerful like that, need to use
toda a sua força em cima duma mulher	all his strength against a single woman
sozinha... por quê?...	... why?...
CREONTE — Você quer saber?...	CREON — You want to know?...
JOANA — Por quê?	JOANA— Why?
CREONTE — Por medo...	CREON — Out of fear...
JOANA — Medo de mim?...	JOANA— Fear of me?...
CREONTE — Medo de você	CREON — Fear of you
sim, porque você pode investir a qualquer	yes, because you can charge at any
hora. Tá calibrada de ódio, a arma na mão	time. You're calibrated by hate, gun in hand
E a vida te botou em posição de tiro	And life has put you in a firing position

(continued)

Só falta a vítima, mais nada. Então prefiro	The only thing left is the victim, that's all. So I'd rather
virar pr'um outro lado a boca do canhão	turn the cannon's mouth elsewhere
Não gosto de guerra nem vou facilitar	I don't like war and I won't be incautious
diante de quem está se achando injustiçada	facing someone who is feeling wronged
[...]	[...]
Joana come um bolo; agarra-se aos filhos; cai com eles no chão; a luz desce em seu set; sobem, brilhantes, luz e orquestra da festa onde todos, com a maior alegria, cantam Gota d'água; *vai subindo de intensidade até o clímax, quando se ouve um grito lancinante... É Corina que grita; ao mesmo tempo Creonte bate palmas e a música para.*	*Joana eats cake; clings to her children; falls with them to the ground; the light descends on their set; brightly turn up both light and orchestra of the party where everyone enthusiastically sings* Drop of water; *the intensity goes up until the climax, when a piercing shriek can be heard... It's Corinna screaming; at the same time Creon claps his hands and the music stops.*
CREONTE — Atenção, pessoal, vou falar rapidamente	CREON — Listen up everyone, I will speak quickly
Jasão... vem cá... Meus caros amigos, agora, aproveitando a ocasião e aqui na frente	Jason... come over here... My dear friends, now, taking advantage of the occasion, in front
de todo mundo, quero anunciar que de ora em diante a casa tem novo dono. A cadeira	of everyone, I want to announce that from now on the house has a new owner. The chair
que foi de meu pai e foi minha vai passar	that belonged to my father and used to be mine will pass on
pra quem tem condições, e que é de minha inteira	to whom is capable, and has my complete
confiança, para poder continuar	confidence, to be able to continue
a minha obra, acrescentando sangue novo	my work, adding fresh blood
Portanto, sentando Jasão aí eu provo:	Therefore, sitting Jason there I confirm:
não uso preconceitos ou discriminação	I do not have recourse to prejudices or discrimination
Quem vem de baixo, tem valor e quer vencer	Who comes from below, is worthy, and wants to win
tem condições de colaborar pra fazer	can collaborate to make
nossa sociedade melhor... Senta, Jasão.	our society better... Sit down Jason.

(continued)

(continued)

Jasão senta; um tempo; ouve-se um burburinho de vozes; entra Egeu carregando o corpo de Joana no colo e Corina carregando os corpos dos filhos; põem os corpos na frente de Creonte e Jasão; um tempo; imobilidade geral; uma a uma, as vozes começam a cantar Gota d'água; *reversão de luz; os atores que fazem Joana e filhos levantam-se e passam a cantar também; ao fundo, projeção de uma manchete sensacionalista noticiando uma tragédia.*	*Jason sits down; for a while; a buzz of voices can be heard; Aegean enters, carrying the body of Joana in his arms and Corinna carrying the children's bodies; they put the bodies in front of Creon and Jason; for a while nobody moves; one by one, the voices begin to sing* Drop of water; *light reversal; the actors who play Joana and the children rise and join in the singing; in the background, the projection of a yellow press headline reporting a tragedy.*

Joana justifies her refusal to accept a monthly pension from Jason by saying that she does not want to accept Creon's money. She does not believe that the money comes from Jason's art, but is convinced that it is the money with which he has been manipulated to become part of Creon's system, as the colloquial expression "Você é coisa de pau e corda que Creonte vem e toca"—"You're a wood-and-string thing that Creon came and played with"—conveys.

The most important passage of this dialogue is Joana's comment on Jason's hit song, his samba "Gota d'água": Jason's explanation that he is only joining Creon's camp to help his people with his political songs from a position within the system is countered by Joana's sharp remark that when, for the sake of overt political commitment, political reality is trivialized, any political effect vanishes and what remains is "samba brocha, samba escroto".

This final altercation between Joana and Jason renders the limits of an understanding of "theater as metaphor" in Chico Buarque and Paulo Pontes' play explicit: the distinction between the moral and the representative dimension of action might be difficult, yet it is always real. The theatrical metaphor weakens as the distance between the two dimensions broadens. As Joana points out: Jason is aestheticizing his behavior as a committed artist who claims that he needs to become part of the system in order to criticize the system from within.

Chico Buarque's 1975 play does not radically oppose morality to theater; it does not intend to enclose theatrical activity within a static structure. Nowhere in Chico Buarque's text can a hint about the restriction of the social scope of theater be found. On the contrary: precisely because Chico Buarque was so keenly aware of the great influence it can exercise on social life, he insisted on the differentiation between theater and reality.

Erika Fischer-Lichte
From *theatrum mundi* to Theatricality

The seventeenth century, just as the turn of the nineteenth to the twentieth century, can be characterized as a period during which the prevailing symbolic order underwent a process of collapse. In the first case, the episteme of resemblance lost its popular appeal, and gradually was replaced by the order of representation. In the second, it was that very order of representation that entered a state of crisis.[1] While in the seventeenth century the metaphor of "theatrum mundi" or "theatrum vitae humanae" and a related new concept of theater served as an answer to the crisis, at the turn of the nineteenth to the twentieth century the introduction of the concept of theatricality—as well as the avant-garde theater movements—fulfilled a similar purpose.

In Elizabethan England, professional public theater emerged at a time when the episteme of resemblance was no longer prevalent. The old rituals it was based on failed to work, or, if they still did, they were denounced either as pagan (as with the rites of May), as conscious deceit (as with exorcism rituals), or as superstition (as with the Eucharist). The underlying principle of "significando causare", rooted in the teaching of similarities, was no longer generally accepted.

In these turbulent times, a public theater was established. It was open throughout the year and took place in special buildings located either on the other side of the river Thames in the south of the city, or beyond the city limits in the north. The new theater had an ambivalent relationship to the old rituals. On the one hand, it broke away from them implicitly by asserting a very particular concept of theater; explicitly, it took recourse to the old rituals by ridiculing and reviling them, or even by altering them in a particular manner. Shakespeare, for instance, transforms the ritual structure of the rites of May in *A Midsummer Night's Dream*; in *Twelfth Night* he makes fun of rituals of exorcism, which in *King Lear* he turns into a dramaturgical function. Webster in *The Duchess of Malfi* relates to charivari; he denounces its practices as instruments of power, of which individuals make use in order to push for their own, often insidious interests. They could hardly be misunderstood as meaningful community-building rites.

A new concept of theater emerged in which the principle of "significando causare" was superseded by that of "agendo significare". The actions on stage

---

1 See M. Foucault, *The Order of Things: An Archaeology of the Human Sciences*, tr. F. Durand-Bogaert, London 2002.

were to be received as signs—not, however, as signatures within the episteme of resemblance but in terms of the binary model of the sign as it was later elaborated by Descartes, the *Logique de Port Royal*, or Leibniz.

This might lead us to conclude that the emergence of a professional public theater paved the way for overcoming this crisis. Yet this conclusion holds true only to a certain extent. It does not take into account the devices through which Elizabethan theater sought to create—on stage and in the minds of the spectators—the illusion of a fictive world. In *A Midsummer Night's Dream*, the play of the craftsmen presents a form of theater unable to achieve this and therefore it does not live up to the standards of this new concept of theater. Peter Quince's long prologue robs the spectators of any chance to get involved in the actions that follow. He reveals everything beforehand, "At the which let no man wonder".[2] In order to prevent any narrative illusion from emerging in the minds of the spectators, Wall confides in them "[t]hat I, one Snout by name, present a wall, / And such a wall; as I would have you think".[3] Lion finds soothing words: "You Ladies, you, whose gentle hearts do fear".[4] Moon breaks character and declares frankly: "All that I have to say is to tell you that the lanthorn is the moon; I, the Man i' th' Moon; this thorn-bush, my thorn-bush, and this dog my dog".[5] Thisbe, finally, rather politely says goodbye to the spectators in the play before she dies: "(Stabs herself) And farewell, friends; Thus Thisbe ends; Adieu, adieu, adieu. (Dies)".[6] All of them exploit so excessively the medieval convention of directly addressing the audience that the difference between the actor and the character remains glaringly evident the entire time, so that no illusion of a fictive world can take shape. It is small wonder that the spectators therefore respond with ironic comments that relate to these devices:

> Demetrius: Well roar'd, Lion.
>
> Theseus: Well run, Thisbe.
>
> Hippolyta: Well shone, Moon. Truly, the moon shines with a good grace.[7]

---

[2] William Shakespeare, *A Midsummer Night's Dream*, ed. S. Chaudhuri, London and New York, NY 2017, V.1.133. The first quarto edition of the play dates to 1600.
[3] Ibid., V.1.155f.
[4] Ibid., V.1.156.
[5] Ibid., V.1.250–252.
[6] Ibid., V.1.336–338.
[7] Ibid., V.1.257–260.

While in this case the external communication between actor and spectator dominates, drawing the spectators' attention to the device of representation, the internal communication between the characters is supposed to serve as guiding principle in professional theater, allowing the spectators to focus their attention on the fictive world represented on stage. The actors are expected to act in such a way that the spectators will be able to receive and understand their actions as those of the characters they are playing. The spectators should never become aware that they are watching the work of actors but follow the illusion of fictive characters. For the entire duration of the performance the spectators should take for granted the transformation of the actors into their respective characters.

Hamlet's address to the actors can be read along those lines:

> Speak the speech, I pray you, as I pronounced it to you, trippingly on the tongue; but if you mouth it, as many of our players do, I had as lief the town-crier spoke my lines. Nor do not saw the air too much with your hand, thus; but use all gently; for in the very torrent, tempest, and, as I may say, the whirlwind of your passion, you must acquire and beget a temperance that may give it smoothness [...] Be not too tame neither, but let your own discretion be your tutor; suit the action to the word, the word to the action; with this special observance, that you o'erstep not the modesty of nature; for any thing so overdone is from the purpose of playing, whose end, both at the first and now, was and is, to hold, as 'twere, the mirror up to nature; to show virtue her own feature, scorn her own image, and the very age and body of the time his form and pressure. Now this overdone, or come tardy off, though it makes the unskillful laugh, cannot but make the judicious grieve [...].[8]

The theater will function as a distancing model for the spectator only if the actor plays his role in a way that enables the spectator to focus solely on the character and not on the actor. Yet this approach is not to be mistaken for, say, David Garrick's psychological-realistic style of acting or that described in Diderot's *Paradox of Acting*.

It seems, therefore, that theater did not, in fact, overcome the crisis. The crisis rather unfolded in an unforeseen manner and thus manifested itself in a very special way. The episteme of resemblance had become obsolete, while the new concept of representation, although foreshadowed, had not yet established itself.

The actor playing a role appears to be participating in the magic of the old rituals and thus disguises the crisis of the approach based on similitudes. At the same time, his roleplay reveals the latter as a delusion. For it launches a

---

[8] William Shakespeare, *Hamlet*, ed. A. Thompson and N. Taylor, London and New York, NY 2016, III.2.1–7, 14–32. The first quarto edition of the play dates to 1603.

seemingly unsolvable game of deception between being and appearing, which lays open the ineffectiveness of the category of similarity. All that is in the world no longer seems to be connected to each other by way of similarity; on the contrary, the similarity is exposed as mere appearance that does not correspond to any being. On stage a boy plays the part of a girl; because of his girlish appearance spectators might take him to be a girl. In front of the spectators this girl dresses up as a boy and declares that s/he will play this role—she, who "in reality" is a boy. In this case, is role-play disguise or transformation? Does it grant access to a person's true self or does it obstruct such an understanding? And which self would that be—the roleplaying actor's, the character's, or the perceiving and interpreting spectator's?

The crisis of the episteme of resemblance in Elizabethan England not only resulted in the foundation of professional public theaters where experts of transformation, disguise, and deceit displayed their art. It also led to the publication of a flood of treatises dealing with self-knowledge, such as John Frith's *A Mirror or Glasses to Know Thyself* (ca. 1533), Sir John Davies' *Nosce Teipsum* (1599), or the English translation of Philippe de Mornay's *The True Knowledge of a Man's Own Self* (1602).

The acting thus exposed the ambivalence surrounding the new concept of theater with regard to the crisis of the episteme based on similitudes; on the one hand, it exacerbated the problem and, on the other, it veiled it; it added fuel to the fire while at the same time appearing to overcome it. It was this ambivalence that gave a new topicality to the old saying of *theatrum mundi* or *theatrum vitae humanae*. The old symbolic order of similarities was already crumbling and losing its meaning, while the new symbolic order of representation had not yet taken hold. Theater was seen as a model for dealing with problems arising in the real world as well as in daily life, which might explain the proliferation of the theater metaphor in the seventeenth century.

In the late nineteenth century, however, the model of representation that had developed over the course of the seventeenth century entered into a crisis of its own. The best-known formulations of this crisis in German literature came from Nietzsche and Hugo von Hofmannsthal: Nietzsche's *Vierte Unzeitgemäße Betrachtung* (1876) and Hofmannsthal's *Brief des Lord Chandos* (1902).

From our perspective, we can summarize the crisis in the following three sentences:
1) The available signs are not analogous to the objects they are meant to signify; i.e. they are unable to represent them adequately.
2) The link between signifier and signified is not stable, as was assumed before, but fundamentally unstable; signifiers can float freely and may be connected to different signifieds.

3) Since the ego has made the disturbing experience "that he is not even master in his own house" (Freud), the subject is unable to constitute a stable self; it decenters and dissolves into a sequence of momentary, fragmentary selves.

These three sentences describe the crisis of representation as a crisis of perception, knowledge, the subject and his/her identity.

This cultural crisis resulted not only in the emergence of different forms of avant-garde theater that used this watershed moment as their point of departure, but concomitantly also led to the formulation of new theories of theater. The Russian theoretician Nikolaj Evreinov (1879–1953), for example, developed a theory of theatricality, which was meant to explain such crises as fundamental to all forms of culture.

In 1908 Evreinov introduced the term "teatral'nost'" (theatricality), which was already being used in other contexts, in a lecture entitled "Apologia for Theatricality", held at the theater of the eminent actress Vera Komissarzhevskaya (1864–1910) in St. Petersburg. Evreinov had received his law degree in 1901 with a dissertation on the history of corporal punishment in Russia, and entered the service of the Ministry of Railways as a lawyer, a job he quit in 1910. He gave the lecture at Komissarzhevskaya's theater in his part-time position as director succeeding Vsevolod Meyerhold, who had left the theater in 1907, as his artistic principles could no longer be reconciled with Komissarzhevskaya's. By that point, Evreinov was already rather experienced in matters of the theater. He had founded his own theater, the "Old Theater", which, as the name suggests, placed a programmatic focus on updating past epochs of European theater for the contemporary stage. Its first season (1907/08) centered on medieval French theater, while the second one, which came about only in 1911/12, addressed the Spanish theater of the Siglo de Oro. His work on the concept of theatricality also mostly fell into this period, which is reflected in his many writings. In our context, besides the "Apologia", the two essays "The Theatricalization of Life" (1911) and "Theatrocracy" (1915) are of importance.[9]

These treatises do not debate theater as a specific art form—though this is also discussed—so much as they define the term theatricality as a fundamental human instinct. Evreinov writes in his essay "Theatrocracy":

---

[9] See S. Lukanitschewa, *Das Theatralitätskonzept von Nikolaj Evreinov: Die Entdeckung der Kultur als Performance*, Tübingen and Basel 2013; as well as E. Kalisch, "Teatral'nost' als kulturanthropologische Kategorie: Nikolaj Evreinovs Modell des theatralischen Instinkts vor dem Hintergrund seiner 'Geschichte der Körperstrafen in Russland'", in: *Herrschaft des Symbolischen: Bewegungsformen gesellschaftlicher Theatralität. Europa—Asien—Afrika*, ed. J. Fiebach and W. Mühl-Benninghaus, Berlin 2002, pp. 141–163.

> Beside the survival, sexual and other instincts, I have succeeded in discovering the instinct for transformation in human beings, i.e. the human instinct to respond to images received from outside with other images, which they have randomly created at the level of pre-aesthetic transformation of visible *nature*. After careful consideration, I have named this the instinct for theatricality [...] to be understood as the absolute law of creative metamorphosis of our perceived world.[10]

The instinct for theatricality is here defined as the instinct for metamorphosis—*preobrashenie*—and for transformation—*transformacia*. Both terms evoke a very specific semantic field. *Preobrashenie* points towards the holiday of the transfiguration of Christ, which is celebrated on August 6 in the Orthodox Church. The term further serves as translation of the Greek *metamorphosis* and implies the corresponding range of meanings, which largely tally with those of the term *transformacia*.[11] The instinct for theatricality can thus indeed be described as the instinct for metamorphosis.

In his various writings Evreinov attempts to prove that this instinct is innate to human beings and therefore present in all cultures. As a result, his examples span human history from "early man" and "indigenous peoples" to the—mostly European—religious, social, and political history up to his own present. Based on a host of ethnological literature that was available at the beginning of the twentieth century, Evreinov draws the conclusion that "early man" was virtually gripped by a "mania of metamorphosis". This was evidenced by

> tattoos, piercings of the skin, cartilage and teeth in order to insert feathers, rings, pieces of crystal, metal or wood (pelele), knocking out of the incisors, pulling out of hair, deformities of the skull or the feet [...].[12]

Not just the jewelry, which Evreinov first refers to, but the most important events, situations, and stations in the life of "early man" were determined by the desire "[t]o be someone other than yourself!"[13]:

> Early man, just like man in late civilization, turned almost everything into a purely theatrical performance—the birth of the child and its education, hunting and marriage, war, tribunal and punishment, religious ritual and, finally, burial. His whole life consists of

---

10 Nikolaj Evreinov, "Theatrokratie", in: Nikolaj Evreinov, *Theater für sich*, ed. S. Sasse, tr. R. Kühn, Zurich and Berlin 2017, pp. 13–32, p. 14.
11 See Kalisch, "Teatral'nost'", p. 144.
12 Nikolaj Evreinov, *Teatralizacija žizni*, in: Nikolaj Evreinov, *Teatr kak takavoj*, 2nd ed., Moscow and Berlin 1923, pp. 25–59, p. 31.
13 Ibid.

that [...]. He theatricalizes life and it thus achieves its truest meaning: its metamorphosis into *his* life.[14]

As he continues through human history via the history of the Greeks and Romans, during which "theater [...] was at the forefront of public interest" and "dominated and ousted [...] all others",[15] as K. Borinski, whom Evreinov quotes, asserts, Evreinov addresses the Church's battle with "this dominant position of theater":

> It eagerly wanted this dominant position in everyone's lives for itself. But the idea of theater achieved a decisive and incontestable victory at the beginning of this significant battle. The lot fell on the Christian ascetics to first express their contempt for martyrdom publicly—in the circus arena!—and the faithful sons of the Church had to first show themselves to the heathen world—as actors in this tragedy foisted on them!—, in a bloody public display. This is what the fatal debut of the Christian martyr looked like given that the ancient world lusted for circus games.
> Of course such scenic performances did not cause the Church to develop a taste for the theater and yet it had to structure its entire liturgy according to theatrical principles, whether it initially liked it or not.[16]

The "invasion of theater into the liturgy"[17] that Evreinov notes here is further made plausible with references to Nietzsche's *Gay Science* and relevant studies of the historians M. Reisner, M. Burckhardt, and K. F. Tiander. In his above-quoted essay "The Theatricalization of Life" Evreinov expands his perspective to include cultures outside of Europe. He claims that in China "the intensity of theatrical sentiment is so high that no banquet can be held without the participation of actors who offer the guests a true theatrical menu consisting of fifty to sixty plays."[18] For the Indian cultures he mentions as an example the performances of the great epics in Pondicherry, "which go on for four to seven consecutive nights" without the five to six thousand spectators leaving the venue in between, because, as Evreinov or his source assumes, they "have no strength left to leave this place of greatest temptation and go home".[19]

In the remainder of the essay, Evreinov returns to European cultural and social history. He mentions the Spanish and French cultures of the seventeenth and

---

14 Ibid., p. 33.
15 Qtd. in: Evreinov, "Theatrokratie", p. 18.
16 Ibid., p. 19.
17 Ibid.
18 Evreinov, *Teatralizacija žizni*, p. 36.
19 Ibid.

eighteenth centuries respectively as particularly pertinent examples for the almost comprehensive theatricalization of life. He thus claims that in Spain literally

> everything turned into theatre: an inquisitional trial with masked judges and hellish instruments of torture, grandiose burnings of heretics [...]; where even the crude trade of the butcher became a beautiful performance of bullfighting.[20]

To Evreinov, courtly life in France appears thoroughly theatricalized—to an extent that in his opinion

> the rivalry between real life and life on stage went so far that nobody could tell which of the two was more theatrical. Here and there you relied on the most fustian, rehearsed phrases, on the camp refinement of bows, smiles and gestures. Here and there you wore costumes for the purpose of self-exhibition that were as decorative as rooms, castles and gardens. Here and there you saw a lot of white and red make-up. Beauty patches, lorgnons and very few 'real' faces [...]. Here and there you wore incredible wigs [...] and, finally, here and there you had a culture of courtesy that produced creatures of a wholly different nature from those created by God.[21]

Interestingly, Evreinov sees the French Revolution as an event that was to draw awareness to "the theatrical affectation of this hierarchy of life"[22] without, however, breaking with the principle of theatricality itself. Instead, he defines the Revolution as a form of theatrical egalitarianism. It

> merely changed the production and exchanged roles by bringing everyone together on a scenic common ground: to depict each other as equals. In order to generate a purely theatrical egalitarianism they first tackled the costumes: the painter David painted the costume of the 'free citizen,' the actor Talma adapted it for the stage and the people [...] got changed. The wigs were burned, the pigtails were chopped off and you started greeting each other with a clenched nodding of the head that alluded to those who had died on the guillotine. The passion for theatricality did not even spare the corpses of the beheaded. They were placed in painterly compositions: in poses of conversation, as if flirting with each other, in pathetic and pornographic poses. They played with them, sang to them, danced, laughed and made fun of the absurd appearance of these actors who knew to play their ridiculous roles so very badly. [...] In short, the Great Revolution was as political as it was theatrical.[23]

The instinct for theatricality not only dominates religious, social and political life but also affects all other cultural aspects—even including economics. Only theatrocracy could explain

---

20 Ibid., p. 38.
21 Ibid., p. 39.
22 Ibid.
23 Ibid.

the tremendous success of advertising, the specific phenomenon of our epoch, the essence of capitalist society, which characterizes the entire modern order so garishly [...]. That the entire miracle of advertising, which serves as justification for spending 100,000,000 Francs in France and several hundred million dollars in the United States of America, that their whole secret, which now embarrasses dozens of honorable scientists, lies in the simple art of a printed *mise-en-scène* of the advertised object, in other words— in applying elements of *theatrical* seduction, of demonstrative illustrations down to the garish, compressed, powerfully animated language of advertising. For only the theatrical form holds the *optimum power to seduce* the masses.[24]

From "early man's" jewelry to the advertising strategies of contemporary capitalism, Evreinov seeks to prove that the instinct for theatricality has existed in all human beings at all times and in all cultures as the instinct for metamorphosis out of which ultimately all cultural creativity arises. The point is not to create a "counter world" to the "real" world via theatricality. Rather, Evreinov sees all cultural manifestations as being enabled and made possible through the instinct for theatricality. For this instinct aimed to turn the conditions found in one's—initially natural—surroundings into cultural creations or to contrast existing cultural creations with others that spring from one's imagination. Culture was ultimately to be seen as a product of the instinct for theatricality. Therefore, the term theatricality must advance to the single-most important keyword of cultural studies. Without it the process of permanent change in the most diverse of cultures could hardly be explained.

Attempts to trace back the origins of culture to a single source—here, the instinct for theatricality—are, however, always subject to accusations of simplification. At the same time, they are frequently debated anew, mostly in order to prove that they are unsuitable as a general explanation.

In this respect, Evreinov's theory is an exception. Though he was occasionally criticized for simplifying the discussion in Russia before the October Revolution, his theory was hotly debated. After the Revolution, however, Evreinov still emerged as a highly successful director, evidenced impressively by his mass production *The Storming of the Winter Palace*, which took place on the original site in Petrograd on the third anniversary of the October Revolution on November 8, 1920, and attracted 160,000 spectators.[25] Yet he did not develop his theory of theatricality further—with one exception, which I will come back

---

24 Evreinov, "Theatrokratie", p. 27.
25 For further reading on the performance see, amongst others, M. Dalügge, *Die Manöverinszenierungen der Oktober-Revolution in Petrograd: Theatralität zwischen Fest und Ritual*, Tübingen 2016, pp. 329–384, and E. Fischer-Lichte, *Theatre, Sacrifice, Ritual: Exploring Forms of Political Theatre*, London and New York, NY 2005, pp. 97–121.

to later. It was forgotten or intentionally disregarded even before his emigration to Paris (1925).

Later theories that revolve around the concept of theatricality partly do not even mention Evreinov. The sociologist E. Goffman's book *The Presentation of Self in Everyday Life*, which in its German translation bears the apt title *Wir alle spielen Theater* (literally "We are all playing theater", meaning "All the world's a stage"), was published in 1956, i.e. three years after Evreinov's death in Paris, and explains daily interactions with recourse to the theater metaphor without mentioning Evreinov's works.[26] However, the concept of theatricality fundamentally differs from the theater metaphor insofar as it assumes that the instinct for metamorphosis is an anthropological given, or it defines it as such. A wider discussion of Evreinov's theory as well as attempts to productively develop his concept of theatricality further only took place in the 1990s.[27]

Four aspects that seek to flesh out and at the same time modify Evreinov's concept of theatricality can be distilled from these theories:
- that of the *performance*, which is defined as the process of representation through body and voice in front of physically present spectators and comprises the ambivalent interplay of all factors involved;
- that of the *mise-en-scène*, which is defined as the specific mode of the use of materials and signs in the production;
- that of *physicality*, which results from factors pertaining to the representation and the material
- that of *perception*, which refers to the others, to the audience members, the spectators and their role and perspective as observers.

Since a performance comes into being as the interplay of the other three aspects mentioned, theatricality could also be defined as the specific *mise-en-scène* of bodies with regard to a particular form of perception, which on the one hand is performed, but can, on the other, also be used in texts, images, film and other

---

26 See E. Burns, *Theatricality: Study in Convention and Everyday Life*, London 1972.
27 See here the two titles mentioned in n. 9 as well as the section entitled *Theatricality* (guest ed. E. Fischer-Lichte) in *Theatre Research International*, vol. 20, 1995, pp. 85–118, with contributions by M. Carlson, E. Fischer-Lichte, M. Quinn and H. Schramm; E. Fischer-Lichte (ed.), *Theatralität und die Krisen der Repräsentation*, DFG symposium 1999, Stuttgart and Weimar 2001; R. Münz, *Theatralität und Theater: Zur Historiographie von Theatralitätsgefügen*, Berlin 1998; T. Pearson, "Evreinov and Pirandello: Twin Apostles of Theatricality", in: *Theatre Research International*, vol. 12, 1987, pp. 147–67; Pearson, "Evreinov and Pirandello: Two Theatricalists in Search of the Main Thing", in: *Theatre Research International*, vol. 17, 1992, pp. 26–36; H. Schramm, *Theatralität und Denkstil: Studien zur Entfaltung theatralischer Perspektiven in philosophischen Texten des 16. und 17. Jahrhunderts*, Berlin 1995.

media—as, for example, in advertising, as Evreinov points out. In this respect comparable to H. Plessner's hypothesis of self-dissociation, of establishing distance from oneself,[28] theatricality could also be understood as an anthropological condition that calls for metamorphosis: Human beings face themselves/ another in order to compose an image of themselves as another, which they can then reflect on through the eyes of another or see reflected in the eyes of another. Theatricality therefore means a process of metamorphosis that simultaneously aims at the perception of one's self through others.

One more aspect of Evreinov's concept of theatricality is that it lays open transformation as a fundamental principle of culture. Unlike evolutionary theory, which highlights transformation in a particular direction—from "lower" organisms to higher and more complex ones—, the concept of theatricality focuses on cultural processes of transformation that are initiated and carried out by human beings. Accordingly, they cannot be described and defined as quasi-natural processes of development but represent creative processes that aim to deliberately change given circumstances.

That is to say that any symbolic order, once established, will necessarily culminate in a crisis. For the instinct for metamorphosis proves to be decisive for all cultures, since it is an anthropological given. According to the theory of theatricality, there will always be transformations—however, it remains unpredictable which ones will take place, what turns they will take and what kinds of crises they will lead up to. While the metaphors of "theatrum mundi" and "theatrum vitae humanae" successfully served the purpose of dealing with the crisis of the episteme of resemblance, the concept of theatricality was intended to provide an explanation for the inevitable fact that all symbolic orders ultimately end in crisis, since human beings are always in need of transformation.

---

28 See H. Plessner, "Zur Anthropologie des Schauspielers", in: H. Plessner, *Gesammelte Schriften*, ed. G. Dux, O. Marquard, and E. Ströker, Frankfurt/Main 1982, pp. 399–418.

Notes on Contributors

Ekaterina Boltunova is an Associate Professor in the Faculty of Humanities at the National Research University Higher School of Economics, Moscow. Professor Boltunova was a 2017–2018 Visiting Professor at the University of Illinois at Chicago; in 2008–2009 she taught as a Fulbright Scholar at Columbia University. She has given lectures at Yale University (2017), Smith College (2017), Amherst College (2017), and the University of Illinois, Urbana-Champaign (2009) and participated in multiple international research projects. Her research interests include the cultural and political history of the Russian Empire and the USSR; the topography and semiotics of power; the imperial discourse of war; historical memory; and Soviet as well as post-Soviet reception of the imperial space. She is the author of *Peter the Great's Guard as a Military Corporation* (2011, in Russian); "Reception of Imperial and Tsarist Spheres of Authority in Russia, 1990s–2010s", in: *Ab Imperio*, vol. 2 (2016), pp. 261–309; "Russian Officer Corps and Military Efficiency: 1800–1914", in: *Kritika: Explorations in Russian and Eurasian History*, vol. 16 (2015), pp. 413–422; "Imperial Throne Halls and Discourse of Power in the Topography of Early Modern Russia (late 17th – 18th centuries)", in: *The Emperor's House: Palaces from Augustus to the Age of Absolutism* (2015), pp. 341–352, and many other texts.

Kirsten Dickhaut is a Professor of Romance Literatures at the University of Stuttgart. Her main fields of research are intermediality, drama in early modern times, and magic/sorcery/witchcraft. Recent publications: K. Dickhaut (ed.), *Art of Deception. Kunst der Täuschung: Über Status und Bedeutung von ästhetischer und dämonischer Illusion in der Frühen Neuzeit (1400–1700) in Italien und Frankreich* (2016); "Plaire et instruire ou comment Molière présente les valeurs religieuses dans L'École des femmes", in: *Le fait religieux dans les littératures française et québécoise: Présences, résurgences et oublis* (2017), ed. G. Dupuis, K.-D. Ertler, A. Ferraro, and Y. Völkl, pp. 61–84.

Erika Fischer-Lichte is the Director of the International Research Center 'Interweaving Performance Cultures' at Freie Universität Berlin. She is a member of the Academia Europaea, the Göttingen Academy of Sciences, the German National Academy of Sciences, the Berlin-Brandenburg Academy of Sciences, and the American Academy of Arts and Sciences. Research fields: history and theory of theater; aesthetics. Her main book publications include *Transformative Aesthetics* (2018); *Tragedy's Endurance: Performances of Greek Tragedies and Cultural Identity in Germany Since 1800* (2017); *The Politics of Interweaving Performance Cultures* (2014); *Dionysus Resurrected* (2014); *The Transformative Power of Performance* (2008).

Andrey Golubkov, cand. phil., is a philologist and literary critic. He serves as a Senior Researcher at the Gorky Institute of World Literature (Russian Academy of Sciences), and as an Associate Professor at the National Research University Higher School of Economics, Moscow. Academic interests include the French literary sphere in the ages of the Renaissance, the seventeenth century, and the Enlightenment; the French cultural tradition of *galanterie*; and the history of the anecdote in Western culture. He has penned a number of articles on the above topics and is author of the book *Preciosity and the Gallant Tradition in the 17th-Century French Salon Literature* (2017).

Julia V. Ivanova is an Associate Professor at the School of Philology and a Leading Research Fellow at the Poletayev Institute for Theoretical and Historical Studies in the Humanities at the National Research University Higher School of Economics, Moscow. She has written on Neo-Latin humanist literature, Counterreformation political thought, and Renaissance medicine. Her more recent publications are dedicated to the history of method in the early modern humanities, Prospero Alpini's idea of Egyptian medicine, and G. Vico's juridical thought.

Joachim Küpper is Professor of Comparative Literature and Romance Literatures at Freie Universität Berlin. He has published widely on literary, historiographical, and philosophical texts from Homer to the twentieth century. His most recent publication is a book dealing with a network theory of cultural dynamics (*The Cultural Net*, 2018). In the course of his career, he has been awarded the Heinz Maier-Leibnitz prize as well as the Leibniz prize of the Deutsche Forschungsgemeinschaft. In 2010, he received an Advanced Grant from the European Research Council, Brussels. Küpper was the founding director of the Dahlem Humanities Center, Berlin. Currently, he serves as the director of the international network 'Principles of Cultural Dynamics'. He is a member of the Göttingen Academy of Sciences, the North-Rhine-Westphalian Academy of Sciences, the German National Academy of Sciences as well as the American Academy of Arts and Sciences.

Olga Kuptsova, PhD, is a Professor at the National Research University Higher School of Economics, Moscow as well as a Senior Researcher at the Russian State Institute for Art Studies; in addition, she has been a visiting professor at the *Maison des sciences de l'homme*, Paris. Her publications include: *From the History of Soviet Theater Criticism, 1917–1926* (1984); *Essays on Russian Theatrical Culture* (2003); *The Life of the Estate Myth: Lost and Found Paradise* (2008); "Le théâtre à Moscou: voie sans issue ou periode de transition", in: *Revue russe* (2000), pp. 35–43; "Meyerhold et la France, lettres des années 1920–1930", in: *Les voyages du théâtre: Russie / France* (2001), ed. H. Henry and E. Galtsova, pp. 101–118; "Theaterspiele in Garten und Parkanlagen russischer Landsitze um 1800: Versuch einer Typologie", in: *Die Gartenkunst* (2013), ed. A. Ananieva, G. Grünig, and A. Veselova, pp. 173–180.

Peter W. Marx holds the Chair for Media and Theater Studies at the University of Cologne. He is also the director of the *Theaterwissenschaftliche Sammlung Köln*, one of the largest archives for theater and performance culture in Europe. His research focus is on theater historiography, Shakespeare in performance, and the formation of theater as a cultural practice in the early modern period. His most recent book, *Hamlets Reise nach Deutschland*, was published in 2018.

Jan Mosch was a member of the ERC-funded research project 'Early Modern European Drama and the Cultural Net' at Freie Universität Berlin and is finalizing his doctoral thesis, which explores how the post-Reformation 'scribbling age' (Robert Burton) informs the uneasy negotiation of heteronomy and individual agency in plays by Shakespeare and Racine. As a junior lecturer, he has been teaching classes on British literature, particularly contemporary fiction. He has been a theatrical reviewer for the *Yearbook of the German Shakespeare Association* since 2012, and he is the co-editor of a recently published collective volume titled *History and Drama* (2018).

Elena Penskaya is a Professor of Russian and European Literature at the National Research University Higher School of Economics, Moscow. She also serves as a Principal Researcher in the Theater Studies Laboratory at HSE. From 2010–2011, Prof. Penskaya was a visiting professor at the Sorbonne; in 2016, she lectured as a visiting professor at Humboldt University, Berlin. She is the Executive Editor of the *Education Studies Quarterly* (HSE), and a member of the editorial board of the *International Encyclopedia of Literary Museums*. Her research is dedicated to the crossroads of Western European and Russian historical, cultural, and literary contexts from the nineteenth through the twenty-first century. Further scholarly interests: intellectual history; Russian and Western European literature and drama; comparative studies. Her most recent books are on the Russian entertainment culture of the Silver Age (1908–1918); the anti-formalist campaign of the 1930s; the era of 'removal'; Russian formalism and modern humanitarian knowledge; the historio-sophical discourse in Fielding's farces.

Petr Rezvykh is a Leading Research Fellow at the Poletayev Institute for Theoretical and Historical Studies in the Humanities of the National Research University Higher School of Economics, Moscow, and an Associate Professor in the Faculty of Humanities of the School of Philosophy (HSE). Main publications: P. Rezvykh and P. Ziche, *Sygkepleriazein: Schelling und die Kepler-Rezeption im 19. Jahrhundert* (2013); P. Rezvykh, "Absolute Affirmation and Conditions of Meaning: Logical-Ontological Paradoxes of F. W. J. Schelling's 'Identity Philosophy'", in: *Russian Studies in Philosophy* (2011), pp. 41–64.

Sandra Richter has been Professor and Chair of the department 'Modern German Literature I' at the University of Stuttgart since 2008. She specializes in modern German and comparative literature (1600 until the present), poetics, aesthetics and literary theory, and intellectual history. Her main publications include the monographs *Eine Weltgeschichte der deutschsprachigen Literatur* (2017) and *A History of Poetics* (2010). Since 2019, she serves as the director of the Deutsches Literaturarchiv Marbach.

Tatiana Smoliarova is an Associate Professor of Russian Literature at the University of Toronto. Her main areas of interest are the Age of Enlightenment and its legacies in Russia and Europe, poetry and poetics, and theatricality and spectacle in cultural history. Her first book, *Paris 1928: Ode Returns to the Theater* (2000), examined Sergei Diaghilev's ballet *Ode* (1928). She is also the author of *Lyrics Made Visible: Derzhavin* (2011), a book on visual culture in Russia at the turn of the nineteenth century and on one of the era's foremost poets. Her latest book, *Three Metaphors for Life: Derzhavin's Late Poetry*, was just published by Academic Studies Press, Boston.

Pavel V. Sokolov is an Associate Professor at the School of Philosophy and Leading Research Fellow at the Poletayev Institute for Theoretical and Historical Studies in the Humanities at the National Research University Higher School of Economics, Moscow. He has published on late scholasticism, early modern Biblical hermeneutics, and political thought. His more recent publications deal with eighteenth-century Dutch medicine, the reception of Th. Hobbes's political ideas in the Netherlands, and G. Vico's conception of heroism.

Juana Christina von Stein is an Assitant Professor in the Department of Romance Studies and the Petrarca Institute at the University of Cologne. She wrote her doctoral thesis on Baudelaire and Flaubert (*Melancholie als poetologische Aliegorie*, 2018) and is currently working on the reception of Dante in France as well as on a book which deals with the myth of Don Juan.

Susanne Zepp is a Professor of Spanish, Portuguese and French literatures at Freie Universität Berlin. At FUB, she is also the Director of the Gulbenkian Doctoral Program for Portuguese Literature and Culture, and a Principal Researcher at the Friedrich Schlegel Graduate School for Literary Studies. From 2003–2015, Prof. Zepp held the position of Deputy Director of the Simon Dubnow Institute for Jewish History and Culture at Leipzig University. At present, she serves as the Academic Coordinator of Freie Universität's Strategic Partnership with the Hebrew University of Jerusalem. Prof. Zepp teaches literary and historical texts in Spanish, Portuguese and French that range from the sixteenth to the twentieth century. She has published on Borges, Montaigne, Eça de Queiroz, Lispector and Albert Cohen, amongst others. Her most recent books include an *Introduction to Portuguese and Brazilian Literary Studies*, the first collection of critical essays on Claude Lanzmann, and a monograph on early modern Jewish literary creativity.

www.ingramcontent.com/pod-product-compliance
Lightning Source LLC
Chambersburg PA
CBHW031803220426
43662CB00007B/515